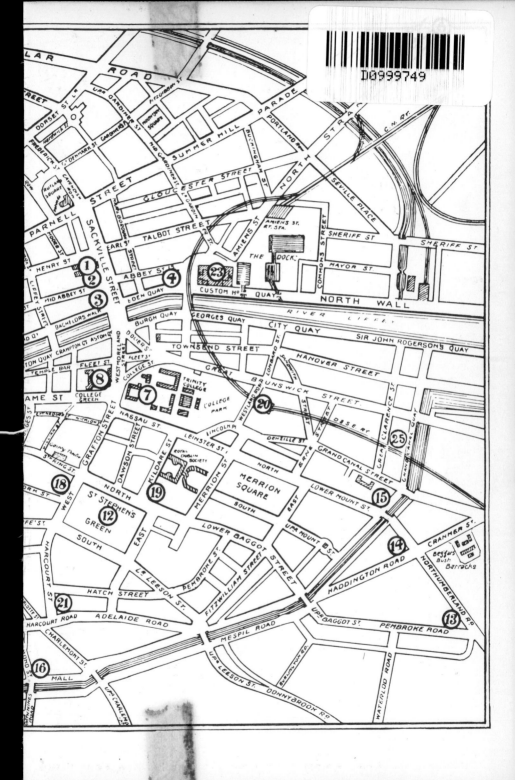

The Easter Rebellion

MAX

CAULFIELD

The

Easter

Rebellion

HOLT, RINEHART AND WINSTON

NEW YORK CHICAGO

SAN FRANCISCO

Designer: Ernst Reichl
81324-0113
Printed in the United States of America

This book is for my father

Malachy Caulfield

who remembers it all

Acknowledgments

So many people gave of their time and trouble toward the making of this book that it is almost invidious to single any out.

Both in England and in Ireland, I was received with great courtesy and hospitality by everyone in a position to help with the research. Many people went to great trouble to look up documents or write accounts of their recollections.

In Dublin one was almost washed away with hospitality, but I would particularly like to thank Mr. Michael MacDonagh, then editor of the Dublin *Sunday Review*, Mr. Erskine Childers, Jr., and Mr. Desmond Ryan, himself a historian of the Rebellion, who went to great trouble to put me in touch with sources and to advise in general. Mr. William Cosgrave went to exceeding trouble to show me over the site of the battle at the South Dublin Union and General Richard Mulcahy aided me with personal recollections and several interesting documents. No one could have been more helpful than Mr. Frank Robbins, who gave me much information and helped me with sources in relation to the Irish Citizen Army. Nor could anyone have been of greater assistance than Commandant Brennan Whitmore who not only gave me the benefit of his most lucid interpretation of events, but has allowed me access to his personal memories.

Magnificent hospitality was shown me by Mr. James Doyle at his farm in Wexford and by Mr. Thomas Walsh, at his home in Dublin. Both Jack Shouldice and his brother Frank went to immense trouble to procure me every possible detail of the fighting in North King Street and have left me with warm memories of Dublin. Mr. Garry Holohan, Mr. Thomas Sherrin, Mr. Joseph

Brady, all put themselves to a great deal of inconvenience, as did Mr. Simon Donnelly.

My enquiries were no less well assisted in England. My researches took me into a belt of the country with which I was not terribly well acquainted and it was interesting to note the character and social nature of the people vis-a-vis their counterparts in Ireland. Here, away from the acerbities of London, I found the same warm-hearted courtesy and hospitality, particularly in Nottinghamshire and Derbyshire. I am exceedingly grateful to Captain Frank Pragnell of Nottingham, Major William Foster, of Southwell, Notts, Colonel J. S. Oates of Besthorpe, Notts, and Colonel M. C. Martyn, of Wentworth, Yorks, for the trouble and time they took to give me their accounts and lend me books and documents. I am particularly indebted to Captain A. E. Slack of Chesterfield, Derbyshire, whose enthusiasm and cheerfulness gave me many valuable leads to sources.

My thanks, too, to the staffs of the Imperial War Museum, the British Museum, the National Library of Ireland and the Dublin City Public Library whom I put to considerable inconvenience.

London, 1963

The Easter Rebellion

At four minutes past noon on Easter Monday, April 24, 1916, a Red Cross nurse, returning to duty at the wartime hospital which had been set up in Dublin Castle, paused at the main gate. Half jokingly she asked the policeman on duty, "Is it true that the Sinn Feiners are going to take the Castle?"

"Ah, no, miss," answered Constable James O'Brien of the Dublin Metropolitan Police (D.M.P.). "I don't think so. Aren't the authorities making too much fuss?"

The nurse smiled and walked on into Upper Castle Yard through a stone archway surmounted by an imposing statue of Justice, standing with her back to the city—a fact which Dubliners of rebellious sympathies liked to insist was significant. Upper Castle Yard itself was a quadrangle 280 feet long by 130 feet wide, enclosed by the various Crown administrative offices and by the Irish State Apartments. Among these were the gilded Throne Room and the age-worn St. Patrick's Hall, where for centuries the Viceroys of Ireland had given magnificent state balls, looked down upon by some rather undistinguished murals depicting the submission of the Irish chieftains to King Henry II—a measure of the time England had wielded paramount influence in Ireland. Inside this short perimeter, then, lay the heart of British power in the sister isle.

At this same moment Mr. H.S. Doig, editor of the Dublin *Mail & Express,* busy writing a leader on Shakespeare's Tercentenary, heard one of his staff exclaim, "Good God! The Citizen Army are parading in spite of MacNeill's letter!" Doig, whose windows faced the Castle Gate, rose in time to see

3

a small detachment of armed men and women breaking ranks. They were wearing dark green uniforms and Boerlike slouch hats pinned up at one side with the Red Hand, their union badge. He watched Constable O'Brien walk forward with his hand upraised, imagined that he must be saying, "Now, boys, you shouldn't be here at all." The Citizen Army men stepped back and raised their rifles. Doig was not prepared for what happened next. A rifle cracked and the big policeman slumped to the ground, blood streaming from his head. Then, as the insurgents seemed to hesitate, their leader roared, "Get in!"

The military sentry inside the Gate fired into the air to warn the guardroom, then ducked for cover as the rebels opened fire on him and began pouring in. Doig watched a passing priest make a heroic effort to stop them. The rebels, however, simply shoved past him, leaving him bewildered. As they opened a haphazard fire on the Castle, the priest rushed over to O'Brien to administer the last rites.

Inside the enormous, straggling barracklike complex of buildings, in a fusty Victorian office scarcely twenty-five yards away, Sir Matthew Nathan, His Majesty's Under-Secretary for Ireland, Major Ivor Price, the Military Intelligence Officer, and Mr. A. H. Norway, the Secretary of the Post Office, were discussing their plan to arrest the leaders of the political conspiracy known as Sinn Fein—a decision to seize them having been reached at a conference held the previous night in Vice-Regal Lodge by Lord Wimborne, the Lord Lieutenant. This had climaxed an extraordinary week-end, during which Sir Roger Casement had been captured after landing from a German submarine and the Irish Volunteers had canceled their Easter Sunday maneuvers—maneuvers obviously intended to cloak something more serious. The likelihood of real trouble developing in Ireland had therefore receded—or so Sir Matthew and his colleagues thought. Yet they considered it still advisable to take punitive measures. Permission to proceed with the arrests had been asked for by cable and the reply of the Chief Secretary for Ireland, Mr. Augustine Birrell—whose concurrence was constitutionally necessary—had just been received from London. On Major Price's arrival at a quarter to twelve, Sir Matthew had telephoned Mr. Norway and invited him to join the talks. Mr. Norway had immediately quit his office in the newly renovated and remodeled General Post Office (G.P.O.), opened to the public again only six weeks before, and had arrived at the Castle precisely at noon. Now, suddenly, the sound of shots shattered an exceedingly comforting illusion.

"They've commenced it!" shouted Price, and leaving Nathan and Norway open-mouthed, he hurled himself from the office. He reached the Yard in time to see half a dozen insurgents breaking their way into the guardroom. Hastily emptying his revolver in their direction, he at once retreated.

The six men on guard duty had been quietly heating stew for their midday meal when the shots interrupted them. They had grabbed their rifles and were rushing outside at the double when a homemade bomb, lobbed through the window, exploded and temporarily stunned them. Before they could recover, six insurgents, led by a man called Tom Kain, piled in on them. In a moment the guards found themselves trussed up like chickens—with their own puttees. Yet curiously, the insurgents made no attempt to penetrate farther into the Castle. Possibly they were overawed at the thought of capturing a citadel which had so arrogantly defied its enemies for seven hundred years. More likely they were afraid of running blindly into the considerable forces they believed were in the Castle. Certainly they had no idea that the place lay almost entirely at their mercy, that fewer than twenty-five soldiers sat idling around the corner in Ship Street Barracks. As it was Easter Monday and there was an excellent card at Fairyhouse—including the Irish Grand National—perhaps they should have guessed that the garrison would be at reduced strength. Indeed, the only two officers left in the place were a colonel and Major Price. There were sixty-seven war-wounded soldiers in the Red Cross hospital, but they were hardly in a condition to fight. The Castle was, in fact, almost entirely in the hands of civil servants, most of whom had spent their morning idly gazing out at the impeccable sky and envying the holiday-makers at Dalkey or Malahide. Yet instead of reinforcing Kain and capturing the entire Castle, the leader of the insurgent detachment, John Connolly, split his forces, sending one

5

unit to occupy the premises of Henry and James, outfitters, at the corner of Parliament Street (which dominated the Castle Gate), another to charge up the stairs of the *Mail & Express* offices on the opposite corner and eject the startled Doig and his staff at bayonet point, while the main body, which he led himself, retreated into the unoccupied City Hall, using a specially impressed key.

Back in Sir Matthew's office, Major Price was summoning every available soldier from Ship Street Barracks, expecting the insurgents at any moment to come bursting through the door. Sir Matthew himself took a revolver from his desk and prepared to assist in selling their lives dearly. The rebels, however, never appeared. Instead, a military party turned up at the double—Major Price was taken aback in counting only twenty-five men when he had expected two hundred. He grabbed Sir Matthew's private telephone, which had a direct line to Military Headquarters at Parkgate, to call for reinforcements, conscious of the terrible blunder that had been made in not doubling the garrison or at least stoppping all leave that morning. He held the receiver to his ear for perhaps three full seconds. Then a wild look crossed his face and, turning to Sir Matthew, he exclaimed in desperation, "My God! They've cut the wires!"

Bugler William Oman of the Irish Citizen Army had sounded the "fall in" for the main insurgent army at exactly 11:30 that morning. The notes had risen stickily into the calm air of Beresford Place and had sounded hoarsely along the dingy corridors of Liberty Hall, headquarters of the Irish Transport and General Workers' Union and its militant off-shoot, the Citizen Army. Sergeant Frank Robbins, who was trying on a new pair of trousers, had them only half on when he heard the call. It was followed by a sudden rush of feet along the rough boards outside the door. Heart in mouth, Robbins, who was only twenty, slung his bandolier over his shoulder, took up his rifle, and raced down the stairs, still buttoning his trousers. He found the place in an uproar. Bicycles were parked everywhere, in some cases a dozen deep; girls were rushing about, carrying haversacks stuffed with food

6

and medical supplies; wives and sweethearts were thrusting cigarettes or chocolates upon their men as they bade them farewell.

Down in the square in front of Liberty Hall two hundred and fifty men and boys were shuffling themselves into a martial double column. One of them, Tommy Keenan, was only twelve years old. Behind them, bisected by the ugly Loop Line railway bridge which links termini at Amiens Street and Westland Row, rose Gandon's graceful Custom House, in the sunlight a dazzlingly white-and-shadowed affair of slender dome and sweeping perpendiculars. Over the Liffey, mirrored as a lake, swung the lazy, drifting gulls, like flowing polka dots.

The insurgents, despite the enhancing effect of a glorious morning, hardly resembled an inspiring army. Men are no braver, perhaps, for being in uniform; yet because it shows that they have been trained and are probably well disciplined, it creates a degree of confidence. Fewer than a quarter of these men and boys, however, were clad in the dark green of the Citizen Army or the heather-green of the Irish Volunteers. One or two had tried to give themselves a military appearance of sorts by covering their legs with puttees; some had donned riding breeches, but the best most of them had been able to do was to sling a bandolier over the right shoulder or wear a yellow brassard upon the left arm. Their armaments, too, looked astonishingly primitive. In the bright sunlight the high gleam of pikes proved a great deal more eye-catching than the dull glint of rifles, which appeared only a trifle less antique than the pikes. There were a few modern short Lee-Enfields (filched or bought clandestinely from the military), some Italian Martinis (smuggled in from the Continent among blocks of Carrara marble) and an odd Lee-Metford. There were plenty of single-barreled shotguns; but the predominant weapon was the brutelike Howth Mauser—so called because it had formed part of the cargo of German rifles landed at Howth in July, 1914, from Erskine Childers' yacht *Asgard*. This rifle, manufactured for the Prussian forces of 1870, was a single-loader, firing a soft-nosed lead bullet which struck with all the effect of a dum-dum. It would drill a neat hole in a man as it entered, but tear out at the other side like a plate,

7

and its use would cause the British army angrily to accuse the rebels of firing outlawed bullets.

In short these men, like almost any insurgent army anywhere, looked a forlorn and desperate lot. No one, perhaps, realized this better than James Connolly himself, commander of all the rebel forces in Dublin. As he clattered down the broad staircase of Liberty Hall—a stocky little man wearing the full uniform of a commandant-general, his bandy legs encased in highly polished leggings, ready to sacrifice his life for his passionately held principles—he stopped to say goodbye to his friend William O'Brien. In a half-whisper, so that the men nearby could not overhear him, he added, "Bill we're going out to be slaughtered."

"Is there no hope at all?" asked O'Brien, knowing full well that the question was superfluous.

"None whatever," Connolly answered cheerfully, and with a quick slap on O'Brien's shoulder, strode on.

At exactly 11:50 A.M., the first body of rebels moved off at Connolly's sharp order: "Left turn! Quick march!" Twenty-eight men and eight boys comprising a detachment under Captain Richard MacCormack, flung their shoulders back and, like true soldiers, marched straight toward Butt Bridge, the nearest one over the Liffey. This, unfortunately, was not right, and Connolly had to run after them shouting, "Not that way, Mac! You'll get slaughtered! They might be fighting in some places already." MacCormack wheeled his men about and led them up Eden Quay. With Robbins in the column was James Fox, aged nineteen. A few minutes earlier, an old man had pushed his way forward, leading a young man by the hand. "Frank Robbins," said Patrick Fox, "here's my lad. Will you take him with you? I'm too old for the job myself."

It was 11:55 A.M. when Patrick Pearse appeared, followed by his younger brother Willie and behind them the bizarre figure of dying Joseph Plunkett, his throat still swathed in bandages from a severe operation for glandular tuberculosis three weeks previously. A filigree bangle glittered on his wrist and he wore two enormous antique rings. By then Mac-Cormack's column was well over O'Connell Bridge, moving almost at the double. The Castle detachment followed. Then

8

John Heuston, aged nineteen, leading twelve young men, all of about his own age, tramped off to occupy the Mendicity Institution on the south bank of the river. Until then the main force had scarcely thinned, but as forty men under Commandant Michael Mallin moved off to occupy St. Stephen's Green—his second in command, Lieutenant Countess Markievicz, flamboyantly following with her own troop of Boy Scouts—the numbers decreased perceptibly. Hardly one hundred and fifty men, in fact, were left in Beresford Place—the grand army with which Pearse hoped to establish the headquarters of an Irish Republic in Sackville Street.

Patrick Pearse, thirty-six-year-old Commander in Chief and President of the Provisional Government, paused on the steps of Liberty Hall to take in the thin, shabby ranks. Beyond them were two drays, laden with an extraordinary assortment of weapons and working implements, including pickaxes, sledges, and crowbars and some brand-new wicker hampers. A closed cab hung funereally about on the outskirts, stuffed to the roof with similar odds and ends. Not satisfied with a soldier's ordinary equipment, most of the men had also loaded themselves down with two rifles (one over each shoulder) or alternatively a rifle and pickax, or a shotgun and pike. A member of Plunkett's staff, Captain Brennan Whitmore, could not help staring at them in astonishment, wondering how they hoped to do battle if they were suddenly called upon to defend themselves. Before he could do anything about the matter, however, a dust-whitened touring car swung into Beresford Place and came to a halt amid ringing cheers. Down from the high running board stepped The O'Rahilly, Treasurer of the Irish Volunteers, his flushed appearance at this twelfth hour as encouraging to the insurgent army as it was utterly unexpected, for it was known that he opposed an uprising. He had, indeed, spent the last forty-eight hours doing his best to prevent one—his efforts taking him in a wild night drive to the provincial commanders in Wicklow, Wexford, Waterford, Tipperary, and Limerick with dispatches from Professor John MacNeill, President of the Volunteers, ordering them not to move. Now, however, as he leaped eagerly up the steps of Liberty Hall to shake hands with Pearse and Plunkett, he gasped in explanation, "Well, I've helped to wind up the clock, so I might as well hear it strike!" Delighted Volunteers and Citizen Army men at once began to load weapons, implements, and homemade bombs into his car. The time then was just two minutes to twelve. Then a trivial yet quite extraordinary incident followed.

To Patrick Pearse, his thoughts fixed intently on somberly magnificent ambitions, it must have seemed as though the Furies themselves were determined to make a last oddly twisted attempt to thwart him. He had neither wife nor fiancée to distract him from his duty. He had, however, a mother and four sisters, and now, as he waited for James Connolly to give the order to march, one of these girls mounted the steps beside him and began to plead hysterically, "Come home, Pat, and leave all this foolishness!" Embarrassed, Pearse turned away in silence. In the front ranks there was some uneasy shuffling. Connolly, recognizing the plight of the Commander in Chief, bawled out, "Form fours!" which gave Pearse an excuse to brush past his sister and take his place at the head of the column. He was followed immediately by Plunkett, his Chief of Staff, the mercurial brain behind the military planning and strategy of the Rebellion, who dramatically unsheathed a saber as he took up his position. Then Connolly, having satisfied himself that everybody was at last ready, took position between Pearse and Plunkett. Behind the three commandant-generals (as they had ranked themselves) came the rest of the column in orthodox fours, with Captain Brennan Whitmore on the extreme left and next to him Plunkett's aide-de-camp, Michael Collins, an energetic young officer who, until recently, had been an employee of the Post Office in London. Further back stood little Sean T. O'Kelly, who would one day find himself President of Ireland, and still farther back young Thomas MacEvoy, aged seventeen, a grocer's assistant, who marched into insurrection under the blithe impression that he was taking part in nothing more exciting than an ordinary route march. Meanwhile Captain Michael O'Reilly, Brigade Deputy-Adjutant, tightened his grip on the magnificent sword which had cost him all of thirty shillings and hoped that the words with which he had com-

10

forted his wife and four children ("Don't worry now, when I come back I'll be Minister of Defense,") would turn out to have real substance. In the column, too, were Connolly's fifteen-year-old son Rory and his loyal, if rather school-marmish, secretary, Winifred Carney, the only woman in the entire procession. The rear—behind the closed cab, the drays, and The O'Rahilly's car—was brought up by two motor-cyclists, young Jack Plunkett, the youngest of the three Plunkett brothers, and Volunteer Fergus O'Kelly, who had orders direct from Joseph Plunkett to set up a wireless transmitter. Connolly snapped out, "By the left, quick march!"—which drew an ironical outburst of cheering from the crowd of urchins and grownups who had been watching them parade.

The rebels stepped out briskly, and considering their weird impedimenta, even quite impressively. Most, after all, had had some military training. Many had been drilled regularly by the Volunteers for the past three years while some had had service in the British Army; one, Major John MacBride, had even fought with the Boers. They had, therefore, an appreciation of order and discipline, despite their ridiculous parapher-nalia, despite even the pikes.

Yet, as Volunteer Patrick Colwell clattered up Abbey Street, he wondered where they were all marching to and what for. He was a Kimmage man—one of the fifty-six young men who, for the past three months, had been living rough—sleeping eight to a mattress in some cases—in an old mill on the farm of Count Plunkett at Kimmage. They were young Irish-men who had left their homes and jobs in Glasgow, Liverpool, and London when conscription was introduced there on the principle that, if they had to fight for anybody, they preferred to fight for Ireland. At Kimmage, where the Plunketts had set up a crude arsenal, the men had been put to work making weapons. Eventually they had even attempted a field gun, using twelve feet of rainwater piping bound with copper wire and a heavy chain. To test it they had put a charge of gun-powder into the breech, rammed the ammunition—pieces of metal of every description, including old razor blades—down the muzzle, and then touched it off. It had, of course, blown up immediately, scattering metal over a wide area, and almost

11

killing Count Plunkett's daughter as she emerged from the door of the farmhouse. After that they had restricted themselves to the less complicated, if more unrewarding, task of making six-foot pikes or crude bayonets, or manufacturing homemade bombs from such unpromising material as old tea canisters and tobacco tins.

That morning all fifty-six of them, led by their captain, George Plunkett, had marched from the old mill at Kimmage to the suburb of Harold's Cross and, somehow or other, squeezed aboard a tramcar. While Plunkett had flabbergasted the conductor by asking for fifty-seven tuppenny tickets ("Why bother to pay? You've already captured the tram!" the man had expostulated), Volunteer James Brennan stationed himself behind the driver, and prodding him gently in the back with a shotgun, ordered him to keep going without a single halt until they reached O'Connell Bridge.

"I've more sense than to argue with a gun!" said the driver, and did as he was told. There were complaints from the passengers, however. Some wanted off. One large woman, struck in the face by swinging equipment, lost her temper and shouted at the conductor, "I demand that you put these men off!"

"Perhaps you wouldn't mind doing it yourself then, ma'am?" he suggested mildly. "I seem to be rather busy."

The long march up Abbey Street, for all its subsequent significance in modern Irish history, passed like a dream for most of the men in the column that morning. As the front ranks reached Sackville Street, people stepped back to let them march through. A few raised a cheer, but most remained indifferent.

As the traffic mainstream halted, Connolly led his forces out into the great street and then briskly along the west side. A few British cavalry officers idling outside the Metropole Hotel grinned broadly as they came into sight. At the main door of the G.P.O., Second-Lieutenant A. D. Chalmers, 14th Royal Fusiliers, remarked to a friend, "Look at that awful crowd!" He then pushed his way inside to send a telegram to his wife in London. Thirty seconds later the rebels were abreast the building—a Palladian structure of Ionic columns supporting a stu-

12

pendous classical pediment surmounted by Hibernia, Mercury, and Fidelity (known colloquially as the Three Apostles). Suddenly, in the hoarse, bitten-off shout of a regimental sergeant-major, James Connolly gave the command: "Company halt! Left turn!" Then, as his men briskly obeyed, he loosed a shout, flaming with the pent-up passion of a lifetime: "The G.P.O. Charge!"

At once the whole incongruous column broke formation to hurl itself toward the great façade, rifles, pikes, and bayonets swinging in short, bright, menacing arcs. They swept through the main doorway in a cheering, triumphant mob and spilled out over the marble floor, while the public and the staff froze behind the broad teak counters, stupefied. At the telegram counter, Lieutenant Chalmers felt a sharp object prodding his backside and swiveled around to find a pike pointing straight at him, held by a scowling rebel who seemed determined to run him through. Indeed, he might well have been spitted there and then upon the archaic weapon had not Captain O'Reilly instructed the pikeman sternly, "That's not at all necessary."

Then Connolly shouted, "Everybody out!"

Yet for a moment no one moved. Instead, a woman's voice could be heard insisting that she wanted to buy stamps. Then the staff stampeded. A few vaulted the counters; others bolted, leaving their coats and hats behind. Mr. E. A. Stoker, a Grafton Street jeweler, who had been standing outside the G.P.O. when the insurgents charged, sought to enter the building, believing that the attack was only an exercise. He managed to fight his way through the people flooding out, only to be brought up short by a youth who punched a revolver into his stomach.

"Get out!" said the youth shortly.

"What's up?" asked the unbelieving Stoker.

"Hands up, or I'll blow your heart out!" replied the youth, driving him back out the door.

Michael Collins left Plunkett (who at this stage could scarcely raise a smile and had to support himself against a wooden ledge) and crossed to the telegram counter, where he informed Chalmers that he was a prisoner and must submit

13

to a search. Chalmers, conscious of his dignity as a British officer, surrendered without protest. Then, while Brennan Whitmore kept him covered, Collins crossed to a telephone booth in the center of the office and yanked out the cord. With this he first bound the Englishman, then, hoisting him on his back, carried him over to the telephone booth where he dumped him, facing out toward Sackville Street. From the other end of the counter, where he had been watching everything in frozen silence, Constable Dunphy of the D.M.P. pleaded as Collins advanced toward him, "Please don't shoot me . . . I've done no harm."

"We don't shoot prisoners," said Collins shortly, and ordered two Volunteers to take him upstairs. As he was led away, Connolly shouted, "Smash the windows and barricade them!"

A frenzy of destruction followed. Men flung themselves delightedly at the big windows, smashing them with rifle butts. Glass crashed, and tinkled. A man staggered out of the melee holding up his bleeding wrist. Pearse, as exhilarated as anyone, hardly sobered up even when The O'Rahilly told him, "We haven't seized the telegraph instrument room yet."

With a flicker of sheer happiness on his face, Pearse ordered Volunteer Michael Staines to take six or seven men and occupy the second floor.

Quickly Staines led a small party up the wide stairs which led to the instrument room. Some girl telegraphists were on their way down. Only one girl, however, who knew Staines slightly and appeared to have rebel sympathies, yelled, "That's the stuff to give them, Michael!" With a slight feeling of resentment at this meager support, Staines led his men on. They burst out onto a landing and suddenly found themselves covered by seven rifles. Instinctively a Volunteer fired and shot the sergeant of the guard, who fell as though poleaxed. Then, to Staines' astonishment, the entire guard dropped their weapons.

"We've no ammunition!" shouted a corporal in explanation. Staines quickly checked their guns and ammunition pouches and discovered that this was true. He backed them against a wall, then ordered two insurgents to take the wounded man

14

to the hospital. The sergeant, however, sat up and declared that he had no intention of quitting his post.

"I'm on guard here until six o'clock this evening," he said stubbornly, "and I dinna leave ma post until I'm relieved."

Staines left the obstinate Scot and his disarmed men under guard and pushed on into the instrument room. Most of the staff had already left—all, in fact, except the woman supervisor, another indomitable Scot. When she, too, resolutely refused to leave, Staines rasped, "Stay if you like, but don't touch those instruments!"

"Can I not send out these death telegrams?" she asked, pointing to a sheaf of messages.

"No, some of my men will do that," said Staines.

"Oh, then, in that case . . . !" she said, and flounced out.

Meanwhile, the ground floor had become a shambles. Tables, chairs, desks—anything solid or heavy—had been pushed against the windows. All along the front and sides of the great building, the massive ground-floor window frames enclosed little more than a gallery of enormous holes. Men had climbed onto the tables and desks and were knocking out the upper panes; others had piled books, ledgers, pads of money orders, and even correspondence files into the empty spaces below and were flattening themselves behind the debris to check what protection it gave. Brennan Whitmore, high on a table, wiped the sweat from his face as he looked out into Sackville Street. Beside him, Michael Collins, wielding a loose telephone receiver, smashed another pane and even as the glass shattered onto the pavement a woman cried; "Glory be to God! Would you look at them smashing all the lovely windows!" Collins laughed boisterously. It was such an infectious laugh that within a moment half the people in the Post Office were roaring their heads off. Then, in the middle of all the uproar, somebody let off an accidental shot which plowed its way into the ceiling.

Winifred Carney had settled herself on a high stool behind the brass grille of a stamp counter; here, an enormous Webley within easy reach, she began typing Connolly's orders. Sean T. O'Kelly stood by himself in the middle of the big room, waiting to be assigned specific duties, for, although he held the

15

rank of captain, he considered himself more of a politician than a military man. At the outset he had attached himself to his Irish Republican Brotherhood (I.R.B.) protégé, Pearse, as A.D.C.; but so far these duties had consisted solely of following Pearse up to the second floor when he had gone to talk to Tom Clarke and John MacDermott, fellow members of the Provisional Government, then following him downstairs again. Now he was delighted when James Connolly noticed that he was not doing anything and shouted, "Are you busy, Sean?"

"No, not at all," replied O'Kelly hopefully.

"Well, will you go to Liberty Hall and bring me back a couple of flags?"

"Glad to," said O'Kelly. And having been told where he would find them, he trotted off.

He was back shortly, carrying the traditional green flag of Ireland and the Sinn Fein tricolor of green, white, and orange (signifying the union of Catholic Ireland with Protestant and Orange Ulster).

"Here!" said Connolly to a Volunteer officer when O'Kelly handed them over. "Have them hoisted up on the flagpoles."

O'Kelly sauntered outside to see the effect. He watched the tiny figures of Volunteers suddenly make an appearance above the massive tympanum which bore the Royal Arms of England. He watched them move across the left-hand corner of the roof. Around him the crowd in the street gazed up, eager not to miss a single move in this quite extraordinary business. For an instant the flag as it was run up, rested at the top of the flagpole, a dark, nondescript blob, then jerkily broke out at the masthead, only to flap down listlessly in the warm midday air. A few halfhearted, half-mystified cheers greeted its appearance, but not until a sudden breeze stirred it gently could anybody make out what it was—a green flag with a golden harp in the center and across it in bold Gaelic lettering, half gold, half white, the quite incredible legend:

IRISH REPUBLIC

16

Ireland—which has probably the oldest continuing national consciousness of any nation in Western Europe—had always been a puzzle and a source of continual anxiety not only to Dublin Castle but to every English Government over the previous eight hundred years; and it was not as though England were in Ireland for any reason other than for Ireland's own good. Or so Englishmen liked to think. As far back as the reign of Henry II, Pope Adrian IV, the only Englishman ever to sit on the throne of St. Peter, had recognized the chaotic state of the country and the inability of the Irish to govern themselves and had issued a bull bestowing the island upon those who could undoubtedly run it better. Yet, good Catholics though the Irish were—and few over the centuries had been more tenacious for what they believed —they had somehow never been able to accept the legality of England's rule.

They had almost rid themselves of the incubus during the reign of the first Elizabeth, but the eventual failure of the great Hugh O'Neill, Earl of Tyrone, after years of continual victories, had led to the breakup of an ancient Gaelic order whose roots lay in prehistoric society. Worse, it had led to a policy of annexation and colonization by successive English Governments so that eventually two Irelands emerged—that of the English landowners (the Anglo-Irish) and that of the dispossessed natives. But although apparently well and truly tamed by the end of the sixteenth century, the country had risen in rebellion twice in the seventeenth and once in the eighteenth century. Napoleon, indeed, was to lament that he had not attacked England by landing in Ireland where he would have been warmly received, instead of wasting his time in Egypt. By the eighteen-forties, however, war, waste, conquest, and the stoutly resisted Act of Union with England and Scotland of 1801 had so operated upon the country that the Irish had become the poorest people in Europe. Even the Duke of Wellington could say, "There never was a country in which poverty existed to so great a degree." This was the age of the Anglo-Irish rakes; rapacious landlords who, with the one hand built elegant Palladian mansions, planted innumerable avenues of glorious trees opening onto vistas of glittering fountains, and with the other gulped down such oceans of claret that they could only sprawl senseless in their own vomit; an age when rich men quarreled and dueled at the rear of coffeehouses, gamed and wenched in common alehouses, and, for bloody excitement, matched gorgeously appareled fighting cocks; erecting the whole grand edifice of extravagant living upon rents which rose higher and higher even as the population mounted. This was a time when Ireland presented "the extraordinary spectacle of a country in which wages and employment, practically speaking, did not exist. There were no industries; there were very few towns; there were almost no farms large enough to employ labour . . . greens were unknown, bread was unknown, ovens were unknown. The butcher, the baker, the grocer, did not exist; tea, candles and coals were unheard of." Men lived on patches of land for which they paid preposterous rents and grew potatoes as their only crop. On this diet alone, the population somehow managed to thrive—from some four million in the second half of the eighteenth century, it grew to over eight million by the eighteen-forties. Then the crop failed; and within ten years, four million Irish had vanished—either into the cities of America or into coffins.

Three times in the bustling, expanding nineteenth century —a time of unparalleled misery for the farming people of Ireland—the wilder spirits made a protest in arms. Each was hardly more than a skirmish, a brush with authority, a puny thing bordering on farce. Their objective, stripped of all qual-

18

ifications and reservations, was the end of English rule. The twentieth century, however, opened with hope. There seemed an excellent chance that a Home Rule Bill might at least be granted; and this, it was felt on both sides of the Irish Sea, small measure of local government though it might be, would appease all Irish national sentiment. In addition, the attractions of English social and commercial order, now being more fully extended to Ireland, had helped to soften many bitter memories. The lifting of penalties against Catholics; the disestablishment of the Protestant Church of Ireland; the efforts of Englishmen—such as the Liberal Gladstone with his three attempts to push Home Rule Bills through Parliament, and of the Tory George Wyndham, whose land act had converted the peasants into a class of small proprietors—had all had their inevitable effect. The Famine became only a dark remembrance; the land agitation, with its evictions and boycotts, a matter for history. Great Protestant—and therefore Ascendancy—names such as Wolfe Tone, Robert Emmett, Dean Swift, Oliver Goldsmith, and Charles Stewart Parnell became enshrined as those of national heroes. Catholic Irishmen received their own university. Self-governing boards, divorced from the control of Dublin Castle, were set up in various counties. Wealthy people began to act and think as the English upper classes did, and the British Army found a fertile recruiting ground among the idle and unimaginative. In the minds of the majority of English and Irish people, therefore, in the first decade of the twentieth century, Ireland had at last become an integral part of the United Kingdom; Dublin as much a British city as Manchester or Leeds, Edinburgh, or Cardiff. A sixth of the House of Commons at Westminster were Irish members and Home Rule had become the great moral touchstone of English politics. At long last, it began to look as though the two countries were about to embark upon a new era of mutual respect and good will.

There were only three things amiss with this otherwise beautifully ordered picture. The English Conservative Party was against any kind of independence for Ireland; the Protestant Orangemen, who had enjoyed a local majority in the four northeastern counties since the great Plantation of 1603 (when Irish lands had been seized and given to English or Scottish settlers) believed that Home Rule meant Rome Rule —to which, of course, hell was preferable; and there were young men in the rest of Ireland who still resented any integration at all of their country into Britain's political and economic structure with the consequent disappearance of their own nationality. The seeds of action lay with the Conservatives. As far back as 1885, when Gladstone was preparing his Home Rule Bill, Lord Randolph Churchill, father of Sir Winston, had privately voiced his opinion that "if Gladstone went for Home Rule, the Orange card would be the one to play." Gladstone, of course, did go for Home Rule and the Tories played their trump. The Orangemen (a society named for the Protestant champion, William of Orange, who defeated James the Second at the Battle of the Boyne in 1690) were stirred to fury by a succession of demagogic meetings and made it plain that they would not stomach Home Rule at any price. The House of Lords, as might have been expected, adopted a similar attitude, and Gladstone's Bill was aborted.

In 1905, however, an Irishman of Welsh descent, Arthur Griffith—a round-faced pince-nezed, brushily mustached journalist—inspired by ideas which had enabled Hungary to achieve her independence from Austria, published a revolutionary proposal. The Hungarians had gained their objectives simply by refusing to send representatives to the Parliament in Vienna: the Irish should follow their example and ignore Westminster. Members of Parliament could begin by withdrawing from Westminster and setting up an Irish Council; after that Irish courts, banks, a civil service, a stock exchange could be established to function alongside their British counterparts until the latter withered away through lack of use. The King of England, of course, could remain King of Ireland—in a dual monarchy—but that would be all. Griffith named this policy Sinn Fein (pronounced Shinn Fain) whose literal meaning is "We Ourselves"—that is, "We rely on ourselves."

His proposals were received enthusiastically by several disparate groups of Irishmen who were vaguely groping toward a better Ireland. All were anxious to make certain that Ireland did not lose its separate national identity. There were those who wanted to see a revival of the Gaelic language (Gaelic had ceased to be the spoken language of the country by the beginning of the nineteenth century) and of the native culture of the Golden Age. Others merely looked for a political and economic policy which would lift Ireland from her trough of poverty. Still others could only recall the misdeeds of England down through the centuries and feel themselves less than men because they were not free to rule themselves. All these found in the principles of Sinn Fein some expression of their aspirations. Far more important for Ireland eventually, however, was the interest displayed in Griffith and his ideas by two militant organizations. The first was the Irish Republican Brotherhood, a secret society formed in the United States in 1857 and intimately linked with Clan na Gael, an open Irish-American organization. The second was the Irish Transport and General Workers' Union. Housed in the worst slums in Europe and paid farcical wages, the victims of police oppression and frequent brutality, these trade unionists, militant and tough, supported the idea of a separate Ireland. Yet everything might have remained just a matter of talk and argument and general old blether if it had not been for two significant developments.

When, in 1911, the Liberal Party again found itself in power in Great Britain, it had a majority so small (forty-three) that, without the support of the Irish Party's eighty-four members, it would not have found it possible to govern at all. As the price of his support, John Redmond, leader of the Irish Party, demanded that the Government introduce another Home Rule Bill; this time it could not fail as Gladstone's bill had, because concurrent legislation was to be introduced making it impossible for the House of Lords any longer to block a bill once it had been passed by the House of Commons three times. The Tories responded to this development with a terrible vehemence. They enlisted the services of Sir Edward Carson, K.C., who set about rousing a new generation of Orangemen. In a grand gesture of sheer theatricality "King" Carson persuaded eighty thousand Belfastmen to sign a Solemn League and Covenant against Home Rule, some of

21

them in their own blood. (Many Englishmen did the same later.) Then he organized them into the Ulster Volunteers, an independently armed, drilled, and disciplined body—probably the most significant action to occur in Ireland since the eighteenth century. Finally, with the direct encouragement of Mr. Bonar Law, the Canadian-born leader of the Conservative Party (whose forebears were born in Ulster), Carson and his Orangemen pledged themselves to resist Home Rule by force. They announced that they would fight Great Britain in order to *remain part* of Great Britain, which was being a great deal more Irish than the Irish themselves. They even went so far as to set up their own Provisional Government to take over and administer "Ulster" (as they described the counties near Belfast) as an integral part of the United Kingdom if it should become necessary.

Suddenly civil war threatened not only Ireland but even Great Britain herself. Bonar Law informed King George V that he would advise British Army officers to refuse any orders which directed them to take action against Ulster. Winston Churchill, First Lord of the Admiralty and—in contradistinction to his father—a supporter of Home Rule, ordered the Third Battle Squadron to stations off the west coast of Scotland and threatened that if Belfast showed fight he "would have the town in ruins in twenty-four hours." In the Curragh, County Kildare (the main camp for the British Army in Ireland) fifty-eight senior officers "mutinied," that is, they declared they would resign their commissions rather than fight against Ulster. And then the Orangemen smuggled in three thousand German rifles and three million rounds of ammunition.

The time was April, 1914. In Berlin, Kaiser Wilhelm II and his advisers watched the unfolding drama with keenest interest. With England deep in the mire of unresolvable Irish politics, irregular armies threatening civil war or revolution, the regular armed forces mutinous, the two great political parties ready to fling themselves at each other's throat, what had they to fear from her? In August, the Kaiser struck—a month after a conference of all parties, called by King George at Buckingham Palace, had broken down in immutable intransigence.

22

Long before this, of course, the southern Irish had delightedly responded to the challenge thrown down by "King" Carson. "There is only one thing more ridiculous than the sight of an Orangeman with a rifle and that is a Nationalist without one," declared Pearse. If it were legal for Orangemen to take up arms and defy the Government, then surely it must be legal for southern Catholics to take them up in its defense. The south decided to form its own armies.

The Dublin trade unionists were first in the field. Led by James Larkin, a great hulking man of extraordinary eloquence, and James Connolly, his first lieutenant, they formed the Irish Citizen Army. Originally intended to be simply a protective force against the Dublin Metropolitan Police, it was not until Larkin went to America in 1914, leaving Connolly to take command, that the Citizen Army began to be trained seriously as a revolutionary body. At his headquarters in Liberty Hall, Connolly studied the great insurrectionary battles of Paris and Moscow. He established a rifle club to which his men contributed sixpence a week. He bought guns illegally from British soldiers of the Dublin garrison. He got his women helpers to make the army's dark green uniforms. He led route marches through the streets of Dublin in defiance of the police and mounted dummy attacks against prominent public buildings. With the assistance of ex-regular army noncommissioned officers and reservists, he rapidly made his Citizen Army a small, tough, creditably efficient force.

The poets and professors, the intellectuals and professional men—all the Sinn Feiners, in fact—but above all, the Irish Republican Brotherhood, were also stirred to action. In November, 1913, they founded the Irish Volunteers, electing John MacNeill, the eminently respectable Professor of Archaic Gaelic at the National University of Ireland, President of the Executive Committee and Chief of Staff. But without MacNeill's knowledge three key members of the I.R.B., Patrick Pearse, John MacDermott, and Edmund Kent, managed to get themselves elected to the Committee. Cynically they planned to take over the whole organization and use it as a revolutionary weapon. Left to themselves, of course, they had little hope of gaining sufficient adherents to form even the

23

tiniest of armies, for most Irishmen had forsworn methods of violence. Joining the Volunteers, however, appeared to be a different matter and by the end of 1913 membership had risen to 10,000. Redmond, jealous of the organization's increasing power and influence, demanded a share in its control, and when his nominees were finally admitted to the Executive Committee, membership quickly reached 160,000. The Volunteers, in fact, appeared to be such a respectable body—their field commander was Colonel Maurice Moore, brother of the novelist, George Moore—that when those who could afford uniforms marched through the streets of Dublin in their light green dress and stiff-peaked caps, the Castle authorities, if they hardly relished the sight, could discover little cause for alarm, especially as the organization had few arms and little hope of getting more following an embargo which had been imposed after the Orangemen's gun-running exploit.

Yet a month before general war broke out in Europe, the Irish Volunteers managed to run in fifteen hundred Mauser rifles and forty-nine thousand rounds of ammunition (most of it outlawed by international convention and therefore unusable). The landing of this cargo at Howth was followed by an incident in which regular troops opened fire on a crowd of jeering women and children. By this time, Parliament had passed Home Rule and the Bill needed only the formality of the Royal Assent. Mr. Asquith's Government suddenly found itself up against the inevitable dilemma: whether to impose the Bill on the whole country at once—and thereby clash with the Orangemen; or, by means of an Amending Bill, exclude Ulster for the time being—in which case they could expect trouble from the already incensed Irish Volunteers. Before the shotguns could go off in Ireland, however, the greater cataclysm was to divert men's minds elsewhere.

In the House of Commons, on that dark and dreadful day when Britain declared war on Germany, Sir Edward Grey, the Foreign Secretary, felt able to announce: "The one bright spot in the very dreadful situation is Ireland. The position in Ireland—and this is a thing I should like to be clearly understood abroad—is not a consideration among the things we have to take into account now."

24

Grey had every reason to believe that he was right. The Ulster leaders, through Bonar Law, had immediately pledged themselves to call off their Home Rule revolt and to support the Government loyally—at least for the duration. John Redmond, driven to say something equally generous, suggested that Britain could safely withdraw her forces from Ireland and leave the defense of the island to the Volunteers. This announcement was misinterpreted by an emotionally charged Commons as a pledge of absolute Irish support for the war. As for the contentious Home Rule Bill, all parties were agreed that it should be deferred.

Redmond had no doubts as to where the real interests of Ireland lay. He believed that Irishmen should support Britain and the Empire to the hilt, thereby demonstrating a loyalty and friendship which was certain to be rewarded when the guns were eventually stilled. His recruiting speeches were persuasive enough. Some two divisions of Irish troops voluntarily agreed to go to France, despite the malignant attitude of Lord Kitchener, the War Minister (an Irishman himself), who, while allowing the Ulster Division to fight as a single unit and to use the Red Hand of Ulster, the ancient symbol of the Province, as their emblem, refused the southern recruits permission to form their own separate divisions or to sport the Irish harp. Yet power to speak for Ireland was already passing from the parliamentarians. At a meeting held on September 5, 1914, the Supreme Council of the Irish Republican Brotherhood decided to stage an insurrection and to accept whatever assistance Germany could give. No specific date for this uprising was fixed. It was simply agreed that it should take place (1) if the Germans invaded Ireland, (2) if the English tried to force conscription on the country, or (3) if the war looked as though it were coming to an end. The insurrection would be accompanied by a declaration of war on Britain and a demand that the Provisional Government be represented as the envoys of a belligerent nation at the Peace Conference which must inevitably follow the end of hostilities.

British authority in Ireland rested principally upon the shoulders of three men. There was young Ivor Churchill, Baron Wimborne, a Liberal peer who had only recently been appointed Lord Lieutenant (or Viceroy) of Ireland and who, as the Monarch's personal representative, lived in opulent state at Vice-Regal Lodge, driving through Dublin in an open carriage escorted by Household Cavalry and Hussars. Like the Sovereign, he was a figurehead, possessing no executive authority.

The men who really bossed Ireland were the Chief Secretary for Ireland, Mr. Augustine Birrell, a genial politician and littérateur, and his assistant, Sir Matthew Nathan, the Under-Secretary, a former Governor of Hong Kong and an ex-Chairman of the Board of Inland Revenue. Until the war, Birrell had appeared to be handling Ireland with superlative skill, possessing as he did a genuine regard for the country and its people—a feeling reciprocated by most Irishmen. He had, in his seven years of office, pushed through Parliament fifty-six bills dealing specifically with improvements in Irish agriculture, housing, and education. He had given Catholics their first university. He had invariably treated alike north and south, Catholic and Protestant, refusing to make the invidious distinctions which former Chief Secretaries had made, and he enjoyed a reputation for geniality and wit in a country bursting with genial wits. When he proclaimed that "Orangemen have no more religion than a billiard ball," all southern Ireland had roared with laughter. The worst his Irish opponents could say of him was that he was "trying to kill Home Rule by kindness."

The chief difficulty facing the Castle after 1914 was the fierce opposition of the Irish to the threat of military conscription. Sinn Fein organizers found it easy to recruit members, as most young Irishmen were reluctant to sacrifice their lives for a nation toward which they felt no loyalty. Those who appreciated exactly what the struggle between Germany and Great Britain was about wanted no part of it; the attitude of the rest is perhaps best summed up in a statement issued by Bishop O'Dwyer of Limerick after a party of Irish men and women emigrating to America had been jeered at the Liverpool docks as shirkers: "Their crime is that they are not ready to die for England. Why should they? What have they or their forebears ever got from England that they should die for her? This war may be just or unjust, but any fair-minded man will admit that it is England's war, not Ireland's." It was a view which became more popular as Britain's military position grew increasingly parlous and the enormous losses on the battlefields of France caused British politicians and military leaders to cast about for new sources of manpower. In England, thousands of young men of military age had to be exempted from duty because they were skilled workers; the Irish, for the most part, were technologically unskilled, and would therefore make ideal cannon fodder. In the last weeks of 1915 over two thousand young men enrolled in the Irish Volunteers.

By this time Redmond and his party had formed their own organization. The rump rapidly grew more vocal and belligerent under the direction of the I.R.B. Organizers such as Mac-Dermott stumped the country spreading anti-British and anti-recruiting propaganda, helping to break up recruiting meetings and promising young hotheads that a "day of action" was coming soon. Newspapers and magazines—they included publications such as the *Spark, Honesty, Scissors & Paste*—published material which Dublin Castle could only regard as out and out pro-German propaganda. Plunkett's *Irish Review*, for instance, described the war as "a blessing" and said that it "approved" the possible "conquest" of Ireland by Germany. Alongside defaced British recruiting posters all over Dublin, fresh newspaper bills appeared, announcing "England's Last Ditch," "England's Growing Hypocrisy," and similar sentiments.

Mr. Birrell, as a member of the Cabinet, found it necessary to spend most of his time in London. His visits to Dublin had become increasingly rare and were, in fact, generally undertaken only at holiday times (drawing a complaint from the *Irish Times* that he was not earning his £4,000 a year salary). In Dublin, Sir Matthew Nathan, upon whom the day-to-day running of the country devolved, did what he could to keep the Sinn Fein agitation within bounds—short of attempting to disarm the Volunteers or arrest their leaders. He closed down one seditious newspaper after another—only to find them reopening under other names. He prosecuted Sinn Fein organizers such as Terence MacSwiney for seditious utterances—only to see an Irish magistrate let him off with a shilling fine. He banned the import of all arms and ammunition—only to discover that he had no means of preventing English

27

firms from importing what they liked. On one occasion an innocent-looking case labeled "Hardware," dispatched from a reputable firm in Sheffield to a respectable firm in Dublin, was found to contain five hundred bayonets. But on the whole he set his course by Mr. Birrell's policy—which was to refrain as much as possible from upsetting the delicate balance of order in Ireland despite having seen evidence that the Volunteers were growing increasingly more cocksure. On St. Patrick's Day, 1916, when they commandeered the entire center of Dublin to stage a march past their Chief of Staff, they had behaved with the contemptuous assurance of men who believed they could capture the whole city if they wanted to.

And then, on the night of March 20, the guns finally blazed. The incident occurred in the village of Tullamore, just outside Dublin. The trouble began on the nineteenth when some young men jeered the 7th Leinster Regiment, departing for France. The crowd turned on them and, the following night, waving Union Jacks, converged on the local Sinn Fein hall and stoned it. The defenders replied with shots, which brought the local police to the scene, and in the ensuing fracas some thirty shots were exchanged. Even Sir Matthew was shaken. Major-General L. B. Friend, G.O.C. Irish Command, ordered a detachment of infantry to stand by to raid Liberty Hall, Headquarters of the Citizen Army. But before General Friend could move, Mr. Birrell had dispatched an angry countermanding order from London.

Even when Major Price, early in April, produced a copy of a letter which had fallen into his hands, written by a Sinn Feiner to a friend abroad, and hinting at an early insurrection, Sir Matthew had no hesitation in writing in the margin: "The outbreak in the summer I look upon as vague talk." The Chief Secretary was more emphatic. "The whole letter is rubbish!" he wrote in the margin. He foresaw nothing but a few small outbreaks of homemade bomb throwing. Yet Sinn Fein drills and marches became more frequent; articles were published in the Irish Volunteers' official organ or James Connolly's *Workers' Republic,* telling men how to fight in the streets or to conduct guerilla warfare in open country.

From the imposing suite in Phoenix Park, where from the

28

windows could be seen the memorial to yet another man of destiny, Wellington, who had actually been born in Ireland, Lord Wimborne almost daily bombarded Nathan with reminders that the country was a powder keg. Repeatedly Sir Matthew replied that there could be brought against the Sinn Fein leaders no charges which would stick in any court; that there was nothing in the Defence Regulations to cover the situation. Sir Matthew probably hoped that the storm would blow itself out, though such hopes should have been dashed finally on Spy Wednesday, April 19, 1916. On that day a Dublin newspaper attempted to publish a document which, it claimed, had been copied from the official files of the Castle. It gave specific details of a directive signed by General Friend, ordering an extensive swoop on all Sinn Fein premises in Dublin. The censor killed the story at once, but that afternoon an Alderman Kelly, who was handed the document by the newspaper's editor, read it to a meeting of the Dublin Corporation. It produced an immediate uproar—proof of the Castle's desire to provoke an insurrection so that the British Government might be absolved from implementing Home Rule when the war ended. Sir Matthew, of course, knew that the document was a forgery, but it came near to achieving its real end. Professor MacNeill—who had all along been adamantly against any violence unless the Government *first* moved against the Volunteers—issued a general order to all Volunteers to stand ready to defend themselves.

Sir Matthew should have realized then what was happening, particularly in view of an Admiralty message which had flopped on to his desk five days before. This stated baldly that "a German ship and escort had left on the 12th, was due to arrive on the 21st, and that a rising had been planned for Easter Eve," and added: "But the Admiralty is sceptical of the reality of such an intention."

Wimborne had found it all so vague that he thought the ship was coming from America. Nathan, of course, took no action. The casual manner in which the message arrived had not helped. General Friend had received it from General Stafford, C in C Southern Ireland, who had taken it, again apparently quite casually, from the Admiral Commanding at

Queenstown. None appeared to appreciate that it was an inter-cept of messages passing between Clan na Gael in New York and the German Foreign Office in Berlin, which had been secured by Naval Intelligence's Room 40—that famous room where Admiral Sir Reginald Hall and his brilliant team of cipher experts had managed to crack the German codes; where everything passing between the German Embassy in Washington and the Foreign Office in the Wilhelmstrasse had long been an open book.

Physically, for heroes, the men who led the Irish insurrection were quite an extraordinary lot. One would be hard put to find a more unlikely collection of revolutionaries anywhere. Clarke was a small, frail man, aged fifty-eight, broken in health after fifteen years of confinement in an English jail. Pearse, tall and full of the dignity of his own destiny, was squint-eyed. MacDermott, dark-haired and almost handsome, limped as the result of polio; and Plunkett was dying of glandular tuberculosis of the throat. Of the three remaining members of the Provisional Government, only James Connolly possessed that robust health and tough, overpowering dynamism which are the usual marks of a true leader.

Without Clarke and MacDermott, however, it is highly unlikely that there would have been any insurrection at all. These men were its main architects—Clarke the old revolutionary master, MacDermott his zealous pupil. In his own person Clarke was a living link with the revolutionary effort of the previous generation, the dynamitards of the eighteen-eighties. Sunken-cheeked, wearing cheap glasses and with a drooping, seedy mustache, he looked for all the world like a downtrodden clerk or a petty shopkeeper—which is exactly what he was. Yet he was the most singularly dedicated of all the rebel leaders and generated enormous driving force. On his release from an English prison in the eighteen-nineties he had gone to the United States where he might easily have remained for the rest of his life. However, at the urgings of his old friend John Devoy, a former Fenian and the head of Clan na Gael, he had returned to Ireland. Once home, he had become the doyen, the old man of wisdom, the unresting force.

His greatest friend and ally was John MacDermott, who had begun life as a barman. MacDermott was an articulate speaker, who possessed energy and zeal. Perhaps his greatest asset was his charm. He is still remembered as "a delightful man"; yet he was also a person of hard and practical common sense. As a paid organizer of the Irish Volunteers (salary £150 per annum) he traveled about the countryside, speaking on the aims of Sinn Fein and the I.R.B., and enrolling young men. It was a key position and allowed him to appoint members of the Brotherhood to many of the top Volunteer commands. When the rising came, such men were to take their orders directly from Pearse.

Thomas MacDonagh was Professor of English at the National University and a stylish minor poet and dramatist. His presence among the leaders helped to lend the Irish Rebellion a certain poetic ambience. By nature he was an excitable and temperamental little man, given to exaggerated gestures, and sometimes perhaps a trifle too flamboyant, even arrogant. His moods alternated between gloom and high exultation. Normally, however, his conversation was rapid and full of learning and wit. His poetry, on the other hand, revealing more truly the real man, shows him as inwardly full of gloom, one who had the death wish. Indeed, he once wrote a poem called "The Suicide."

When Home Rule again became an issue in British politics, MacDonagh was content to be a happily married man with a young son, Donagh, (today a well-known playwright) and a predominating interest in European literature plus a half-hearted one in the revival of the Gaelic language. The attempts of the Conservative Party to block Home Rule, however, utterly incensed him and finally drove him along the path which eventually led to the firing squad.

The father of Joseph Mary Plunkett was a papal count and Director of the National Museum among many other honors and emoluments. The Plunketts had antecedents: a forebear was Blessed Oliver Plunkett, who may one day be canonized by Rome; kinsmen were Sir Horace Plunkett, who reorganized

Irish agriculture at the beginning of the century, and Lord Dunsany, the writer. Joseph and his two brothers, George and John, were imaginative and talented boys. Early in life Joseph discovered an aptitude for excellent minor poetry. As boys they played a great deal with toy soldiers, and while planning imaginary campaigns in the drawing room, Joseph is said to have worked out the basis of the rebel strategy during Easter Week—although it is more probable that he found inspiration in plans made by the United Irishmen in the eighteenth century and by Robert Emmett. Certainly he fancied himself as a military thinker. After he left Berlin in 1915 (he had paid a secret visit there to negotiate a cargo of arms), an exasperated member of the German General Staff was heard to exclaim: "That blowhard Plunkett! Imagine! He was trying to tell us how to conduct the war!"

Edmund Kent (Eamon Ceannt) remains perhaps the most shadowy of all the rebel leaders. By trade he was a £300-a-year employee in the Treasurer's Department of the Dublin Corporation; a zealous and sensitive man who possessed a passionate love for the Gaelic language and for that extraordinarily tuneless instrument known as the Irish pipes. Dressed in a saffron kilt, he once gave a recital for the Pope.

Towering above the others, however, stood Patrick Pearse and James Connolly—Pearse the young dreamer and idealist of whom many who knew him say, as of a saint: "He would never have made a success of anything in this life"; Connolly, the tough Socialist, the iron-willed man who would have gone out in rebellion with only a hundred men. At forty-six, Connolly was a thickset, round-faced, heavily mustached, bandy-legged Ulsterman. He could produce the most blistering language either with his pen or his tongue and reveled in audacity. From the age of eleven he had earned his own living and his education—while not inconsiderable—came wholly from voracious reading on his own account. When James Larkin, the Irish trade-union pioneer, left Dublin for America in 1914, Connolly inherited both the Irish Transport and General Workers' Union and the infant Citizen Army, which marched under the proud banner of the Plough and Stars. His first action as boss of Liberty Hall was to hang a banner outside the building declaring: "We serve neither King nor Kaiser, but Ireland." A stanch believer in the equality of men and women, he would allow no distinctions in Liberty Hall; even chose a woman to be a commander—Constance, Countess Markievicz, daughter of Sir Henry Gore-Booth, Bart., and a friend of the poet W. B. Yeats. By 1915, Connolly had converted part of Liberty Hall into a munitions factory where he made bayonets, steel bars (for forcing doors), and bombs. His speeches and writings, meanwhile, underlined his determination to use them. So much so that the Republican Brotherhood grew anxious. Scared that he might stage a small-scale effort on his own before they were ready ("What could he do by himself but stage a riot?" demanded Pearse, exasperated), they asked Connolly to meet them. The talks (held in a house in south Dublin) lasted for three days, and in the end Connolly was made a member of the Brotherhood and preparations for an insurrection were handled as a joint operation. Yet all that happened was that Connolly grew more reckless.

On Palm Sunday, April 16, he staged an elaborate ceremony at which the old flag of Ireland—a golden harp upon a green background—was hoisted onto the roof of Liberty Hall. The entire Citizen Army paraded in full dress. Thousands of Dubliners cheered and wept openly as Miss Molly O'Reilly, her long red tresses dancing in the wind, climbed out onto the parapet and hauled on the lanyard which sent the flag billowing in the wind.

That night Connolly delivered a last lecture to his troops on tactics. "I'm going to fight the way I want, not the way the enemy wants," he announced. "It'll be a new way, one the soldiers haven't been trained to deal with. We'll use the rooftops for a start. But remember this: if you do snipe your man, don't get enthusiastic and stand up and cheer, for if you do it'll probably be the last cheer you'll ever give." Then he reminded them: "The odds against us are a thousand to one. But if we *should* win, hold on to your rifles because the Volunteers may have a different goal. Remember, we're out not only for political liberty but for economic liberty as well. So hold on to your rifles!"

It is hardly likely that Pearse went into battle knowing that

Connolly had these reservations. Patrick Henry Pearse remains a most improbable insurgent leader. This thirty-six-year-old son of an Englishman (the family originally spelt the name Pierce), born of an Irish mother, was an introspective idealist who, even from childhood, foresaw his tragic destiny. While still a boy he knelt on a prie-dieu with his adoring brother Willie and swore an oath someday to "free Ireland or die fighting the English!" He grew up tall and well built, with a slightly stooping head and deep, profound eyes —the left one marred by a slight cast. What greatness, if any, he possessed was rarely apparent at first meeting: he was inclined to be aloof and reserved unless he happened to be addressing a large body of people, in which case the burning passion within him would blazon forth. It was largely because of his oratorical gifts that he eventually became prominent in Sinn Fein politics, although his actual delivery was not especially good—he never quite managed to overcome a slight lisp, which meant that he had always to speak slowly and fairly deliberately. In private life he was an ascetic. He neither drank nor smoked and normally he restricted his social pleasures to the delights of good conversation and the tumultuous subject of Irish independence. Once MacDonagh managed to lure him to a music hall and, out of sheer irreverence, insisted on breaking into his embarrassed reveries with comments on the physical attractiveness of the young ladies on the stage.

"Begad, Pat, isn't that a fine leg?" said MacDonagh.

"Like the limb of an angel," agreed Pearse.

"What fine eyes, Pat," said MacDonagh.

"Indeed, indeed, the eyes of an angel," replied Pearse.

"Beautiful lassies," persisted MacDonagh desperately.

"Angels, angels, every one," echoed Pearse reverently. Yet he had once managed to fall in love—and indeed treasured the memory of the girl all his life—his lost, drowned love.

> O lovely head of the woman I loved
> In the middle of the night I remember thee;
> But reality returns with the sun's awakening
> Alas, that the slender worm gnaws thee tonight.

And in a poem called "I Have Not Garnered Gold" he also wrote:

> In love I got but grief
> That withered my life.

Early in life he had become fascinated with the Gaelic language and with that lost culture of Ireland which once produced such visual masterpieces as the *Book of Kells* and the *Cross of Cong*. In young manhood he liked to dress himself as a tramp and go into far Connaught to study the ancient language and the people who still spoke it, and to take down some of the old songs and stories. He became wrapped in this "beauty of the Irish world" until finally this half-legendary society dominated his very life and thoughts.

His great work was the establishment of St. Enda's, an experimental, bilingual school at Rathfarnham. He founded it as a protest against the existing national school system which he said was an English one, and not a very good English one at that, complaining that it was intended simply to turn all Irishmen into good little Britons. He described it as a worse offense against Ireland "even than the Famine," insisting that Irish education must possess a soul of its own, molding Irish character as the English public-school system molded upper-class English character. In pursuit of his theories he covered the walls of St. Enda's with murals depicting the deeds of ancient Irish heroes, blazoning across them, too, the words of Cuchulainn (accurately echoing his own ambitions): "I care not if my life have only the span of a night and day if my deeds be spoken of by the men of Ireland." Here he practiced the most modern methods of bilingual teaching, dreaming that someday everybody in Ireland would speak with two tongues, English and Irish; yet even so, failure haunted him, and the school was deeply in debt when he marched out into Sackville Street. Shortly before Easter, 1916, confiding to a friend that he might be forced to close the school, he confessed that he hated the idea because he did not want to be pointed out in the streets of Dublin as a failure.

In 1912, Sean T. O'Kelly had him formally enrolled in

the I.R.B. By 1914, when war began in Europe and the Home Rule Bill lay suspended, Pearse was declaring: "If the English trick us again, there'll be war in Ireland; yes, by God! even if I have to lead it myself!" And shortly afterward he wrote: "The European war has brought about a crisis which may contain, as yet hidden within it, the moment for which the generations have been waiting. It remains to be seen whether, if that moment reveals itself, we shall have the sight to see and the courage to do; or whether it shall be written of this generation, alone of all the generations of Ireland, that it had none among it who dared to make the ultimate sacrifice."

By that time he had turned St. Enda's into a hotbed of revolution and sedition. Here MacDonagh and the other I.R.B. leaders met with him to work out their plans. On one occasion he declared: "My God, rather than go on living as we are, I would prefer to see Dublin in ruins." Yet behind this bloody intention remained the gentle scholar: "Wouldn't it be a grand thing to have no ambition whatever and to be a clerk with £2 a week? Yes, I should enjoy that—no worries and at ease among my books."

Like Connolly, he realized from the outset that an insurrection would fail in a military sense. On an afternoon in the winter of 1915, when he was standing with his mother on the first floor of St. Enda's, gazing out at the magnificent view which extended west to the Dublin mountains, he said, "How beautiful is all that has been created by God, Mother! Look at the slanting sun and the play of its shadow on the hills." Then he moved to the middle of the room, talking about the flowers, the trees, and the beautiful grounds surrounding the house.

"Soon, Mother, that will be no more for me . . . for us. The day is coming when I shall be shot . . . swept away like that . . . and my colleagues, shot like me."

"And Little Man, our Willie?" asked his mother.

"Willie? Shot like the others, Mother. We will all be shot."

In January, 1916, as Director of Organisation, he instructed all battalions of the Irish Volunteers to prepare for special maneuvers at Easter. MacNeill asked him directly if he were planning an insurrection and on receiving an assurance that he was not, returned to his medieval studies content to leave the running of the organization to Pearse as before. He should have known his man better. He should have remembered Pearse's words at the graveside of O'Donovan Rossa, an old Fenian whose body had been brought back from America for burial: "They think they have pacified Ireland. They think they have purchased half of us and intimidated the other half. They think they have foreseen everything: but the fools, the fools, the fools!—they have left us our Fenian dead, and while Ireland holds these graves, Ireland unfree shall never be at peace."

Until Holy Thursday, April 20, the great insurrection promised to be a really serious and impressive affair. If every Irish Volunteer, in the event, had answered the call, ten thousand would have been in action. If, in addition, once the fighting had started, Redmond's National Volunteers had joined in—as was hoped—there would have been more than one hundred thousand men under arms.

As it was, Pearse and Connolly went into action with the two hundred Citizen Army men and less than a tenth of the full membership of the Irish Volunteers, although Plunkett's military plan for Dublin alone had called for at least five thousand men. In addition, they marched out short of modern rifles and ammunition and without even a machine gun. Until Holy Thursday they had expected a substantial cargo of arms and ammunition, *including artillery,* from Germany. They had hoped, too—against admittedly forlorn hope—that the Germans might land an expeditionary force.

Their original over-all plan had hinged primarily on the successful landing of the German arms in the southwest of Ireland and the denial of the ports of Dublin and Kingstown to the Government by the use of at least one German submarine—whose efforts they intended to reinforce themselves by sinking blockships. They had earmarked the arms for their provincial battalions, which were even more abysmally supplied than the Dublin units (in County Limerick, for instance, some rebels possessed only enough ammunition to sustain

38

a five-minute action). Then, with the provincial Volunteers properly armed, they would establish a line based roughly on the River Shannon and from there advance upon the capital, reducing military and police barracks as they marched. This, although an ambitious strategy, was considered feasible enough because the British Army in wartime Ireland was standing substantially below strength.

In Dublin itself the principal buildings were to be seized and a series of fortresses established in an inverted crescent across the southern suburbs of the city, commanding the roads and railways by which military reinforcements were certain to enter the capital. If pressure ultimately proved to be too strong, these fortress garrisons were to fall back upon G.H.Q.; if that, too, eventually failed to hold, a line of retreat was to be kept clear northward as far as County Tyrone, where a link-up with northern units was to be made and the fight developed into guerilla warfare in open country. Connolly as a Socialist firmly believed that a capitalist government would never use artillery because of damage to property, and this became a cardinal tenet of the rebels' strategy. So, joyously his Citizen Army was able to parade through the streets of Dublin in the week before Easter, bravely singing:

> "We've got the guns and ammunition
> We know how to use them well,
> And when we meet the Saxon
> We'll drive them all to hell.
> We've got to free our country
> And to avenge all those who fell,
> And our cause is marching on.
> Glory, glory to old Ireland,
> Glory, glory to our sireland,
> Glory to the memory
> Of those who fought and fell,
> And we still keep marching on."

A bored British seaman patrolling the southwest coast of Ireland just before Easter, 1916, summed up the desolate environment as "nothing but rocks, sea, and Sinn Feiners." The Admiralty, however, knew a great deal better.

On February 10, 1916, Von Skal, a member of the German Ambassador's staff in Washington, had sent to an agent in Rotterdam a dispatch containing an extract from a letter written by John Devoy from New York and intended for the German Government. Devoy had reported: "Unanimous opinion is that action cannot be postponed much longer. It has therefore been decided to begin action on Easter Saturday. Unless entirely new circumstances arise you must have your arms and ammunition landed between Good Friday and Easter Saturday. Expect German help immediately after."

On March 4, the German Foreign Office had replied by cable to its Washington Embassy: "Between 20th and 23rd April, two or three steamers could land 20,000 rifles, ten machine guns with ammunition in Tralee Bay. Irish pilot boat to meet the trawlers at dusk north of the island of Inishtooskert at the entrance of Tralee Bay and show two green lights close to each other at short intervals."

Three weeks later another cable had reaffirmed that "three trawlers with a small cargo steamer capable of carying 1,400 tons will be sent." Furthermore, the message had stated that beginning April 8, Nauen wireless station would broadcast every midnight the code word "Finn"—meaning that the cargo had started—or the word "Bran" if a hitch had occurred. In reply, Devoy had dispatched urgent messages on March

18, 19, and 20 asking that Easter Sunday be fixed as the date for the delivery of arms and inquiring about the possibility of a submarine being sent to Dublin Bay. A suggestion that Germany should try to land troops "possibly from an airship" had drawn the tart reply from Berlin: "Sending German submarine to Dublin harbour impossible. Landing troops equally out of the question." (How amateurish of the Irish rebels to suppose troops could be dropped from the air!)

On March 21 the German Admiralty had finally decided to send only one ship and had selected the man to command her. He was Lieutenant Karl Spindler of the Imperial Naval Reserve; the ship, the *Libau*, formerly the *Castro*, was an impounded allied vessel. On April 9 the *Libau*, disguised as the *Aud*, a neutral Norwegian ship, sailed from Lubeck. Three days later, Sir Roger Casement and two companions left Wilhelmshaven in a submarine.

Admiral Sir Lewis Bayley, C in C, Queenstown, had an idea of all this, thanks to Room 40. From St. Patrick's Day onward he had taken special precautions along the west coast of Ireland. An array of sloops lay out to sea in a wide intercepting arc, and smaller craft constantly scoured every inlet and river mouth along the highly indented coastline. On Holy Thursday, in addition, he dispatched the cruiser H.M.S. Gloucester, plus three destroyers of the Grand Fleet, to watch for any vessel acting suspiciously.

The *Aud* took her time about reaching Ireland, steaming through the Kattegat and the Skaggerak and up the North Sea, in order to evade British blockade patrols. On her run down toward Ireland she was scrutinized by a British warship, but not stopped. Passing Rockall, she again came under surveillance, but once more was allowed to proceed. At 4:15 P.M. on April 20 she reached Inishtooskert, an uninhabited island in the northwest corner of Tralee Bay, where she was to rendezvous with Casement's U-Boat. Spindler saw no submarine, however, and after a half hour's wait steamed into the Bay. When dusk fell, he flashed a signal toward the shore, but got no reply from darkened, sleeping Fenit. For some hours he sailed about the Bay repeating the signal, but when the coastline remained stubbornly in darkness, dropped anchor at 1:30 A.M. in the lee of Inishtooskert, realizing that the plans had somehow misfired.

As Good Friday dawned, luck finally ran out for him. An armed trawler, *Setter II,* spotted him and drew alongside. Spindler remained calm and decided to bluff the Englishman. He explained that he had been forced to anchor because of an engine breakdown; then showed his forged papers which looked convincing enough, and finally opened up part of his cargo—some of the pots and pans mentioned in the ship's manifest. The Englishman, his suspicions lulled, bade him a cheery good-bye and resumed patrol. Spindler decided to wait for darkness, then move out into the Atlantic to evade the signaling stations strung along the coast, and make for Lisbon. Soon after 1 P.M., however, he received a second shock: a small steamer was racing toward him from the north end of Tralee Bay, a gun poised on her fo'c'sle. This was the armed trawler *Lord Heneage* whose skipper, Lieutenant W. H. A. Bee, R.N.R., had just picked up a message from Loop Head signaling station, warning him that a suspicious vessel had been spotted in Tralee Bay. A second message from Smerwick, relaying information that the foreigner was heaving things overboard, confirmed Bee's suspicions. As the furious Bee bore down on him, Spindler raised anchor and ordered full speed ahead, and despite his chief engineer's warning— "If you go on like this, the boilers will burst"—he kept at it until he began to pull away from his pursuers. In desperation the *Lord Heneage* opened fire at long range, Bee meanwhile sparking out a message: "Suspicious vessel sighted south of Tearaght, steering south-west." At 4:30 P.M. two sloops, *Zinnia* and *Bluebell,* hastened to intercept. At 5:40 P.M. *Bluebell* sighted the *Aud* racing toward the southwest and at 6:15 closed in, but *Zinnia,* finding a three-island tramp flying the Norwegian flag, and with the Norwegian colors painted on her sides, signaled her to proceed. *Zinnia*'s commander (Lieutenant-Commander G. F. Wilson, R.N.) decided, however, to shadow her, pending further orders from the Admiralty. When these arrived they were: "If *Aud* sighted she is to be brought into port for examination." Wilson at once asked Spindler to show his papers, but the German pretended not to understand and Wilson, thinking him a tiresome fellow, ordered *Bluebell* to escort him into Queenstown. Spindler, however, was far from finished.

"I am bound for Genoa," he signaled. "May I proceed?"

"Wait," replied *Bluebell*.

"Why?" demanded Spindler.

"Follow me to Queenstown, course S.60," replied *Bluebell*.

Once again Spindler attempted to dissimulate by pretending that he did not understand but Lieutenant Martin Hood, *Bluebell*'s skipper, his patience exhausted, fired a shell which just cleared the German's bows. This time Spindler obeyed, but at 9:25 next morning, the day calm and beautiful and both ships just off the Daunt Rock Lightship outside Queenstown Harbour, he suddenly halted. As *Bluebell* backed a cable's length to find out what was wrong, Spindler lowered his boats. Into them scrambled his crew, dressed now in German naval uniform. Then the smoke of an explosion burst into the air from charges laid in the *Aud*'s hold. Within ten minutes the ship had sunk. Down with her went twenty thousand rifles, a million rounds of ammunition, and ten machine guns, the spoils of Hindenburg's great victory over the Russians at Tannenberg and the last hope the insurgents had of entering the conflict on something like equal terms, at least so far as small arms were concerned.

The two green lights which should have blinked out at Spindler still hung idly in the Rink, the Volunteers' drill hall in Tralee.

Three weeks earlier, Patrick Cahill, Vice-Commandant of the Tralee Battalion, had traveled to Dublin to obtain the two green fishing lamps from John MacDermott. On his return, Austin Stack, his commandant, had ordered him to hang them in the Rink, adding that they would not be needed until sometime between the afternoon of Holy Saturday and the early hours of Easter Monday. Even the pilot, Mr. Matt O'Leary of Castlegregory, was not engaged until the day the *Aud* actually sailed in. Indeed, as Mr. O'Leary tramped home after taking on the job, he spotted a large, two-masted vessel lying about a mile off Inishtooskert. He had been told, however, that the

German ship would be small and that she would not arrive before Easter Sunday, so he decided that this was a British decoy ship and went on home and forgot about it.

Mr. O'Leary could hardly be blamed. What in fact had happened was that the Provisional Government and the German Admiralty, between them—aided and abetted by a difficulty in communicating—had managed to get their timings confused.

Direct communication between Dublin and Berlin was not, of course, feasible in wartime. Officially Ireland, as part of the United Kingdom, was Germany's enemy. The conspirators therefore had been forced to send their messages—and receive the answers—through John Devoy, the seventy-year-old head of Clan na Gael. Realizing that the British Government would probably break their codes if they used the Atlantic cables, the insurgents had decided upon a more cumbersome, if apparently safer, method of getting their messages through: they had employed personal emissaries. Early in March, Tommy O'Connor, a steward on an Atlantic liner, had carried a message to Devoy, giving Berlin the date of the rising. In addition this message had asked the Germans to land their arms between dusk on Holy Thursday and dawn on Easter Monday. In the first week of April, unfortunately, Pearse and his colleagues had developed second thoughts. If the arms arrived on Holy Thursday, they decided, Dublin Castle would be certain to find out before Sunday. The alternative was to ask the Germans to delay the landing until the insurrection (timed to start at 6:30 P.M., April 23, in Dublin, 7 P.M. in the provinces) had actually begun. Accordingly they sent Joseph Plunkett's niece, Philomena, to New York with fresh instructions. She arrived in Manhattan on April 14, exactly five days after the *Aud* had left Lubeck, two days after Casement had quit Wilhelmshaven. On receipt of a frantic message from Devoy, the German Admiralty—behaving rather more offhandedly than one would have expected of a service trying to raise a revolution in the enemy's rear—decided that, as the *Aud* had no wireless, there was nothing they could usefully do, and informed Devoy accordingly. The old man has sworn that a messenger was dispatched to Ireland to warn Pearse of this misfortune, but there is no record that the message was ever received; and, indeed, Pearse and his colleagues continued to act as though everything were all right. It was not until Good Friday, for example, that Plunkett sent three specialists to Kerry with orders to dismantle the Government radio at Valentia and set up their own transmitter in a remote spot in order to contact the arms ship as she came down the west coast. Yet they can scarcely escape censure for not ordering someone to keep a watch in Tralee Bay from Thursday onward as a simple, indeed, elementary precaution.

While Spindler lingered between Inishtooskert Island and Fenit pier, the German submarine U-19 began nosing her way into Tralee Bay; aboard her were Sir Roger Casement and two companions, Robert Monteith of the Irish Republican Brotherhood and Sergeant Daniel Bailey of the Royal Irish Rifles, who, while a prisoner of war in Germany, had been induced to join Sir Roger's Irish Brigade. For some reason Lieutenant Weisbach, commander of U-19, made no attempt to communicate with Spindler, although he had sighted him off his starboard beam just before dusk. For the next hour and a half, then, U-19 also joined in the search for the two green lights, while Casement and his companions stood in the conning tower straining their eyes into the darkness. The night was murky and the sea calm; quite ideal, Monteith thought, for running guns ashore, but as time passed and the pilot did not appear, he heard the German officers swearing into the night. Casement's face took on a cold, drawn, and hopeless look. Finally, anxious for the safety of his ship, Weisbach informed Casement that he intended running deep into Tralee Bay and landing them somewhere along the deserted shore.

In Dublin, Bulmer Hobson, Secretary of the Irish Volunteers, was working late at his office in Dawson Street that evening when two Volunteer officers, J. J. O'Connell and Eimar Duffy, burst in upon him with startling news.

"Several of the country companies have received orders to take part in an insurrection next Sunday," exploded O'Connell.

The announcement staggered Hobson. "We must see Mac-Neill at once!" he exclaimed angrily.

They drove straight to Rathfarnham and at 11 P.M. knocked

on the door of a large Victorian villa in Woodtown Park. MacNeill greeted them in his pajamas. Inside Hobson explained what had brought them. When he had finished, MacNeill thundered, "My authority must not be flouted! I must see Pearse at once and tell him what I think of him!" And although it was well past midnight, they drove out to St. Enda's where MacNeill pounded on the door until he had gained admittance.

"I've just learned that you've issued orders for an insurrection!" he immediately accused Pearse when they were led into the study.

Thrown off balance by this unexpected intrusion, Pearse fumbled for a moment. Finally he admitted, "Yes, a rising is intended."

MacNeill lost his temper and for the next few moments subjected Pearse to a blistering abuse. Finally the latter interjected, "Yes, you've been deceived. But it was necessary."

"Well, there'll be no rising!" MacNeill rasped out. "There'll be no waste of lives for which I'm directly responsible. I'll not allow a half-armed force to be called out. I can promise you this: I'll do everything I can to stop a rising—everything, that is, short of ringing up Dublin Castle." And with that and an angry wave of his fist, MacNeill stamped out.

Behind him he left a chastened and dejected Pearse, slumped wearily behind his big desk. Through the great picture window at his back night obscured the low Dublin mountains and the grounds of the school—grounds where his hero, Robert Emmett, had paid court to Sarah Curran more than a century before.

After a while his mother had come in. "Is there anything wrong, Pat?" she asked gently.

"Nothing, Mother; nothing much," replied Pearse. "I've had some trouble with MacNeill, that's all. But it'll all come right in the end, you'll see. So don't worry." And with that he rose and got ready to go into Dublin. By the time he left, he had fought the last battle with his conscience, had made the fatal decision from which there could be no turning back.

At 2:30 A.M. on Good Friday, 1916, U-19 finally hove to a mile or so offshore and a small tublike collapsible boat was lowered into the water. Sir Roger, looking down at it, said encouragingly, "Well, it'll be a much greater adventure going ashore in this cockleshell, anyway." Then he jumped in and took a seat in the stern while Monteith and Bailey slipped into the front seats. All three donned life belts and strapped their coats and kits to the seats—each kit containing a Mauser pistol, a pair of Zeiss binoculars, and a sheath knife. From the conning tower there were shouts of good luck and then U-19 edged away to be lost in the darkness.

The three men believed that with luck they should be able to get safely ashore, however stringently the coastline was patrolled by police and other government agents. Their intention was to reach Tralee shortly after breakfast and there contact Commandant Austin Stack. When they had been rowing for about an hour, Casement declared he could see the coast ahead. Then the sea suddenly grew rough, great green hissing caverns opening up all around them and even as he shouted, "Only two hundred yards more," a giant wave overturned the boat. They all might have drowned if it had not been for the life belts. As it was, Monteith managed to touch the flatbottom, which miraculously righted itself and they scrambled aboard. Wet, miserable, and exhausted they allowed themselves to be carried toward shore.

When the boat grounded, only Monteith and Bailey had enough strength left to crawl from it. Monteith, up to his waist in water, held the craft steady while Bailey carried the coats and kits ashore. Casement was too weak to struggle and had to be helped by Bailey while Monteith tried to scuttle the boat. This proved impossible, however, and he gave up, stumbling out of the water to find his companions stretched on the sand. Casement, hardly conscious, lay half in, half out of the water. His eyes were closed and without his beard (he had shaved it off in order to avoid recognition) Monteith thought he looked like a sleeping child. He chafed Casement's legs and body until he revived sufficiently to move about by himself. But Monteith was to regret for the rest of his life that he had not left him there to die by the water's edge.

Sir Roger Casement, of course, was among the most distinguished Irishmen of his day. Born in Ulster of Protestant stock, he had won fame in the opening years of the century by courageously exposing the atrocities practiced against natives by rubber planters in the Belgian Congo and the Putamayo area of Peru. Upon retirement from the British consular service, he had become a founder member of the Irish Volunteers and its first treasurer. Early in 1914, he had left Ireland for the United States, hoping by lectures, cajolery, and charm, plus his own great personal prestige, to raise funds.

By this time he had swung violently to the view that the Irish insurrectionary movement should seek Germany as an ally. Following the outbreak of war in 1914, he traveled to Berlin, where he gave the German Foreign Office some information (which they already had) that a group of nationalist-minded Irishmen had organized themselves into an armed and disciplined body and hoped soon to rise in rebellion. He underlined the advantages Germany would gain from an insurrection in Ireland, especially if they assisted with an expeditionary force. The German Government, however, showed itself lukewarm. Casement asked if they would send some experienced officers to Ireland; with German officers to lead them, the raw Volunteers might cause real embarrassment to the British Army, but this suggestion, also, was left pretty much in the air by the Germans.

In March, 1916, while Casement lay ill in a Munich sanatorium, his hopes of raising a strong Irish Brigade from among Irish-born prisoners almost dead, he was informed that the date of the Rebellion had at last been fixed. Quitting the hospital at once, he got in touch with Monteith, who informed him that the Germans not only had decided *not* to send an expeditionary force (although they were anxious to land the fifty-odd members of the Irish Brigade raised so far) but that they had no intention of dispatching even artillery. Incensed at such pusillanimity after his many years of effort, Casement stormed into both the German Foreign Office and the Admiralty, demanding much greater support. "All they want is cheap Irish blood," he complained bitterly to Monteith.

Angered by Casement's increasingly outrageous demands, the General Staff finally turned on him. Captain Nadolny, their spokesman, bluntly informed him that Germany had no idealistic interest in Irish freedom. "If it were not for our hopes of a military diversion, we would not even send the rifles," he explained cynically. "As it is, we may well cancel the shipment altogether and leave your countrymen in the lurch." Staggered by this show of Germanic ruthlessness, Casement decided to return to Ireland as soon as possible. On April 12, two days before Miss Plunkett arrived in Manhattan, he set sail from Wilhelmshaven. Such was his elation at leaving Germany, where he had suffered such desperate disillusionment, that he lightheartedly noted in his diary that evening: "Left Wicklow [code name for Wilhelmshaven] in Willie's yacht."

It was undoubtedly the last time he would ever feel even so remotely happy.

At 4 A.M. on Good Friday, the collapsible was discovered floating on the tide. For no particular reason John MacCarthy, a farmer, had awakened at two o'clock that morning and had decided to do something he had never done in his life before— walk to a Holy Well along Banna Strand to say his prayers. When he sighted the collapsible, he called Pat Driscoll, a neighbor, who helped him to drag it in. They found a dagger lying in the bottom and, in the sand nearby, a box containing a thousand rounds of ammunition. Farther up the beach they found MacCarthy's small daughter playing with three loaded revolvers. Their most significant discovery, however, was the footprints of three men in the sand. As there was no sign of them, MacCarthy asked Driscoll to fetch the local police.

Sergeant Thomas Hearn and Constable Bernard Reilly spent the better part of that morning making a thorough search of the neighborhood. At 1 P.M. they finally reached a prehistoric castle known locally as McKenna's Fort, a circular stone ruin surrounded by a trench, the interior thickly covered with bushes. As Reilly worked cautiously around this fort, he sighted a crouching man and immediately covered him with his rifle, threatening to shoot.

"That's a nice way to treat an English visitor," said Casement casually, rising to his feet. "I'm not armed, you know. I won't do you any harm."

49

Reilly called the sergeant.

"What are you doing here, anyway?" Hearn demanded when he came over.

"What's your authority for asking me that?" countered Casement.

"I can ask you any questions I like," said Hearn firmly. "I could arrest you under the Defence Regulations. What's your name?"

"Richard Morton, of Denham, Buckinghamshire," lied Casement. "I'm an author."

"Oh," said Hearn. "What books have you written?"

"One on the life of St. Brendan the Navigator," replied Casement. Hearn, however, had noticed that his trousers were wet and that there was sand on his boots. He ordered Reilly to search him and a slip of paper was found in his waistcoat. There was writing in a strange language on it.

"This isn't Irish, anyway," said Reilly.

"I've no idea what it is," murmured Casement. "I've never seen it before."

At Ardfert a further search disclosed that he possessed five sovereigns and eleven shillings in English money, but apart from the arms and ammunition found near the collapsible, the only incriminating evidence against him consisted of two sheets of typewritten paper which he had tried to dispose of as he was being led away from McKenna's Fort. These bore a series of numbers written in a foreign script. There were also phrases corresponding with these numbers, which indicated that this was some kind of code. The phrases included "await further instructions," "further ammunition needed," and "send another ship to."

Sergeant Hearn, who had as yet not guessed the prisoner's real identity, telephoned Tralee for instructions (at a time when Monteith and Bailey were already in the town seeking help). The Tralee authorities, on the alert immediately, ordered the prisoner to be sent forward, and later that evening they put him on the train for Dublin, en route for the Tower of London.

In Dublin, Patrick Pearse, faced with the wreckage of all his plans, sought out MacDermott and MacDonagh, and early on Good Friday morning, accompanied by both, bearded Mac-Neill in his home. He found the professor still in bed, but quite ready to talk—though only to MacDermott; he would have nothing to do with Pearse. Ushered into the bedroom, Mac-Dermott came at once to the point. A cargo of German arms was about to be landed in Kerry; MacNeill must bow to reason.

"I'm against a rising and I intend to do everything I can to stop one," the professor said with determination.

"Look," said MacDermott patiently, "the fact is that we control the Volunteers and we just won't let you. Anyhow, it's too late for you to interfere now. Hostilities are inevitable."

MacNeill digested this. An arms landing in Ireland at this juncture was certain to bring the wrath of the Government down on them. Bloody force would be used if necessary and the whole Volunteer movement disarmed.

"Well," he said firmly after brief deliberation, "if we have to fight or be suppressed, then I suppose I'm ready to fight."

"Thank God for that!" replied MacDermott fervently.

He went downstairs to tell the others, leaving MacNeill to get dressed. Later, when MacNeill entered the drawing room, he approached Pearse, shook him by the hand and, amity restored, he invited them all to stay to breakfast.

A dispatch saying that the *Aud* had been scuttled landed on Sir Matthew Nathan's desk shortly after ten o'clock on the

51

morning of April 22, Holy Saturday. Beside it was one reporting the arrest of a certain "Richard Morton," and another which said that Commandant Austin Stack, trying to secure "Morton's" release, had been arrested in Kerry. Even Sir Matthew suddenly realized that he had a crisis on his hands.

Then the telephone rang. It was Vice-Regal Lodge.

Although Lord Wimborne had worked with Nathan without actually falling out with him, he had found the latter's supine attitude toward the current unrest in Ireland annoying. It seemed to him thoroughly ridiculous to suggest that, simply because Britain had her hands full in Europe, peace in Ireland had to be purchased at any price. Firm action by the Government—the arrest of the Sinn Fein leaders, the disarming of the Volunteers, the introduction of conscription—should, in his opinion, have been carried out several months ago. As it was, thousands of shirkers were simply getting away with it. Conscription had worked in England. It had languished in Ireland only because Birrell and Nathan had behaved pusillanimously. At a time when the Empire needed every man it could lay its hands on, a policy of restraint could only be construed as weakness.

Now, speaking from his regally magnificent residence in Phoenix Park, Baron Wimborne could scarcely conceal his anxiety. These reports certainly clinched matters, he said. The Sinn Feiners could now be charged with "hostile association with the enemy" under a section of the Defence Regulations. All the necessary evidence was available.

Sir Matthew listened carefully, but at the end of the conversation he resolutely refused to commit himself.

Twice again that day Sir Matthew had a golden chance to act decisively. On both occasions he hesitated. His first opportunity came when he motored to Vice-Regal Lodge, taking with him the startling news that "Richard Morton" was none other than Sir Roger Casement. It was a climactic moment for the British Imperial interest in Ireland when Nathan and Wimborne sat down in Vice-Regal Drawing Room to decide what they should do. Casement's arrest, plus the scuttling of the *Aud*, was certainly proof that the Sinn Feiners were in league with the Germans. And yet . . .

And here Sir Matthew had paused. The loss of the *Aud*,

he said tentatively, really meant that there would be no uprising now. With their arms and ammunition at the bottom of the sea, their most distinguished leader under arrest, even the Sinn Feiners must realize that there was no point in going on. Sir Matthew, watching the Lord Lieutenant's countenance, saw that this line of reasoning was being well received. Yet he was agreeably surprised all the same—aware as he was of His Excellency's very strong views—when Lord Wimborne said he agreed that a rebellion must now be considered unlikely. Indeed, added Wimborne thoughtfully, all this probably marked the collapse of the Sinn Fein movement.

And with this note of optimism ringing in his ears, Sir Matthew took his leave.

Neither of them was right, of course. By midafternoon Pearse and his colleagues knew the complete extent of the disaster and reacted quickly. Far from changing their plans, they considered it more imperative than ever to go ahead. The Castle, they decided, would be certain to order their arrest and thereby wreck the whole carefully built-up movement for national independence.

At this point The O'Rahilly took a hand in the drama. Handsome, wealthy, gallant, he became angry when he learned that the I.R.B. had kidnaped Bulmer Hobson, presumably to keep him out of harm's way while they went ahead with their plans. On Friday evening, while Pearse sat alone in his study, the door suddenly opened and The O'Rahilly stood before him, drawn revolver in hand.

"Whoever kidnaps *me* will have to be a quicker shot," he announced with a theatrical flourish.

Pearse stared at the enraged face above the gun barrel pointed directly at his heart and replied calmly, "No one wants to kidnap you, man. Sit down and throw away that gun!"

And such was the quality of his personality that The O'Rahilly, a trifle shamefacedly, lowered the revolver. For a while the two of them sat and argued, failing, however, to reach agreement. Pearse's arguments, maintained The O'Rahilly, were those of a poet and idealist, not of a practical man of affairs.

Early on Saturday morning, The O'Rahilly, still furiously

determined to stop Pearse, made his way to Woodtown Park in an effort to convince MacNeill that "the insurrection *could* and *should* be averted." He found the chief of the Volunteers "terribly agitated." Skimpy press reports from Kerry, relating to the capture of a man who had landed from a German submarine, had been enough to persuade him that something had gone seriously wrong down there. He paced the room, almost distraught, as The O'Rahilly enumerated reasons why he should intervene.

MacNeill at last announced that he would ask all Volunteer staff officers to meet him at Dr. James O'Kelly's house on the Rathgar Road at 9:30 that evening. Then he sat down to write out a series of countermanding orders for dispatch to all battalions throughout the country, convinced that they would be enough to prevent a rebellion.

At fifteen minutes past six that evening, hoping to provide further moral support for MacNeill, The O'Rahilly brought him two Volunteer officers, O'Loughlin and Fitzgibbon, who had just returned from Kerry. They possessed full details of the capture of Casement and the scuttling of the *Aud* and their stories reinforced MacNeill's convictions. But Pearse, he decided, must be given a last chance. He therefore asked The O'Rahilly to drive him to St. Enda's immediately. On arrival he was received, alone, by Pearse and they had a short but animated conversation. Then, still arguing fiercely, they came out together and halted at the top of the steps. Neither made any attempt to conceal his bitterness.

Angrily, almost rudely, Pearse shouted, "We've used your name and your influence for all they're worth. Now we don't need you any more. It's no use your trying to stop us. Our plans are laid and they'll be carried out."

"Your plans are so well laid," retorted MacNeill acidly, "that the police at Ardfert have already upset them. Anway, I'm still Chief of Staff of the Irish Volunteers and I'm going to forbid tomorrow's mobilization."

"Our men, at least, will never obey you," said Pearse.

"Well, if they don't, that's your responsibility," answered MacNeill. "If you should want to see me again, I'll be at Dr. O'Kelly's house on the Rathgar Road from nine o'clock tonight." And with that he left abruptly.

Bidding the boys of St. Enda's and members of his own Volunteer company good-bye, Pearse said, "And always remember this: if you're ever free, it's the son of an Englishman who will have freed you."

At the gate, as he and his brother mounted their bicycles to ride into Dublin, his mother warned, "Now, don't do anything rash, Pat!"

Dutifully Pearse replied, "No, Mother."

When ten o'clock had passed without word from Pearse, MacNeill indicated that his countermanding order should be dispatched at once. It read:

WOODTOWN PARK
RATHFARNHAM
CO. DUBLIN

22 April, 1916.

Volunteers completely deceived. All orders for special action are hereby cancelled, and on no account will action be taken.

Signed:
Eoin MacNeill,
Chief of Staff

The O'Rahilly jumped into his car and began a whirlwind drive which took him through six counties before he ended up in Limerick city the following morning. Other couriers left Dublin by train and taxi. Then at 10:30 P.M. MacNeill took an irrevocable step; he composed an announcement for publication in a Dublin Sunday newspaper:

Owing to the very critical position, all orders given to Irish Volunteers for tomorrow, Easter Sunday, are hereby rescinded and no parades, marches, or other movement of Irish Volunteers will take place. Each individual Volunteer will obey this order strictly in every particular.

And to make certain that this was published, he personally cycled down to the *Sunday Independent* offices to see the editor.

55

At 7 P.M. Sir Matthew Nathan again visited Vice-Regal Lodge, only to discover that Lord Wimborne had changed his mind. Now he wanted an immediate swoop on Liberty Hall —under the impression, apparently, that this was the headquarters of all subversion and that if he raided it, he was bound to catch all the plotters together. Sir Matthew, palpably unnerved at this, could only repeat his earlier advice against "precipitate action" and add that he was not prepared to accept responsibility for a raid which could easily be a spark to set the country alight. He was still mentally balancing the pros and cons of this argument when he returned to Dublin Castle.

Easter Sunday morning dawned in all the soft beauty of an Irish spring. The altars of the Dublin churches, immaculate in their adornments of starched white linen and solid gold candelabra became even more beautiful with the addition of immense sprays of Easter lilies. Among the communicants were hundreds of Irish Volunteers.

Nora Connolly returned from Mass to find her father up and dressed in his general's uniform, quietly singing to himself:

> "We've another saviour now,
> That saviour is the sword."

She had arrived in Dublin early that morning after a frantic all-night train journey from the north. Late on Saturday, Mac-Neill's order had reached hundreds of Volunteers gathered at Dungannon and Nora had at once left for Dublin to see her father in order to find out what had happened. Connolly had reassured her: "Pray God, Nora, if there's no Rising, may an earthquake swallow up Ireland," and had then calmly gone back to bed.

Like a dutiful daughter, Nora prepared breakfast, as members of the Provisional Government turned up one by one. The last to arrive was Pearse. He had already breakfasted at Sean T. O'Kelly's home where he and Willie had stayed the night. While the others were still eating, a Citizen Army girl entered the room with a copy of the *Sunday Independent*.

56

"Look, Mr. Connolly," she said. "The *Independent* says 'No maneuvers today!' "

"What's that?" said Connolly and grabbed the paper from her. He paled as he read MacNeill's announcement.

"Let me see it," said Pearse. He read the paragraph, then looked at Connolly and said, "I knew nothing about this."

The other leaders had risen to their feet, and Connolly led them to the Council Room. Tom Clarke took the chair and immediately proposed that they should go ahead with the insurrection as planned, arguing that once the fighting had begun in Dublin, Volunteers throughout the country would join in. Pearse disagreed and MacDermott, for once deserting his old friend and mentor, supported him. Connolly finally cast his vote in favor of postponement, arguing that it would be impossible to get enough men out now anyway. Eventually a decision was reached to rise at noon the following day.

Tom Clarke, returning to his tobacconist's shop in Great Britain Street, after the agonizing conference ended at 1 P.M., confided to his bodyguard, Vice-Commandant Pierce Beasley, "MacNeill has ruined everything—all our plans. I feel like going away to cry."

Dublin looked serene and lovely that afternoon—as all spacious and well-ordered cities did before the advent of motorcars. Open-deck tramcars provided almost the only mechanical means of travel in Sackville Street. St. Stephen's Green was filled with leisurely strollers, men in curly-brim bowlers, women in wide hats and ground-sweeping hobble skirts. Great trees rustled gently, casting shade broken by shifting discs of sunlight. Cab horses munched peacefully at the "hazards."

In Liberty Hall flatbed presses were rolling off a thousand copies of the Proclamation of the Republic. Type was scarce and the printers—Christopher Brady, Michael Molloy, and William O'Brien—used sealing wax to turn a capital F into a capital E. Countess Markievicz grabbed a copy with the ink still wet on it and read out the contents from the steps, characteristically disregarding the detectives mingling among the crowds.

By the late evening Lord Wimborne had decided to make a last desperate attempt to carry out his clear duty in the teeth of Sir Matthew's continuing opposition. At 7 P.M. when Nathan returned to Vice-Regal Lodge along with Colonel H. V. Cowan—military commander in Dublin while the Commander in Chief was in London—Wimborne asked his opinion about raiding Liberty Hall.

"Well, sir, I couldn't get in without fighting my way in," admitted Cowan. "And to do that I'd need a field gun. The nearest, unfortunately, is at Athlone."

"How many men have you available?" asked Wimborne.

"There are always four hundred standing to arms in Dublin barracks," said Cowan.

Wimborne hesitated. Then in a grandly theatrical gesture he called his private secretary and canceled an official trip to Belfast for the following day. "I'm not leaving Dublin until I've secured the arrest of these Sinn Feiners," he declared.

"In that case, I'd like to consult with some of my staff as well as the Commissioner of the Metropolitan Police," said Cowan. "May I return at ten o'clock?"

Wimborne grimly nodded agreement.

At ten o'clock Sir Matthew again arrived at Vice-Regal Lodge for the meeting. He was ushered into the Drawing Room where he found six men waiting, including his Excellency.

"I want between sixty and a hundred of the ringleaders arrested tonight," said the Lord Lieutenant, as soon as the group was seated.

"On what charge?" demanded Sir Matthew. "To hold them on a charge of 'hostile association' would need the agreement of the [British] Home Secretary."

"They could be kept on remand," snapped Wimborne. "Anyway, I'll sign the warrants and accept full responsibility." And having thus steam-rollered his way through Sir Matthew's first objection, he got down to the real business of the meeting. The obstacles to the actual physical arrest of the Sinn Feiners were formidable. An immediate raid on Liberty Hall was, of course, out of the question, as Cowan had pointed out, because, without artillery, the loss of life would be high. Major Price also mentioned that it was unlikely that all the Sinn Feiners would be together under one roof anyway. For over an hour the discussions continued before it was decided to put into operation a plan proposed by the Commissioner of Police. This involved a joint military-police swoop on the homes of the Sinn Fein leaders about two o'clock some morning when they were certain to be asleep. The raid, however, could not be carried out at once—it would take a couple of days to make the necessary arrangements.

It was well after midnight before the meeting broke up. It had been agreed that Nathan would cable Birrell first thing in the morning, and that meantime the military and police would begin preparations.

In the early hours of Easter Monday, MacDonagh issued a final order to the Dublin battalions: "The four city battalions will parade for inspection and route march at 10 A.M. today. Commandants will arrange centres. Full arms and equipment and one day's rations."

Shortly afterward a whistle blew in Liberty Hall and sleeping men sprang to their feet, rifles ready. It was only a false alarm, however. Outside, the streets lay dark and empty, the Liffey glistening under the gaslight. At 2 A.M. scouts posted near British barracks reported that all was quiet within. The city slept and had no premonitions.

Garry Holohan planned to explode five bags of gelignite in the Magazine Fort in Phoenix Park to signal the start of the Rebellion. The idea was not really very spectacular, not very violent—not in a world already inured to violence. This was the two hundred and sixty-fifth day of the second year of the First World War. It was the sixty-fifth day of the Battle of Verdun. Along the Meuse, the Germans would use flame guns against the French, explode infernal mines near Souchez and win a bloody footing in British trenches. At Loos, Arras, and Ypres a series of spectacular artillery duels would take place while farther along the front historic French chateaux would be systematically pounded to rubble. It was not a world where there was much latitude to indulge delicate susceptibilities.

Nevertheless, on the home front affairs were being conducted in an atmosphere of near-normality. In England, for instance, their Majesties spent the holiday, as usual, at Windsor. In Brighton and Southend, piers and cafés were packed with Londoners who had swarmed in from early morning. Along Carlton House Terrace, convalescent officers, sitting out in wicker chairs or propped up in beds at open windows to enjoy the sun, cast a shadow of the war. In Ireland, despite a few scarcely felt food shortages, it was even more difficult to imagine that there was desperate trouble in the world although the recruiting posters—torn by Sinn Fein sympathizers—offered these reminders:

In addition to the Fairyhouse race meeting, the Spring Show of the Royal Dublin Society was opening at Ballsbridge. In the afternoon, St. John Ervine was offering a matinee performance of Yeats' *Cathleen Ni Houlihan* at the Abbey. That night, too, the D'Oyly Carte Opera Company was due to open a season at the Gaiety—in fact four theaters proposed to give Dubliners and the many visitors from out of town a chance to forget their troubles.

Holohan, still in bed at half past nine, was aroused by his friend Paddy Daly, who was an expert on the Magazine Fort. Six months earlier he had wangled himself a job with Sir Patrick Shortall's building firm when extensive repairs were being carried out at the fort, and he had seized the opportunity to map the interior and learn the drill of the guard. He had also found out where the keys to the high-explosive store were kept.

"Get up for God's sake!" said Daly. "We're going out at twelve!"

"Surely the Rebellion isn't until this evening?" said Holohan.

"That's all a mistake," said Daly. "Get up!"

Having roused him, Daly left to see about mobilizing other men while Holohan dressed, thinking that his first job must be to get hold of Volunteer Tim Roche and tell him to commandeer a car and have it beside the Fort, engine running, by half past eleven. Next he would have to help Daly with the mobilization. Apparently he had misunderstood John Mac-Dermott when he had talked to him on Sunday at Liberty Hall. MacDermott had said, "Everything is off for twenty-four hours," and Holohan had taken this literally. Smarting

61

at his blunder, he jumped on his bicycle and went off to see Roche. Having made the arrangement with him, he set out to assist in the mobilizing. By 11:05 A.M., however, he had found only three men at home and moodily made his way to Liberty Hall to report the situation to Commandant Connolly. The Commandant-General gave him a note to the commandants of the four city battalions, allocating him a man from each, so by 11:45 he had an additional four men. The last, a lad named Barney Mellowes, begged for a chance to say good-bye to his mother.

"There isn't time!" Holohan shouted in exasperation. "For God's sake, man, get on a tram at once!"

Dispirited, he turned toward home, certain that the idea of blowing up the Fort as a signal would have to be canceled. Indeed, as he passed through St. Stephen's Green, he saw Commandant MacDonagh's men mobilizing to seize Jacob's biscuit factory. When he reached home, however, he was pleasantly surprised to find thirty lads waiting for him. Paddy Daly was there giving them final instructions. The party was to split into three detachments—the first and second going by tram to Phoenix Park, the third traveling there by bicycle. All were to meet on the playing fields beside the Fort, and to make it appear that they were assembling to play football.

At five minutes past twelve Holohan and Daly stopped at Whelan's shop near the Four Courts and bought a football. At twelve fifteen they entered Phoenix Park and approached Thomas's Hill, on the brow of which squatted the low stone Fort. Roche was waiting in the driveway—although without the motorcar. He explained that he had managed to steal one all right, but on the way up to the Park had driven it straight into a lamppost. Unhurt, he had jumped out and hailed a passing jaunting car. Holohan, glancing at the waiting jarvey, wondered if they could really get away safely. Well, there was nothing to do now but make the best of it.

The men stood bunched together at the fence circling the Fort. Holohan punted the ball and they began scrambling for it. It was 12:17 now and down in the city—and all over Ireland, Holohan hoped—the Rebellion would have begun. On the far side of the Liffey the spires of St. Patrick's and

Christ Church glittered boldly against the sky. The ball was kicked around the corner of the Fort within sight of the sentry on the main gate. It was kicked again and this time landed near him, skidded against the fence, and came to rest at his feet. The sentry grinned. He had no time even to stiffen his muscles before they all piled on top of him. . . .

Daly led the way inside. Once in the long passageway, which ran through the length of the building, he turned right, into the guardroom. Holohan continued straight on until he emerged into a bright quadrangle with a raised platform four feet high, running around the walls. There were short flights of steps at each corner. On one side stood a soldier, his back toward Holohan, a small hut partially screening him. Holohan yanked out his automatic and shouted, "Surrender!"

The soldier swiveled. But for the hut, he could probably have picked Holohan off easily. He shifted right to get in a better shot, then suddenly changed his mind and pulled out his bayonet. Holohan, running toward him, squeezed the automatic twice and watched him go down, clutching at his thigh. As Mellowes raced in, the wounded man cried out, "Sirs, sirs, don't shoot me! I'm an Irishman myself and the father of five children!"

"You'll be all right," Mellowes said. They lifted him to his feet, but he collapsed immediately, blood welling from his thigh.

"We'll just have to leave him," said Holohan. Then, turning to the wounded man, he said, "Don't worry—we'll let your pals know." And with that he leaped down off the platform and retreated across the quadrangle. Inside the guardroom he found ten military prisoners, all young, all frightened, one weeping.

"One of your chaps is hurt," he said, jerking a thumb toward the quadrangle. Then he asked where Daly was.

"In the small-arms store," said a young rebel.

In a little room off the main passageway, he found Daly. With him were two Volunteers—Holohan's brother Pat and a friend, Edward Martin. Daly had had wretched luck. He had easily overpowered the guard, had rounded up Mrs. Isabel Playfair, wife of the Fort's Commander (on active service in

France) and her two boys and a girl, and had warned her that he was going to blow the place up. He had allowed her exactly six minutes to get out. Then, with success apparently in his grasp, he had reached for the key to the high-explosives store, only to find the hook empty. The key had been taken by the officer in charge, who had gone off to Fairyhouse. Thoroughly chagrined, Daly took, instead, the key to the small arms, and by the time Holohan arrived had placed bags of gelignite next to the wall of the high-explosives store and piled belts of ammunition on top of them. With luck, the explosion would blast through the wall and send the whole lot up.

Daly ordered Holohan to set the fuses. This done, they all returned to the guardroom where Daly warned the prisoners, "When we let you out, don't try to follow us or raise the alarm!" The rifles which had been captured from them lay neatly stacked in a long rack and he had these taken outside. Then together he and Holohan shepherded the disarmed soldiers through the door, where Daly ordered, "Now clear off!"

The soldiers showed no desire to stop and argue, and left rapidly, while the young insurgents, waving the captured rifles and bawling out "The Soldier's Song," streamed down the hill. At the foot, the rifles were dumped into the jaunting car. Then six or seven rebels climbed aboard while the rest scattered through the Park.

"Off you go now!" yelled Daly, and the terrified jarvey whipped up his nag and drove toward the gate. Holohan, following on his bicycle, suddenly noticed a young fellow running some distance ahead of them.

"That's young Playfair; we'd better stop him," shouted Daly.

The boy ran toward the park gate, darted outside, and crossed to the middle of the road, where he spoke to a policeman on traffic duty. Holohan, leaving the rest to make their way into the city, pushed hard on the pedals: there were two military barracks close by—Islandbridge and the Royal Barracks—and either could intercept them. He swerved left at the gate past the policeman, following Playfair, who by this time had reached the corner of the Islandbridge road. When Holohan himself reached the corner, Playfair was running across the road at an angle, making for a row of large houses. He glanced around, saw Holohan, and immediately put on a spurt. He reached the first house, fumbled at the gate for a moment, then burst up the path and battered on the door.

Holohan leaped from his bicycle, letting it crash to the ground. From the doorway, a desperate face glanced back at him. As the door opened and a woman stood framed in it, Holohan squeezed his automatic three times, and young Playfair, barely seventeen years old, crumpled on the doorstep, dying.

Even as Daly and his party trotted along the Quays in their jaunting car, behind Holohan somewhere, back toward the Park, there was a dull explosion. It was not very loud; not loud enough, certainly, to be heard any great distance away.

Across the river in the South Dublin Union, Commandant Edmund Kent again looked at his watch, waiting for the signal. When five minutes had passed and there was still no sound, he shrugged philosophically. "Ah, well, it hasn't worked," he said.

A big bang might have cheered him. As it was, he felt depressed at facing an impossible task. The South Dublin Union (Workhouse) consisted of an extraordinary sprawl covering some fifty-two acres, the better part of it wide lawns and open fields, the whole enclosed by a great stone wall. It constituted an amazing ramification of streets, alleyways, and courtyards, studded with residences, halls, dormitories, wards, sheds, and even two churches. It was, in fact, a small town and its population that morning, excluding officials and insurgents, was 3,282, which is larger than most Irish towns. Kent's Fourth Battalion had mobilized at eleven o'clock that morning in Emerald Square—a small inappropriately named group of workmen's cottages in southwest Dublin, an area of tall distilleries and factories, back-to-back terrace houses, sleazy-looking pubs, and small huckster shops, all dominated by the giant complex of Guinness's Brewery. Out of a nominal battalion strength of seven hundred hardly one hundred and twenty men had turned out. Nominal Volunteer strengths, of course, usually meant little—they varied a great deal with political shifts. When the Army launched a fresh recruiting campaign or the Government hinted that they might extend conscription to Ireland, there was always an upsurge in attendance. When things were quiet, the attendance fell off. The hard core of enthusiasts, however, rarely varied. These were the men who for several reasons regarded the Volunteers as the mainspring of their existence. Some had enrolled because they were patriots, others because they enjoyed drilling or learning to fire a rifle. Others still had baser motives—believing that membership in the Volunteers might lead to a good job or prevent conscription. There were saints and sinners in the organization. Even so, Kent knew, under more auspicious circumstances he would have had a turnout of at least five hundred.

The men who had reported for duty, however, had responded magnificently to his short address: "Today you're going into action! An Irish Republic has been declared and we are marching on the South Dublin Union." Most of them had waited a long time to hear words like that.

They had moved off at 11:35 A.M., Kent, tall and lean, leading a party of ten cyclists by a back route; Lieutenant William Cosgrave, a Dublin city councilor, guiding the main party which was under Vice-Commandant Cathal Brugha, the small but ferocious son a Yorkshireman. Cosgrave, who lived in the district, took them through back streets to avoid attention. On the way small parties dropped off at three important outposts—Jameson's Distillery in Marrowbone Lane, which was occupied by Captain James Murphy with twenty men; Watkin's Brewery in Ardee Street, taken over by a pugnacious little man called Con Colbert, with about the same number; and Roe's Distillery in James Street which was broken into by Captain Thomas MacCarthy also with twenty men. From the whole complex the insurgents could control movement along the Liffey quaysides and command Kingsbridge Railway Station and the Royal Hospital, Kilmainham. Kingsbridge was the terminus for trains from the Curragh, the British Army's main camp in Ireland; the Royal Hospital, one of the most architecturally pleasing buildings in the city, the headquarters of the General Officer Commanding, Ireland.

66

Kent waited until noon to approach the back entrance of the Union with his cyclists. This was at Rialto Bridge, one of many small bridges crossing the Grand Canal (Dublin is encompassed by two canals—one, the Royal, threading its way through the northern suburbs; the other, the Grand, through the southern; both running from west to east in a line roughly parallel to the Liffey). There was no opposition beyond a porter who refused to hand over the keys. Kent brushed the man aside and took them from their rack. Courageously the porter tried to telephone the police only to discover that the line was cut. Leaving a party of nine Volunteers under Captain George Irvine to guard this entrance, Kent walked half a mile to the front gate where he found Brugha and the main party. The strains of a military band could be heard from Richmond barracks a little way up the river. "They don't know yet," Kent said to Brugha, but the words had scarcely left his mouth when the music stopped. "Oh, that's ominous," he added.

His ideas for the defense of the Union, of course, had rested on the assumption that he would have many more men. Brugha had already barricaded the big front gate, which gave entrance to the grounds, and had sent a party to occupy the offices arching over it, which made up the Union's short frontage on James Street. Men were already tunneling through the walls so that the whole frontage could be traversed without their having to leave cover. Now Kent deployed thirty-eight officers and men throughout the Union grounds, an extraordinary prodigality in the circumstances. His main idea was to prevent British troops moving in through the southwestern suburbs. These forces—in the opening stages anyway—would probably march in either from Richmond or Islandbridge barracks, or possibly both, moving along the southern banks of the Liffey. In this event they would come under fire from Roe's Distillery. If they took the parallel inland route, along Old Kilmainham and then up the slight rise of Mount Brown, they would have to pass the Union. Before reaching it, however, they would march some five hundred yards alongside open fields on the right called MacCaffrey's Estate, a part of the Union grounds. At the foot of Mount Brown lay Brookfield Road, leading to Rialto Bridge and the South Circular Road. If the military swung right here, they could outflank the Union, but would come under fire from Jameson's Distillery.

Edmund Kent, however, was not the kind of man to let the enemy outflank him without at least making an effort to prevent them. First he placed an officer and four men at the extreme point of MacCaffrey's Estate—at the corner of Mount Brown and Brookfield Road where they were concealed by a low wall dropping steeply on the other side to the pavement. Back nearer the Union, hidden behind hedges, he placed another officer and eight men. At the Rialto Gate, where he had already placed Irvine and his men, he now held a three-hundred-foot-long tin shed used by the Union authorities to house male lunatics, with a single Volunteer in a shallow trench opposite the gate in support. An officer and five men guarded the Canal wall at the rear of the Union while five Volunteers guarded the eastern boundary wall. Finally he placed eight Volunteers in the big, isolated permanent building known as Hospital 2-3, two hundred and fifty yards from the Rialto Gate, where two men occupied the ground floor, six the upper.

Cosgrave approached Vice-Commandant Brugha. "Look," he said, "isn't this hopeless? Surely, we can't hope to hold the whole Union—we haven't got the men."

"What do you suggest?" asked Brugha laconically.

Cosgrave pointed to the Night Nurses' Home, a solid, three-story, stone-built structure on the west side of the courtyard and at right angles to James Street. "It's the strongest building in the Union," he said, "and it's in the right position. From the back we can control MacCaffrey's, Mount Brown, Brookfield Road, and even the Rialto Gate."

"Get the men in at once," said Brugha. "Kent will want to make that headquarters."

By 12:25, when Daly's gelignite blew up, the Battalion had started working on its defenses. In the front offices work had begun breaking through the party walls. Inside the Nurses' Home, windows had already been smashed and the empty frames barricaded. In the Rialto sheds the Union Wardmaster had herded all his lunatic charges into one of the six dormito-

68

ries, leaving Irvine free to throw up mattresses at all the windows.

At the bottom of MacCaffrey's Estate, Section-Commander John Joyce hid behind the low wall and gazed up Old Kilmainham. There were three men here under Lieutenant William O'Brien. For ten minutes now they had been listening to the "separation women" (army wives who received separation allowances while their husbands were in France) hurling abuse at them. In the beginning this had merely consisted of mild suggestions that they should "join the British Army and fight like men," but has progressed to a point where their ancestry was being freely aspersed. Finally one Volunteer shouted "Go to Hell!" at which the women's voices rose to a terrible screech.

Then suddenly they scattered and Joyce heard one of them shout, "Yez'll bate it now, me boyos. Here's the military!"

"Get your heads down, boys!" warned O'Brien. "And remember, for God's sake, don't fire till I tell you—d'ye hear that!"

Before Joyce flattened himself down, he caught a glimpse of khaki figures coming down into the dip in the road, three hundred yards away. He was able to count about twenty of them before he lowered his head. They were marching with all the cheerful precision of the British Army and their bayonets gleamed brightly in the midday sun.

At 11:45 Commandant Edward Daly, commanding the First Volunteer Battalion, walked out of Colmcille Hall into the bright sunlight, his aides at his side, and briskly saluted his men. He spoke crisply and in a matter-of-fact tone. "I have to tell you, men, that you will be shortly going into action," he said. "At twelve o'clock today the flag of the Irish Republic is to be raised. Now, I don't want any cheering and I also want to make it clear"—and here his eyes strayed anxiously over the desperately sparse ranks—"that if anybody wants to withdraw now, then he is at liberty to do so." For fully five seconds there was no movement in the ranks. Then Volunteer John Alwright shouted, "Well, I don't like this," and stepped out. When nobody else moved, Daly gave the command: "Left turn, quick march!"

69

His principal objective was the Four Courts, home of Ireland's Judiciary, where a massive dome, 64 feet in diameter, looms over the river. Daly's problem was to decide which outposts he should try to seize and hold with his small forces. He decided to dispatch twenty men under Lieutenant Joseph MacGuinness to take the Four Courts itself while he divided the rest into five small parties to occupy positions in the streets around. He himself established temporary headquarters in the Convent of St. John.

The Angelus bell was ringing as MacGuinness led his men toward the Four Courts. They anticipated little resistance, and met none; the Volunteers, in fact, were to marvel at the ease with which a city, even a capital like Dublin, steel-ringed with military barracks, could be captured. Those who knew of the efforts to persuade the Germans to send an expeditionary force could only feel despair when they realized how easy it would have been for them to take all Ireland. MacGuinness, ignoring twenty D.M.P.'s watching him from the Bridewell Police Station, marched to the Chancery Place entrance where Lieutenant Thomas Allen, with drawn revolver, forced a policeman to hand over the keys. They entered the building with less difficulty than if they had been litigants. Volunteer Charles Beavan and a party of three went to the front where they occupied the Lord Chancellor's chambers facing upriver. They smashed the tall windows and barricaded them with leather-bound tomes from the Chancellor's library.

In the surrounding streets, other rebels had begun erecting barricades. A lorry was commandeered and driven onto Church Street Bridge, partly blocking it. In Hammond Lane, bedsteads were linked across the road in a crude fence. In other streets cobbles were prised up and built into a wall. Broken bottles were scattered on the roadways to prevent a cavalry charge. Trams were stopped at the entrance to Church Street and the passengers made to alight. Then a tram was heaved over on its side. The main effort, however, was concentrated at the intersection of Church Street and North King Street. The latter runs roughly parallel to the river, the former intersecting it at right angles. The whole constitutes an area of narrow streets, small houses, pubs, and little shops.

70

Here the insurgents soon discovered that a rebellion is a matter of hard and backbreaking effort—plus insults. There was plenty of foul language when the poor people of the area saw their possessions being dragged out to make barricades.

"But the Republic will repay you, ma'am!" Lieutenant John Shouldice was forced to repeat.

People's sympathies were divided. Some helped when they heard a Republic had been declared; others became hostile. Patrick Kelly of "C" Company had to draw his revolver to protect himself against women of the neighborhood when he halted a regular soldier.

"Go on, can't ye—take away his gun!" they shouted at the soldier. "Take away his gun and he'll run!" Kelly kept the soldier covered and eventually he turned away.

Then into it all blundered the regular cavalry.

A troop of the 5th and 12th Lancers, part of the 6th Cavalry Reserve Regiment stationed at Marlborough Barracks (Phoenix Park), had been dispatched early that morning to the North Wall railway terminus as escort for a small munitions convoy. Even as Pearse and Connolly marched away from Liberty Hall, the troop had begun their trek back along the quays, five low carts laden with rifles, rifle grenades, and bombs rumbling along in their midst. Lances bobbed disdainfully, hoofs clattered spiritedly. In Liberty Hall, a small party, left to guard food and ammunition reserves, saw from a window a perfect target approaching, but Lieutenant Frank Thornton's orders were to avoid action until the main forces had consolidated themselves in the Post Office. He allowed the convoy to pass, therefore, and unaware that behind the silent windows of Liberty Hall rifle barrels were trained intently on them, the Lancers trekked proudly on. At O'Connell Bridge rebel scouts also allowed them past.

Watched by the Volunteers, the troopers clattered across the end of Sackville Street and along Bachelor's Walk. They had not gone far, however, when a man shouted at Second-Lieutenant Hunter, officer in charge, "Look out for yourselves! The Sinn Feiners are out! They're up ahead!" Discounting this as mere Irish nonsense, Hunter continued his disdainful march. To the rebels, hard at work erecting barricades around the Four Courts, the Lancers proved a startling sight. In a sheer panic, the men at the Church Street Bridge barricade knelt in the roadway and set off a fusillade.

It surprised the Lancers utterly. Several troopers were unhorsed; animals plunging and rearing, whinnying in terror, threatened to unseat the rest. Lieutenant Hunter wheeled his horse and ordered his men toward a side street. A few charged toward Chancery Place, hoping to find refuge in the Four Courts. Volunteer James Byrne, on guard at the gate there, opened fire from behind his flimsy barricade, and his Howth rifle, with its reverberating echo, sounded like a small cannon. Beside him, two shotguns flung out a hail of metal, but everything missed and the cavalry galloped past, followed by several riderless horses. Some found themselves in Charles Street, where Hunter led them down the narrow street toward Ormond Markets, an open space. Once again they came under insurgent fire and were forced to turn back. For a few chaotic moments men, horses, and lorries milled around in a confined space, all order and discipline gone. Hunter, rallying his men bravely, ordered them to break into the Collier Dispensary and the Medical Mission opposite. Bunched together, the troopers rushed the doors which gave way under their weight. Once inside they flung up everything they could gather behind the windows and prepared to repel attack. Strangely enough, none came and eventually they were able to unload the ammunition lorries and bring the boxes inside.

Meanwhile, in the streets nearby, other wounded or unhorsed troopers of the shattered column were being taken prisoner. Two men charged down North King Street, not knowing where they were going, and found themselves galloping toward a barricade. In a panic, one of them shot off his carbine. The bullet hit a child, killing her instantly. Alerted rebels at the corner of Church Street replied with a ragged volley as the Lancers swerved right, hoofs flying wildly. At the corner of North Brunswick Street, Section-Commander Philip Walsh and Commandant Daly opened fire together. Daly's shot dropped the first Lancer, while Walsh's bullet carried the second man out of the saddle and sent him sprawling into the gutter. Volunteers ran out into the road and

72

grabbed the horses. Daly slapped one on the rump and sent it back down Church Street to throw confusion into any cavalry following.

In triumph the dead trooper's lance was borne back to the corner of Church Street and North King Street where it was stuck into a manhole in the center of the road and the tricolor of the new Republic hung victoriously from it.

So keyed up at the thought of action was Section-Commander James Grace, aged twenty-six, that he had been unable to eat his breakfast that morning. He left home in full Volunteer uniform and was the first man to arrive at his particular mobilization point; this was at Earlsfort Terrace, directly opposite Mr. Augustine Birrell's new National University. Here he waited, a solitary if determined figure, armed with a long Lee-Enfield and fifty rounds of .303 ammunition. These were moments when a man could feel both a trifle scared and a little ridiculous. Supposing a policeman were to challenge you? Supposing nobody else turned up? It was with a feeling of relief, therefore, that he saw the tall, fair-haired figure of Lieutenant Michael Malone come along on his bicycle.

At twenty-eight, Mick Malone was a comrade in arms likely to inspire men under stress. A good-looking man, he was both quiet-spoken and serious-minded. He had long-fingered, elegant hands; fingers that remained nerveless along the barrel of a rifle or upon a trigger, and no doubt helped to make him what he was—easily the best shot in the battalion. He was a bachelor because "the organization" (as its members called it) had always encouraged its recruits to keep clear of women. He was wearing uniform and carrying a Mauser rifle-pistol known as a "Peter the Painter." When he mentioned that he, too, had been unable to eat breakfast, Grace felt a great deal better.

Not that Grace was without military experience—if only briefly. During a visit to the United States in 1913, he had moved up into Canada and joined a territorial regiment in order to learn how to use a rifle; three months later, on receiving a letter from home saying, "We are waiting for you," he

73

had wrapped his long Lee-Enfield in a canvas bag and caught the *Cathaginia* to Glasgow.

The rest of "C" Company, Third Battalion, collected casually, almost as though they were merely gathering for a charabanc outing. When Lieutenant Simon Donnelly appeared, however, he wore a worried look upon his dark face. He explained that, as the regular captain had refused to turn out, Commandant de Valera had been forced to promote him. By 11:20, indeed, it had become clear that quite a few men were not going to turn out—in fact there were only thirty-four present. Nevertheless, at 11:50 precisely, a thoroughly downcast-looking Donnelly gave the order to march.

"C" Company moved off in two sections—Donnelly leading with twenty men, Malone following with the fifteen members of the Battalion's Cycle Corps. They marched eastward for about a mile until they reached Upper Mount Street, where Donnelly halted and waited for Malone to catch up. Here Dublin is an oasis of quiet Georgian charm set amid genteel opulence, a part of the city preserved virtually intact in splendid eighteenth-century elegance. The streets are broad and usually empty, the squares tree-lined and gracious, and on this particular Easter Monday hardly a human being stirred. In the far distance a cab loped by, the jarvey's head jogging happily in rhythm with his nag's movements.

Donnelly and Malone held a brief conference, then resumed their march separately. Donnelly cut down through Stephen's Place to Boland's Bakery, which De Valera had chosen as his headquarters. Malone marched up through Mount Street Crescent to the Canal where he wheeled left toward Mount Street bridge, and there halted his four section-commanders —George Reynolds, James Grace, Denis O'Donoghue, and Patrick Doyle. Following a brief conference, Grace, with two boys, Paddy Byrne and Michael Rowe, marched over the bridge and up Northumberland Road for three hundred yards to the intersection of Haddington Road. Two hundred yards east, toward the railway and the sea, lay Beggar's Bush military barracks; Grace's orders were to keep its main gate under observation until the rest of the party had a chance to take up positions. Section-Commander Patrick Doyle with

74

three men occupied St. Stephen's Parochial Hall, two hundred yards up Northumberland Road on the right-hand side, and Section-Commander O'Donoghue occupied schools on the left-hand side. Section-Commander Reynolds, preparing for action, slipped his blood-poisoned left hand from a surgical sling and pointed to a house on the corner of Clanwilliam Place.

From a military position Clanwilliam House, a large three-story stucco-fronted corner residence could scarcely have been better sited. Here, where the main Dublin-Kingstown road is carried along by Lower Mount Street and Northumberland Road, the two long, almost-straight avenues are linked by Mount Street Bridge. Clanwilliam House, therefore, dominated the Canal, as well as the schools on the far side, Northumberland Road as far as Haddington Road, and, most important of all, the bridge itself. It was brilliantly positioned for an Irish Thermopylae.

Reynolds pushed his bicycle up the pathway, mounted the steps, and pressed the bell. A maid opened the door.

"May we come in, please?" asked Reynolds.

The maid giggled.

"Bring in your bikes," ordered Reynolds, and before the girl could prevent them, five young men stood in the hallway. Reynolds ordered Volunteers James Doyle and William Ronan to search the house. "If you find anybody, send them down," he said.

On the first landing the two men met a middle-aged lady —a Miss Wilson, whose mother owned the house.

"What's all this about?" she asked sternly.

"Will ye go downstairs, please, ma'am?" said Ronan. "No harm'll come to you." Even as he spoke old Mrs. Wilson herself came out onto the landing and querulously demanded to know what all the fuss was about.

"If ye'll please go downstairs, ladies," insisted Ronan.

When he and Doyle had searched the house, Reynolds called the men into the front sitting room, a large, bright room with an oil painting over the fireplace and a photograph of a regular officer in full uniform on the mantelpiece.

"One thing I want you to remember," said Reynolds,

75

"we're the representatives of the Irish Republic, so don't behave like hooligans. I want you to be respectful to the residents of this house. Don't break the windows and do as little damage as you can." And to show them what he meant, he crossed to the window, and with great care raised the lower sash. Then he waved a hand around the room. "Now, quick, get some of the furniture over here beside the windows—but don't make it obvious that we've taken over the place."

Meanwhile Malone had led Grace and the two boys into No. 25 Northumberland Road, an empty, terraced mansion on the corner of Haddington Road. The owners, sympathetic to Sinn Fein and warned that the premises might be needed, had evacuated the place. Malone and his men at once set about barricading the front door with furniture and loopholing the windows.

In the street outside, twelve-year-old Gerald Morrissey and his friends, tired of waiting for something really exciting to happen, returned to their game of cowboys. The policeman patrolling his beat in the area had sensed that this might be an unhealthy district in the not-too-distant future and had already made himself scarce.

One hundred and fifty yards east of Clanwilliam House, Commandant Edward de Valera, thirty-four-year-old New York-born mathematics professor, had established himself in Boland's Bakery, a single-story, low-lying building fronted on Grand Canal Street. His position was hardly an enviable one. Plunkett's original plans had called for him to occupy sixteen outposts in the Ringsend area, including several Canal works, a railway station and two-mile stretch of line plus signaling cabins, gasworks, a granary, a railway locomotive shop, dockmilling premises, several warehouses and mills, and the bakery—a nightmarish task for an amateur commander, even with a full-strength battalion. As it was he had only one hundred and twenty men.

Both farce and tragedy had marked his occupation of the area. He had picked the Grand Canal Dispensary as his personal quarters. When he and five men climbed the wall separating the Dispensary garden from the Bakery at about

76

12:10 P.M., the doctor's wife happened to be alone in the house. Terrified, she watched the men, led by the tall swarthy-looking De Valera, brandishing a sword, come running across her garden.

"You have five minutes in which to pack your valuables and leave the premises, ma'am," De Valera announced peremptorily, after he had entered the house. Faced with what she took to be a gang of cutthroats and murderers, Mrs. Healy threw a fit of hysterics. Professor de Valera, for all his learning, was no expert on women. He turned to his nearest aide and said, "You'd better handle this." Then he left swiftly and crossed back over the wall.

Mrs. Healy's hysterics continued, indeed, until the return of her husband, Dr. Healy, who was admitted on the clear understanding that he would leave again immediately, taking his wife with him. Reassured by his presence, Mrs. Healy quieted down, but the doctor, sensing that he stood in little danger, decided to delay his departure in the hope that some form of help might arrive.

"What'll happen if my property's destroyed or damaged?" he demanded.

"The Irish Republic will recompense you," said Lieutenant Joseph O'Byrne.

"H'm," said the doctor doubtfully, and sat down to compose an inventory of his possessions. When he had finished, he asked O'Byrne, "Can I have a receipt for these things?"

"You're not getting any from me," said O'Byrne shortly, "because we're not going to steal anything."

When the doctor and his wife had departed, the insurgents discovered six gold sovereigns lying loose in a desk drawer. Determined to show him that they were honest men, fighting only for their rights, they carefully locked the coins in the desk and scribbled a note telling him where to find them.

The actual seizure of the Bakery had been a relatively easy matter, the only serious opposition springing from the bakers who, to begin with, had refused to take the rebels seriously. Indeed, it was not until Donnelly threatened to shoot them that they realized he was in earnest. Then they pointed out that they had a thousand loaves of bread baking in the ovens and that if these were allowed to spoil, the people of the district would go hungry.

"All right," said Donnelly, "three or four of you can stay; the rest go."

Even then, it looked for a moment as though the disgruntled bakers might decide to have it out with them, but a bayonet shoved against one man's throat soon persuaded them to leave quietly.

From the outset the great fear nagging De Valera and his aides was that they would be subjected to a prompt attack from Beggar's Bush Barracks. Almost the first thing Donnelly did, therefore, after the bakers had been got rid of, was to make emergency postings of four or five men in each corner of the Bakery, retaining a small mobile reserve. After this he ordered a number of bread vans pulled to Grand Canal Bridge and the wheels taken off, thus creating a formidable barricade facing up Clanwilliam Place toward Mount Street Bridge. His main job, however, was to arrange for the erection of a gangway from the Bakery to the main Dublin-Kingstown railway line, which sliced straight through the position. The tracks here were elevated, banked to a height of sixteen feet. Donnelly first breached the brick wall separating the Bakery from the embankment and then made a ramp by propping earth-filled flour bags under a causeway of planks; this gave De Valera quick and easy communication between his headquarters and his outposts.

Within ten minutes, tragedy had struck. Tom Walshe of "B" Company was busy unloading "the stuff" from a donkey cart when a soldier on his way back to Beggar's Bush Barracks crossed the road and asked, "What are you up to?"

"Clear off!" shouted an insurgent from the top of the Bakery wall.

The soldier sturdily stood his ground. To get rid of him, a rebel shouted that a republic had been declared.

"You're nothing but bloody traitors!" said the soldier.

"You know, that fellow'll have to be shut up," the rebel murmured, and raised his rifle. "Will you go away now?" he asked.

"Traitors!" shouted the soldier.

78

The rebel pressed the trigger and the soldier dropped in his tracks. Walshe stared down at him, surprised, and then slowly back at the smoking rifle. It was the first time he had ever witnessed an act of violence. Strange how little effect it had on him, he noted.

"Let's get on with it," said the other rebel nonchalantly, and with a shrug Walshe handed him a parcel of bombs.

A big millworker who had seen the shooting came over and said, "Why don't you put him in your cart and take him to Duns?" When they ignored him, he persisted, "You can't leave him here!"

Walshe said, "I'm not taking him anywhere until I've finished this job."

The big millworker lifted the soldier, and staggering under his weight, set off up the street. When he reached the corner, a crowd rushed forward to help and Walshe heard them cheering.

Less than half a mile away Volunteer George Lyons was doing his best to prevent the 12:15 to Kingstown from leaving Westland Row terminus. Like many another rebel that morning he had found the public inclined to regard the idea of a rebellion facetiously—until they found themselves threatened suddenly with violence.

Lieutenant John Quinn and the rest of "B" Company had seized the station a few minutes after noon, occupying the main incoming platform before either staff or public were aware of their presence. While Quinn continued on down the line to put the signaling cabins out of action, Lyons, making a cup of his hands, bawled out, "Leave the train! Go to the waiting rooms! Attention! Go to the waiting rooms!"

People poked their heads out of the carriages, but none moved. "I'll count ten," shouted Lyons, aiming his rifle at the occupants of the nearest carriage. Mystified and a little frightened, the people began filing toward the waiting rooms.

One man, however, started across the rails toward Lyons shouting; "You're interfering with my business, do you know that?"

"Go back or I'll shoot!" said Lyons, turning the rifle toward him.

"What the hell do you mean threatening me with a gun!" shouted the man. "I'm a better man than you any day of the week—a better soldier if it comes to that."

Lyons called out to his men, "Use your bayonets on that fellow!" Two rebels advanced upon the man, but without any great show of determination. "Ah, now, like a good man, can't you go back there and do as you're told!" they pleaded.

"Damned if I'll back an inch!" said the man stubbornly. They argued for a moment, then one of the rebels shouted, "He's a member of the Citizen Army!"

"Well, then, in the name of God, tell him to report to his officers!" answered Lyons. "He ought to be out with the rest of us."

He had hardly finished dealing with this customer when a top-hatted gentleman, who said he was the stationmaster, shouted, "Are you going to let this train leave?"

"No," said Lyons.

"Are you going to let us do any business here today?"

"No!"

"Are you going to let the public stay?"

"No—and you neither! You'd better go home now."

"Thank you," said the stationmaster with heavy sarcasm. "Thank you very much. But I'm in charge of this station and I intend to stay."

"We're relieving you of your responsibilities," said Lyons.

"There's money in this station, and I'm responsible for it," objected the stationmaster. "I'm not leaving, and that's that!"

Lyons had to admire the man's stubbornness and devotion to duty.

Meanwhile the public, ordered to leave the station, began crowding out through the main door, and Lyons found himself facing a new problem. A party of priests was pushing through the crowd toward him. Lyons shouted, "Reverend sirs, please turn around and leave the station. At any minute the military might rush the place. Everyone of us here is in danger!"

Two priests began climbing the barrier.

80

"Retire!" shouted Lyons desperately. "Soldiers, prepare to fire!"

But only two men raised their guns.

"Can't I speak to you?" a priest asked.

"You can give us your blessing, Father," said Lyons.

"What are you doing here anyway?" asked the priest.

"Fighting for Ireland, Father. Ready to die for her."

"But people will be slaughtered—innocent people. And the country ruined," said the priest.

"We want to make Ireland independent, Father," said Lyons.

"Well, promise me you'll stop fighting if you find you can't win? You do realize that you're morally bound to yield to superior odds to prevent useless sacrifices?"

"If we can't hold our ground, then we'll give in!" promised Lyons. "But not before—I can tell you that."

Suddenly they were interrupted by one of Lyons's men who dashed forward and knelt at the feet of the priest. "Will you hear my confession, Father?" he pleaded.

The priest knew he had won. "We demand to be allowed to minister to the spiritual needs of these men!" he said.

Reluctantly Lyons said, "Well, if you promise to confine your business to hearing confessions and don't try to give them any advice about what they're doing."

"That I agree," said the priest.

"All right, then," said Lyons, and opened the ticket barrier. Quickly the priests filed onto the platform, then slowly they moved down it, listening to the muted words of the confessing rebels, who knelt, still gripping their rifles.

Down the line Peter Nolan, twenty, ripped up rails with a sledge hammer to make certain that no trains ran. Other men got busy smashing signaling mechanisms, or closing level crossings.

Volunteer Joseph Guilfoyle, eighteen, guarding a railway bridge, watched people walking on the roadway beneath, unconcerned at the thought of armed rebels above them. Once Commandant de Valera came down the line, tall, foreign-looking, tensed. As he passed, he called out curtly, "Remember, shoot anything you see in uniform!" Guilfoyle had the impulse to ask if that order included postmen, but he decided that the Commandant was not likely to enjoy the joke.

Farther down the line Guilfoyle's brother, John, a lieutenant in "A" Company, started on the most ambitious and back-breaking task of all. Ordered to invest Beggar's Bush, he had decided to occupy a shop opposite the main gates. There was only one way into it, and Guilfoyle began boring through a row of cottages backing onto it. It took him six hours to do it, but inside Beggars' Bush that evening the harassed military, watching spurts of rifle fire from the shop window, wondered how in the devil the rebels had managed to get there.

[7]

James Joyce, a thirty-five-year-old private in the Citizen Army, thought of himself as among the most miserable of men. He worked for an "ould slave driver" called Davy, who owned a public house at Portobello Bridge, and twelve hours a day, seven days a week, he languished in Davy's cellar, washing bottles. The job might have been just bearable if the "ould blackguard" had been "half-dacent." But Davy would not even give Joyce a Sunday off to parade with the Citizen Army, which meant everything to him. Used to the continual contempt of his fellows, he had discovered in the Army a degree of dignity and companionship for which his soul deeply longed. Boys like Paddy Buttner or Charlie D'Arcy would listen wide-eyed as he vividly described how someday he would shoot "ould Davy."

Davy was beyond the pale, of course; he had even given Joyce a final warning that, if he took another Sunday off, he could take a week's notice.

On Tuesday of Holy Week, General Connolly had provided Joyce with the most important moment of his life so far. On that evening, shortly after eight o'clock, Joyce had been summoned to Mr. Connolly's room in Liberty Hall—a sparsely furnished room with a plain table, a few chairs, and a cot in the corner where the General slept. Waiting in the room with Connolly were Captain Richard MacCormack, Captain John O'Neill (who had once served in the British Army), Lieutenant Michael Kelly, and two sergeants, Frank Robbins and Joseph Doyle. As usual, Connolly had wasted no breath. He explained that an insurrection was to be launched in Dublin at half past six on Easter Sunday evening. The main body of the Citizen Army were to occupy St. Stephen's Green under Commandant Mallin and the Countess Markievicz, and as the first military threat to the Green would probably materialize from Portobello Barracks, he wanted Captain MacCormack to secure certain outposts and hold on to them just long enough to allow Mallin and the Countess time to prepare their defenses. Therefore he was ordering Sergeant Doyle and sixteen men to occupy Davy's pub ("Including you!" said Connolly, pointing at Joyce). Lieutenant Kelly would support them from the railway bridge overlooking the Canal while MacCormack himself would seize Harcourt Street railway terminus.

To Doyle, Connolly added, "Don't fire on the military until you see the whites of their eyes!" To Robbins, he explained, "I want you to prepare an escape route for these fellows when they are forced to fall back. Barricade Hatch Street at both ends. Find a way out for them into Stephen's Green through some of those big houses—I suggest Iveagh House." Finally, turning to Joyce, he said, "What would you do if a British soldier was chasing you, threatening to ram a bayonet up your backside? You'd take the shortest way out, wouldn't you? Well, that's what I want you to do for these fellows. Get them out of that pub the quickest and safest way you know."

At 11:55 A.M., then, this Easter Monday, Joyce found himself marching with Captain MacCormack's detachment up Grafton Street. Beside him trotted fifteen-year-old Paddy Buttner. All continued well until they debouched into St. Stephen's Green, where a haughty young military officer accompanied by an orderly clopped toward them on horseback. "Lording it as usual!" murmured Joyce. "Keeping down the natives."

"What do you think we'll do?" asked Buttner nervously.

"Wait and see," said Joyce.

As the officer came abreast, Captain MacCormack saluted smartly. The British officer instinctively returned the salute, and he and his man had clattered past before they realized exactly what happened. Once past, however, the officer reined in his horse. Glancing over his shoulder, Buttner saw them

84

looking back suspiciously. When he looked again, both were following.

At the station, MacCormack ordered Doyle to take eight men and two boys and proceed to Davy's pub; he marched his main body inside. The military rode past, stopping a short distance away to see what would happen next. Doyle muttered, "We'll fix that fellow!" At the next corner, he knew, he might get his opportunity. Here, just before a left-hand turning into the road leading to Portobello Barracks, a small street offered a short cut. Everything, therefore, depended upon the officer's choice of route: if he chose the short cut, they would be unable to do anything; if he took the main turning, they could nip through the short cut and head him off. They held their breaths as they watched him near the short cut. He rode past. "Right, fellows, at the double!" shouted Doyle.

They cut through and reached the main road well ahead of the two mounted men. Doyle ordered them to fix bayonets and spread across the road. The horsemen rounded the corner, and came on slowly. While still half a dozen yards away, the officer spurred his horse. Private James Kelly lunged with his bayonet, shouting, "Begod, you won't," then fired. The shot missed; but the officer swung around and galloped away.

"To Davy's—at the double!" roared Doyle, and Joyce led the way. When he reached Davy's, he kicked in the door. Davy himself was standing behind the bar, serving customers. Joyce strutted forward masterfully. "Ould Davy" banged the counter with his fist and roared, "I'm giving you a week's notice, Joyce!"

"And I'm giving you five minutes, Mister Davy!" shouted Joyce, and opened fire at the bottles on the shelves. As Davy ducked in terror, glass showering all round him, his customers fled.

The famous Long Bar of the Shelbourne was filled with people. The atmosphere was one of neat whiskies and gins, horses and military talk. Cavalry leggings, red tabs, and white whiskers mingled with the heavy tweeds of the landed gentry

85

up for the Ballsbridge Show. Overbred voices hummed with pre-lunch chatter.

Through the tall, graceful windows the trees of St. Stephen's Green Park, new-leaved, stirred sweetly in the hazy sunlight. The green lawns glittered, and heavy scents rose from the mingling rosebeds, high protecting shrubberies, and the great shading elms, chestnuts, and copper beeches. White-bonneted babies, watched over carefully by uniformed nannies, crawled about on the grass or gurgled in their prams; old men on the park benches read their papers; Air Mechanic Alfred Pratt, Royal Flying Corps, and his young lady sat watching the antics of ducks on the pond.

Mallin's men filtered into the Green in twos and threes through eight different entrances. At the west entrance the park-keeper stopped Mallin saying, "You can't come in here."

"I'm sorry, but we mean to," said the Commandant.

"Well, at least wait until I get the women and children out," replied the park-keeper.

When the public had been shepherded out, Mallin ordered all the gates closed and barricaded with park benches. Rebels stacked their rifles and commenced digging shallow trenches. Air Mechanic Pratt and his young lady sat on, watching it all with interest until, suddenly, they were spotted.

"I'm sorry, miss, but you'll have to go," said a rebel. "And you, mister, I'm afraid you're a prisoner."

"But we're enjoying it," said the young lady. "Can't we stay and watch?"

"Damn it all, miss, this is a rebellion, don't you understand? We're fighting for Irish freedom! *He's* a prisoner. *You* can go home."

"Aren't you simply carrying out maneuvers?" asked Pratt.

"No!" exclaimed the insurgent angrily. A look of astonishment crossed Pratt's handsome face. Dazedly he allowed himself to be escorted toward a summerhouse where he was told to sit on some steps. He looked up and found he was sitting under a statue of George the Third.

Countess Markievicz arrived with an air of triumph, entering boldly by "Traitors' Gate," [it had been erected as a memorial to Irishmen who fought against the Boers] almost as though she owned the place. In that moment she was unforgettable—tall and dark, hardly beautiful by modern standards perhaps, yet still an embodiment of that "wild Irish girl" the Anglo-Irish aristocracy once bred with a proliferating regularity. Behind her loomed a girlhood spent among wealth and privilege—of gay parties and the hunting field; of Lissadell, her father's great house in Sligo where she had entertained the poet Yeats. All this she had forsaken to marry Casimir, Count Markievicz; but at least it had brought its compensations. She had found herself in the genteel world of Dublin's artistic salons and its literary high teas and then, through the ferment of emergent nationality, in the soup kitchens of Liberty Hall, where she had appeared like a flaming angel, ministering and exhorting during the worst moments of the 1913 transport strike. Now she marched into St. Stephen's Green at the head of her troops, dressed theatrically, to suit the occasion, in a dark green woolen blouse trimmed with brass buttons, dark green tweed knee breeches, black stockings and puttees, and around her waist a cartridge belt from which, on one side, dangled a small automatic pistol and from the other a convertible Mauser rifle-pistol—the whole topped by a black velour hat trimmed with coq feathers. It hardly mattered that the troops she led were only Boy Scouts and women; she still marched them through the gate with the imperious confidence of a woman whose ancestors had been conquerors.

With the arrival of the Countess's contingent, a commissariat and a Red Cross post were rapidly established. Miss Margaret Ffrench-Mullen set up the Red Cross First Aid Post in the summerhouse, while Miss Mary Hyland and Miss Kathleen Cleary commandeered a conservatory where they laid out sandwiches, cheese, meat, ham, and cake.

For the Countess, there were no purely feminine activities. Here, in these few acres of city park, in acceptance of James Connolly's advanced ideals, women would stand beside men. The Countess had no scruples about shooting the enemy. She even looked forward to it, and as things turned out she would not have to wait long. Within five minutes Constable Michael Lahiff tried to enter the Green at "Traitors' Gate."

He was warned to go away, but he refused to. Informed of his attitude, the Countess rushed to the railings and took aim with her rifle-pistol. As she fired, two shots also rang out beside her. Lahiff slumped to the pavement, hit by three bullets. The Countess was delighted. "I shot him!" she shouted. "I shot him!"

From the door of the summerhouse Miss Chris Caffrey watched the women laying out the first-aid equipment; the sunlight playing over the green lawns; the people strolling past, stopping now and then to look in, and found it almost impossible to believe that this was the beginning of an insurrection. A few yards away she saw Commandant Mallin, a pale, slight figure with a tight, clean-cut walk (he had served for a time with the Indian Army as an N.C.O.), stroll among his men, aiding and exhorting them, cracking jokes quietly. She was unable to conceive then, of course, exactly how complicated Mallin's task was. Connolly and Plunkett had ruled that the Park should be considered vitally important. No fewer than ten streets led into it—three of them essential to any penetration of the city from the south: Merrion Row, Leeson Street, and Harcourt Street. If the military, for example, advancing from Kingstown, were to meet stubborn resistance from De Valera in his headquarters, and decide to outflank him by crossing the Canal by a bridge farther up, they must funnel down Merrion Row or Leeson Street on their way toward Sackville Street; troops from Portobello were likely to work down Harcourt Street.

Mallin quickly realized that the Park would be an indefensible stretch of open ground, particularly if the military managed to seize houses around its perimeter. He decided, therefore, to occupy some houses himself. With the help of the Countess and a small party he smashed the ground-floor windows of several houses and placed men inside—occupants could leave or stay as they wished. This done, he began blocking off streets. All traffic was halted and motorists, draymen, cabbies, and tramwaymen were ordered to add their vehicles to the four barricades which eventually blocked the entire perimeter. Two trams left derelict outside the Shelbourne helped to prevent any movement.

Tweedy gentlemen, emerging from lunch at the hotel, suddenly found themselves prisoners—although in most cases they were quickly set free again. Military men, of course, were given different treatment. A khaki uniform appearing on the porch immediately drew a pot shot. One or two drew their own revolvers and shot back, but wiser counsels prevailed, and it was decided to conserve ammunition as much as possible in case the rebels decided to rush the hotel.

For all his reputed skill and experience, Mallin made no attempt to take the Shelbourne, although it was easily the most prominent building in the Green, and by virtue of its height, certainly the most commanding. Instead, he continued to allow his men to dig in in the Green where, crouched in their shallow holes, they were able to gaze up at the brilliant façade, its stonework picked out in rich cream paint, and envy the wealthy who ate there and slept there. He was to regret it, of course, for soon, and during all the hard days that would follow, it was to stand there and mock him.

The plans to isolate Dublin, originally drawn up with care, had been bungled.

For weeks before Easter, Captain Dermott Lynch, a Volunteer staff officer, had been collecting information about the telephone and telegraph lines in the city, with the help of such men as Richard Mulcahy, an employee in the Post Office Engineering Department. On Holy Thursday a small group of Volunteers and Citizen Army men were detailed for various jobs. Mulcahy was ordered to cut the cable and telephone lines to Belfast and Great Britain at Raheny, outside Dublin. Brothers George and Sam King were to blow up manholes in Lombard Street and Palace Street, cutting the Castle's private wires to London and other parts of the country. Michael King was to destroy the main telephone manhole outside the Telephone Exchange in Crown Alley which would cut off most of the city's internal telephone system.

At 12:10 A.M. George and Sam King blew up the manholes as instructed, cutting Sir Matthew's direct circuit to Mr. Birrell in London and almost—but not quite—isolating the Castle. Mulcahy cut the cables and telephone wires at Raheny.

But Michael King found himself unable to carry out his task, for the men who were to assist him failed to turn up. He told Pearse and Connolly.

"In that case, fall in with Mallin's men," said Connolly, already deciding on another plan.

When he had occupied the Post Office, he dispatched a small party to seize the entire Central Telephone Exchange. The attempt failed because of an old woman. As the party turned into Crown Alley, she rushed forward, shouting, "Go back, boys, go back, the place is crammed with military!" Taking her at her word, the rebels fell back.

Five hours later the military sent a garrison to occupy the Exchange, which had stood undefended all day long.

Yet the bungling was not all on the rebel side.

In the early hours of Easter Monday, the District Inspector of the Royal Irish Constabulary at Tralee reported to Dublin Castle that the second of the three men who had landed from the German submarine had been captured and had turned out to be a Sergeant Daniel Bailey of Casement's Irish Brigade. He had talked freely. He said that an insurrection was about to be staged and that the Castle itself would be attacked. Wimborne urged Nathan to strengthen the guards on the Castle and at Vice-Regal Lodge. Once again, however, the Under-Secretary demurred, and when 10:30 A.M. passed without incident, Wimborne did not press the point. Revolutions, he felt, usually occurred immediately after breakfast and as nothing had happened so far, Bailey's warning appeared to be valueless.

Even when, an hour later, reports of damage to railway lines and communications began to flow in from as far south as Kildare, neither Wimborne nor Nathan displayed any real sense of alarm. Their attitude was reflected in the behavior of Colonel Kennard, O.C. troops, Dublin, who in fact was absent from his office when the insurrection began, and by his deputy, Colonel H. V. Cowan, Assistant Adjutant-General. Cowan believed that if the Sinn Feiners had been prepared to start anything, they would almost certainly have attempted to rescue Casement when he had passed through Dublin on

Saturday night. No extra precautions, therefore, were taken. Only normal measures, which had been in force for some time, were in operation at noon on that day—an inlying picquet of 100 men from each regiment in Dublin was standing by, 400 men altogether.

The military forces in Dublin that morning amounted to 120 officers and 2,265 men—not all of them completely trained, but certainly all efficient enough to be turned out. These numbers were made up as follows:

At Marlborough Barracks, Phoenix Park: 35 officers and 851 other ranks of the 6th Cavalry Regiment.

At Richmond Barracks: 18 officers and 385 other ranks of the 3rd Royal Irish Regiment.

At Portobello Barracks: 21 officers and 650 other ranks of the 3rd Royal Irish Rifles.

At the Royal Barracks: 37 officers and 430 other ranks of the 10th Royal Dublin Fusiliers.

By 12:10 the Dublin police—thanks to the failure of the insurgents to seize the Telephone Exchange—had telephoned military H.Q. at Parkgate with the news that the Castle was under attack. Colonel Cowan, assisted by Major Owen Lewis of the General Staff, ordered a cavalry detachment from Marlborough Barracks to proceed at once to Sackville Street. Then he ordered forces from Richmond, Portobello, and the Royal Barracks toward the Castle. It was unfortunate, certainly, from the rebel point of view, that an attempt also to destroy the telephone junction at Parkgate Street—through which all Irish Command lines ran—had not been pressed with resolution.

There was nothing that could be called panic in either the Government itself or its branches, the military and police, although all, undoubtedly, were caught on the wrong foot. Certainly adrenalin began to course freely through a number of port-encrusted veins and there was a great deal of confusion. Wimborne, warned that Nathan was besieged in the Castle and that an army of rebels was marching on Vice-Regal Lodge, called for military protection; he also dispatched troops from Marlborough Barracks to put out the fire in the Magazine Fort. He felt overwhelmed, however, by the difficulty

91

of knowing exactly how many rebels were out, whether the country was going to rise in their support, and even if Irish recruits in the Army were likely to go over to them. Above and beyond anything else, what of Germany?

According to insurgent calculations made on the morning of the insurrection (these have been amended over the years to something like twice the size), there were just over seven hundred rebels out in Dublin altogether. The military forces therefore outnumbered the rebels from the start by at least three and a half to one; by late afternoon the odds had lengthened significantly and within forty-eight hours the military would be outnumbering the rebels by something like twenty to one. Yet the authorities made no real move to crush the rebels immediately, but rather nervously cast about for overwhelming reinforcements.

At 12:30 P.M. Colonel Cowan succeeded in getting through to the Curragh before the lines were cut, and asked that the sixteen-hundred-strong Mobile Column in reserve there be dispatched immediately to the capital. He then attempted to call London, but was unable to get through. A junior officer volunteered to dress in civilian clothes and bicycle through the insurgent lines to Kingstown, where there was a naval wireless transmitter. He reached Kingstown, seven miles away, shortly after one o'clock. At 1:10 precisely the news was flashed to London.

By then troops had already clashed with the rebels and the jittery Cowan had called for further reinforcements. These consisted of a battery of 18-pounders from Athlone, the 4th Battalion of the Dublin Fusiliers from Templemore, a composite battalion of New Army recruits from Belfast (one thousand men) and an additional thousand, apart from the Mobile Column, from Curragh. The rebels had asked for it. And now certainly they were going to get it.

92

At a window of the Imperial Hotel in Sackville Street, a young bride and her husband watched as Pearse and Connolly emerged from the G.P.O. and halted under the massive portico.

Mrs. Thomas Dillon had a fervent interest in the scene before her. Three of her brothers, the Plunkett boys, were inside that great gray building. Joseph, perhaps, was closest to her; she had kept house for him, and they had planned to hold a double wedding—she to Tom Dillon, he to the artist, Grace Gifford, whose enormous antique ring was one of the two he wore on his finger and to whom the will that lay next his heart bequeathed everything. They would almost certainly have been married as arranged on the previous day despite his illness, had it not been for the special circumstances.

The honeymooners could see little but a jostle of Volunteers and Citizen Army men under the portico. They continued to watch as a crowd gathered and a sudden hush fell over the street.

From the low step of the G.P.O., Patrick Pearse began to read the Proclamation of the Republic:

"POBLACHT NA h-EIREANN

THE PROVISIONAL GOVERNMENT

of the

IRISH REPUBLIC

TO THE PEOPLE OF IRELAND

93

"IRISHMEN and IRISHWOMEN: In the name of God and of the dead generations from which she receives her old tradition of nationhood, Ireland, through us, summons her children to her flag and strikes for her freedom.

"Having organised and trained her manhood through her secret revolutionary organisation, the Irish Republican Brotherhood, and through her open military organisations, the Irish Volunteers and the Irish Citizen Army, having patiently perfected her discipline, having resolutely waited for the right moment to reveal itself, she now seizes that moment, and, supported by her exiled children in America and by gallant allies in Europe, but relying in the first on her own strength, she strikes in full confidence of victory.

"We declare the right of the people of Ireland to the ownership of Ireland, and to the unfettered control of Irish destinies, to be sovereign and indefeasible. The long usurpation of that right by a foreign people and government has not extinguished the right, nor can it ever be extinguished except by the destruction of the Irish people. In every generation the Irish people have asserted their right to national freedom and sovereignty; six times during the past three hundred years they have asserted it in arms. Standing on that fundamental right and again asserting it in arms in the face of the world, we hereby proclaim the Irish Republic as a Sovereign Independent State, and we pledge our lives and the lives of our comrades-in-arms to the cause of its freedom, of its welfare, and of its exaltation among the nations.

"The Irish Republic is entitled to, and hereby claims, the allegiance of every Irishman and Irishwoman. The Republic guarantees religious and civil liberty, equal rights and equal opportunities to all its citizens and declares its resolve to pursue the happiness and prosperity of the whole nation and of all its parts, cherishing all the children of the nation equally, and oblivious of the differences carefully fostered by an alien government, which have divided a minority from the majority in the past.

"Until our arms have brought the opportune moment for the establishment of a permanent National Government, representative of the whole people of Ireland and elected by the suffrages of all her men and women, the Provisional Government, hereby constituted, will administer the civil and military affairs of the Republic in trust for the people.

"We place the cause of the Irish Republic under the protection of the Most High God, Whose blessing we invoke upon our arms, and we pray that no one who serves that cause will dishonour it by cowardice, inhumanity, or rapine. In this supreme hour the Irish nation must, by its valour and discipline and by the readiness of its children to sacrifice themselves for the common good, prove itself worthy of the august destiny to which it is called.

"Signed on behalf of the Provisional Government.

THOMAS J. CLARKE

SEAN MAC DIARMADA	THOMAS MACDONAGH
P. H. PEARSE	EAMONN CEANNT
JAMES CONNOLLY	JOSEPH PLUNKETT"

When Pearse had finished, Connolly took his hand and shook it, saying, "Thanks be to God, Pearse, that we've lived to see this day!" A few ragged cheers hung in the air, but the poet, Stephen MacKenna, who heard Pearse read the words, has recorded that he felt sad for him, for the response from the crowd was chilling. There were no wild hurrahs, no scenes reminiscent of the excitement which had gripped the Bastille mob. The Irish had listened and shrugged their shoulders or had sniggered and glanced around waiting for the police to appear.

James Connolly beamed, however. He stepped out onto the pavement and looked up at the roof where the two flags flew—the green at the left corner of the G.P.O. (on Princes Street) the Tricolour at the right (on Henry Street), and chuckled to Miss Carney, his secretary, "Isn't it grand!" Around him young insurgents were posting copies of the Proclamation. One copy, held down with stones, was placed on the ground beside Nelson's Pillar so that everybody could read it easily.

Slowly the crowd began to break up. Some strolled over to the Pillar and idly began reading the Proclamation, others just stood and stared up at the unfamiliar flags. Quite a few, bored with the whole thing, simply wandered away.

By the early afternoon, however, big crowds had gathered in Sackville Street. People sat on the parapets of O'Connell Bridge or collected at the corner of D'Olier and Westmoreland streets waiting tensely for the military. There was a constant flow of people past the G.P.O. Boys and girls flirted as they walked under the walls and their laughter floated up to the rebels on the roof. Dublin, it was clear, was *en fête* and thoroughly determined to enjoy itself. Now and then a shrill cry of "Here's the military!" or "Here's the soldiers!" would cause a slight panic until it proved to be a false alarm.

Inside the G.P.O., there were constant alerts. Each time, the insurgents were forced to down tools, pick up their rifles or shotguns, and run to the windows. In the confusion, it was hardly to be expected that the inexperienced recruits would always find it possible to control their weapons. Rifles and shotguns were continually going off, until Captain Brennan Whitmore began to feel that it might be safer outside the building than in.

Outside, all around the building, the crowd was thickening. Many were "separation women," mainly from the poorer class, who wore black shawls over their heads and shoulders. First they hurled abuse at the rebels, who answered them in kind; then they began to squabble among themselves. Inevitably they began to fight. Delightedly the rebels watched two "shawlies" hit out at each other. When they began pulling each other's hair, wild cheers greeted their efforts.

Then suddenly the crowd appeared to stagger. People began pushing into each other as others pressed forward, and in a moment the squabbling shawlies had been carried roughly away. Brennan Whitmore saw that a line of priests, their hands linked, had spread across the width of Sackville Street and as they advanced steadily from the far side of the Pillar, the crowd was falling back in disorder toward O'Connell Bridge. Like an encroaching wave, the priests came forward. The crowd solidified into a black, bobbing mass of heads. Some broke into the side streets where they waited until the clergy had passed and then flowed in behind them again. Just short of the bridge the priests halted; they had driven most of the crowd onto it. They turned and began walking up Sackville Street again. Their faces stern and unyielding, they forced the crowd back once more.

Inside the G.P.O. the rebels sang:

"Soldiers are we,
Whose lives are pledged to Ireland . . ."

Rifle fire crackled from across the river, from the direction
of Dublin Castle, as the priests pressed on. Now, however, a
different mob faced them—a wilder, more ragged lot, a slum
crowd excited and exhilarated by the breakdown of order.
Their front ranks stood firm, while behind them more shawlies chanted ribald songs. At the Pillar, the line of priests
split temporarily. Grabbing the initiative, the mob surged
forward. The priests were sent reeling, then swept away like
bubbles on surf.

Suddenly there was a yell and the crowd scattered. Whitmore heard the shout, "The Lancers! The Lancers!"

A sack of coal, intended for a barricade, slipped from his
hands, and he reached for his rifle. The G.P.O. had become a
frenzy of movement. Men dropped whatever they were carrying and grabbed their weapons. Officers bawled orders. Whitmore dropped flat on a table, poked his rifle through a loophole, and sighted along the barrel. He could see little; his field
of vision was narrow, barely stretching from Clery's shop opposite to the plinth of the Pillar on the left. Some of the crowd
had taken cover in doorways while a few, more daring, stood
in the roadway poised, ready to run. Whitmore found his
mouth dry. It was the first time he had been under fire, and
like so many before him, he wondered how he would acquit
himself.

He could hear Connolly's voice rising above the noise:
"Don't fire until I give the command! Let them gallop the full
length of the building. . . . Is that clear? . . . And whatever
you do, don't fire until I tell you!"

Two hundred men of the Royal Irish Regiment under Major Edward Warmington and Lieutenant Alan Ramsay halted some hundred and fifty yards from the place where Section-Commander John Joyce of the Irish Volunteers and four comrades were huddled behind a low wall. As the two officers scanned the rise of Mount Brown, Joyce dug himself closer to the earth, almost afraid to breathe. He felt no sensation of fear; even today he remembers nothing beyond a certain pulsating excitement.

A party of twenty men, with bayonets fixed, moved forward from the ranks of soldiers. With a sergeant leading, they began to advance slowly, fanning out across the road. They made no attempt to utilize cover, clearly relying on their own alertness to minimize surprise. Although in a magnificent ambushing position, Joyce felt uneasy about the open fields behind him. He itched to raise his head to see where the military were, but when he moved even slightly, Lieutenant O'Brien hissed, "Heads down!" Joyce could still hear the "separation women" shouting and he imagined that they must be trying to warn the oncoming troops. Every now and then O'Brien, screened by the hedge, would take a quick peek over the wall.

Then suddenly, without warning, the soldiers began to scatter. As Joyce popped his head up, an uneven fusillade rang out beside him and three soldiers dropped.

Once in action, Joyce became so tense that he could not focus properly on any of the darting, crouching, running figures. They reached the far side of the street without additional

98

loss and began breaking into houses there. Joyce could not help but admire their sergeant's cool behavior. His back to the rebels, he stood his ground unflinchingly, directing his men as they forced the flimsy doors of the small houses or crashed bodily through the front windows. Joyce tried to line the sergeant in his sights, but the man shifted about so much that he became an almost impossible target. Joyce finally fired and watched his bullet kick into the brick just above the sergeant's head. Neither by sign nor gesture did the man show that the bullet had almost hit him. After that Joyce fired rapidly, if at times a trifle wildly. More bodies appeared on the roadway. Then, abruptly, firing ceased as the enemy gained cover.

The lull lasted for almost fifteen minutes. O'Brien and his men felt quietly jubilant. They realized, however, that, as yet, they had not been exposed to anything like a full onslaught. The continued lull, in fact, appeared slightly ominous.

They had reason to be apprehensive, in fact. Annoyed at the treatment meted out to his advance party, Major Warmington had decided that a frontal attack was no longer feasible. Two hundred and fifty yards to his left stood the Royal Hospital, the official residence of the Commander in Chief, and, incidentally, Dublin's oldest public building outside the Castle. (Charles II had built it as a retreat for veteran soldiers.) From its roof and its great dormer windows the rebel positions could be easily enfiladed. Warmington therefore dispatched a party to take positions there. Then he sent his main party under Lieutenant Ramsay to attack the Union from the rear.

Ramsay doubled back along Old Kilmainham until he reached O'Connell Road running off to the left, which led him onto the South Circular Road and eventually to Rialto Gate. Here he divided his men into several small parties, which entered houses opposite the Gate. He also disposed fifteen men into the Rialto Buildings on the other side of the Canal, while he himself crouched down behind garden walls with the rest of his forces and prepared for a quick dash across the road toward the Gate.

At almost exactly five minutes to one the assault opened.

99

One second there was only brooding silence; the next the air seemed filled with fury. To Joyce, lying under the wall, under really severe fire for the first time in his life, the effect was utterly unnerving. To fight England, to do battle for Ireland, had until now seemed merely a simple, elemental matter of give and take—success and survival depended upon one's own rapidity and accuracy of fire. There had been nothing in his experience to prepare him for the veritable wall of bullets which swept over his head, coming not only from the front, but also from the rear and flanks. Were they encircled? In that first awful instant, Joyce could only feel a sense of utter helplessness; a sense of having nowhere to hide.

Time and place and their meaning appeared to vanish. It was difficult to see anything to fire back at; the military seemed to have disappeared into thin air, yet from the bullets spattering all about him Joyce knew they could see him. O'Brien, fortunately, kept cool, and Joyce instinctively obeyed him as he shouted, "Spread out! Spread out!"

He glanced around, searching for cover in the bare fields, but it seemed impossible for a man to survive out there in the face of such fire. Yet there was no alternative. A few slight ridges and dips in the ground offered hope and he made a sudden dash, hurling himself toward a depression barely twenty yards away. Over and over he rolled in the grass, firing wildly toward the enemy. Spread out across the field, he saw other comrades lying on their stomachs, firing as rapidly as their antiquated weapons would allow, then retreating in short, sharp, running bursts, only to fling themselves flat again almost immediately. The explosive crackle of rifle fire sounded continuously. Under the wall from which they had just retreated lay the still body of John Owens, aged twenty-four, fatally wounded. Suddenly a new sound became apparent. There was the quick chatter of a Lewis gun and a stream of bullets arced over the field in a wide sweep. With this machine-gun fire now coming from the roof of the Royal Hospital, normal movement became impossible, and any retreat (the general line was diagonally back toward an auxiliary hospital) had to be carried out in a series of belly wriggles. Even at that, men were hit. Joyce heard continued shouts of pain, each showing that another bullet had found a mark.

100

At Rialto Gate a ferocious assault had been launched to coincide with the main frontal firing. Irvine's party, holed up in the tin sheds near the gate, found themselves no better off than if they were in the open; bullets passed through the corrugated iron clean as a whistle. In a moment the sheeting looked like a sieve. Inside, bullets ricocheted wildly as they struck against iron bedsteads. There was an outlandish racket, a chaos of badly tuned gongs and rattling smacks; and in a matter of minutes the ears of the rebels were singing. The only safe position was flat on the floor. Bullets fired by the military from the other side of the Canal ripped through the gable, catching them in a fierce cross fire. A bullet went through the Wardmaster's coat as he lay flat among his lunatics in No. 6 dormitory.

Irvine soon discovered that the hasty defenses he had erected were giving his men only minimum protection. Within moments of the commencement of battle, seventeen-year-old John Traynor, the best shot in the company, dropped, mortally wounded. Irvine rushed to help him, but found blood pouring from his chest. As Traynor fought for breath, the rest of the party left their posts and gathered round him to say a prayer. Irvine, a Protestant, joined with them, as Traynor, gasping, "May Jesus have mercy on my soul," died.

Backed by strong rifle fire from the Rialto Buildings on the far side of the Canal and the machine-gun fire from the Royal Hospital, Lieutenant Ramsay sent one party doubling across the road and along the Canal bank where, screened by the high stone wall of the Union grounds, they edged toward a small gate two hundred yards away.

Ramsay, a veteran of Gallipoli, led the assault on the main gate, backed up eventually by a second wave led by Major Warmington. Rialto Gate itself was locked and barred, but a small wooden door beside it was easily broken down and Ramsay led his men through at the double. Coming immediately under fire from the sheds and from the solitary insurgent who had dug himself in opposite the gate, he fell, shot through the head. The rebel fire directed onto the narrow entrance gradually forced the military back. In a lull which followed, a stretcher party was permitted to go inside and carry away the wounded officer. Told that his lieutenant had only a few minutes to live, Major Warmington vowed to exact vengeance. He lined up a party behind him and at a signal charged through the small door. He was hit immediately and fell dead. His men, seeing him fall, broke under the heavy fire and so for the second time the military retreated.

Meanwhile the military attempting to break in by the Canal wall were enjoying a mixed success. As they began smashing down the stout wooden door, bullets suddenly kicked into the wall or, falling short, sizzled into the water beside them. This fire was coming from Captain James Murphy, holed up in Jameson's Distillery in Marrowbone Lane. It caused immediate casualties and the troops, caught without cover, could only flatten themselves along the grassy bank and attempt to return the fire. A few men tried to scale the ten-foot wall. Once on it, though, they were raked by rebel fire. One officer succeeded in getting his leg over the wall but toppled back, shot through the head. A private scaled a telegraph pole, with bullets gouging out splinters of wood at his heels, but he was difficult to hit because the pole partly hid him. When he was finally hit, he fell in an awkward cartwheel, his body hitting the path before bouncing into the water.

Eventually, the door was stormed and soldiers, pouring through, fanned out rapidly across the open field. Succeeding waves, however, were still forced to scamper through rapidly in the intervals between fire, or creep in lying on their bellies. Six insurgents, placed in the field by Commandant Kent, with only trees or bushes for cover, now began to retreat. Their problem was to cross the open ground lying between them and Hospital No. 2-3, the nearest of the outlying Union buildings. They could make a dash for it or wriggle across it slowly. Either way they would expose themselves to the fifteen-man military party in the Rialto buildings on the far side of the Canal, who were now in a position to fire down on them. They chose to try it slowly. But as they began to emerge into the open, crawling on their bellies, earth spurted up all around them. First hit was Richard O'Reilly, who had a brother, John, in the Nurses' Home. (His other two brothers were fighting in France."Funny," said John later, "that day there were two of us fighting *for* England, two of us *against!*") The

102

first bullet wounded him slightly, but a second clipped the life from him. Volunteers Brendan Donelan and James Quinn were hit shortly afterward and their bodies were to lie for the rest of the day where they had fallen.

The troops were closing in fast now, their firepower proving immensely superior. At Rialto Gate, Irvine decided the situation was hopeless and sent a messenger to ask Commandant Kent for instructions. The man somehow got through to Kent. He even managed to return with a message ordering Irvine to retire. By now, however, it was too late. The military, as though apprised of what was happening, had increased their pressure. Rebel rifles grew so hot, resisting, that the men had to take turns ceasing fire to allow them to cool. With the rebel fire lessening dramatically, the military mounted their final assault. The door of the hut strongly barricaded, kept them at bay, but in the end, three soldiers, using a heavy lawn mower as a battering ram, broke it down. The troops charged forward into the dangerous gap as George Irvine called out in a desperate voice, "Don't shoot! We surrender!"

Miss Lucy Stokes, blonde, attractive and long-limbed, ate her breakfast at 8:15, then dressed herself in a neat blue costume, put up her hair in a bun, pinned on her hat, and caught a tram to the North Circular Road, arriving exactly at 9 A.M. at the military hostel where she worked as a V.A.D. (member of the Volunteer Aid Detachment). Girls of her class (Miss Stokes came from a well-known Dublin medical family and was a Trinity College graduate) considered it their duty to help in the war effort, and assisting to clean the hostel was part of her contribution.

Shortly after midday, feeling, as she put it, "like a dried hemlock from weariness," she started back home for lunch. She walked down to the Quays, intending to catch a tram there, but after waiting for some time and seeing no trams, she asked some "excited-looking people" what had gone wrong with the service. Were the tramwaymen playing a game, or what?

"There's no trams, miss," a man explained. "The Volunteers has the city; they have all the stations taken and the

Bank of Ireland, the General Post Office, the Castle and the Green, and they have killed two of the polis, blown up a train and all in it, and sure, isn't Sackville Street strewn with corpses! Don't make any mistake and get on a thram! . . . There now, did you hear them? The Volunteers in Guinness's Bathin' House, shootin' the soldiers—they're after shootin' two in the thram and the ladies in it with them."

Miss Stokes had never heard such exciting news, although she didn't believe a quarter of it. She set off to walk along the Quays, pausing for a moment at the first bridge she came to, where some men were crowded around a barricaded pub. The men inside told her to "hurry out of that" to safety. But at that moment she heard a crackle of rifle fire and, looking northward across the river, she saw soldiers emerging from the Royal Barracks and taking cover behind the opposite Quay wall. A few, hunched down, started across the bridge toward her. The crowd around her at once grew excited: "The military's coming out—their bayonets fixed! Lor', they'll take us for Volunteers!" To prove that they weren't, they broke into a cheer as the soldiers approached. They even gave advice: "Go round the back, ye'll catch them there. Kape to the wall or ye'll be shot dead!" The soldiers passed on as though they had heard nothing, leaving the crowd to change its attitude to one of disgust. "There now, d'ye see that!" insisted one man. "Such muddlin'! Isn't it aisy to believe in the muddlin' at the front!"

Miss Stokes decided to follow the soldiers, but two polite officers stopped her and suggested that she take a different direction. So she crossed over the river to the north side and walked along the Quays past the Four Courts toward Sackville Street. She watched the troops on the side of the river she had left edging their way cautiously toward Dublin Castle.

These were men of the 10th Royal Dublin Fusiliers, ordered forward by Colonel Cowan. Leaving Royal Barracks, which lay on the north bank of the river, facing Guinness's Brewery, a small party had crossed the river under fire from a token force of rebels ensconced in the Brewery. Meanwhile their main body filtered along the northern Quays, intending to cross the river lower down and make a direct assault along Parliament Street to the front gates of the Castle. But before they could do this, they came under fire from the Mendicity Institution on the south bank, held by John Heuston and his party of youths. The approach to the Mendicity—a converted mansion used to house the poor of the city—had to some extent been blocked off by half-finished barricades which the troops made no attempt to test.

Ignorant of rebel strength, the military were not to know that, emerging from their barracks almost two hundred strong, they appeared an overwhelmingly powerful force to the dozen youths locked up in the old building. A resolute charge might have carried the place, but as Heuston's men opened a wild and inaccurate fire, the troops took cover. Some found a refuge in deserted tramcars, but the majority crouched down behind the Canal walls or sought cover in side-street doorways. The exchanges were scattered. After a while, leaving a strong covering party behind the low river wall, the main force commenced filtering again along the Quays until they reached Queen Street Bridge. They still came under fire as they crossed this, but the Castle's relief now looked certain.

When the 12:20 from Kingstown jolted to a halt at the disused Sandymount Station just inside the city limits, John J. O'Leary, a newspaper reporter, thought it was to check tickets, and began fumbling in his pocket. He had been ruminating on the changing character of Irish Easter Mondays. Once, in the old days, he remembered, Kingstown would have been packed on a holiday; as it was, the railway station had looked virtually empty. Were tastes, he wondered, changing in a subtle way?

When a collector did not appear, O'Leary glanced out of the window. He saw that some passengers had alighted and decided to join them. Together they stood around wondering what was happening until a guard came stumbling along the line.

"What's up?" asked O'Leary.

"We're not going any farther; that's all I know," said the guard, and strode away quickly.

105

Sensing a story, O'Leary decided to walk along the line and find out what was wrong. At the next station, he found another halted train. A porter told him, "The Sinn Feiners have taken the city and occupied Westland Row." Then, pointing to the nearby Rugby grounds, headquarters of the Irish Rugby Union, he said, "Look, you can see them ripping up the rails." O'Leary saw a bunch of shirt-sleeved men working with picks and shovels. He decided, therefore, to take to the main road and walk on into the city. As he grew nearer to the center, he saw extraordinary scenes. Knots of people were standing about everywhere talking together excitedly. Near Mount Street Bridge he saw a line of deserted trams. A little farther on he heard his first shot.

In the suburb of Donnybrook, a region of well-kept lawns and solid Victorian houses, Mrs. Margaret Taaffe put down the telephone and, turning to her son Michael, remarked, "Avice says Stephen's Green and the G.P.O. are full of rebels. Sinn Feiners, I suppose. You know how your aunt exaggerates, but all the same I'm going down to Northumberland Road to see if Mother is all right."

When she had ridden off on her wooden-rimmed bicycle, wearing a large and quite unsuitable velvet hat, thought Michael, he decided to go into the city himself.

His first discovery was that the Donnybrook trams had stopped running. Halfway down Leeson Street (which leads into St. Stephen's Green), he heard a shot. He ducked right toward Merrion Square, making for the Lincoln Gate at Trinity College where he was a student. Massey, the porter, dressed in the traditional peaked velvet cap and brass-buttoned coat, let him in.

"What's going on inside?" asked Taaffe.

"Ah, they're all up at the Front Gate, arranging what I heard tell was a plan of campaign," said Massey. " 'Tis quiet here, anyway," he added.

Taaffe hurried across College Park and found the Front Gate shut and locked. A khaki figure, complete with a short leather cane and a Military Cross gleaming on his tunic, bounded out of the Porter's Lodge.

"Well, thank God for that!" grinned this apparition. "Another medical student's turned up! Jolly good! Come to win the war?"

From somewhere outside Trinity there was the sound of shots and Taaffe jerked a little nervously. "Can't have too many men," barked the figure in khaki. "Got to defend the library at all costs, y'see."

Taaffe had a sudden vision of a last stand at the library windows, ammunition spent, while a horde of rebels with fixed bayonets swept across the Fellows' Garden. "What can I do to help?" he asked uncertainly.

"Well, you'd better come up to the Regent House and see Lawford," said the figure in khaki.

Upstairs, sunk in a chair in the magnificent room over the Front Gate, Taaffe found an ancient Fellow, fast asleep, a rifle between his knees. At a table under the high windows sat Tom Lawford, a brewer, in his captain's uniform, busily writing.

"Are you in the O.T.C.?" asked Lawford, who wore a Military Cross.

"I'm afraid not."

"Oh, well. . . . Anyway you'll want to see what's going on above. You can get to the roof if you go out that way. But watch yourself."

Taaffe climbed through the trap door onto the leads. Keeping his head well down for fear of snipers, he crawled forward. Abruptly, he was confronted by the dirty face of a divinity student known to him as Pinky Wilson.

"Thank God you've come!" said Wilson. "Another five minutes an' I'd have given in."

"Why, what's wrong?"

"If I don't get to the lavatory this minute, I'll not be responsible for what happens! You'll find the gun an' all up there in front. Orders are to treat everyone you see who isn't in khaki as a rebel."

"You mean—*shoot* at them?"

"Of course, that's what you're here for!"

"Have you been shooting at everyone?"

" 'Course I haven't, but those are the orders. I think it's that bloodthirsty little sod with the M.C."

107

Wilson left and Taaffe inched forward to the parapet where he found a .303 rifle, several clips of ammunition, cigarettes and matches. Sixty feet below lay Dame Street, leading up to Dublin Castle. Taaffe scanned the roofs. They seemed deserted enough. Gingerly he picked up the rifle, checked that there was a bullet in it, then put it down and lit a cigarette. After a while he picked up the rifle again and sighted along the barrel at the Bank of Ireland opposite, pretending that he was focusing on a rebel. Suddenly the rifle jumped and on the other side of the street, high up on the stone façade of the Bank, a little cloud of dust appeared.

"What the hell do you think you're shooting at?" hissed Wilson, emerging from the trap door. . . .

As far out as Ballsbridge, where the Royal Dublin Society's Spring Show was in full swing, the Right Honorable Frederick Wrench, P.C., took immediate steps to organize resistance in the event of a rebel attack. With the assistance of Robert Bruce, the Agricultural Superintendent, he rounded up some workmen and got them to get a giant hose into position. Wrench told everybody that there must be "no funking a fight."

James Stephens, poet and novelist, was on his way home to lunch when he noticed an unusually large number of people standing about in small groups, gazing apprehensively toward St. Stephen's Green. His thoughts, however, were preoccupied with a dulcimer with which his friend Professor Thomas Bodkin had just presented him, so it did not occur to him that anything out of the normal was happening. It was not until he had eaten lunch and was on his way back to the library where he worked that he noticed that crowds were still congregated near the Green and decided that there must be something really wrong.

"Has there been an accident?" he asked a tough-looking, red-mustached man.

"Don't you know? The Sinn Feiners have seized the city. The Green is full of them!" said the man.

"My God!" said Stephens. With some courage he made for the Green, despite the sound of rifle fire.

108

The place was in a state of siege—barricades made out of motorcars and carts had been thrown across the street and empty tramcars lay deserted all around the perimeter. At the Shelbourne Hotel, he saw three rebels dash from the Green and halt a chauffeur-driven car. He heard them courteously apologizing to its occupants, a man and a woman, whom they made alight. Then they told the chauffeur to lodge the car in the barricade.

"What's the meaning of all this?" Stephens asked a rebel, a young man of twenty, whose face was grimy with sweat.

"We're expecting a military attack at any moment," replied the rebel. Then, pointing to a crowd gathered at the far gate of the park, he said, "But imagine—those people won't go home for me!"

Miss Stokes, still trying to reach home, halted at the same barricade a few minutes later to watch another "splendid motorcar" held up and a dignatory of the Catholic Church step down as a rebel saluted and said, "I beg your pardon, my Lord, but it's my orders."

She thought she might see Germans, for on her way up Grafton Street an army recruiting sergeant had warned her, "The Germans have the Green, ma'am, and are after sendin' off a volley." By now, incredibly, many Dubliners were convinced that "all the trouble" was due to a German landing. Volunteer Richard MacAuliffe, for instance, wandering down Westmoreland Street on his way to the G.P.O., heard an old woman call out, "A corpse of Germans has landed on the Green!"

While Miss Stokes lingered at the barricade, yet another car came whirling down the side of the Green. Trapped, the driver slammed on his brakes.

"Drive to the barricade!" shouted a rebel, as the driver, struggling with his steering wheel, tried to turn around. When he refused to obey, a rebel shot at his tires and burst one open.

"Now, drive it on the rim!" shouted the rebel, and the driver, left with no alternative, drove slowly forward and lodged his car with the others.

Beside Miss Stokes an elderly gentleman said, "If those

109

ruffians had shot him, I'd have shot them," and he showed her a small revolver he had hidden in his sleeve.

Patrick Doyle was busy in his greengrocer's shop at the corner of North King Street and Church Street when he heard galloping hoofs and saw a riderless horse flash past. A moment later, a neighbor put his head in the door and shouted that a lancer had been shot dead. Doyle went to the door and saw armed men busy up Church Street dragging cabs, milk floats, and lorries from Moore's, the coachbuilder's. He watched them enter Murphy's, the chemists in North King Street, and roll out empty oil drums and wooden barrels; then saw them take chairs, tables, and beds from some houses and pile them up in the street. They were making two barricades— one across Church Street at No. 77, and another across North King Street at No. 159. A little later a party of rebels entered the shop and said they had come to commandeer a bed. Doyle did not argue. He watched silently as they carried his bed across to Father Matthew Hall, where they had set up a Red Cross post. Some of them came back and ordered him to get into the back of the house.

"But I haven't any back rooms," protested Doyle, and pointed out that his premises were on a corner so that all windows faced the street. "And I've two sick children up-stairs," he complained, explaining that his wife had gone with his mother-in-law to Fairyhouse and had left him to take care of young Jimmy and Margaret, now in bed with measles.

"Well, get back as far as you can," they told him. "There's going to be trouble." He watched them break his windows in order to leave themselves a clear field of fire. Then they carried in sacks of flour which they had commandeered from Monk's Bakery and began loopholing the windows. Finally they flung themselves face down and poked their rifles out. And there they waited.

[10]

The troop of Lancers halted at the head of Sackville Street, immediately beneath the smooth obelisk commemorating Parnell, while Colonel Hammond, their commanding officer, cautiously surveyed the street. He saw people surging back toward O'Connell Bridge, some seating themselves on the parapets or scaling lampposts to get a better view. High over the Post Office flaunted two flags which were strange to him. Then he went forward, with his obedient troops following.

They were a stern and martial sight. Their horses, high-spirited, silken-coated, groomed magnificently, trotted forward in an even line, their hoofs ringing sharply on the roadway. The troopers sat like ramrods, their tall, slim, pennanted lances somehow emphasizing their superb correctness. Carbines jerked in their holsters with every movement of the horses. Harness jingled pleasantly; bits and spurs glittered. Colonel Hammond affected an air of self-assured arrogance almost as though he were on the parade ground. The very perfection of the ensemble should have been sufficient to shatter the insurgents' morale—as it was, indeed, certainly calculated to.

Inside the G.P.O., men rushed to the windows and to the parapet on the roof. On the far side of Henry Street, which forms the northern boundary of the building, Volunteer James O'Brennan flattened himself on the roof of the Tower public house and poked forward a single-bore shotgun. Inside the Imperial Hotel, Mrs. Dillon almost fell out of the window in an effort to obtain a superior view, but her bridegroom put a protecting arm around her. Back in the G.P.O., Con-

111

nolly's sharp orders were taken up by his officers and sent echoing through the building. The atmosphere became charged with excitement. Until now, rebellion had meant nothing more than a prosaic matter of lugging coal bags about to block up windows, or pushing chairs and desks and tables into position, while avoiding the many accidental rifle shots which threatened to leave the British Army with nothing at all to do.

This was the moment chosen by the Rathfarnham Company of Volunteers, arriving late for the battle, to make a dash across Sackville Street from Lower Abbey Street. Youngsters had been cheering them and one tough-looking Dubliner had encouraged them: "Up the Volunteers! Hammer the sh-- out of the f-----s!" They started their dash just as the Lancers broke into a quick trot, but most of them reached the Princes Street entrance of the G.P.O. before the troopers charged. Shouts of "Who are you?" from inside, greeted the desperate men.

"We're from Rathfarnham!" shouted Lieutenant Bulfin. "For God's sake open up."

"To hell with that!" replied a rebel. "Break the blasted windows and inside with you, you bloody fools!" So they smashed the nearest window—which had not yet been loopholed—and the company began scrambling in.

As they did so, the Lancers approached the Pillar at a sharp gallop and amid a hail of huzzahs! The callow, easily excitable rebels lost their heads and, despite Connolly's explicit orders, opened a ragged volley. Had the men behind those crude fortifications been seasoned troops, Colonel Hammond and his troops must have been decimated. As it was, four Lancers toppled from their saddles; three dying before they hit the ground; the other being fatally wounded.

A second volley poured into them caused no casualties. A bullet fired by rebels posted on the other side of Sackville Street, however, entered the telephone booth where Lieutenant Chalmers was held captive and buried itself in the woodwork above his head. Another bullet caught a sixteen-year-old member of the Rathfarnham Company as he waited his turn to climb into the Post Office; in the ensuing scramble, Volunteer John Keely accidentally shot himself in the stomach. Even as this was happening, a Lancer spurred his mount madly past Nelson's Pillar. Captain Brennan Whitmore, peering through his loophole tried to catch him in his sights, but the horse stumbled and fell, flinging its rider over its head. The man picked himself up and staggered toward the footpath. Reeling drunkenly, with his hand up to his head, he vanished from sight down North Earl Street opposite. Whitmore made no attempt to shoot him.

Meanwhile Colonel Hammond, his sword flashing in the air, was trying to restore order among his disjointed forces. "Get back! Get back!" he yelled, and the milling troopers, wheeling about, their splendid order gone, galloped back to the head of Sackville Street, leaving their casualties behind them.

A newsboy ran into the street where a trooper's carbine lay near the Pillar; Whitmore watched him pick it up and come toward the G.P.O. A shawlie grabbed at him, but the newsboy swung the rifle and clubbed her. She collapsed, screaming, as the boy ran up to the front of the G.P.O., shouting, "Here yez are! Here yez are!" and flung the carbine through a window.

Casualties among the insurgents had been negligible. A man at a second-floor window was shot dead—probably by a comrade on the other side of the street. A homemade bomb blew up in Lieutenant Liam Clarke's face just as he was about to fling it; although his face was made bloody, it was obvious he would survive, which drew from one rebel the wry comment: "So much for those bloody canisters! If poor Clarke's head wasn't blown off, the divil little else use they'll be— except for moral effect."

Reporters Maurice Linnane and Michael Knightley raced up Sackville Street in the wake of the retreating Lancers. At the Parnell Monument they discovered Colonel Hammond reforming his men. Linnane decided he was going to try another charge, but the Colonel evidently thought better of it, for with a crisp, angry shout of command, he wheeled his mount toward Great Britain Street and was followed by his defeated troop amid the jeers of the crowd. It was clear that the insurgents were determined and had dug themselves in well. A mere display of martial strength obviously was not going to shift them.

113

Outside the G.P.O., the first ambulances appeared, picking up the dead and wounded without hindrance.

With their long skirts hampering them, the Citizen Army women found it no easy job to get into the City Hall, for an iron-trellis gate barred the entrance to the steps before the main door. Throwing modesty to the winds, they hoisted up their skirts and scrambled over. Emily Norgrove, for one, split her skirt.

Once inside, Miss Helena Moloney set up quarters in the caretaker's kitchen and began allocating duties. She asked some women to fill buckets or baths with water, others to prepare bandages, while the rest she detailed to see to the cooking. Miss Norgrove was ordered to do sentry duty in the main entrance hall. It proved to be a lonely post, with nothing much to do but listen to the sound of shots from the men on the roof and sporadic answering fire from somewhere across Castle Yard.

To those besieged inside the Castle, however, it seemed as though half Ireland had risen in rebellion and had seized the surrounding roofs. Firing, if not particularly heavy, was at least continual. Hard upon the shooting of Constable O'Brien came the death of Sergeant-Major Brosnan, who, dressed in mufti, was mistaken for a rebel and shot by a soldier. His death seemed the more poignant because he should not have been in the Castle at all. That morning he had said good-bye to his wife and children and was about to leave for Buncrana, County Donegal, where he was a musketry instructor, when the attack on the Castle opened. He had at once gallantly offered his services.

At 1:40 P.M. the first relief arrived at the Ship Street entrance—180 men of the Royal Irish Rifles and the Dublin Fusiliers, thereby destroying any hope John Connolly's men had ever had of taking the Castle or even neutralizing it.

A V.A.D. who served in the Castle during the insurrection has left a vivid account of these moments:

I ran into the Sterilising Room to see what was happening at the back. A troop of soldiers had arrived and were drawn up in

114

Barrack Yard. The heavy solid gates were closed and also shut across, with a sentry at each peep-hole. Outside, instead of men with bayonets, were small children, staring with open mouths at the massive gates. Rifle shots were heard at intervals but we could not see where they came from. At First Dinner there was a general atmosphere of unrest. Conversation flagged, although a few people kept up constant questions—chiefly asking if we had seen the policeman's helmet in the hall, and the holes made by the bullet. There was a noise of people rushing down the corridor and the sisters ran out to see if they were needed. Several times during the meal stretchers passed up and down the corridor outside and each time we asked the same question: "Killed or wounded?" and someone came in and said: "Dead," or "Very bad."

My only conscious sensation at the moment was of a burning desire to go out and have a shot at the rebels myself. Instead I remarked prosaically to one of the V.A.D.s: "It doesn't look much like the theatre tonight?" "Hush!" she said, "don't suggest to anyone that it would not be safe; it'll be all right by then and we must go." We could not cross the Yard to our rooms after dinner, so I took a tour through the Picture Gallery and Throne Room, where all the windows were thronged with spectators. The Throne Room faces the Front Gate and from there I could see that the Gate was locked and guarded by rebels. Otherwise things looked much as usual; only rifle shots rang out at intervals. "Look! you can see the sniper; watch the roof of that house", said one of the men next to me. Presently something popped up on the roof—a puff of smoke—bang! When I came back to the Supper Room I found a nurse in great agitation. "I was nearly killed." she exclaimed. As there did not seem any immediate danger, I asked how. "I was leaning out of the Sterilising Room window, and a bullet whizzed right past me—look at the mark on my apron!" She pointed to a rent, which I was convinced had been there all morning, and tactlessly said so. "Well, it passed very near me, anyway," she protested, "and I got such a fright."

It was just after two o'clock when the insurgents investing the Castle lost their leader, John Connolly—a small lean man, who had been an Abbey actor of great promise.

Helena Moloney, Jenny Shanahan, and Bridget Davis were

on the roof at the time. Anxious to see what was happening, they had daringly climbed up onto the balustraded balcony which rimmed the great dome. Here, solitary and remote, Helena Moloney remembers, she felt safe so long as she crouched down behind the dome. Connolly stood only three or four yards away from her, peering out cautiously now and then, to take a shot.

As she turned to speak to Bridget Davis, she suddenly saw him slump sideways. "Oh! Oh!" she gasped, and crept along the rim toward him. She spoke, but he made no answer. "Go and get Dr. Lynn," she said to Bridget.

Dr. Kathleen Lynn, a member of the Citizen Army, was with Mallin's forces in St. Stephen's Green. As the girl left, Helena Moloney breathed an Act of Contrition into Connolly's ear. He was still alive, moaning faintly, when Bridget returned with Dr. Lynn. The two women had to crawl on their knees to reach them. Before they could negotiate the difficult passage, Connolly was dead. "I'm afraid he's gone," said Dr. Lynn gently. A few yards away, also on his hands and knees, crouched the dead man's brother, fourteen-year-old Matthew Connolly, fighting back his tears.

That afternoon Lord Wimborne, snatching a moment from his other duties, wrote to Mr. Birrell:

The worst has happened, just when we thought it averted. If only we had acted last night with decision and arrested the leaders as I wanted, it might have been averted. The Post Office is seized —Nathan is still besieged in the Castle but I hope he will be out soon. Almost all wires are cut. Everybody away on holiday. Bridges blown up. Fortunately we got the Curragh before interruption and about 2,000 are arriving. The situation is not yet in hand, but if we get through the night, I hope we shall settle them tomorrow. No news from the provinces, but there is sure to have been trouble. I fear, too, a raid [*from Germany*]. This is too audacious to have been undertaken without hope of support. We must have troops. At least a brigade. I should prefer a division. I am attempting to form a Privy Council quorum to proclaim Martial Law or whatever now corresponds to it. I shall take the most energetic and

116

sternest measures consistent with my resources. The situation is very serious and we need energetic help. So far, no general rising or sympathy with the Sinn Fein, so far as I can hear, but one never knows what may be developed.

There was, indeed, something not far from panic at times among the highest military quarters in the capital. No one knew just how many rebels were out—or how many might come out; the situation in the country remained obscure because of the breakdown in communications. Worst of all, as no one was capable of believing that the Sinn Feiners would be mad enough to attempt anything without a guarantee from Germany, news of an invasion was awaited hourly. This sense of being about to be overwhelmed transmitted itself even to the military barracks in the city. The extreme audacity of the rebel moves; the skillful way in which they had seized the most important strategic points in the city, plus the nature of the fight they had put up wherever the military had encountered them, led everyone to believe that their actions were based on careful plans made by Germany. When Major Sir Francis Vane hurried back from a pleasant lunch at Bray to help organize the defense of Portobello Barracks, he found the place in a state of dire confusion; the news was that the Germans had landed on the west coast and that huge insurgent armies had joined them and were even now marching on Dublin. This confusion and panic was compounded, of course, by the presence of innumerable refugees, military and civilian, and the fact that the total force in the barracks was just under six hundred men, compared with a normal peacetime establishment of two battalions.

Luck, however, had not entirely deserted the authorities. Pearse and Connolly, handicapped by their shortage of men, blundered on from one mistake to yet another. They even failed to appreciate the vital importance of Trinity College as a strategical position, though it sat astride their communications with St. Stephen's Green. Here the authorities were to gain gratuitously a lodgment in central Dublin.

Trinity was put into a state of siege by the University O.T.C. within less than an hour of the start of the rebellion. In the

117

early afternoon a handful of Canadian and Anzac soldiers, in Ireland for a brief furlough, made their way into the place when they heard it was being held for the Government. Several more were recruited by Trinity students who paraded the streets in mufti, looking for any who would help. Young Ernest O'Malley, a Dubliner, was stopped by three students he knew.

"What do you think of these damned Sinn Feiners?" asked one.

"Well, I don't know," said O'Malley, "but I suppose they'll soon be chased out of the place."

"Well, we're collecting people to defend Trinity. Will you come along? We'll give you a rifle—we've plenty belonging to the O.T.C."

O'Malley, however, had not made up his mind. "Oh, I'm on my way home now," he said, to put them off. "But look—I'll come back later."

(11)

It was late in the morning when Professor Liam O'Briain and his friend Captain Harry Nicholls of the Irish Volunteers, who had been left out of the mobilization, climbed over the railings of St. Stephen's Green and joined Commandant Mallin's men. They found Mallin himself, a small, quiet man, who gave an impression of efficiency and deep, thoughtful judgment. He was brisk but not hasty in making decisions and after welcoming O'Briain and Nicholls warmly, he ordered them to be given rifles and positions. Nicholls was told to dig a trench at the corner of the Green opposite Cuffe Street. O'Briain was told to report to Lieutenant Bob de Coeur, who handed him a pick and ordered him to get busy. It was the first time in his life, remembers O'Briain, that he had ever done "a decent day's work," and it irked him to see Citizen Army fellows, most of whom were accustomed to using their hands and muscles in their various trades, always more anxious to give up the back-breaking stuff and do sentry duty than he, a soft-palmed, un-muscled linguist—he was Lecturer in Romance languages at National University.

"I'll go sentry now, Bob," he heard them volunteer time and again, while he had to console himself with the thought that the ache in his back was the least he could offer Ireland.

Passers-by continued to stop and look in through the railings all afternoon. They stared at the rebels curiously, almost as though they expected them to turn suddenly and bite.

As the day wore on, O'Briain discovered that for the most part his fellow rebels were far more eager to discuss politics than they were to dig trenches. Few Irish Volunteers had

119

thought deeply about the kind of Ireland they wanted to see if the Rebellion succeeded; all that mattered was that the shackles should be flung off and that Irishmen once again should be able to walk freely with their heads as high as anyone else's. O'Briain discovered that the Citizen Army men were much more concerned about the economic and social aspects.

"I thought the military revolution was to be followed by the industrial revolution," said a man called O'Leary.

"Indeed!" replied O'Briain, flabbergasted. "The industrial revolution—what industrial revolution?"

"A general strike," said O'Leary.

It was the first time O'Briain had ever heard the expression and when O'Leary explained what it meant, O'Briain deemed it a wonderful idea; it would certainly shake the Castle a great deal more than a bomb or two.

The shadows lengthened. A tall old man, very straight, with a mustache and side whiskers à la Franz Josef, came to the railings and shouted, "Can anybody join in this or is it a private fight?"

"You can come in," replied O'Briain, "if you know anything about it."

"I was seven years in the American artillery," answered the old man proudly.

"Begod, in that case come right on in!" said O'Briain, and went over to help him—a move he was later to regret when he found that the man, a returned Yank called Sullivan, was slightly crazy.

During the afternoon, Mallin, wakening at last to the weakness of his position, ordered Sergeant Frank Robbins to seize the Royal College of Surgeons, a well-proportioned building with a fine classical façade, dominating the west side of the Green.

The military now began moving in from just north of the city. By midafternoon, forces under Major A. F. Sommerville, Commander of the School of Musketry at Dollymount, had seized the North Wall railway station, main terminus for all dock traffic. A second party, sent down the Great Northern railway line toward Amiens Street Station, ran into one hundred rebels at Clark's Bridge over the Royal Canal. The rebels were under the command of Captain Tom Weafer, Second Battalion, and were escorting a convoy of weapons and medical supplies to the G.P.O.

Weafer, a sensible, level-headed fellow, kept his wits magnificently when the military stumbled into him. He ordered his advance guard to engage the enemy, a second group to seize defensive positions near Ballybough Bridge—which would enable them to control road and rail approaches to the city and also to protect their battalion headquarters—and with the rest of his party he gathered the scattered convoy together and pushed on to the G.P.O. The forces he left behind took up positions commanding Annesley railway bridge, by entering corner houses in North Strand, Spring Garden Street, Annesley Place, and Leinster Avenue. When the military, flushed with success after scattering the convoy at Clark's Bridge, reached Annesley Bridge, they were met by heavy fire. Caught on the open railway line, they attempted to get their machine gun mounted, but rapid fire by the rebels put it out of action before it could even reply. The military then sought cover in the side streets. Some two hundred yards north of the bridge, they dug in and prepared for a rebel attack.

Taking advantage of their lack of aggression, the rebels slipped away from their positions and made their way also to the G.P.O.

Mr. St. John Ervine, the noted Ulster playwright and then manager of the Abbey Theatre, had gone to his office early that day to deal with the mountains of correspondence which had piled up during the company's recent English tour. In the afternoon, he intended to present a gala matinée performance of Yeats's poetic play, *Cathleen ni Houlihan*. Shortly before the performance was due to begin, however, a stage hand entered his office.

"I don't think we'll be able to hold a performance, sir."

"Why not?" asked Ervine.

"I think there's a rebellion or something on—anyway the Sinn Feiners are out! Listen."

121

Ervine heard the dull sound of rifle fire. He left his office then and stepped out into the street in front of the theater. He saw small knots of people standing about at the corners and noticed that there were no policemen anywhere. Well, this is damn funny! he thought.

Hearing a rumble of carts, he looked down a lane and saw an extraordinary convoy approaching. Two carts piled high with vegetables, principally cauliflower, were being escorted by armed youths. The idea of rebels stuffing themselves with interminable cauliflower seemed to him highly amusing and he burst into laughter.

Late that afternoon Lord Wimborne published a proclamation:

Whereas, an attempt, instigated and designed by the foreign enemies of our King and Country to incite rebellion in Ireland and thus endanger the safety of the United Kingdom, has been made by a reckless, though small, body of men, who have been guilty of insurrectionary acts in the City of Dublin:

Now, we, Ivor Churchill, Baron Wimborne, Lord Lieutenant-General and Governor-General of Ireland, do hereby warn all His Majesty's subjects that the sternest measures are being, and will be, taken for the prompt suppression of the existing disturbances, and the restoration of order:

And we do hereby enjoin all loyal and law-abiding citizens to abstain from any acts or conduct which might interfere with the action of the Executive Government, and, in particular, we warn all citizens of the danger of unnecessarily frequenting the streets or public places, and of assembling in crowds:

Given under our seal, this 24th day of April, 1916.

WIMBORNE

From the roof of the G.P.O. the contents of this Proclamation were shouted across to Volunteers O'Brennan and Mc-Gaham on the roof of the Tower bar.

"Ah, the ould cod!" yelled back O'Brennan. "Send us over some more bombs!"

122

The rebels, of course, knew that it was essential to let the world—and especially the United States—know what they had done. Joseph Plunkett, therefore, had prepared elaborate plans to send out the news by wireless transmitter. To this end he had at first enlisted the services of three men—Fergus O'Kelly, David Bourke, and Con Keating—to help set up a pirate transmitting and receiving station at his father's Kimmage farmhouse. O'Kelly had served with the Army Signalling Corps and the other two were trained Marconi operators.

They had found it impossible to construct a transmitting set, although they had managed to build a crude receiving apparatus, using a gramophone motor. This, however, had failed to work. Plunkett's original intention had been to use this pirate radio to pick up any messages broadcast by the Germans concerning the *Aud*. When the set would not work, he sent Keating and Bourke to Kerry to seize the Government's apparatus at Valentia. On their way, Keating lost his life when the car in which they were traveling took a wrong turning and plunged into the sea, Bourke luckily escaping.

Late on Monday afternoon, then, when it had become clear that the authorities had neither the will nor the strength to crush the insurrection promptly, Plunkett ordered O'Kelly to occupy the Dublin Wireless School of Telegraphy on the other side of Sackville Street. This had been closed at the beginning of the war by the authorities, parts of the apparatus being dismantled and the doors sealed. O'Kelly took six men (among them a Cockney, Lieutenant John O'Connor, known as "Blimey," and Arthur Shields, the Abbey Theatre actor and brother of Barry Fitzgerald who became a Hollywood film star) and climbed the stairs to the school. This was on the top floor of a building known as Reis's, in the block between Lower Abbey Street and the river. They broke the seals and entered. David Bourke set to work to reconnect the apparatus —a long and tedious task.

O'Kelly walked out on the roof and found that the aerial had been taken down. The two poles, however, lay on the roof and a Volunteer was sent to search electrical shops in the neighborhood for the proper wire. O'Kelly, examining the position from a military viewpoint, thought it far too exposed for comfort. It was dominated by the pagodalike dome of the Dublin Bread Company's (D.B.C.'s) Restaurant two doors away; if the military were to seize this, the School would be untenable, so he sent a man back to tell Connolly. The Commandant's reaction was to order Captain Tom Weafer to occupy the entire block.

The danger, it appeared to Connolly from his vantage point in the G.P.O., was that the military might launch an attack up Lower Abbey Street from the direction of Amiens Street railway terminus (which he had not been able to occupy) and isolate this block; so he told Weafer to barricade the mouth of Lower Abbey Street, blocking access to Sackville Street. Two hundred yards down Abbey Street, Weafer found large rolls of newsprint in the *Irish Times* warehouse, and he pushed these out onto the street. Next he "commandeered" £5,000 worth of brand-new motorcycles from a shop and piled them up beside the newsprint. The barricade drew the anger of the mob. They came up from the tenements around Gardiner Street and booed and booed the rebels as they went about their task.

(12)

Eighteen-year-old Volunteer James Doyle, crouching in the back bedroom of Clanwilliam House and gazing down Lower Mount Street, idly wondered if it would be long before he died. A long way off there was rifle fire. Once he jerked nervously as shots sounded nearby.

A little later Volunteer Willie Ronan, his bald pate shining pinkly, put his head round the door and said, "You're to go in to George in the front room."

Doyle found Reynolds kneeling at the middle window, watching Northumberland Road through field glasses. Following the direction of his gaze, Doyle saw a number of khaki-clad figures lying prone on the pavement near Haddington Road. They appeared to be either dead or seriously wounded. "Don't fire, anybody!" warned Reynolds.

The khaki-clad soldiers were, in fact, members of a Home Defence Force known as the Georgius Rex (irreverently christened by Dubliners "The Gorgeous Wrecks"). They were mostly elderly men, many of them British Army veterans, drawn from respectable business or professional circles. That morning, they had taken part in a sham exercise near Kingstown, using rifles, *but no ammunition*. When news reached them that rebels had taken the city, they had at once marched on Dublin.

Nearing Beggar's Bush Barracks about 4 P.M., they decided to split their forces. The main party, led by Major Harris of Trinity College O.T.C., forked right and marched along Shelbourne Road (which borders the railway line and runs parallel to Northumberland Road) where they came under fire from

125

Captain John Guilfoyle's company up on the railway embankment. Major Harris and a few of his men, however, managed to reach the main gate of the barracks, while the rest, ordered to retire up Landsdowne Lane, succeeded in climbing over the barracks wall. All in all eighty-one men and nine officers slipped out of the rebel trap. Inside, they found Beggar's Bush in a condition of near-panic; among them the garrison had only seventeen Lee-Enfields and were glad of the six carried by the G.R.'s. The G.R.'s themselves were advised to use their old Italian rifles *as clubs* if the Sinn Feiners attacked.

The second party of forty men, under the command of Mr. F. H. Browning, marched straight into trouble. Forking *left* as they neared the barracks, they came down by Northumberland Road. What happened then has been best described by a woman resident of the district, who, contemporaneously, wrote:

As I stand at the drawing room window, I see a small detachment of G.R. veterans. The afternoon had been warm, they looked hot and tired. A sharp report rings out, and the man in the foremost rank falls forward, apparently dead and a ghastly stream of blood flowing from his head. His comrades make for cover—the shelter of the trees, the side of a flight of steps. Bullet follows bullet with lightning rapidity. The road is unusually deserted until one of the veterans dashes across the road, falls at the feet of a woman who sets up a wail of terror. I cannot bear to look and yet I feel impelled to do so. Of six men by the tree only one is now standing—they must have lain down—but now, they have fallen on their backs, one over another—they are all wounded! Oh, the horror of it all—what does it mean? A wounded man is being borne in the direction of our house—we rush to open the door and offer assistance but they take him next door. I cannot watch any longer—I must go back to my mother, who is sitting quietly by the fire. She is very old and frail and must not know of what is passing so I try to appear as usual. After chatting to her for a short time, I return again to the window just in time to see a bareheaded white-coated doctor drive up in a motor-car. He disappears into one of the houses where he tends the wounded, some of whom are

126

carried off to the hospital; the crowd which had gathered at the cross-roads gradually melts away.

It was an unfortunate incident; Lieutenant Malone and Section-Commander Grace ceased fire immediately when they realized that the G.R.'s carried no ammunition. News that the rebels had attacked a body of unarmed elderly men, however, produced a violent public reaction. That night Pearse tried to rectify the damage by issuing an order expressly forbidding the rebels to fire on anyone who was unarmed—whether they were in uniform or not.

But the G.R.'s did not stand around mourning their losses. Aided by the garrison in Beggar's Bush, they climbed onto the barracks roof and, from several vantage points, opened a hot fire on Guilfoyle's men. One man, indeed, daringly worked his way over the barracks wall and through the rear gardens until he reached the back of No. 28 Northumberland Road, almost directly opposite No. 25. Malone and Grace, disturbed to find bullets kicking through their windows, tried to locate him. Then Grace heard Malone's "Peter the Painter" tearing out shots, and jerked his head up in time to see the sniper fall inside the room of the house opposite, pulling the window curtains down with him as he crashed.

Normality eventually returned to Northumberland Road. Gerald Morrissey and his friends scampered up to the corner of Haddington Road and helped to pick up the rifles dropped by the G.R.'s. These they handed over to the Volunteers holding the Parochial Hall. A little later George Reynolds ventured out the back of Clanwilliam House, dropping over the garden rail onto the pavement, so as not to disturb the barricaded front door. On his way to see Malone, he stopped to ask Section-Commander O'Donoghue what orders he had received about firing on unarmed men.

"My orders are to attack only armed men trying to force their way into the city," said O'Donoghue.

"That's my view, too," said Reynolds. "I'm going to take no notice of men who are not prepared for war, even if they are in khaki."

Inside the Schools the time passed slowly. Late in the afternoon excursionists began to pass in toward the city on their way home after their day out. Long shadows fell across the Canal and O'Donoghue decided to eat. Food was scarce because the boys who made up half his garrison had not thought to provide themselves even with sandwiches. He handed over his revolver to one of the youngsters and told him to keep watch. While O'Donoghue ate, the lad interrupted him every few minutes, shouting, "There's a car coming, what'll I do?"

In disgust O'Donoghue roared at him, "Don't fire at all—at anything. If you see the entire British Army coming down the road, *don't fire!*"

Inside Clanwilliam House, Reynolds knocked on the dining-room door and when Miss Wilson opened it, he suggested that she might feel happier if she gathered all her valuables together and put them in a suitcase, which could then be locked up in a room.

"That is very kind of you," said Miss Wilson courteously.

With the assistance of her maids, she collected silver and other valuables, filling *two* suitcases, which young Doyle carried to a rear bedroom at the top of the house. Reynolds then locked the door in Miss Wilson's presence and handed her the key.

Shortly afterward Reynolds had to face his first crisis. The youngest member of his party, a lad of seventeen, began to show signs of nerves. He sat shivering on his hunkers at the back of the room, his face pale and glistening with sweat.

Reynolds said casually, "Would you like to go home for a while? When you're feeling better, you can always come back."

His face ashen, the boy nodded.

"All right," said Reynolds, "you can get out the back way." And without a word the boy hurried away.

"We're better without that fellow," explained Reynolds. Young Doyle glanced around. Only four of them were left now. He himself had never fired a rifle in anger before—or, indeed, in any other way; the only rifle practice he had ever had was on a miniature range.

He thought rather enviously of the lad who had left.

128

Little Willie Nolan was in a high state of terror. He was certain the Sinn Feiners were after him. So he hoisted his red-painted, official Post Office bicycle up onto the parapet of the Halfpenny Bridge and let it drop into the Liffey. It struck the water with a splash and with a feeling of relief Willie watched it disappear. All he had to do now was to get rid of his uniform. . . .

Willie—he was only four feet, eight inches tall—had spent the better part of the morning delivering a telegram to the suburbs. On the way back, he had taken a short cut through an alleyway which brought him out at the rear of the Post Office building. In Princes Street he had stopped abruptly. Two armed men in trench coats and soft black hats turned up at the side, barred his way.

"What do *you* want?" growled one.

"I work here," said young Willie.

"Well, you don't any more," said the man. "Don't you know we've declared a Republic?"

Willie shook his head.

"Well, you know now," said the man. "Now get to hell out of here—and take that British uniform off if you don't want to get shot!"

Willie had bolted back into the alleyway. He was halfway down it when he heard shooting and decided: They're after me. He was so scared, indeed, that he did not know whether he should jump on his bicycle and ride it or whether he should wheel it; one thing was certain, however, so long as he had it in his possession, he stood in danger of being identified as a British official and shot. After dropping the machine into the Liffey, however, he felt a great deal better. . . .

He hurried home, anxious to get rid of his uniform, too. He found his mother almost distracted, for all sorts of rumors were sweeping the neighborhood. He told her what he had done with the bicycle.

"My God!" she said. "You'll get five years for that—destroying Government property. We can thank the bloody Sinn Feiners for this."

But when his mother went out to discover from neighbors what was happening, he took off his uniform and burned it. I'd far rather go to jail, he decided, than be shot by men in soft black hats.

At 4 P.M. the first military train from the Curragh drew into Kingsbridge Station to the accompaniment of heavy rifle fire. Aboard was a draft of one thousand troops of the Mobile Column, among them Captain Carl Elliotson of the 3rd Reserves Cavalry Regiment.

As horses and gun-limbers had been left behind owing to the hurried entrainment, Captain Elliotson's first duty was to commandeer trolleys to handle equipment and ammunition. He secured three luggage trolleys on a promise to return them. As loading commenced, heavy firing broke out somewhere in the neighborhood. At 5:30 the advance on Dublin Castle began cautiously. The column, with a fan of scouts ahead, moved down the southern bank of the Liffey and past Guinness's Brewery without meeting opposition. Detouring through side streets, the column had arrived safely within half an hour at the Ship Street entrance to the Castle.

With the new arrivals, Cowan had the rebels outnumbered by at least five to one, though he did not know it. His problem remained: Exactly how many rebels were there, and would the country rise? Even more important, when and where would Germany strike?

Kent's forces, desperately defending the South Dublin Union, were being allowed no respite. All that hard day—that long, brilliantly sunlit, death-hunting day—hunger and thirst had waxed among them and utter weariness, even despair, had begun to replace that earlier sense of exhilaration. The fighting had become a game of cat-and-mouse—a nerve-racking, heart-stopping battle of unexpected death, with never a second's rest. A sense of purpose, the flame of patriotism still flickered strongly, but the abstract had given way to the real, and battle had been bared to its true components.

It was just five o'clock when the military launched the final assault of the day, a move designed to clear Section-Commander Joyce and perhaps a half-dozen men from the Women's Infirmary. It was an incongruous battlefield. Although the Union authorities had courageously fought to evacuate most of

130

the patients, some women still remained when Joyce and his comrades flung themselves down on the floor at the intersection of Wards 16 and 17 and made ready to pick off the military who were breaking their way in below. It was a desperate plan; its only chance of success—which was remote—being that the military, caught in the narrow entrance to Ward 16 might be made to suffer such heavy casualties that they would be forced to retire.

The smell of wax polish touched Joyce's nostrils gently as he lay there, hardly conscious of the patients who, after a hysterical hubbub, had surrounded themselves with beds in a corner. Then suddenly the military stood in the doorway. For a second they halted, like tiny, brown gnomes. Joyce fired. The crack of rifles opened up all around him. The women screamed. Then he was scrambling back with his comrades and helping to slam the ward door shut. The military gave them no time to think. They banged on the door, demanding, "Surrender, in the name of the King!"

Joyce and his men flung themselves down as several bullets came through the door. Only a thin partition divided them and they found themselves pinned to the floor. Joyce was hardly conscious of what he was doing; one thing was certain, though, he had no intention of surrendering.

The firing ceased abruptly and an educated voice shouted, "I'll count five. Either surrender or we're coming in."

Joyce listened to the count: "One . . . two . . . three . . ."

Then somebody shouted, "Quick! this way!"

He got to his feet and ran. A locked door barred their way, but they blew it open and ran on. At the end of this ward they stopped and lay down again, firing on their pursuers. Joyce flung himself sideways as bullets spattered against the wall. There was a wild melée, with both sides groveling on the floor trying desperately to take accurate aim.

In the end the rebels had to make a scattered retreat. Joyce's memory of what happened next has become vague. He remembers racing into an empty part of the building, along bare corridors, and finally finding himself outside in the grounds. The sounds of pursuit had by then died away. A final dash

131

across an open courtyard and then he was safely inside the Nurses' Home.

The party collapsed, exhausted and trembling—and utterly weary. They had something to eat for the first time that day—corned beef, followed by reviving draughts of hot tea. Their battered spirits were enormously cheered by Kent's announcement that the Rising was going well; indeed, the Republic was in the ascendant everywhere, and the military had been held back. When Kent finished speaking, he posted sentries. Then the whole garrison knelt down and recited the Rosary.

"Hooroosh! Hooroosh!" shouted the drunken old woman. "They're raiding Noblett's!" Her shawl-covered arms flapped excitedly like two great black wings.

Up out of the slums, the worst in Europe at that time outside the stews of Naples; from the tenements of Gardiner Street and Marlborough Street; from the back streets behind Moore Street and off Great Britain Street, swarmed the underprivileged—or as 1916 knew them, the poor. The women outnumbered the men by at least four to one. There were old crones in their black shawls and young girls in their bare feet. The men wore mufflers round their throats and even their caps were ragged and dirty. The backsides of urchins showed bare through their ragged pants and the little girls had grubby pinafores.

Suddenly, with a tremendous crash, the plate-glass front of Noblett's, a confectioner's on the corner of Sackville Street and North Earl Street, splashed onto the pavement.

A cascade of sweets spilled out and men, women and children scooped up handfuls of chocolates, Turkish delight, glacier mints, fruit bonbons. Boxes were ripped open and strewn over the street. The mob went wild with excitement. As the news of the spoils available spread rapidly, the crowds swelled in size. In the middle of all the looting somebody shouted, "The soldiers are coming!"

There was a terrible scattering; women and children trampling each other down. They surged toward O'Connell Bridge in a black tide, but the panic eased when they reached it. Then, when there was still no sign of the military, like a flock of vultures they surged back toward Noblett's.

Once one shop had gone, there was no halting the destruction. Two more were quickly broken into, the noise of their crashing plate glass sounding the louder because of the new and awful stillness that seemed to have fallen over the city. Guttersnipes ran out of Dunn's, the hatter's, bedecking themselves in silk hats, straw hats and bowlers. One urchin danced to the edge of the pavement with the three different varieties perched perilously on his head, one on top of the other. A second made a swipe at him and knocked the lot over. As the hats were flung into the gutter, other urchins made footballs of them. Several drunken women reeled from the Saxone Shoe shop, brandishing satin slippers and knee-high Russian boots. Merchandise lay strewn over the pavements in prodigious profusion. Women clasping boxes of shoes fought their way out of shops only to find that they had grabbed a whole series of left-foots.

Lieutenant Bob de Coeur marched over to the trench where Professor Liam O'Briain was engaged in argument with two Citizen Army men, and bawled, "Fall in!"

O'Briain and the two Citizen Army men stepped from their shallow trench and presented arms. They waited at attention as Commandant Mallin came up, followed by Countess Markiewicz. De Coeur seemed pleased about something; what it was became clear in a moment.

The news was exciting, Mallin declared. The whole country was up. The West was up; Kerry was up; Limerick was up; so was Cork. The Boys of Wexford were on the march again— 118 years after their epic stand at Vinegar Hill. Murmured O'Briain to the man beside him, "Begod, this is the biggest thing since 1690." Then Mallin, having stirred their blood and sent their spirits leaping, smiled at them pleasantly and walked back with the Countess to the headquarters hut. Behind them they left an excited buzz of speculation. Ireland, indeed, had seen nothing like this for centuries. Could it be really happening? Was the apparently impossible actually on the verge of being achieved? Excitement reached new heights when somebody announced as pure gospel that the Germans would be sailing up the Liffey at 3 A.M.

With this exhilarating news clanging about his ears,

134

O'Briain was picked out with twenty men and ordered to march to the top of Leeson Street and occupy houses commanding the bridge over the Canal. They were handed homemade bombs and told how to toss them down from the rooftops if the enemy attempted to storm the bridge. As they filed out by the west gate, they were saluted by an old gentleman who leaped to attention, doffed his hat and held it solemnly across his breast. It was a simple gesture which somehow made O'Briain realize for the first time the solemnity and importance of what they were doing.

Led by De Coeur the party advanced cautiously up Leeson Street, splitting into two files of ten men each on opposite sides of the street. O'Briain and De Coeur marched in the middle of the road.

At the top of Leeson Street, the men paired off and began to knock on the doors. O'Briain and De Coeur took the last house. When there was no reply to their repeated knockings, De Coeur lifted his pickax and hacked it into the door, a fine piece of eighteenth-century wood, exquisitely fashioned. Ruined within seconds, the door still refused to give. Annoyed, the two men turned around as the door of the next house opened and a maid looked out. Before she could shut it again, they shoved past her, went swiftly up through the house, out a skylight onto the roof, and along it until they reached the first house. They found it empty and began preparing it for a siege.

"What you need in a revolution is furniture movers," remarked O'Briain, as he pushed at a heavy wardrobe. When they had finished barricading the place, O'Briain wrote a note to the owner, apologizing for what they had done. "Sorry for any damage to the furniture. Hope you approve of the cause," he scribbled.

It was a beautiful night and later, on the roof, O'Briain watched his comrades, squatting cheerfully on the roofs of other houses. Parapets two feet high protected them against falling into the street. Shortly after they had taken up their positions, one of the men, Jem Little, shouted to De Coeur from the next roof, "Hey, Bob, there's an ould fellow down here, a judge or lord or something—anyhow the maids keep calling him 'me Lord'—and he's annoying us."

"What's he done to you, Jem?" asked De Coeur.

135

"He's telling us we should go home," said Little indignantly. "Telling us we've got no right to be in his house. D'ye ever hear the like of that?"

"Oh, we'll soon put a stop to that," said De Coeur determinedly. "William," he said to O'Briain (who had never been called anything but Liam), "William, you know how to talk to these people—go down and tell that ould fellow what this is all about."

"Take me to him, Jem," said O'Briain, and he climbed over the intersecting wall and dropped down through the skylight behind Little. Downstairs in the drawing room he found a portly, highly dignified old gentleman, white-haired and bearded, and dressed in a frock coat, standing in front of a big fire blazing in the hearth. Beside him stood his wife and three terrified maids.

"I understand you've been telling these men to go home?" began O'Briain, as sternly as he could.

"Yes, that is so. You've absolutely no right to be here. The whole thing is entirely illegal. I protest against your presence in my house."

"You realize that this is an insurrection and that we're acting under orders?"

"Yes, that's right," chipped in Little, "we must obey our orders!"

"I'm sorry," continued O'Briain, "but you'll have to make the best of it. We'll do as little damage as we can to your house. If there should be any fighting, I advise you to go downstairs and go to the back of the house. By the way, some of the other houses are giving the men tea."

Judge Drennan Andrews (one of whose ancestors had helped to found the United Irishmen of 1798) drew himself up with great dignity. "I am an old man [he was 83] and I am ill. I cannot prevent you taking anything you want from my house, but if I offered hospitality to these men, it would mean that I should be giving them permission to be here—and that I shall not do."

"Well, all right, sir," said O'Briain. "In that case we won't disturb you." And followed by the incongruous proletarian figure of Jem Little, he withdrew.

136

It grew cold on the roof after a while, so O'Briain and De Coeur came down and went into an upper bedroom, which they found a great deal warmer. Neither attempted to sleep. Just before midnight a sidecar came trotting along, the voices of the jarvey and his customer floating up to them quite clearly. The jarvey declared portentously: "I tell you, sir, there's something behind all this."

Shortly after midnight O'Briain heard the measured tramp of an approaching column, from the far side of the Canal bridge. He grabbed a bomb and scrambled out onto the roof. He could see shadowy figures stealthily taking up positions along other roofs. He crouched close to the parapet, the nose of his rifle just topping it, the bomb immediately beside his hand. Then, as the approaching column reached the bridge, De Coeur shouted, "Fire!"

There was an earsplitting uproar as twenty antiquated weapons spewed lead onto the bridge below. O'Briain swung his arm in a quick, jerking arc and there was a stunning noise from below as the bomb exploded. Then somebody shouted up, "Stop shooting, we're Volunteers! Stop shooting!"

"Cease fire!" bawled De Coeur.

The firing stopped. From below they could still hear shouts as the scattered column reassembled. Along the roofs the men crouched down, softly cursing into the night at their mistake.

At Dublin Castle, late in the evening, the situation had begun to resolve itself a little.

Inside the Castle, Captain Carl Elliotson carefully reconnoitered the position. Huddling close to the buildings, he edged toward the main gate, stopping to examine the lines of fire which might enable him to dominate the City Hall and Rates Office opposite it. In double-quick time he had a Vickers gun set up in a concealed position and had begun firing. A jet of bullets streamed toward the City Hall. Inside, Helena Moloney and Dr. Kathleen Lynn, happening to look out, thought the weather had changed; it seemed to be hailing. Then they realized "the hail" was simply bullets. As the firing grew more accurate the effect became nerve-racking; bullets sizzled through the windows, banging and ricocheting around the walls like stones in a bucket. Plaster crashed from the ceiling; sections of cornice and wall rumbled down in clouds of dust that made the place as dark as midnight.

Young Annie Norgrove, aged sixteen, whose father, George, was fighting on the roof, had spent most of her day trotting from the kitchen to the roof, carrying food and water to the men. As the fight wore on, she saw the men's lips puff up with thirst and their faces blacken from gunpowder. Some of them tied handkerchiefs around their hands to protect them from the overheated rifles. During one machine-gun burst she herself was almost hit. "Down Annie—down for God's sake!" shouted one of the men, and she ground herself into the roof as the bullets kicked and ripped around her. A chimney pot showered into pieces over her head. After that, she was no longer asked to go up on the roof.

Downstairs Dr. Lynn spent much of her time trying to cope with eighteen-year-old John Coyle, who had been severely wounded. As bursts of fire intensified and the whole City Hall appeared to be coming down around their ears, his body began to shake violently. "Oh, don't leave me!" he moaned, each time Dr. Lynn attempted to move away. To give him a feeling of protection she and Helena Moloney propped him in a high wooden-backed chair, then moved it against a pillar, placing it so that he was shielded by the pillar in front and the chair back in the rear.

The Castle defenders had already mentally prepared themselves for a long siege. A great cheer went up, therefore, when a milkman entered Upper Castle Yard rolling a big can with the evening's milk supplies; nobody had expected him to get through. Morale rose immediately, except possibly among some badly wounded cases in the Red Cross Hospital. One soldier declared, "We might as well go back to France!" Another said, "I'm getting out of here tomorrow and going home!"

Eventually, toward dusk, an order was given to pull down all blinds and dowse the lights. The defending troops were going to launch an attack on rebel positions and a terrific noise might be expected. "After a while," wrote the V.A.D., "I peeked out and saw an officer and some men congregated near

138

the main gate. I heard the officer giving orders and then saw two or three men dash toward the Gate and disappear, followed an instant later by two or three more."

All told, the military were to employ two hundred troops in the assault on the City Hall—almost seven times the number of insurgents occupying *all* the besieging positions. One hundred men were involved in the first frontal assault. They quickly succeeded in taking the Provost-Marshal's house (it was found to be empty), but the attempt to recapture the guardroom failed because of rebel barricades.

Captain Elliotson's machine-gun crew swept the City Hall from the roof above Mr. Birrell's office as the second assault party raced out onto Cork Hill and around to the front entrance of the City Hall, seeking a way in there. They were caught in a concentrated fire poured from the roofs of the *Mail & Express* office opposite the castle gate. Several men, including the officer in charge, fell. Command was taken over by the troop sergeant, who ordered a retirement. More than twenty khaki-clad figures were left lying in the roadway, most of them dead, a few severely wounded. Rebel fire proved so hot that a support group waiting in the lee of the main gate were unable to advance at all.

Because of the realization that the rebels were not going to be shifted easily, Red Cross patients and their beds were moved from the Picture Gallery and the Throne Room to the comparative safety of St. Patrick's Hall. Here, in the great room where Queen Victoria, and afterward her son, King Edward the Seventh, had once received their Irish subjects in solemn state, the wounded were laid down, twitching as the familiar sounds of battle brought back unhappy memories of the Western Front. Soon the corridors leading to the Operation Room were packed with casualties. V.A.D.'s sat and talked to the men, trying to take their minds off their troubles.

One man said, "I'd like to get every one of those Sinn Feiners and torture them, and then turn machine guns on them."

As it was the rebels inside the City Hall were suffering enough agony even to satisfy him. Conditions on the ground floor, where most of the women and the wounded lay huddled behind the pillars, had become appalling. To the noise of heavy machine-gun fire there was added a new sound, that of exploding hand grenades. Troops ordered to attack the rear of the City Hall partly outwitted the rebels by advancing through the Castle cellars. This brought them out into a small area just under the City Hall windows. From here the troops began throwing bombs with the idea of "softening-up" the garrison. Finally they decided to rush it. As they launched their assault, the rebels on the roof had their first chance to fire on them; but in moving out from cover, big Jack O'Reilly, six feet six inches in height, who had taken over the rebel command after John Connolly's death, was shot.

On the ground floor the situation had become so dangerous that Emily Norgrove (no less than five members of the family were "out") firmly believed the great dome was coming down on their heads. The din grew fantastic as the military, attempting to get in by the rear windows, were met by terrific fire from rebels ordered down from the roof to meet the threat. Although the first wave was stopped, a second assault followed immediately, and this time the defenders were forced back. They retreated in haste to the first landing, waiting as the military came crashing through the dust and rubble. Then a concentrated volley met the British and sent them reeling down the stairs again.

As the military fell back in confusion, they collided with the second wave of their own forces. In the darkness and noise, the two parties mistook each other for rebels. They opened fire at close quarters and bayonets slashed out wildly. As they fought each other, the rebels poured volley after volley into them from the landing above. For a few moments it seemed to the rebels that a miracle had saved them, but the military discovered their mistake. Quickly their officers restored some order. They retreated to the rear windows to sort themselves out, then, with great courage, launched yet another charge. This time the small, gallant rebel party on the landing was easily wiped out. An abrupt silence descended on the City Hall.

On the roof, the rest of the rebels, thoroughly exhausted by now, welcomed the respite gratefully. Downstairs, as a little of the confusion died away, a voice rang out through the darkness, "Surrender in the name of the King!" A torch, shone through the choking dust, swept round the battered interior of the City Hall, picking out a handful of terrified women and wounded crouching behind the pillars.

"Hands up or we'll fire!" shouted an officer.

Dr. Kathleen Lynn, shaking off the grasp of young Coyle, slowly advanced into the circle of light. Behind her the others followed slowly, their hands raised.

"We surrender!" she shouted. "We surrender!"

With the torch firmly beamed upon her, she was permitted to advance. Soldiers stepped forward, bayonets ready, suspicious of a trap. One party searched behind the pillars and reported that there were no fighting men there, only some wounded.

"Is this really all there is?" asked the officer in surprise.

"I'm afraid that's all, sir," replied the soldier.

"Oh, well then, line them up!" said the officer, in a resigned voice.

While military stretcher parties carried away the wounded, the women were marched out through one of the great broken windows at the rear; they had to scramble over rubble and debris, and received no assistance from the military. They were led by a devious route into Upper Castle Yard and thence to Ship Street Barracks, where they were lodged in a vermin-ridden wing which had lain unoccupied for years; they were expected, apparently, to lie upon a few dirty cushions. As they tried to sort themselves out in the filthy place, two soldiers came in with tea and hardtack, and for the first time they began to realize the enormity—in their captors' eyes—of what they had done. Lewd suggestions and coarse remarks by the soldiers reinforced a growing realization that they had sacrificed their privileges of citizenship and that even their lives, indeed, might now be forfeit.

After the rebels on the ground floor had surrendered, a military detail, advancing cautiously up through the different floors, discovered Jenny Shanahan. Jenny, although a rebel, was not in uniform, and the officer of the detail incorrectly assumed that she had been held prisoner.

"Are there many of them up here?" he asked, adding solicitously, "Have they treated you badly?"

Realizing his mistake, Jenny said, "Oh, no, sir—they've

treated me well enough. But there must be hundreds of them up there on the roof!"

"H'm," murmured the officer thoughtfully. He hesitated for a moment, then gave orders to his men to retire below; nobody —after all that had already happened—relished a night battle among the rooftops. Downstairs he announced that the final clearance of City Hall must await daylight.

Miss Shanahan's new status did not last long. With great politeness she was escorted to Ship Street Barracks, where it was intended that she should identify the women rebels. Her appearance, however, was greeted by the other women with shouts of recognition.

"Oh, so you're *one* of them!" shouted her escort angrily, and she suddenly found herself being propelled forward roughly with a shove in the back.

Two hours after they had first attempted to enter the locked guardroom, the military finally forced the door. Inside they found the guard still trussed up, their rifles and ammunition gone—and no sign of the rebels. There was no mystery about how they had left. A press had been pulled back from the wall, disclosing a small iron grating. The rebels had removed this and crept down the piping.

Tom Kain was at that moment, in fact, encamped with his men less than twenty yards away. Emerging from the pipe, they had found themselves in Castle Street. They sneaked along the side of a wall and entered the first premises they came to—plumber Lahiff's—where they made their way into the cellar. They decided to stay there until things had quieted down. They had access to drinking water, for a pipe ran through the cellar, and Kain managed to make a small hole in it with a pin.

Above them, in Castle Yard, the military built two large watch fires about fifteen yards apart. Here, as the night grew cold, the soldiers stamped on the ground and warmed their hands at the blaze.

On the roof of City Hall, shivering rebels watched for a sniper's flash from the high Bermingham Tower, certain now that on the morrow they would die.

142

(14)

To obtain a better view, William Redmond-Howard, nephew of John Redmond, decided to move from the Metropole Hotel, where he had been staying, to the Imperial Hotel on the opposite side of Sackville Street. Here, as at the Metropole, there was bewilderment and confusion, but amusingly a different collection of rumors. First, he was told that his uncle had been taken prisoner and shot; then that the Castle was in flames; then that Father O'Doherty, one of the priests from the Pro-Cathedral, had been shot in the head when he ventured forth, fully vestmented and with a cross in his hand, to remonstrate with the rebels. Hurriedly Redmond-Howard went to his room to note down as many incidents as he could.

Shortly after 9:30 P.M. he saw the first flicker of fire reflected in the windows of the Metropole. Leaning out of his own, he saw that the Cable Shoe shop next door was on fire. He went down into the street, joining a crowd of some two hundred people who were watching the place burn down. High up on the face of the building, a chink of light, shining from a curtained window, showed that there were people living in the flats upstairs. The blaze was crackling merrily through the lower floors, belching out black, suffocating smoke.

Realizing that the people above were as yet unaware of their peril Redmond-Howard raced to a side door giving access to the upper floors. He found it locked and pounded on it for a moment without avail. He then called for assistance, but the door resisted even the combined weight of three men. The kicks and hammerings had some effect, however, for a window snapped up and a man angrily popped his head out.

"The place is on fire!" yelled Redmond-Howard.

143

"My God!" said the man. "There are women and children sleeping here!"

At 10:06 the Dublin Fire Brigade led by Captain Purcell, their chief, reached the scene. By then the side door was open and Redmond-Howard was assisting the trapped women down the smoke-filled staircase into the street. He had run into unseen difficulties, however, in the shape of an expectant mother, already in labor, who refused to leave her bed. Even the experienced Captain Purcell had never before been confronted with such a problem, but he firmly ordered his men to remove the woman whether she wished it or not. Screaming and hitting out wildly, she was carried down through the smoke and flames. Part of the staircase had by then caught fire and the whole place was being consumed so rapidly that two more sections of the Brigade were called out. By 10:59 the fire was under control. The firemen had hardly finished their task, however, when looters set a second shoe shop on fire, and wearily they had to begin all over again.

When Redmond-Howard returned to the Imperial, where the manager had offered rooms to the evacuated families, he found that sleep was out of the question and sat down at his bedroom window. Below, the hungry crowds had grown even more turbulent. First a tobacco shop went; then a jeweler's. Within seconds, urchins were diving in among the ruck of legs and flying elbows and coming out again with watches and rings, which they began bargaining off at ludicrous prices—solid gold watches, for example, were sold for 2/6d.

Down in Boland's Bakery and all along the railway line from Sandymount to Westland Row Station the Volunteers had had a hard and wearing day. Commandant de Valera, already strained and haggard-looking, roamed about with his shotgun in hand, a restless, dissatisfied, and slightly worried figure. Captain Simon Donnelly began to feel that if De Valera continued like this, he was likely to drive himself into such a state that he would no longer be able to lead them.

Ripping up rails, digging trenches, building ramps, and ordering bakers about hardly helped De Valera to instill in his men a real hatred for the enemy. It was almost with relief that they watched a small party of military from Beggar's

144

Bush emerge on the railway line; but a few shots, delivered at random, quickly put them to flight.

Panic, however, swept some of the positions just before midnight when once again the British tried a feeble advance. This was quickly repulsed, however, and the sector was again quiet for a time. During the lull, a rather curious order was passed along the line. If an aeroplane flew overhead during the night, no one was to fire on it—it would be German. At midnight, De Valera issued orders for the first of the on-again, off-again projects which were to distinguish his tense, constantly anxious leadership during the insurrection. He instructed Donnelly to take four or five men and scout toward Kingstown in order to find out whether there were signs of military reinforcements from England. Donnelly picked four men, made certain that they had full equipment—rations, full water bottles, rifles, and, as a precaution against his raw, rather jittery troops losing each other in the dark, made each man rub flour on the back of the man in front of him. But just before they were due to move out, De Valera changed his mind and ordered the expedition canceled. During the week, his officers were to become used to this erratic quality in his make-up.

Captain Brennan Whitmore sat on the roof of the Pillar café, which earlier in the evening he had been ordered to occupy, and gazed down at the silent street. By now the last drunks had gone reeling into the night, although every now and then a lone voice could be heard caterwauling somewhere above Nelson's Pillar. The street lamps still shone and, seen from behind his parapet, they gave a garish red glow, strangely reflected in the slight mist hanging high and motionless in the sky—a weird picture which was to etch itself into his memory.

Across the street, the G.P.O. lay dark and heavy; inside, the lights had been cut off and the men were burning candles. Sentries were visible at the windows and Whitmore could see shadowy figures passing to and fro. A strange feeling of isolation crept over him.

A few doors away Redmond-Howard still kept vigil. He and

Mr. Marsh, manager of the Coliseum Theatre, had been asked to share a room and they had decided to take turns watching and sleeping. Fifty yards away the G.P.O., etched by the street lamps in pale blues and greens, looked for all the world like the backcloth in a theater. Redmond-Howard's impression was of sitting in the dress circle of some gigantic opera house. Now and then a rattle of rifle fire broke the stillness.

Inside the G.P.O., a Volunteer asked James Connolly how he thought the fight was going.

"They're beaten," said Connolly, as always superbly terse and confident.

At 3:45 A.M. on Tuesday, Brigadier-General W. H. M. Lowe, Commanding the Reserve Cavalry Brigade, arrived at Kingsbridge from the Curragh with troops of the 25th (Irish Reserve Infantry Brigade) and assumed command of all forces in the Dublin area. In Cork, General Stafford took over direction of operations in the south of Ireland, while in Belfast, Brigadier Hackett-Paine undertook responsibility for Ulster. The arrival of Lowe's reinforcements brought the total of military forces in the capital to 4,650 men—which meant that the rebels were now outnumbered by almost five to one.

Some two hundred fifty miles away, Field Marshal Lord French, Commander in Chief, Home Forces, was again relishing the smell of battle. For six weary months he had languished at a desk in Horse Guards Parade, busying himself —rather drearily—with the hypothetical defense of Britain, working out measures to stop the Zeppelin nuisance and training raw battalions for Kitchener's New Armies—in support of his successor Sir Douglas Haig. Late on Monday afternoon he had been handed a wireless message stating that rebellion had broken out in Ireland. There were no other details, but for the former British Commander in Chief in France, it had been a happy moment.

Like an old war horse, he had leaped into action. From a chat with the Irish C in C, General Friend, who had been in to see him on Saturday, French had gathered that the situation was rather tricky in Ireland, on top of which there had been the business of Casement over the weekend. A rebellion at any time in Ireland was a serious matter for the British Army; in wartime, of course, it was unthinkable.

French's first action was to dispatch an alert to the 59th (North Midland) Division which, under Major-General A.E. Sandbach, C.B., D.S.O., was then encamped in billets around Watford, St. Albans, Hemel Hempstead, Luton, Wheathampstead, and other towns and hamlets in Hertfordshire. The 59th was a mobile division (nicknamed "The Lost Division" by those in it because they had long ago given up any hope of getting to France) made up of three Brigades: the 176th (2/5th, 2/6th South Staffs Regiment, 2/5th, 2/6th North Staffs); the 177th (2/4th and 2/5th Lincolnshire Regiment, 2/4th, 2/5th Leicestershire Regiment) and the 178th Infantry Division (2/5th, 2/6th, 2/7th, 2/8th Sherwood Foresters). Convinced that the Germans were eventually bound to try something on the east coast of England, Kitchener, as War Minister, had placed the 59th astride two railway systems, the London, Midland and Scottish and the London and North-Western, so that it could be shunted north at an instant's notice; trains were held in a state of readiness at Watford and other stations in the vicinity. The division, a second-line one, had lost substantial drafts to the first-line regiments in France, and was now made up of old hands who had had plenty of practice digging trenches and firing Japanese rifles, and of recruits under the Derby scheme, whose only musketry drill was at miniature ranges, and whose average length of service was less than three months.

Shortly after French had alerted General Sandbach, General Friend—who, completely unaware of events in Dublin, had been enjoying a stroll in St. James Park—entered his office. It was possibly the worst moment in Friend's whole life. His discussion with the Commander in Chief was sharp and brisk and he left hurriedly for Ireland, aware that his career there had very likely been ruined for good. When he had gone, French confirmed orders that two of the Brigades were to move as quickly as their transport could be arranged. In doing so, he noted: "I was aware that I was acting beyond

147

the powers which were delegated to me, but I considered the situation to be so critical that it was necessary to act at once without reference to the Army Council."

The 59th Division was hardly prepared for such an order. To the normal English passion for an extended weekend was added the complication of the Easter holidays. Shown the message by the Battalion Adjutant, Captain G. J. Edmunds, O.C. "A" Company, 2/6 Sherwood Foresters, could only comment bitterly, "The damn fools would have to go and have an entraining at this particular time." He and the Adjutant, in fact, were the only two Battalion officers left in camp. Even the Brigadier, Colonel E. W. S. K. Maconchy, was absent. Practically everybody was on leave which would not expire until midnight.

Messages were hurriedly flashed on screens in canteens and cinemas: "All 178th Brigade men return to billets immediately." Redcaps and patrols scoured pubs and clubs; soldiers with their girls in Cassiobury Park, Watford, suddenly heard the barked order, "Back to camp, you! At the double!"

Amid uproar and confusion, the 59th Division gradually sorted itself out. There were Lewis guns, Vickers tripods, iron rations, blankets, ammunition, limbers and mules for heavy guns, officers' valises, company books to be dealt with and billets to be paid up before the 178th, the first Brigade due to leave, was ready to go. In the middle of the preparations there was a Zeppelin alert and all lights had to be dowsed and air-raid patrols sent out. Staff-Captain Godfrey Tallents swore like a trooper as he endeavored to get heavy wagons, regimental cookers, and water carts lifted onto the railway trucks. He called for the stationmaster. "Look," he said. "Put these bloody lights on."

"I can't, sir," said the man. "There's an air raid on London."

The first train, carrying the 2/6th Sherwoods, left Watford at 4 A.M. The rest of the Brigade followed on trains at 8:30 A.M. and 10 A.M. It was a strangely sober crowd of young men who departed for what to them was God knows where. There was the inevitable attempt to be cheerful, but on the whole there was little horseplay. Few of the officers and none of the men knew they were on their way to Ireland; all took it

148

for granted they were going to France. When it was discovered that the trains were traveling north, there was renewed speculation. In Captain Oates's carriage everybody plumped for Russia. When the train stopped at Crewe, a little enlightenment was gained. Harold Garbett asked a porter, "Any idea where we're bound for?"

"Ten to one it's Ireland," said the man. "They're fighting like hell over there—the streets are running with blood."

Bernard Boram bought a paper, carrying an Admiralty announcement which said, "During the period between April 20th and April 21st an attempt to land arms and ammunition in Ireland was made by a vessel under the guise of a neutral merchant ship but in reality a German auxiliary in conjunction with a German submarine. The auxiliary was sunk, and a number of prisoners were made, amongst whom was Sir Roger Casement."

At 10 A.M., when the first train reached Liverpool, the dock authorities reported heavy fighting in Dublin. Two ships and a destroyer escort were waiting and both the 2/5th and 2/6th Battalions were embarked, and in the haste and confusion most of the officers' kit, as well as Lewis guns, were left behind.

Taking stock at the quayside, the Brigadier found he was short of everything except men. He had perhaps 50 rounds of ammunition per man and absolutely no bombs. Nor had he maps. He telephoned the Director of Operations at the War Office and explained his position.

"Good God!" said an agitated voice. "How much do you want?"

"Four hundred bombs and ten thousand rounds of ammunition. To be at Kingstown tomorrow morning!"

But maps? Where was he to get them? It struck him suddenly that hotels in the city were likely to have them; he therefore sent a party to scour them for maps of Dublin. A few hours later the party reported that only a handful could be found and that these had had to be torn from hotel guidebooks.

At 3:30 P.M. the Brigadier and his staff, accompanying one and a half battalions, embarked on the *Ulster,* a fast mail boat temporarily diverted from the Holyhead run. During the

149

crossing, the escort commander boarded the *Ulster* to inform Colonel Maconchy that he had news by wireless that the rebels had taken Kingstown and that the landing was certain to be opposed.

At 9:15 the previous [Monday] night, Lord French at dinner with General Sir Ian Hamilton, who had commanded the forces at Gallipoli, had been informed that six Zeppelins had been sighted 40 miles northeast of Cromer, making for London. Four hours afterward, Germany, following up her promises to the Irish rebels, staged the desired "naval demonstration" in the North Sea in support of the Zeppelin attack. At exactly 4:10 A.M. four German battle cruisers with attendant light cruisers and destroyers from Admiral Scheer's High Seas Fleet opened a general bombardment on the English east-coast port of Lowestoft. After half an hour a local coast patrol courageously engaged the enemy, who immediately turned away, apparently in the hope that they might draw major units of the British Grand Fleet out to battle. Later the Admiralty listed the damage to the town as follows:

. . . Despite the heavy guns employed by the enemy, the damage was relatively slight. A convalescent home, a swimming bath, the pier and 40 dwelling houses were extensively damaged and some 200 houses were slightly damaged. Two men, one woman and one child were killed, three persons seriously wounded and nine slightly wounded. Most of the damage was to houses on or adjoining the sea front. The roof and front were partially smashed and interiors were exposed amid wreckage of beams, timbers and plaster. In others, a table was knocked away and copings dislodged. Big holes were made through the walls in cases where shells passed through one or more of the houses in a row. A number of enemy shells, however, were aimed wildly; some went right over the town and fell into Oulton Broad, two miles away.

It really was not the kind of operation which would help the rebels much.

150

15

From his position on the roof of the General Post Office, Volunteer Richard MacAuliffe watched a summerlike dawn rise over a quiet and, at first glance, apparently peaceful city. Up toward the Parnell Monument the roadway was white as though there had been a fall of snow—cardboard boxes and sheets of paper, debris of the looting, lay in drifts, driven there by the night wind. Sackville Street itself was empty. On the far side, high over the Wireless School, the silvery thread of an aerial, which had not been there yesterday, was stretched between two chimney pots. Distantly a clock boomed four. Its notes had scarcely died away when there was a sharp volley somewhere—away up near the Green. The firing lasted for ten minutes, then stopped abruptly.

The shots jerked St. John Ervine from an uneasy doze. He rose and crossed to his window overlooking St. Stephen's Green. Outside there was still not enough light to see properly, but he spotted a huddled heap where an insurgent sentry had stood on guard the night before, and near it a horse he had thought dead struggled to rise to its feet.

Young Patrick Buttner, asleep in a shallow trench inside the park, awoke to an even greater shock—the surprise of machine-gun bullets spurting into the earth beside him. At first he was not able to grasp what was happening; then he realized that the angry buzzing noises around him were flying bullets. He started to rise.

"Get down! Do you want to be killed?" hissed Sergeant James O'Shea. Buttner flopped back onto his belly, terrified. He squinted up at O'Shea and found comfort in his strong, hard face. A moment later he even had the courage to poke his rifle forward and try to pick a target; but he was too close to the Shelbourne to get the right elevation—and besides, of the sixty-two windows winking out of the façade, which one did you fire at?

As the machine guns belted their racket of sound over the park, bullets hit a group of youngsters whom Mallin had sent out during the night to work on a barricade. Volunteer Philip Clarke died immediately. Another boy fell, wounded. Mallin left the trench near the Shelbourne Gate where he had been observing the military fire and ran to his assistance. Buttner watched the Commandant pick up the wounded boy and drag him in, under sustained fire.

For nearly three hours a vicious battle continued. Twice the Countess, lying in the shallow trench with Mallin, temporarily silenced one of the machine guns with her Mauser rifle-pistol. At about 6:30 A.M., she crawled across the grass to O'Shea and Buttner, and shouted hoarsely, "Commandant Mallin's orders are to withdraw to the Cuffe Street southwest corner."

By then Mallin had come to realize that he could no longer hold his exposed positions. The southwest corner, on the other hand, afforded good "natural" defenses—trees, shrubbery, and above all, a mound or ridge of earth. Yet even as Buttner and the two men with him prepared to scramble from their trench, young James Fox, having apparently lost his nerve, dashed for the railings along the north side. Shouts of "Don't do it, Jemmy, you fool!" ripped after him, but the boy, crazy now with fear, continued running. He had begun to climb the railings when the machine gun, scything around in a wide sweep which scattered every duck on the ornamental pond, caught him. Hit several times, he fell back, yelling. O'Shea gripped Buttner firmly by the arm as bullets kicked up the ground around Fox and his agonized screams filled the air. Then abruptly he stopped yelling. Yet he still lived, for Buttner saw him crawl a few inches, a movement sufficient to bring the wrath of the military down on him again. A second swathe of machine-gun bullets cut across him and he stopped moving. The machine gun kept on firing at him.

152

Each time a bullet struck the body it would twitch as though Fox were still alive. The dead, it seemed, would not be allowed to die.

All over the Green, the insurgents were now crouching and huddling into the earth, pinned down completely. On the roof of the College of Surgeons, Sergeant Frank Robbins ate bread and bully beef, the last of his rations, and in between bites fired hopefully toward the Shelbourne. St. John Ervine heard a sudden *boom, boom,* and someone under his windows cry "Oh" four times. Pulling back the curtain he saw a laborer lying shot outside the door—someone, he presumed, who had decided to go to work as usual, unaware or heedless of how serious this rebellion was.

Opposite the Shelbourne, young Buttner slithered out of the trench behind O'Shea as the latter warned, "Keep close to me, and keep your head down." Together they crawled forward until they reached some shrubbery. Here they rose to a crouch in order to make more rapid progress. Bathed in heavy sweat, they eventually gained the mound.

Clusters of tall elms protected the area. Women and boys squatted on the ground, taking every advantage of the luxuriant cover. The Countess, of course, scorned to, and defiantly stood her ground even while bullets clipped branches from the trees. A line of men lay behind the mound, returning fire from the Shelbourne and the United Services Club. Mallin, however, soon gave the order to retreat to the Royal College of Surgeons and his small force assembled near the west gate. If Mallin felt any misgivings about his handling of the situation, no sign of it showed in his quiet, good-tempered face. The move, he had decided, would be made in groups of two or three, and despite the screen of trees and shrubbery, he expected it to be a perilous business, especially for the women, handicapped by their hobble skirts.

The first party got across the road safely enough, but when the Red Cross nurses made their dash, they came under heavy fire, their white skirts and bright red badges making them an easy target. One girl had her skirt torn by a bullet; another had the heel of her boot ripped off.

Buttner, waiting his turn to go, hardly gave a thought to

153

the danger. A long night under the open skies had given him a tremendous appetite, and all he could think of was the cooked hams and custard pies being left behind in the greenhouse. He even considered going back until he saw a man cut down on the roof of the College of Surgeons. Caught by the machine gun, Private Michael Doherty slumped over the parapet. For a moment he teetered and Buttner thought he was going to fall into the street. Instead he hung there, head and arms dangling over the street, his blood staining the face of the building. Unable to stand the sight any longer, Captain Joseph Connolly (brother of John Connolly, who had led the attack on the Castle) rushed across the road to bring him down. Connolly, a fireman, was still wearing Fire Brigade uniform. A moment later Buttner saw the gleam of his helmet just above the parapet, and Doherty was dragged back slowly even as bullets clipped angrily along the stonework, sending up tiny puffs of gray dust.

Doherty had been hit by fifteen bullets and Robbins, who had come down off the roof to help those retreating from the Green, looked down at the bloody face of his friend and said sadly, "I'm afraid you're a goner, Mick. May the Lord have mercy on your soul." It turned out to be a premature judgment, however, for Doherty lived to become a victim of the flu epidemic of 1918.

There was little time for the wounded or dying, however; bullets were still chipping splinters out of the pavement as men and women fled from the Green. Robbins tried to help with covering fire. Suddenly he saw three comrades running toward him, hotly pursued by a mob of civilians hurling insults—and rotten vegetables. He recognized Captain Mac-Cormack, Lieutenant Michael Kelly, and a Volunteer named Donnelly, who had been occupying houses higher up the Green. Leading the mob was a young woman who had spent a good deal of time the previous evening hurling insults at him through the Park railings. On an impulse he ran into the middle of the road, dropped on one knee and raised his rifle, shouting at MacCormack, "Out of the way, Mac!" MacCormack instinctively stepped aside and Robbins had the woman lined up in his sights when Lieutenant Kelly jerked his arm

154

up and shouted, "For God's sake don't shoot, Frank!" Robbins, utterly incensed at the woman, tugged his arm free and once again took aim. Kelly shouted angrily, "That's an order!" Discipline, if looser in the Citizen Army than in the Volunteers, was not so loose that Robbins could ignore an order given to him directly. Reluctantly he lowered his rifle, and the young woman, who had halted, stiff with fear, ran back to join the mob.

By 7 A.M. the evacuation of St. Stephen's Green was complete. Five bodies lay behind in the Green, victims of a grave rebel misjudgment. Few who survived, however, welcomed the change from the bright sunlight and surging green of the Park to the grim, shadowed interior of the Surgeons. Mary Donnelly wrote later: "The classrooms of the College seemed huge and draughty. Everywhere were huge glass cases filled with objects for students, pebbles and specimens. In an adjoining room the jars had parts of human bodies preserved in liquid." Into this uninviting place, with its smell of formaldehyde, more than one hundred and ten women and boys now withdrew. Weary, glad to be out of immediate danger, some ripped up the carpets, wrapped themselves around like mummies, flopped down on the floor of the large lecture room and were soon sound asleep.

In the first flush of daylight, the military began creeping stealthily up the cold stone stairway toward the roof of the Dublin City Hall. Here, less than a dozen insurgents, their faces blackened, their hands raw and powder-scorched, their eyes red-rimmed through lack of sleep, squatted in some disarray. From the roof of the Castle buildings, from the high Bermingham Tower, machine-gun fire had sent them scurrying for cover. Very shortly troops were scrambling through the skylight and fanning out over the roof. In less than half an hour the fighting was all over. Outnumbered, and outgunned, with their successive leaders, John Connolly and John O'Reilly dead, the rebels gave in. Others, of course, still held out in the *Mail & Express* Office and in Henry & James opposite. Despite repeated calls from the military to surrender, only defiant shots came in reply.

155

From their window in the Imperial Hotel, Redmond-Howard and Mr. Marsh watched a party of insurgents leave the G.P.O. in the dawn light and begin stretching wire across the street. A little later James Connolly emerged; they heard his voice, clear and resonant, giving orders. Then for an hour nothing much happened until at last there was a stir up near Nelson's Pillar.

At the head of Sackville Street and down toward O'Connell Bridge, rebels were warning people to "get out of the firing line." At the Parnell Monument a rebel told some people: "The Pillar is about to be blown up." At 7:10 A.M. Redmond-Howard heard a loud explosion and saw a cloud of smoke billow up from the base of the Pillar. The great column never even quivered. Three more explosions followed within the next ten minutes—all equally abortive. Proud Nelson stood steadfast, blandly ignoring those who apparently wanted to pull him from his perch. But all that the rebels were trying to do was to blow down tram standards [poles] in order to get more wire.

Work had continued through the night in the Wireless School and by dawn Fergus O'Kelly and his comrades were able to report success. Apprised, Connolly asked that a message be sent: "An Irish Republic has been proclaimed. Dublin is firmly held and all British attacks have been repulsed."

David Bourke, a trained Marconi operator, transmitted the message on a normal commercial wave length, hoping that it might be picked up by ships at sea. Unable to get the receiving set to work, he had no way of telling whether the message was being picked up or not. Nevertheless, he kept on repeating it at fairly brief intervals.

Brennan Whitmore wakened refreshed and rather well pleased with himself; only one man had deserted during the night, the barricade Connolly had ordered him to erect across North Earl Street had been completed, and his men had successfully tunneled through to the Imperial Hotel. Four *Cuman na mBan* girls had come across from the G.P.O. late the previous night and now he and his men could look forward to a reasonable breakfast.

He was halfway through his bacon and eggs when a messenger from the G.P.O. announced that General Pearse was coming to see him. Whitmore at once rose and went down the stairs. Pearse was crossing the street. Whitmore advanced to meet him, saluted, and then walked beside him toward the barricade.

"It looks frail," said Pearse thoughtfully, as he examined it.

"Try pulling it apart, sir," said Whitmore respectfully. Pearse tugged at a chair, but it held firm; wire which Whitmore had intertwined among its components had given it a deceptive strength. Satisfied, Pearse went back to the G.P.O.

Fifteen minutes later, when Whitmore had just finished his half-cold breakfast, there was a rousing cheer in the street as James Connolly walked across. Resignedly Whitmore went downstairs again. Like Pearse, Connolly wanted to inspect the barricade.

"This is far too small and frail to stop a charge," said Connolly, eying it critically.

"Why don't you try and knock it down, sir?" suggested Whitmore.

Connolly seized the leg of a table and pulled at it vigorously; it refused to budge.

"You can see how I've interlaced it," Whitmore pointed out.

Connolly nodded, apparently satisfied. Then his eye, roaming round, noticed a shoe shop on the opposite corner. "Have you occupied that building yet?" he asked sharply.

"I haven't tried to," said Whitmore. "I haven't enough men. I thought it would be useless to put only two or three men in it."

Connolly considered this for a moment; then he nodded and stuck out his hand. "Good luck," he said. They shook hands and Connolly strode back across Sackville Street. Whitmore never saw him again.

Dublin woke to a morning of irritating inconveniences and the wildest of incredible rumors. Only one newspaper appeared, the pro-Government *Irish Times,* which had its own separate power supply. (Early on Monday, De Valera had deprived the rest of the city of its power by dismantling the Gas Works.) There were no letters delivered or collected. Every shop in the center of the city stayed shut. All traffic ceased. Under such conditions, and in a city boasting perhaps the most loquacious inhabitants in the world, it is not surprising that rumors abounded: The whole country had risen; all the cities of Ireland were in the hands of the rebels; Cork barracks had fallen; the Germans had landed in force at Queenstown and thousands of Irish-Americans, led by German officers, had also invaded the country. In addition, the Lord Lieutenant was being held prisoner in Liberty Hall; and the Pope and the Archbishop of Dublin had committed suicide. Worst of all, the Orangemen had begun to march on Dublin. The tales grew taller and spread rapidly.

The *Irish Times* proved to be of little help. The paper consisted of only six pages and most of these were made up of advertisements and "stock" matter. There was a rather detailed account of the Fairyhouse races, reports of a meeting of the Irish Traders' Assistants' Association, an article on the D'Oyly Carte Company, and a short leader concerning the Spring Show. The only references to the Rebellion were two boldly displayed items on the editorial page—one the Lord Lieutenant's Proclamation, the other a short report which said:

SINN FEIN RISING IN DUBLIN

Yesterday morning an insurrectionary rising took place in the city of Dublin. The authorities have taken active and energetic measures to cope with the situation. These measures are proceeding favourably. In accordance with this official statement early and prompt action is anticipated.

Much worse than the absence of reliable information, however, was a growing shortage of food. Supplies laid in to last over the Easter holidays had begun to run out. In the Church Street and Boland's Bakery area the rebels distributed bread, but most other areas in the center of the city had no bread vans, no milk deliveries, and no butchers. Milkmen who ven-

158

tured out into the streets around St. Stephen's Green had their supplies commandeered at revolver point by Lily Kempson and Mary Hyland, two young Citizen Army women. Thus to the growing list of grievances against the rebels was now added a threat of partial starvation.

Dublin, in fact, had already had enough of its glorious insurrection, and was impatiently waiting for the military to do something about it.

For the young rebels garrisoning Clanwilliam House, morning produced a disagreeable surprise. Sent to pick up extra ammunition, James Doyle reported back that the men in the Schools had apparently left during the night. Acting on their own initiative the party had slipped back to headquarters— a typical example of how loosely command was exercised in the rebel army. When Malone slipped in the back way shortly after dawn, Reynolds pointed out how weak this left the position around Mount Street Bridge. Malone agreed that it needed strengthening and suggested that Captain Donnelly should be asked for reinforcements.

Reynolds dispatched young Daniel Byrne with a request for more men and food. Byrne returned from Boland's with pieces of fruit cake and Reynolds had to send him back again to explain that the urgent need was for *men*, and that they would appreciate something a little more substantial than fruit cake.

Shortly after seven o'clock reinforcements arrived in the persons of Volunteers Patrick Doyle and Richard Murphy. Doyle was a married man with children, Murphy a young tailor engaged to be married. A little later the two Walshe brothers, James and Thomas, also arrived, bringing the garrison strength up to an uninspiring total of seven—young Byrne having skipped off. Among them the seven men had four Lee-Enfields, two Martini rifles, two Howth guns, two .38 revolvers, two .45 revolvers, one .38 automatic, and an ammunition reserve of two thousand rounds.

Malone made a second visit to see how they were faring, and Doyle heard him remark to Reynolds that it would be a pity if the owners of the house were killed, or injured in any way; subsequently Reynolds prevailed upon the Wilsons to leave the house and go to friends nearby. Barricades on the ground floor were then strengthened and two heavy wardrobes placed on the stair landings so that a push would send them toppling and block the stairs. Sheets were torn up to make bandages, and soda-water siphons were filled with water and placed at the window.

In Boland's Bakery, spirits could hardly have been better; everyone was happy to believe a report that the Germans had landed and were advancing to their aid. To the rebel rank and file anything seemed possible. Had they not strong British forces cooped up in Beggar's Bush and had their puny efforts to break out not been easily brushed aside? There had been a few casualties—but not enough to cause any anxiety.

Commandant de Valera, however, shared none of his men's optimism. His long, austere countenance still bore a perpetually worried look. He had not slept, his eyes remained wild and red-rimmed. Shortly after daybreak, he called a parade and announced that all boys under eighteen were to go home, explaining that they were no longer engaged in maneuvers, but in a real act of war. If they went now, he said, they would have performed their duty and would receive their reward eventually from the Republic. It took some time, however, to persuade the boys to leave. Willie Fitzgerald, aged fifteen, was "hunted away" time and time again, and in the end won his right to stay. Richard Pearle, aged sixteen, told his mother when she called at the gate in response to the pleas of officers: "Go home, Mother, this is no place for a woman."

At 9:30 A.M. Pearse issued his first communiqué:

The Irish Republic was proclaimed in Dublin on Easter Monday, 24th April, at 12 noon. Simultaneously with the issue of the proclamation of the Provisional Government the Dublin Division of the Army of the Republic, including the Irish Volunteers, Citizen Army, Hibernian Rifles, and other bodies, occupied dominating points in the city. The G.P.O. was seized at 12 noon, the Castle was attacked at the same moment, and shortly afterwards the Four Courts were occupied. The Irish troops hold the City Hall and dominate the Castle. Attacks were immediately commenced by the British forces and were everywhere repulsed. At the moment of writing this report . . . the Republican forces hold all their posi-

160

tions and the British forces have nowhere broken through. There has been heavy and continuous fighting for nearly 24 hours, the casualties of the enemy being much more numerous than those on the Republican side. The Republican forces everywhere are fighting with splendid gallantry. The populace of Dublin are plainly with the Republic, and the officers and men are everywhere cheered as they march through the streets. The whole centre of the city is in the hands of the Republic, whose flag flies from the G.P.O.

Commandant-General P. H. Pearse is Commander in Chief of the Army of the Republic and is President of the Provisional Government. Commandant-General James Connolly is commanding the Dublin districts. Communication with the country is largely cut, but reports to hand show that the country is rising, and bodies of men from Kildare and Fingall have already reported in Dublin.

There were many inaccuracies, of course, in this communiqué, which was printed under the heading:

STOP PRESS!
The Irish Republic

in *Irish War News,* a four-page quarto-sized sheet issued from the Post Office. The first edition, numbered Vol. 1, No. 1. turned out to be the only one ever to appear. Perhaps the most outrageous invention—although it might well be pleaded that it was necessary to include it for morale—was that the country was rising; outside the city, in fact, there was an almost complete lack of action.

In Galway, late on Monday, the small towns of Athenry and Craughwell were seized and the police barracks in both places surrounded. The railway lines to Limerick and Athlone were cut and a contingent of rebels marched west to capture Oranmore and then to take Galway City. The attempt was crushed, however, when British destroyers shelled the road and scattered the insurgent column. They would have met with a hot reception in Galway City otherwise, for the police were armed and ready and Redmond's Volunteers had declared for the Crown.

North of Dublin there were a few isolated skirmishes. At

Donabate the rebels tried to blow up a railway bridge, but succeeded only in disturbing the rails. At Skerries their activities prevented Mr. John Clancy, M.P., from opening a local fete. On the other hand, they managed to seize Castle Bellingham, County Louth, and take its three constables prisoner.

In the north of Ireland, Brigadier-General Hackett-Pain crushed any hopes the rebels had of seizing the County Tyrone by sending in a flying column of three hundred troops from Belfast.

In the south, Limerick and Clare were quiet; Counties Cork and Kerry, fairly so. At Castlegregory, thirty insurgents turned out on Monday afternoon, but discovering no overt signs of the Irish Republic, and perceiving no way in which they could help to establish one, they went home. The military had Cork City in their hands before the rebels there could move.

In the County Wexford, both Ferns and Enniscorthy were captured by the rebels and the police besieged in their barracks. Stores and other war materials were commandeered, railway lines cut, communications destroyed, trees felled, and roads blocked.

Immediately outside Dublin, fifty Volunteers, under Commandant Thomas Ashe, were able to chalk up several minor victories, but when Pearse wrote his communiqué, they had, as yet, done nothing.

16

An outbreak of cholera in northwest India had forced Lieutenant John Mahoney of the Indian Army Medical Service into the hills. With Captain Baldwin of the First Gurkha Regiment, he was negotiating a narrow path in the Himalayas when Baldwin's pony shied and sent Mahoney hurtling over the precipice. Forty feet below he crashed into a boulder and managed to hold on. After a two-hour struggle, his friends succeeded in tying a rope round him and pulling him up. Nursed by some missionary girls at Dharmsala, he was then sent home to Ireland to convalesce.

At 10:30 on Easter Tuesday morning, he stepped off the train in Harcourt Street station, and finding no cabs or taxis waiting, decided to walk toward St. Stephen's Green. He was wearing full uniform—a light-colored gabardine suit decorated with black gorget patches. He had not gone far when a man stopped him and said, "Don't you know the Shinners are out?" Mahoney had no idea what Shinners meant, but thanked him anyhow and continued walking. He skirted the Green, though, on the man's advice, and was making for the Quays when someone shouted, "Not that way—the Shinners are there!" He stopped, uncertain where to go next. At once a crowd gathered and began to give him advice. "Report to Portobello," said one man. "Go up to the Castle," said another. While he was trying to make up his mind, a clergyman came along, trundling his bicycle. He introduced himself: "I'm Canon Hemphill. You know you're in grave danger, walking around in that uniform."

"What can I do?" asked Mahoney helplessly.

163

The Canon thought for a moment. Then he said, "I think you'd better come home with me."

"Thank you very much," said Mahoney. "That's extremely kind of you."

Canon Hemphill led him through back streets, detouring rebel positions. In Upper Leeson Street, a woman came to the door and warned, "Don't go that way. Captain Ramsay has just been shot up there." She added, "And get out of that uniform at once, for God's sake!"

"That's all very well, ma'am," said Mahoney, "but what am I to put on instead?"

"Wait a moment. . . . Better still, come inside."

Mahoney followed the woman and she gave him a mackintosh, a cap, and a pair of blue serge trousers. He changed, but kept on his khaki jacket.

It was only a short walk from there to the Hemphill home on Ailesbury Avenue, where Mahoney was introduced to the Canon's wife and daughter and invited to lunch.

"Would you mind if I used your telephone to let my sister know I'm all right?" he asked.

Mrs. Hemphill smiled. "I'm afraid there's no telephone— the wires have been cut."

After lunch Mahoney said, "I think I'll take a chance and go."

"Well, if you must, you must," said Mrs. Hemphill. "But if I were you I'd take off that tunic. I can let you have one of the Canon's."

"Thank you very much. But the trousers should be a good enough disguise—along with the mac."

"Well, I still think you're very foolish," said Mrs. Hemphill. "You could easily stay with us until the trouble is over."

"I would if I weren't so anxious about my sister," explained Mahoney. He thanked the Hemphills again, then left and walked to Ballsbridge where he found a garage.

"Could I have a taxi?" he asked the garage owner.

"Well," said the man, "I've got plenty of cars, but I've nobody to drive you. Sure, haven't they all gone down into the city to see the fun."

"It's very important that I get across to Drumcondra," said Mahoney, taking out a pound note.

"Oh, if it's that important," said the man, "I'll drive you myself."

They crossed the Liffey by Butt Bridge and drove past Amiens Street station. Rebels were squatting on the roofs of houses along the main road. As the taxi approached the first Canal bridge Mahoney saw four young men signaling them to stop. The driver pulled up and the men surrounded the car. "We're searching for munitions," one explained.

Mahoney sat quietly while they poked around in the interior. Suddenly one barked at him, "Open that coat!" He had no choice but to pull it open, showing the khaki underneath. The cab driver, lifting his eyes to heaven protested, "Honest to God, boys, I don't know anything about this!" Mahoney, at gunpoint, was ordered out of the car, and the driver sped away. Left alone with the rebels, Mahoney hardly knew what to expect. They ordered him to march to the offices of the Dublin and Wicklow Manure Company, where they brought him before a rebel officer. Recognizing the black gorget patches, the officer said, "Oh, so you're in the Indian Medical Service?"

"I am," said Mahoney.

"In that case, I'm sorry about this—but you're wearing khaki. I've no option but to take you prisoner. Incidentally, I used to be stationed in Secunderabad myself."

Following a brief interrogation, Mahoney was led into a small lavoratory where the door was locked behind him and a guard placed on it. A little later a rebel entered and asked, "Would you like some tea?" Mahoney nodded and the rebel went away but returned shortly with a cup of tea. Soon afterward the same man came back and asked, "Would you like to go in with the boys?"

Mahoney had no idea who "the boys" might be, but anything seemed preferable to where he was at present. "Yes," he said, and was led into a big, comfortably furnished office where a number of rebels squatted on a Turkish carpet, their rifles across their knees. Supporting themselves lazily against a wall were three British soldiers and Mahoney was allowed to talk to them. One was a Royal Irish Fusilier who had been made prisoner while enjoying a drink; his main grievance was that he had not been given time to finish it.

Inside the G.P.O., hardly five minutes passed without someone accidentally discharging a rifle. When a sudden burst of firing broke the otherwise pleasant calm of the morning, James Connolly shouted in dire exasperation, "Would you tell those fellows once and for all that unless they're firing at something useful, they're not to fire at all."

He was driven to the extreme limits of his patience when some Citizen Army men asked permission to leave the building. "Why?" asked Connolly. "Where do you want to go?"

"To work, Mister Connolly," said their spokesman, "now that the holidays are over."

The amazing fact was that most people had still failed to appreciate exactly what was happening. How else explain the carelessness of Lord Dunsany and a friend, Captain Wilson —both in military uniform—who bowled along in their motor-car straight into the rebel barricade at Church Street Bridge shortly before noon. Not until a bullet grazed his cheek did Dunsany apparently wake up to the fact that these disturbances were something more than a mere riot.

Almost at once the entire medical and nursing services of the city, both professional and voluntary, had swung into action.

First to offer their services to the authorities were the Dublin Red Cross Society and the St. John's Ambulance Brigade. But everywhere men and women of good will rushed forward to help, irrespective of whether those whom they tended were members of the military forces, part of the civilian population, or even members of the rebel army. All eighteen metropolitan hospitals made preparations to handle casualties and doctors and surgeons and nursing staffs discarded normal working schedules to be on call at all hours. The Irish Automobile Club offered a complete motor ambulance service. Dr. Ella Webb, Lady District Superintendent of the Red Cross, supervised the transforming of a supply depot into a temporary

166

hospital (which provided one operating theater and thirty beds). Large private houses—those of Miss Fletcher at 35 Fitzwilliam Square, Mrs. Jackson at 11 Bushy Park Road, Rathgar, and Miss Meade at 32 Fitzwilliam Square, for example—were also turned into auxiliary hospitals. Some 184 male ambulance workers and 239 voluntary nurses offered to look after refugee women and children, help prepare surgical dressings, carry stretchers through the firing line, and even ride in ambulances amid a hail of flying bullets.

In the South Dublin Union, the rebels improvised a defiant flag, painting an emerald harp upon a yellow window blind and nailing it to a long pole.

Solemnly this extraordinary emblem was raised from an upper window of the Nurses' Home while the garrison stood to attention and sang "A Nation Once Again."

From their hard-won positions within the Union and from the roof of the Royal Hospital on the far side of the valley of the Camac, the military opened heavy fire. The flag was not damaged, but a woman sitting reading a book in her home in James Street, and a holidaymaker from Belfast, walking along the South Circular Road, were both shot dead.

Shortly before noon Major Sir Francis Fletcher Vane, acting second in command of Portobello Barracks, sauntered into the mess. He found the place empty save for a single officer, who sat slumped over a table, his head between his hands. Vane recognized Captain J. Bowen-Colthurst, a member of the well-known Ascendancy family who owned Blarney Castle. Colthurst had been at the retreat from Mons. Now, as Vane walked over, Colthurst raised his head and said, "Isn't it dreadful, Sir Francis, to have to shoot Irishmen?"

"Indeed," said Sir Francis, and promptly forgot the remark until next day events rather forcibly reminded him of it.

Despite gentle rain, the mobs again crowded Sackville Street. With most offices, shops, and factories still unable to open, young men and women flocked into the city. As early as 10 A.M., Messrs. Frewen and Ryan's Emporium was attacked

167

by looters. Women and children emerged with collars, hats, and caps. Tall silk hats and bowlers arced out into the roadway, only to be kicked about like footballs in a glorious orgy of destruction. Crowds of "better-class people" stood watching them, loath to join in, but enjoying the fun.

Toward one o'clock, Francis Sheehy-Skeffington emerged from the General Post Office, carrying under his arm a bundle of papers, a paste brush, and several walking sticks. He stopped at Smith-O'Brien's monument to paste up a poster. Curiously the crowd gathered around and read:

When there are no regular police on the streets, it becomes the duty of citizens to police the streets themselves and to prevent such spasmodic looting as has taken place in a few streets. Civilians (men and women) who are willing to co-operate to this end are asked to attend at Westmoreland Chambers (over Eden Bros.) at five o'clock this (Tues.) afternoon.

Sheehy-Skeffington moved on, stopping only to chat with his friend, St. John Ervine, on O'Connell Bridge. He offered Ervine a walking stick, explaining the idea of a civilian constabulary armed only with sticks. Ervine considered it characteristic of "Skeffy" to submerge his scruples about violence in order to safeguard his country's honor. But regretfully, he refused the walking stick.

The military had behaved, so far, in a manner puzzling to both rebel and civilian. To the ordinary Dubliner the conception of a handful of Volunteers and Citizen Army boys taking over his city and beating off the British Army was sheer wonder. There were few, however, who thought that by this nightfall at least, there would be any other outcome than that the Army and the police, between them, would have succeeded in chasing every rebel home. Meanwhile, where *was* the Army?

Certainly the military had not acted with any degree of brilliance or audacity. Their movements so far had been marked with a perhaps commendable caution and method. They had ignored the rebels where possible and had slipped into useful positions from which they would eventually be able

168

to exert a stranglehold. Most of the South Dublin Union had been cleared, but only as part of over-all operations to relieve Dublin Castle. The City Hall had been retaken—because it was intolerable that rebels should squat on the Castle's doorstep. During Monday night, too, the forces under the command of Major Somerville had seized the Custom House and the North Wall railway terminus, thus securing the vital dock area. Trinity College had been held by the O.T.C. and soldiers from the Empire. But the operations in the Shelbourne Hotel and the United Services Club, while so far producing surprisingly good results, could hardly be called a really offensive operation. Neither Colonels Kennard and Cowan nor Brigadier-General Lowe, when he assumed command, felt inclined to risk their reputations by precipitate action which, while their uncertainty lasted as to the exact number of rebels fighting and the chances of the Germans landing, might have recoiled upon them disastrously.

With approximately five thousand troops in Dublin under his immediate command, General Lowe, in fact, had the rebels outnumbered by the kind of superior odds which, if they could have been brought to bear on the Western Front, would have ended that war inside a week. But instead of risking all on a series of frontal attacks, Lowe sensibly decided to throw a cordon around the center of the city. He ordered Colonel Portal, in command of the Curragh Mobile Column, to establish a line of posts from Kingsbridge Station to Trinity College via the Castle. With this line, running west to east along the Liffey, he would drive a great arrow-wedge through rebel positions. When more reinforcements arrived that afternoon—the 4th Royal Dublin Fusiliers from Templemore, the composite Ulster Battalion of Belfast and a battery of four 18-pounders from the Reserve Artillery Brigade at Athlone—he commenced operations to establish a second line in the northern suburbs which, when joined with the first, would create a tight cordon around the G.P.O. and the Four Courts and cut off the rebels from their outposts.

The insurgent commanders, utterly in the dark as to these intentions, did little to hamper Lowe. Commandant Kent, driven back into his "fort" in the Nurses' Home at the South

Dublin Union, had already lost touch with his three main out-posts at Jameson's Distillery, Watkin's Brewery, and Roe's Malt House, and even when the military pressure eased, made no attempt to re-establish contact. Captain Cornelius Colbert in Watkin's Brewery, quickly tired of being cooped up with his twenty men in a narrow street, joined Captain James Murphy and his forces in Jameson's Distillery; here nearly one hundred and twenty men, well-armed and supplied, and with a large number of women to cook and render first aid for them, waited patiently for the attacks which were never to develop. The C.O. in Roe's Malt House behaved with even greater pusil-lanimity. Cut off from Kent and short both of inspiration and determination, he abandoned his post and sent his men home. Under such circumstances it was a comparatively easy task for Portal to establish his posts from Kingsbridge Station to the Castle. Here, of course, the situation was more active.

James Connolly, delighted at the spirited fight put up by his men in the City Hall and the buildings around it, had twice reinforced them by detachments from headquarters. A dozen men under Sergeant George Norgrove of the Citizen Army had arrived the previous evening in time to join in the City Hall fight. Early on Tuesday, Connolly dispatched more reinforce-ments to occupy the roofs and windows of hotels and houses immediately behind the *Mail & Express* offices and Henry & James, the outfitters. Even so, the odds remained outlandish. Fewer than thirty rebels held these positions and against them were military forces superior to them in numbers by almost a hundred to one.

The battle of Cork Hill commenced about 2 P.M. when a detachment of 5th Royal Dublin Fusiliers under Second-Lieu-tenant F. O'Neill was ordered to clear the newspaper offices, the chief position still in rebel hands. The attack was preceeded by an ominous silence. Occasionally a bullet cracked down toward Trinity College; now and then a military sniper on the roof of the City Hall shot at a rebel shadow on the *Mail & Ex-press* roof. Civilians, sensing an entertainment, huddled close to the walls in Dame Street or crouched in shop doorways. Suddenly a withering shower of bullets from Upper Castle Yard was poured into the newspaper offices. The rebels replied

170

courageously. The effect on the crowds was comical. People darted away like rabbits; women fainted. Some ran straight into the firing line, causing a sudden cease-fire, and the combatants shouted angrily at them from the rooftops. At ten minutes past two, when the streets had been cleared once more, the military reopened hostilities, machine guns chattering above everything else.

A large crowd collected at the top of Lord Edward Street, some reckless individuals running furtively up Dame Street as far as Eustace Street and Crampton Court, while the military on the roof of the City Hall shouted angrily, "Keep back!" A thick cloud of brick dust rose over the street, as bullets spattered into the walls. Fire was intense, bullets booming, echoing, and crackling in a persistent, relentless barrage. After fifteen minutes of this unremitting onslaught, a score of soldiers with fixed bayonets made a rush from Upper Castle Gate. Six or seven were knocked over and the rest scrambled back. Three minutes later a second wave of khaki hurled itself across the street. Over their heads, a covering fire poured solid sheets of lead onto the roof of the newspaper office in an effort to pin down the defenders. There were exultant cries as the wave gained the protection of the *Mail* wall and forced open the door. Certain individuals, anxious to glimpse the struggle taking place inside the doorway, stepped out into the road— only to be driven back by ricocheting bullets.

"It makes me fidgety to know what they do be doing inside," explained one young woman as she dashed back to safety.

"Begob, ma'am, and if ye had one of them things in you, ye'd have the fidgets, sure enough," remarked a spectator.

Twenty minutes after the start of the battle, a third wave, twice as heavy as that which had preceded it, was launched against the *Mail* office. Although the distance they had to cover under fire was no more than thirty yards, they moved forward with great deliberation, ducking, weaving, crouching, now advancing a step or two, now retreating, making themselves almost impossible to hit. The tactic was effective and casualties were fewer than with the earlier wave. When they reached the other side of the street, however, they were forced to fan out

171

along the wall of the newspaper building and wait because those who had got across earlier were still being held up just inside the doorway. Already the place was blocked with their casualties. Some soldiers had tried rushing the stairs, only to be sent sprawling back by volleys from the upper landings. As the reinforcing troops ducked in, they found themselves enveloped in a riot of smoke and noise.

Fifteen minutes after the third wave had crossed the street, the issue was still undecided. Yet another wave of military —about thirty this time—led by two officers, made the crossing. Noise rose to a new intensity. Stretcher parties scurried back and forth with casualites. A badly wounded soldier, still able to walk, was helped by a comrade. Finally, ten minutes after the preceding assault, twenty more troops dashed across the street and this time they were able to gain an entrance without difficulty; the ground floor had been cleared. One Dublin Fusilier, working his way to the rear, came face to face with his younger brother. Lowering his bayonet, he hissed, "Run, you young fool, run!"

By now the battle had edged away from the front of the building. Running short of ammunition, their rifles unbearably hot, the rebels fought the troops with the butts. These were perhaps the most savage and brutal moments in the whole battle—a period of crude, primitive slugging and killing. On the rooftops, firing continued for some four or five minutes more, but with lessening intensity. Then, at precisely one minute to three, all firing ceased. The crowd, its attention fixed on the doorway, waited to see the captured garrison led into the street. Minutes ticked by and still—ominously enough—none appeared. After five minutes, a laborer remarked to his friend, "Jim, I'm going home for me dinner, the fun's over," and started off down Crane Lane. Some of the crowd, idly wandering after him, saw seven insurgents leap from the side windows of houses at the rear of Henry & James, and make toward the river, where they were quickly lost to view.

Behind them lay twenty-two dead comrades, token of their desperate fight.

"Have a look at our corpse!" said Boyd-O'Kelly gleefully, opening a door next to the porter's lodge in Trinity College.

172

Although, as a medical student, Michael Taaffe was hardened to the sight of dead bodies, he found this one, lying on the floor of a stone-walled niche, somehow different. It was that of a young man, so new to death that he looked as though he might rise at any moment and walk away. There was a small black hole through his temple.

"They came through on bikes, heading toward the G.P.O. during the night," explained Boyd-O'Kelly. "Didn't expect anyone to be here, I dare say. We got this chap and winged another, I think, but he kept on going."

Taaffe, wishing that wars—especially of this kind—could be fought without casualties, returned to his eyrie on the roof of Regent House. Sixty feet below lay deserted Dame Street. He scanned the roofs, but as far as he could see they were as empty as the streets. Sitting there, his rifle at the ready, he saw a party of soldiers coming toward the College from the direction of Grafton Street, hugging the walls, their bayonets flashing. Then an officer with a drawn sword ran into the cobbled yard below, signaling his men to follow. The College gates must have been opened to them because the whole party disappeared below.

Taaffe did not know it, but this was the completion of the first arm of General Lowe's cordon. From now on the rebels in the South Dublin Union, Jameson's Distillery, Jacob's Biscuit Factory, the College of Surgeons, and Boland's Bakery were cut off from Headquarters in Sackville Street.

With the capture of the last rebel positions around Dublin Castle and the completion of the southern arm of his cordon, General Lowe began pushing forward units to establish his northern arm.

The rebel command had made no attempt to create strong points or "forts" in the northern suburbs of the city. They had been content to erect barricades along the North Circular Road and its vicinity at places where there were roads and railway bridges. The role of the northern suburbs, as envisaged by Plunkett, was simply to protect the rebel rear and to keep the way open for a retreat toward Ulster if such a course became necessary.

Two battles developed among these northern outposts during the afternoon. A party of Volunteer Second Battalion men had tried to blow up the Great Northern railway line across the Tolka River early in the morning and, when the explosives failed to do much damage, had begun ripping up tracks farther north. This was shutting the gate after the horse had bolted—for the military, under Major Somerville, had already occupied Amiens Street and North Wall termini.

At 2 P.M. a strong military detachment, in an armored train, pushed out from Amiens Street to repair the ripped-up tracks. They were met by rebels ensconced at Annesley Road Bridge and although for two hours they fought courageously, they, for once, found themselves outnumbered and were forced to retreat, leaving several prisoners behind.

The second engagement was more significant, for it brought the first really ominous sign of the extent of military strength, the first tentative indication that the rebels were not going to be treated tenderly. Despite the views of his colleagues, James Connolly had always insisted that the Government would never employ artillery in Dublin. "A capitalist Government will never destroy property," he insisted.

At precisely three o'clock that afternoon he was to learn that a Government, whether capitalist or otherwise, threatened from within and possibly from without, would not hesitate to utilize every weapon at its command, property or no property. At that moment, an 18-pounder hurriedly brought up from Athlone, commenced firing from the gate of the Medical Officer's Residence at Grangegorman Asylum, near the Broadstone Station. The rebels had set up a barricade on the North Circular Road where it intersected the northward-running Phibsborough Road. Shrapnel began bursting over the heads of the defenders who, simultaneously, found themselves coming under machine-gun fire from the Broadstone Station. The rebels might have dealt with the machine guns, for their position looked down on the Broadstone and they had an excellent field of fire, but sighting civilians—mostly women—on the station platform, they withheld their fire. The 18-pounder again belched and carried away most of the barricade. The fifteen rebels manning it fell back upon a second barricade at Cabra Road Bridge.

Warned by the newcomers that the military were using artillery, the men defending this barricade sent out six scouts, who advanced cautiously along the Cabra Road until they spotted a strong military party moving out from Phoenix Park. In a sudden downpour of rain, the scouting party crouched in shop doorways or flung themselves flat on the glistening pavements, firing on the military. The troops reacted sharply, advancing at a rush and forcing the scouts to flee.

Behind the Cabra Road barricade some thirty men shivered in the rain, waiting for the first glint of British bayonets. Volunteer Joseph Canny, a twenty-six-year-old barman, braced himself to meet a bayonet charge, but the first sign of the enemy was a tremendous volley of bullets against the barricade. The rebels replied as best they could through the curtain of rain, but after a few, sharp exchanges, firing ceased. The rebels thought that they had beaten off the attack but then, abruptly, there was the boom of artillery. At 3:45 P.M. the first burst of shrapnel crackled over their heads, and for three-quarters of an hour the desperate rebels—their barricade carried away within minutes—tried to stem the inevitable. Bereft of cover, their losses mounting rapidly, they broke and fled.

The affair became a rout, with the insurgents fleeing across fields and railway tracks, or trying to lose the soldiers in a maze of back streets or along the Canal banks. A few, when they had regained their nerve, made their way to the G.P.O. Others joined up with Commandant Ashe and his 5th Battalion, operating in County Dublin; but most of them, drenched to the skin and with an understanding, perhaps for the first time, of the weight of men and material they were up against, simply went home and stayed there.

By nightfall, the whole rebel position in the northern suburbs had disintegrated as, threatened by encirclement, the remaining forces holding out in Fairview and at Annesley Bridge, retired upon Headquarters.

De Valera, still tense, still sleepless, still burning up energy recklessly, now produced another offensive idea.

Sitting at a table which had been brought out onto the railway embankment, and surrounded by his officers, he pored over a street map, working on a plan to relieve Mallin's hard-pressed men in the Royal College of Surgeons. Finally he decided to lead a party through the back streets near the Shelbourne Hotel and take the enemy in the rear.

News of the projected sally caused excitement in the Boland's garrison. Action would be a welcome change from sitting cooped up in the bakery or huddled together in the rain in a shallow trench between railway sleepers. Easily the worst part of the rising had become the waiting; a man's imagination worked overtime when he had not enough to do.

De Valera picked twelve men to accompany him and as a morale-builder handed each man a cigar. Then he disappeared somewhere, after issuing instructions that each was to be provided with a modern rifle, fifty rounds of ammunition and a day's rations. The twelve men set out in single file along the railway lines toward Westland Row Station. By now the rain had stopped, although it was still damp underfoot. They had reached the first signal cabin when the Commandant came striding to meet them with disappointing news.

"I'm sorry, but it's all off. The fact is I don't feel justified in leading an attack with only twelve men. With twenty-four I could afford to lose half of you, perhaps, and the safety of our main position would not be seriously affected. But with our numbers so few, I can't take the risk—especially as our chances of succeeding are slight. The whole position could be too easily ruined and no good result come from such a wastage of men. In God's name, therefore, we'll go back and stand by our own area."

The announcement was met by discontented mutterings. It would be pleasant if De Valera could make up his mind and for once stick to it. Unhappily they turned away, even as a sentry posted on the bridge over Great Brunswick Street shouted that a party of mounted police was approaching. De Valera's first thought was for the civilians on the road below, who might be caught in the line of fire. A tall, gaunt, extraordinary figure, he must have looked like a lunatic to the people below when they saw him gesticulating wildly and heard him bawling at them to get off the street. They paid no attention to him, of course; Dubliners, even in normal times, were accustomed to all kinds

176

of queer fellows and another one, especially in the middle of a rebellion, was hardly worth bothering about.

Fortunately De Valera's dilemma was resolved for him. A civilian warned the police, "The Shinners are up on the railway bridge," and they bolted back up the street.

De Valera's humanitarianism brought a welcome warmth to the curious regard in which he was held by his men. Reserved and aloof even with his officers, the rank and file— despite his nervously uneasy manner and his tendency to start something and then suddenly cancel it, which somewhat destroyed their confidence in him—could not help admiring him. There was his willingness to take personal risks; his desire to avoid injuring the innocent or causing unnecessary damage. He had dismantled the Gas Works on Monday evening because he feared an explosion during the fighting which might have caused disaster to the civilian population. Early that day he had ordered Captain Simon Donnelly to make certain that the forty horses belonging to the bakery were fed and well looked after. He had personally released the animals at the Dogs and Cats Pound in Grand Canal Street, knowing that they would face starvation and thirst if the Rebellion continued much longer.

He certainly had plenty of ideas. In the afternoon he asked Section-Commander Denis O'Donoghue: "Do you know anybody who could drive a train?" (O'Donoghue was a railway worker.)

"My brother-in-law," said O'Donoghue.

"If we could get steam up in an engine," remarked De Valera thoughtfully, "we could move it up and down the line with an armed party aboard."

O'Donoghue grasped the point. Rapid hit-and-run raids could be launched against Beggar's Bush Barracks; more importantly, if the military broke in anywhere along the line (and it was so thinly held that this was likely), it would give De Valera a mobility which might well enable him to fling back the soldiery.

"I'll see what I can do, sir," said O'Donoghue.

17

For the slum population, the rebellion remained a great and glorious spree. Having extracted what fun and monetary advantage they could from Frewen's Emporium, the mob drifted off into Upper Sackville Street, seeking fresh excitement. Like wild children they now concentrated upon the garish delights of Lawrence's Toy shop.

To Redmond-Howard, Sackville Street had suddenly two faces: one of tragedy, the other of infantile comedy. South of the Pillar where the rebels had begun fortifying the whole of the east side of the street from Brennan Whitmore's position at the corner of North Earl Street down to Hopkins and Hopkins', the jewelers on the corner of O'Connell Bridge, the great street had now the arid, deserted look of a battlefield, with the warlike wire stretched in front of the Post Office to hold back the crowds. North of the Pillar it was a veritable nursery-land. As the mob smashed its way into Lawrence's, mothers squatted on the dead horses and watched their grubby children emerge, carrying bundles of Union Jacks which they dumped into the road. Soon hundreds of flags had risen in a great mound on the tramlines. Then a flame leaped up and in an instant a giant bonfire was burning between Nelson's Pillar and Parnell's Monument. The mood of the mob grew wilder as they danced around the fire.

In the midst of the junketing, a burst of heavy firing sounded from the Quays (the military were beginning yet another attack on Heuston and his men in the Mendicity). Red Cross ambulances raced down Sackville Street, and the sight of them and of the mob dancing and singing while the guns thundered,

178

struck Redmond-Howard as the most extraordinary example of combined pathos and humor he had ever encountered.

The beautiful Miss Stokes, pausing in Sackville Street on her way to meet a friend at the Broadstone Station, was stunned by the sight of one of the greatest streets in Europe in the hands of rebels and an unruly mob.

From the barricade at North Earl Street, Brennan Whitmore watched the scenes at Lawrence's grow wilder. He was astonished that even now, twenty-four hours after the flags of the Republic had been run up over the Post Office, half of Dublin still did not seem to know that they were in the middle of a rebellion. The mob appeared to regard the whole affair as a magnificent excuse for letting off steam.

"What's it all about?" a young woman asked him as he stared up the street. "Why don't you all pack up and go home before the military get you?"

Brennan Whitmore attempted to explain. While they talked, a bearded man staggered toward them, wearing a silk hat, clutching a walking stick, and sporting a feather boa about his shoulders and a lady's undergarment on his arm.

"Would you look at that ould reprobate!" demanded the young woman. Then, as the old fellow, his face grave and dignified, came abreast of them, she called out, "It's at home saying your prayers you should be instead of stealing other people's property, you ould fool!"

Without a word or a change of expression, the old man took off the feather boa and handed it to a youngster who snatched at it angrily, then threw it into the gutter, shouting, "You ought to be ashamed of yourself." The old man stalked off with what dignity he could muster, still holding the lady's undergarment.

The mob kept furiously at it. Two more shops in Upper Sackville Street were broken into. Young Ernest O'Malley saw shawlies offering diamond rings and gold watches for as little as a sixpence or shilling.

Rebels on the roof of the Arch bar in Henry Street were faced with the task of ejecting a part of the mob which had broken in. They hesitated to shoot them down. Then Barney Friel had an idea. He carried buckets with water to the edge of the roof, shouted, "Ready!" and fired a shot through the sky-

179

light. The shot scattered the drunken mob, and as they charged through the door, Volunteer Paddy Bracken tipped over the buckets, drenching the invaders thoroughly.

From the Imperial Hotel window, Redmond-Howard watched a great black smoke cloud rise into the sky at Lawrence's. The mob had set the shop on fire and soon the roar of the flames could be heard a hundred yards away. Ten minutes later flames reached the fireworks. Roman candles, Chinese crackers, high-flying rockets fizzled up into the sky or burst onto the street in a holocaust itself as crazy as the mob. Finally a big yellow, blue, and green bouquet shot into the air, falling back into the street in a shower of sizzling sparks, scattering the crowd in all directions.

Sick at heart, Redmond-Howard and Marsh finally withdrew from their window, having watched for four solid hours. Outside, the mob still rampaged and looted and cheered the flames rising above Lawrence's. Marsh suggested a game of chess and took out a pocket set. Redmond-Howard declined. Chess, in the middle of a revolution, seemed too incongruous.

Sometime later, when they were sitting down to a meal, they noticed, crossing the street, two young rebels who had been keeping them under surveillance from the roof of the G.P.O. Redmond-Howard decided that he and Marsh were to be shot as spies and wondered whether to make a dash for it. Woods, the manager, sensing their predicament, crossed to the table and reassured them: "There's nothing to worry about, gentlemen; the rebels tell me that they are simply taking over the hotel."

He had hardly spoken when the dining room was invaded by a party of rebels. Their officer said courteously, "Finish your meal, gentlemen. I must ask you to leave, but there is no need to hurry." Then he ordered his men to the windows. "Two men to every window. Take furniture—tables, chairs, anything you can find—and barricade them. We may have to stand a siege."

"Is there any immediate danger?" asked Redmond-Howard.

"None, sir, save from your own resistance. Civilians are perfectly safe as far as we're concerned; we're only fighting the troops of England. You may find our men firing over your heads as you pass in the streets, but take no notice; these are partly our own signals to give us warning and they're also intended to clear the streets of looters. If you want, you can have a safe conduct out of the city to the north where our guards have orders to allow all civilians to pass. You see, it's possible our positions may be shelled; we might even be gassed."

Redmond-Howard, still curious to know what the rebel insurrection was aiming at, questioned one of the men, but all he would say was, "England has always hated Ireland and now's the time to free her. Otherwise within a couple of years everybody'll be a slave and a conscript."

It was raining heavily when Redmond-Howard and Marsh began walking to the latter's home at Howth, nine miles away. As they passed the Pillar, they saw the Fire Brigade arriving to tackle the fire at Lawrence's. Two long ladders were edged into the air in an effort to reach a woman and child who could be seen clinging to the roof, but they proved short. As the side wall of the burning building showed signs of collapsing, the two men, too sick to watch any more, turned into lower Great Britain Street, where they were caught in a stream of refugees and vividly reminded of pictures they had seen in the newspapers of French refugees at Ypres. As it continued to rain heavily, they were glad to accept a lift in a coal cart.

To the rebels imprisoned in the great gray building beside the Pillar there was nothing particularly ominous in the flames licking high above Sackville Street or the intermittent rattle of muskets and Maxims along the river. Neither by word or deed had Pearse or Connolly hinted that the situation was anything but good and getting better. Connolly, beaming confidently, constantly roamed the building; the garrison—despite the lack of sleep, the continual alarms, and the sheer boredom of waiting—still retained much of the original feeling of high adventure. On the roof, Fintan Murphy lay against the tiles and yawned. Joseph Sweeney turned his face to the dripping sky and thought what an unfortunate country Ireland was in which to try anything—you were sure to get wet. But the scent of victory was in the air.

The whole building, in fact, buzzed with rumors—all of them good: MacDonagh had forced his way into Lower Castle Yard, although driven back temporarily by machine-gun fire.

181

Cork, Kerry, and Limerick were ablaze with revolt. Irish regiments of the British Army were defecting everywhere and declaring for the Republic. Jim Larkin, Connolly's old boss, had landed in Sligo from America and was fighting his way across Ireland with fifty thousand men. The Turks had landed at Waterford. U-boats had sunk a British transport in the Irish Sea. And the Germans had landed in force—their scouts had been seen on the Naas Road. Everything was simply splendid.

Below, in the rain, some urchins lustily sang, "We are the Volunteers and we'll whack the British Army."

In the College of Surgeons, men lay on the floor, wrapped in pieces of carpet, and sang the old rebel song: "Wrap the Green Flag Round Me." To his surprise, Professor O'Briain found himself flicking a tear from his eye.

Twelve-year-old Tommy Keenan returned in triumph after escaping from his family. One of the Citizen Army women had insisted that he go home to tell his parents where he was and what he had been doing. Tommy's father had locked him in his room, but the boy had climbed out the window and scrambled down a drainpipe.

Frank Robbins, with a company of men, began tunneling through the walls from the Turkish baths (which lay halfway along the Green toward Grafton Street) to South King Street at the top of Grafton. This was part of a bold plan by Mallin to burn out the military in the United Services Club. If he were able to tunnel a way through to South King Street, his men might emerge late at night, dart across Grafton Street and set fire to the corner houses on the north side of the Green. Once these were set alight, with luck the whole block would go up— and this would include the United Services Club. The flames, if they got going properly, might jump the intervening gaps of Dawson Street and Kildare Street and burn down the Shelbourne also. In excellent spirits, Robbins handed 7-pound hammers to his men, remarking, "Right, boys, we only need a hole in every wall big enough for a man to crawl through on his hands and knees."

Toward dusk the backbreaking job was completed.

At 5:30 P.M. Francis Sheehy-Skeffington met his wife, Hanna, and together they took tea in one of the teashops which was still open. Then, anxious about their young son, she left him and went home.

Sometime between six and seven, "Skeffy" set out to follow her. Nearing Portobello Bridge, he saw it was guarded by a picquet of thirty Royal Irish Rifles. He remained in the middle of the road, now without traffic, so that he could be clearly seen. The military did not object to his passage and allowed him to cross the bridge. Then someone on the pavement called his name. At once Lieutenant Morris of the 11th East Surrey Regiment, in command of the picquet, called on him to stop and sent two soldiers to arrest him. Skeffington, to his amazement, was hauled unceremoniously into Portobello Barracks and roughly searched. He was then taken before the Adjutant, Lieutenant Samuel Morgan.

"Are you in sympathy with the Sinn Feiners?" asked Morgan directly.

"Yes, but I am not in favor of militarism."

Nonplused, Morgan reported to Irish Command H.Q. He explained that he had questioned Skeffington, but had been unable to find grounds on which to formulate a charge. Was it in order to release him? The answer was a curt "no." Morgan therefore ordered Skeffington to be detained, but entered no charge upon the charge sheet.

At midnight, Captain Bowen-Colthurst approached Lieutenant Dobbyn, captain of the guard, and formally ordered him to hand over the prisoner. This was an illegal act, as no officer could demand the custody of a prisoner without a written order from his commanding officer. Skeffington was hauled out of the guardroom and ordered to say his prayers, Bowen-Colthurst himself praying, "O Lord God, if it should please Thee to take away the life of this man, forgive him for Our Lord Jesus Christ's sake." Skeffington's time, however, had not yet come. Bowen-Colthurt simply wanted the unfortunate pacifist as a hostage while he and a small party of soldiers carried out a raid.

Bowen-Colthurst led them to Portobello Bridge, then ordered his deputy, Lieutenant Wilson, to hold on to Skeffington, adding that he was to be shot immediately if the Sinn Feiners fired on Bowen-Colthurst or his party. With that the captain headed up the Rathmines Road, firing his revolver wildly into

183

the air. At Rathmines Church he spied two boys—one a seventeen-year-old youth called Coade—who had just left the church and were on their way home. Hours earlier Lord Wimborne had proclaimed Martial Law; now Bowen-Colthurst roared at the two terrified youngsters, "Don't you know Martial Law has been proclaimed and that I could shoot you like dogs?"

Anxious to avoid trouble, young Coade tried to get away. At once Bowen-Colthurst screamed, "Bash him!" and a soldier, lifting the butt of his rifle, slashed it across the boy's face, breaking his jawbone. The youngster, senseless, fell to the ground. As he lay there, Bowen-Colthurst whipped out his revolver and shot him dead.

Continuing his rampage, Bowen-Colthurst led his men to Alderman James Kelly's public house. He began by bombing the place, then entered and seized four men he found still alive. Two were barmen, the others magazine editors named Dickson and MacIntyre, who had taken refuge there. Dickson, a cripple, edited *The Eye-Opener;* MacIntyre, *The Searchlight* —both violently Loyalist papers which had strongly supported John Redmond's recruiting campaign. Despite protests, Bowen-Colthurst took them all back to Portobello, where he lodged them behind bars. Then, pleased with his work, he returned to his quarters where, for the rest of the night, he lay sleepless, praying. In the small hours he came across a text in the Bible which seemed to him apt. It was from St. Luke, and said, "But those mine enemies, which would not that I should reign over them, bring hither and slay them before me."

He had the sanction of religion, then, in what he intended to do.

Toward evening, Lieutenant Mahoney was told to line up with the other prisoners—three privates and a civilian—and then under escort was marched to the G.P.O. Brought before an officer, Mahoney was asked to give his name, at which the rebel sneered, "A nice name to be wearing khaki!" His watch and money were taken away (they were returned next morning) and he was led up to the second floor and ushered into the room where Lieutenant Chalmers was held prisoner. He found

184

Chalmers in a "bit of a funk" about "these wild Irishmen"; apparently he expected to be shot at any moment. After a while there was a knock and one of the Sinn Fein women (Miss Louise Gavan Duffy) came in and asked if they would like some tea. Mahoney asked if a message could be sent to his sister in Drumcondra, saying he was safe.

"If you'd like to write it, I'll show it to the Provisional Government," said Miss Gavan Duffy.

When he had finished this, at Chalmers' suggestion both men settled down for the night under a table. Chalmers had some idea that the military were sure to attack during the night and that, if they did, the roof of the G.P.O. might be blown in; he thought the table would offer protection.

Pearse, seated on a high clerk's stool at a counter just inside the main doorway, had worked for several hours on a manifesto to the citizens of Dublin. When the downpour which had cleared the mob off the streets had eased a little, and the crowds were able to emerge from shelter, he strode out into Sackville Street and, with a small escort, walked over to Nelson's Pillar. His appearance caused a rush in that direction and several hundred were milling around as he began reading:

"The Provisional Government to the Citizens of Dublin. The Provisional Government of the Irish Republic salutes the Citizens of Dublin on the momentous occasion of the proclamation of a SOVEREIGN INDEPENDENT IRISH STATE now in the course of being established by Irishmen in arms.

"The Republican forces hold the lines taken up at Twelve noon on Easter Monday, and nowhere, despite fierce and almost continuous attacks of the British troops have the lines been broken through. The country is rising in answer to Dublin's call, and the final achievement of Ireland's freedom is now, with God's help, only a matter of days. The valour, self-sacrifice, and discipline of Irish men and women are about to win for our country a glorious place among the nations.

"Ireland's honour has already been redeemed; it remains to vindicate her wisdom and her self-control.

"All citizens of Dublin who believe in the right of their Country

185

to be free will give their allegiance and their loyal help to the Irish Republic. There is work for everyone; for the men in the fighting line, and for the women in the provision of food and first aid. Every Irishman and Irishwoman worthy of the name will come forward to help their common country in this her supreme hour.

"Able-bodied citizens can help by building barricades in the streets to oppose the advance of the British troops. The British troops have been firing on our women and on our Red Cross. On the other hand, Irish regiments in the British Army have refused to act against their fellow countrymen.

"The Provisional Government hopes that its supporters—which means the vast bulk of the people of Dublin—will preserve order and self-restraint. Such looting as had already occurred has been done by hangers-on of the British army. Ireland must keep her new honour unsmirched.

"We have lived to see an Irish Republic proclaimed. May we live to establish it firmly, and may our children and our children's children enjoy the happiness and prosperity which freedom will bring.

"Signed on behalf of the
Provisional Government
"P. H. PEARSE

"Commanding in Chief the Forces of the Irish Republic,
and President of the Provisional Government."

There were some cheers, but long before he had finished reading, the restless crowds, bored with words and longing for action, had begun to drift away. Some of them, tired of watching the efforts of the Fire Brigade at Lawrence's, crowded over to one of the few unlooted shoe shops left in the street. Shortly afterward this shop, too, broke into flames. Escorted by only a few men, Brennan Whitmore faced the mob and threatened to fire on them if they did not clear off. Two men were particularly obstinate, so he dispatched a messenger to Connolly asking permission to arrest and shoot them both as an example. Meanwhile he held them prisoners, despite the jeers of the crowd. Connolly replied, forbidding him to harm the men, and reluctantly Whitmore let them go.

The thwarted mob now went raging away up Sackville

186

Street, and Connolly ordered a few warning volleys to be loosed over their heads. He really had no time to deal with looters. Although the military had not tried to repeat their Lancers' charge, intermittent sniping on rebel positions in Sackville Street had opened up from three different places: the roof of Trinity College where the Canadians and Anzacs, aided by the O.T.C. and units of the Leinster Regiment were heavily entrenched; from a shop called McBirney's, a little way along the Quays on the far side of the river; and from the tower of Amiens Street Station.

In spite of specific orders not to fire back—Pearse and Connolly still hoped that Irish regiments could be induced to defect—a Volunteer named Gallagher silenced a sniper on the roof of Trinity, and some of the men took an odd pot shot at Amiens Street Station. By now the occasional crack of a bullet no longer scared the mob, possibly because they guessed that the insurgents were only trying to frighten them. But bullets are wild and uncontrollable things, especially in the hands of inexperienced marksmen. Despite Connolly's orders, a man and a woman were shot dead while standing beside the fire engine at the corner of Henry and Sackville Streets; and another man, brother of one of the Brigade turncocks, was killed while standing beside the engine driver in Cathedral Place. Not that all the casualties were caused by the rebels. The military sniper in McBirney's, trying to knock over one of the three-man garrison at Hopkins and Hopkins, missed him and killed a young woman instead.

The crowd did not seem to care much. The possibility of being killed by a stray bullet was a small price to pay for a front seat at an entertainment which would almost certainly never be repeated.

On the whole, the rebels' behavior had been exemplary in so far as looting or drunkenness—the traditional curses of Ireland—were concerned. Although most of the men were accustomed to the borderline of poverty, it is never recorded that any man took or "commandeered" anything other than what was essential for operations. The absence of drunkenness among men supposedly wedded to the enjoyment of a

187

"pint" was striking. Colonel Brereton, a prisoner in the Four Courts, afterward paid tribute to the self-control of men who, although exposed to the temptation of one of the finest cellars in Ireland, resolutely refused to touch liquor. In one instance, while breaking their way through shops toward South King Street, the men under Sergeant Frank Robbins entered a brandy store; not a drop was sampled and the only bottles taken were sent back to the Red Cross post in the College of Surgeons. In the G.P.O., some men were offered bottles of stout by grateful publicans after the rebels had saved their premises from looters. One man, as he raised the bottle to his lips, had it dashed to the floor by an officer, who fiercely reprimanded him for forgetting that his country's honor was at stake.

Shortly after dusk, when Commander Daly learned that the military had carried away his barricades in the North Circular and Cabra roads, he attempted to interfere with their progress by occupying the Broadstone Station. Daly had originally intended to make the station one of the focal points of the area under his command and, indeed, Captain Denis O'Callaghan and a smal party had been dispatched to seize it at noon on Monday. O'Callaghan, however, on his own initiative, had decided to go no farther than North Brunswick Street, believing that he had insufficient men to carry out orders. Now, with twelve men, including young Garry Holohan, he was sent to take it if the military had not forestalled him.

The mission proved abortive; within fifty yards of the main station entrance, Holohan saw a figure flit across the carriage entrance, followed almost immediately by his friend Edward Martin, screaming, "Garry, I'm shot!" After a brisk exchange, the insurgents, deciding that the station was too strongly held, retreated.

Daly's men were again repulsed a little later when they attempted to burn the Lancers, under Lieutenant Hunter, out of the Medical Mission in Charles Street. A party firing from the Chancery Lane gate of the Four Courts, peppered the Mission while two Volunteers, carrying rags and paper soaked in oil, flung their incendiary bundle through a window. The "bomb" proved ineffective, however, being easily dowsed by the military inside, and as the two Volunteers scrambled back to their base, one of them, Paddy Daly, was badly wounded.

At 10 P.M. precisely the rebels in the College of Surgeons began an intensive fire on the Shelbourne Hotel and the United Services Club. The military replied with their machine guns. Meanwhile a small rebel party waited for the signal to dash across the top of Grafton Street and take the premises on the north side of the Green, before setting them on fire. But even while the shooting was at its height, the Countess Markievicz gave an order to cease fire, explaining, "The idea has been abandoned."

When the din had died down, Robbins heard someone shouting loudly in a high-pitched voice, and found that Private Patrick Poole of the Citizen Army, deafened by the firing, still thought he was talking in conversational tones.

Strain and effort, indeed, were taking their toll. Sergeant Joseph Doyle fainted—not surprisingly, as he had been three days without rest and proper food. A little later Robbins himself, having slept for only two hours out of the past sixty, fell asleep with his rifle still pointing toward the Shelbourne.

In the G.P.O., Joseph Sweeney remembers, some of the men began to imagine things, to think that they could see queer faces in the sky. Hunger and weariness were exacting a price with no help from the forces of Government.

Brennan Whitmore had to admire the woman's spirit. He had first caught sight of her when she was halfway across Sackville Street, walking as if to say, "Take this nonsensical Rebellion out of my way." She teetered right past him, without even looking at him, and marched straight toward his barricade. In astonishment, he let her pass, then went after her and stopped her.

"I'm sorry, but I'm afraid you can't go this way," he said, as politely as he could. "The street is blocked."

"And what right have you to block up the street and prevent decent people going home?"

189

"Sure, haven't you only got to walk a few yards farther down the street and then you can get round easily enough. Surely that isn't too much to ask under the circumstances?" he pointed out, trying to be reasonable.

"I've gone home this way all my life and I'm going home this way tonight, and I'd like to see anyone try and stop me."

"You might break your neck," he said, as she strode to the barricade.

"It's my neck," she retorted, "and if I do break it, it's your fault." And with that she began to climb it. The crowd cheered. One man shouted a word of encouragement which led to her undoing. Angrily she turned to answer him and her foot slipped. Down she came in a tangle of petticoats, the crowd roaring hilariously. Furious, she got to her feet, and with arms akimbo, gave them a tongue lashing. Then, to renewed cheering, she returned to the barricade. After slipping once or twice, she reached the crest. On the way down the far side, however, a chair collapsed under her and she again lost her balance. For a second time the predominantly male crowd was entertained by the sight of her pretty underwear; then she rose and roundly abused the "awful Shinners" before continuing on her way.

At midnight Northumberland Road lay quiet and deserted. Lieutenant Michael Malone called James Grace downstairs and said, "Look, Jimmy, we haven't a chance. The odds against us are overwhelming and the Germans haven't arrived. I'd like to send young Rowe and Byrne away. They're not even sixteen yet, and the chances are they'll lose their lives if they stay on in this house."

"I certainly agree with you," said Grace.

Malone called the two boys and explained the situation. A few minutes later they crept through the skylight and slipped away over the roofs. When they had gone, Grace suddenly realized how gray and haggard Malone looked, partly because of strain, presumably, and partly because he had not slept for nearly four nights.

"Why don't you go to bed for a while?" he suggested. Malone, too tired to answer, simply nodded his head.

190

Left to himself, Grace fixed up some booby traps in the hall and on the stairs and then positioned himself at the drawing-room window, rifle across his knees. Shortly afterward he dozed off. . . . It was light when he awoke.

Shortly after midnight sixty-six men who had controlled the suburb of Fairview since noon on Monday joined the main insurgent army in the G.P.O. Their arrival was the first piece of evidence that the military's pressure was becoming effective.

One man, Volunteer Charles Saurin, missed Pearse's welcoming address—during which he declared that Dublin had redeemed her honor—because he had slipped and cut his hand on glass littering the pavement. After his wound had been dressed, he rejoined his battalion and found the women serving large slabs of cake—hardly the most nourishing food for half-famished men. Almost at once members of his battalion were ordered to occupy the buildings between the G.P.O. and Middle Abbey Street, and Saurin was included with the twenty-two men who were lined up in the street and briefly addressed by Connolly. He listened to Lieutenant Oscar Traynor protest that he felt unfitted to command a whole block, and to Connolly reply brusquely, "Isn't it enough for you that I tell you?"

When the party entered the Metropole, two waiters escorted them to Mr. Oliver, the manager, who was in the foyer with his wife. Traynor explained his mission and Mr. Oliver simply shrugged and stood aside. Mrs. Oliver asked Saurin if he could get her a taxi as she wanted to go to Westland Row Station. Saurin replied that he was sorry, but it was not possible. She then asked him if he could provide an escort of Volunteers so that she and her husband could walk safely through the streets. Saurin pointed out that this was certain to get them fired on by the military.

"What about my personal property?" she then asked. "My dresses, my coats?"

"They'll be perfectly safe," he assured her.

"Well, thank you very much for being so nice when you might easily have been otherwise," she said.

191

Downstairs in the smokeroom, a Volunteer prodded a harassed-looking individual up to Lieutenant Traynor. "This man's a spy—a British spy in mufti," he declared.

The prisoner seemed a mild-looking individual. "How do you know he's a spy?" Traynor asked.

"Ah," said the Volunteer, "when I said 'Quick march,' he stepped off with the left foot."

Traynor looked despairingly at the ceiling. Then he turned to the prisoner. "Who are you?" he asked.

"I'm a master at Portora Royal School—and I've never been so outraged in my life."

Traynor patted the Volunteer on the shoulder. "Like a good man, will you let him go?" he said.

Half an hour after midnight, some sympathetic civilians arrived at the G.P.O. and told Connolly that strong military forces had come from Phoenix Park and were now in Parnell Square.

The information proved accurate. Connolly, however, misinterpreted it. He thought it meant a major night attack. Like everyone else in Dublin, both he and Pearse believed that the troops would inevitably charge the G.P.O. So he at once ordered all lights extinguished and every point manned from which a rifle could be fired or a hand grenade flung. For the men it meant the end of the weariness and increasing boredom of the past thirty-six hours. As excited as anyone was old Tom Clarke. Grabbing a rifle, he placed himself at a window. No one could remember him looking happier. He was utterly in his element—laughing, joking, peering out into the black night, praying to God every now and then that He would let the English come so that at last he could have a crack at them.

In Boland's Bakery, Section-Commander O'Donoghue, fagged beyond anything he had ever experienced, tried to snatch some sleep. Around 1 A.M. he lay down, but sleep eluded him. After a while someone kicked the soles of his boots. "Get up," said Captain Guilfoyle, "I want you to relieve an outpost down near Beggar's Bush."

O'Donoghue, his eyelids heavy as stones, scrambled leadenfooted along the railway line toward Beggar's Bush. Guilfoyle had told him to occupy a small white house on the right of the track. Nearing it, he discovered some Volunteers lying between the sleepers. "Get down, you fool!" they hissed. He flopped on his stomach and advanced, first crawling over those in front, then through a network of wire. He was about to sidle over the low railway wall when a revolver clicked and someone spoke into his ear: "Who goes there?"

"Volunteer," he answered quickly.

"You're lucky I didn't shoot you," said De Valera. "What are you doing here?"

"Relieving outposts, sir."

"Get back at once!" muttered De Valera angrily. "Don't you know you should never advance when a retirement has been ordered?"

"I was only obeying orders, sir."

"Well, get back."

At 4 A.M. O'Donoghue once again tried to sleep. He had hardly laid his ear against his knapsack when Simon Donnelly kicked his boots. "I want men to dig trenches up toward Westland Row," said Donnelly. O'Donoghue suggested he could find fresher men, and simply refused to budge. Donnelly again kicked his boots. O'Donoghue allowed him to go on kicking until he got fed up and went away. For a blissful hour O'Donoghue enjoyed a state of unconsciousness. Then the cold awakened him and, shivering like a man with a chill, he got up and looked for something with which to cover himself. He was scarcely on his feet when Donnelly again pounced on him. "The very man I want. I've got a job for you," he said.

"My God!" said O'Donoghue. "What is it this time?"

"Will you go to Robert's Yard, next to Clanwilliam House? Take three men and provisions. I'll show you the position. You'll be under Mick Malone. You mightn't get a chance to get back here, but even if you don't—even if we retire—hold on there. Fight to the end."

"H'm," said O'Donoghue, and looked at the sky. The first streaks of dawn were appearing and, from the look of it, it was going to be a glorious day. Then, having considered what Donnelly had said, he remarked, "Aye, indeed—that's certainly a handy one all right!"

18

A few minutes before eight o'clock on Wednesday morning, a low, gray shape nudged its way up the Liffey and dropped anchor opposite the Custom House. This was the *Helga,* a small fisheries patrol boat acting under Admiralty orders. At exactly eight o'clock she opened fire on Liberty Hall. Her aim was ill-judged and instead of bringing the Citizen Army's deserted headquarters tumbling down around the ears of its only occupant, the caretaker, Mr. Peter Ennis, she hit the Loop Line railway bridge with a resounding clang.

Embarrassing as this was for the red-faced crew of the *Helga,* the sound still echoed over Dublin like the crack of doom. Father John Flanagan, priest of the Pro-Cathedral, Marlborough Street, halted the Introit for a brief moment to glance round at his small congregation of less than a dozen women (and one server), and then, somewhat disturbed, resumed Mass. On the roof of Trinity College, Professor John Joly, who had been watching the antics of a ragged urchin driving a looted toy motorcar round Grattan's Monument, laid down his rifle and decided that this meant the end for the Sinn Feiners. In the G.P.O., James Connolly smacked his fist into his palm and said, "By God, they're beaten!" In Hopkins and Hopkins' the garrison of three Volunteers, afraid to go near the windows because of the sniper in Mc-Birney's, rigged up a periscope to enjoy the fun.

The operation to uproot the rebels who were supposedly in Liberty Hall had been mounted after considerable preparation. It was first decided to employ two 9-pounder field guns—but it was not possible to get them into place in time. But in

194

addition to the big gun of the *Helga,* several machine guns were positioned on the roof of the Custom House, in the tower of the nearby Fire Station, and on the roof of Trinity College, ready to slaughter the Sinn Feiners as they were driven out by bombardment. Troops of the Royal Irish Regiment and the Ulster Composite Battalion waited in the Custom House with fixed bayonets to follow up on the onslaught with a gallant charge across Beresford Place. It was by far the biggest military operation yet mounted against the rebels. No one knew that Liberty Hall was empty.

Aboard the *Helga* the guards fiddled with their sights. Two things obstructed a direct bang at the building—the Loop Line railway bridge and a Guinness cargo boat anchored alongside the quay. The alternative was to lob shells over both. Sights were raised, trajectories checked, and finally a second shot was fired. This time the shell landed squarely on top of Liberty Hall, wrecking the interior, although leaving the outer walls intact. Then the dose was quickly repeated.

Reporter John O'Leary, sitting at a window across the river, saw the side door of Liberty Hall open as immense clouds of dust and debris spurted into the air. A figure darted out into the street—Ennis, the caretaker. Immediately two machine guns opened fire. This—in Mr. O'Leary's own words—is what then happened.

A machine gun is turned on him. Bullets hit the pavement in front of him and behind him, they strike the roadway and the walls of the building along his route and still he runs on and on. I hold my breath in awe as I watch his mad career. Will he escape? He will . . . he won't. "My God!" I exclaim as a bullet raises a spark from the pavement right at his toe. A hundred yards in nine seconds—a record! Nonsense, this man does the distance in five and disappears, his breath in his fist, his heart in his mouth but—safe!

For an hour the *Helga* pounded the area, sometimes hitting Liberty Hall, more often missing. A steady stream of rifle and machine-gun fire was poured into the empty building under the impression that terrified rebels were still cowering there, although not a single shot ever came in reply. All that happened was that hundreds of poor people living in the vicinity ran into the streets, and a few got hit. At the end of an hour, the *Helga* smugly withdrew, leaving a cloud of dust hanging hazily in the air. Liberty Hall still stood, but only as a shell. Northumberland House next door had taken a worse battering. As the haze settled, O'Leary saw twenty soldiers emerge from the Custom House and rush across Beresford Square to seal the victory by climbing over the rubble into the ruined building.

The real success of the bombardment was in the damage it did to rebel morale. For the first time in their lives the young rebels had an inkling of what was meant by the words "greatly superior odds." Until then, most of them had simply envisioned enormous numbers of khaki-clad men advancing toward them in a swollen, easy-to-hit mass. The shock of artillery fire, however, deprived them of this idea of a man-to-man fight. To die for Ireland was glorious. But not to be able to hit back. . . !

James Connolly, listening to the boom of the *Helga*'s guns, tried to be reassuring. "Don't be alarmed," he told the men in the G.P.O., "when the British Government uses artillery in the city of Dublin, it shows they must be in a hurry to finish the job—but there are probably some forces coming to help us." To Willie Pearse, indeed, he passed on the good news "that the Germans were about to land." A little later, up in the Instrument Room, he repeated this story to Michael Collins. The time for fine words and promises, however, was nearly past. Sackville Street was beginning to know the steady clip of machine-gun bullets as the gun on the roof of Trinity College belted away fiercely at the two buildings on the opposite corners of O'Connell Bridge—Hopkins and Hopkins on Eden Quay (on the right-hand side from Trinity) Messrs. Kelly's, fishing tackle and gunsmiths, on Bachelor's Walk (on the left-hand side). The fire scattered the crowd which had gathered daily on the corner of D'Olier and Westmoreland Streets, south of the river since Monday afternoon. Once they had been chased into the side streets, the Anzacs on the roof of Trinity and the sniper in McBirney's, on Aston Quay, began a persistent rifle fire. Bullets zipped into rebel-held buildings all the way

196

along Lower Sackville Street. They tore to shreds the proud Starry Plough which Connolly had raised over the Imperial Hotel at seven o'clock that morning. They spattered against the leaden roof of the cupola of the D.B.C. (Dublin Bread Company) Restaurant, from which a small nest of rebel snipers intermittently replied; whizzed into the Wireless School and made it impossible to continue working the transmitter. Sackville Street had become a battleground. The quiet ebb and flow of the first two days of the Rebellion suddenly vanished, an indication of the frightening coils which the military, like some giant boa constrictor, had flung around the city.

The previous evening General Lowe, secure in the knowledge that a whole British division was already on its way from England, had decided to ignore rebel outposts such as the South Dublin Union, Jameson's Distillery, Boland's Bakery, St. Stephen's Green, and the quite impregnable-looking Jacob's, and concentrate on swiftly reducing the two most important rebel positions in the city, the G.P.O. and the Four Courts. His grand strategy was first to draw a single wide cordon round both these places, then to draw two separate smaller cordons round each of them. The first of the small cordons was to run from the Castle along Dame Street to Trinity College, thence across Butt Bridge to the Custom House, and on to Amiens Street Station; then up Gardiner Street into Lower Great Britain Street, across the top of Sackville Street at the Parnell Monument, thence to Capel Street where it would swing back toward the river and then to the Castle again. The second noose, also starting from the Castle, was to run northward directly over the river, up Capel Street, then swing west along North King Street as far as Blackhall Place where it was to make a right-angle turn to the river, and by way of Watling and James streets, terminate at the Castle.

But before either noose could be drawn tight, two obstacles had to be swept away—first, Liberty Hall, which supposedly would interfere with the projected noose around the G.P.O.; second, the Mendicity Institution, which would interfere with the noose around the Four Courts. Consequently, late on Tuesday evening, when General Lowe had been reinforced with artillery and knew that advance units of the 59th Division

197

had already sailed from Liverpool, he decided to attack these two positions early on Wednesday morning. As a result, even while the *Helga* was lobbing her shells into Liberty Hall, Dublin Fusiliers were knocking quietly on doors near the Mendicity Institution, advising the occupants to leave as operations would be commencing shortly in the area. Farther down the river, a position was being prepared for the two 9-pound field guns, a task which had created some difficulty. In deciding to use field guns against Liberty Hall, Lowe had given no thought to the problem of recoil. Under normal circumstances a gun, when fired, drove a spade-shaped plate of iron into the earth, thus "fixing" itself, but the stones of the city streets did not permit this. Holes would therefore have to be dug, but with the rebels entrenched just across the river, such digging presented difficulties. Sometime before the *Helga* opened fire, six volunteers from Trinity O.T.C., dressed as navvies, went out with picks and spades. To the curious spectators who watched them begin work they explained, "Something has gone wrong with the gas main to Trinity College and we've come to put it right." Strangely enough the sight of men laboring away on the far side of the river failed to arouse the curiosity of the rebels in Hopkins and Hopkins' or in Kelly's. They were too concerned in the brief intervals between digging and boring through walls, with attempting to knock over the sniper in McBirney's. Even so, the Trinity men found it hard to make headway. The paving stones, six inches long by four wide, were so well set in tar that the picks could not prise them loose.

Meanwhile, upriver, Dublin Fusiliers filtered along the streets and lanes at the rear of the Mendicity; took up positions behind the wall on the other side of the river while assault parties prepared to attack across the bridge.

In the G.P.O., young Richard MacAuliffe watched the bullets kicking into the walls of the D.B.C. Restaurant and the Reis building across the street until an officer roared at him to get back to work and make his window absolutely bulletproof. Soon he had a wall of ledgers seven feet deep in front of him.

In the small room which was their prison, Lieutenant Mahoney played three-handed bridge with Chalmers and Lieutenant King of the Royal Irish Fusiliers who had been taken prisoner in Sackville Street while spying. Mahoney soon tired of the game and began reading *The Hunchback of Notre Dame,* which The O'Rahilly had sent in to him. So far their treatment had been exemplary. After an excellent breakfast, The O'Rahilly and the rebels' Quartermaster, Desmond Fitzgerald, had interrogated them. Mahoney had asked, "Are you going to shoot us?"

Both had looked at him in horror. "Good God, no—you're prisoners of war!" burst out The O'Rahilly angrily, to which Mahoney replied, "You know I'm a doctor; you shouldn't keep me prisoner."

"If you're a doctor," said Fitzgerald, "we've something for you to do."

On the other side of Sackville Street, Brennan Whitmore warned his men to keep their heads low and to fire only when they had a definite target. Not that it was easy to locate the enemy, for by now the volume of fire had become heavy. He stopped at a window for a moment to watch a machine-gun burst spatter against Kelly's corner, then had to duck as a stream of bullets cut through the window beside his head.

Over the river, reporter O'Leary also ducked as rebel counterfire, most of it coming from snipers in the restaurant cupola, battered the front of buildings along Aston Quay. Deciding that it had become too dangerous to look out, he rigged up a crude periscope, using two mirrors. Through this, at approximately 11:50 A.M. he saw three young women emerge from the G.P.O. under a Red Cross flag. Firing died away almost instantly and for two minutes not a shot broke the silence as the women crossed to the Hibernian Bank. The moment they disappeared, the rifles and machine guns opened up with renewed fury.

While Sackville Street became a battleground, James Stephens, less than half a mile away was able to walk through the streets and enjoy the sun, stop to read Wimborne's Proclamation of Martial Law (which had been posted everywhere except in rebel-held areas), and chat with friends or acquaintances. He found most people still smiling and gay. Few of his friends had any sympathy for the rebels—"I hope every man will be shot," one woman told him—yet some felt an odd sense of gratitude toward them.

"Of course they'll be beaten, but at least they're putting up a decent fight," explained one man, and this seemed to epitomize the city's attitude toward the rising.

In St. Stephen's Green, small boys darted in and out of the Park gates, picking up rifles and bandoliers abandoned by the rebels, and skipping out again quickly as bursts of fire broke over their heads. All firing ceased, however, when Mr. James Kearney, the park keeper, entered the Green to feed the ducks; twice daily both sides observed a truce to allow him to perform this duty.

In Portobello Barracks, after a night of prayer, Captain Bowen-Colthurst's mind was made up. At five minutes past ten he informed Sergeant William Aldridge of the Dublin Fusiliers that he wanted the prisoners Sheehy-Skeffington, Dickson, and MacIntyre brought into the yard behind the guardroom and shot. He ordered seven men to come with him as escort for the prisoners. As they moved out, Bowen-Colthurst bumped into Lieutenant William Dobbyn of the Royal Irish Fusiliers. Quickly he explained, "I'm taking these men out of the guard-room and I'm going to shoot them. I think it's the right thing to do."

He marched the three unfortunates into the Yard, then ordered them to walk by themselves to the far wall. As they obeyed, he ordered the escort party to present arms, then gave the command: "Fire!"

Dobbyn, hearing the shots, walked into the Yard in time to meet Bowen-Colthurst coming away; the captain seemed calm and not excited. While Dobbyn was examining the three bodies, he noticed a movement in one of Sheehy-Skeffington's legs, and sent Lieutenant Tooley to the orderly room to report this and ask what was to be done. Bowen-Colthurst sent back the message: "Shoot again," and Dobbyn reluctantly stood by while four soldiers complied with the order.

Fifteen minutes later Bowen-Colthurst reported the shooting to Lieutenant Morgan, saying that he had feared an armed attempt might be made to rescue the men. He then mumbled

200

something about having "lost a brother in this way" and "I'm as good an Irishman as they are." As he crossed Barrack Square on the way to the mess, he ran into Major James Rossborough, who was temporarily in command of the barracks, and reported that he had shot three prisoners, adding, "I suppose I'll get into trouble for it." Rossborough, shaken by the enormity of the offense, could only stare at him astonished.

Although the military had the Mendicity completely surrounded, Volunteer John MacLoughlin found it easy to sneak in and out whenever he wished. By this time the youthful garrison were both hungry and short of ammunition, for it had never been Connolly's intention that young Heuston (promoted Commandant on Easter Monday morning, owing to the shortage of officers) should occupy the place for more than a few hours; consequently no stocks of food and ammunition had been laid in. Heuston's role, indeed, as envisaged by Connolly, had been simply to harry any military advancing from Richmond or Royal Barracks and prevent them from attacking the Four Courts before the rebels there could entrench themselves. In pursuance of these orders, Heuston had opened fire on the Dublin Fusiliers on Monday as they marched to the relief of Dublin Castle and since then he had been under continuous siege.

A tall, lanky lad, hardly sixteen, MacLoughlin had been able to move in and out because he was no different from a hundred other youngsters who, drawn by curiosity, wandered at will about the area. He had managed to obtain small supplies of food and extra ammunition for the hard-pressed garrison and to fetch and carry dispatches between Heuston and G.H.Q. Heuston himself—and, indeed, almost his entire garrison—probably could have sneaked out almost any time without the military being any the wiser, but Heuston gallantly never thought of this alternative. By Wednesday midday, however, there was no longer any question of anybody getting out.

MacLoughlin had sneaked through early that morning with a dispatch for Commandant Connolly. Toward noon, on his way back via Queen Street Bridge, he heard the attack beginning on the Mendicity. On the bridge itself large forces of troops were moving across under heavy fire. Despite the bullets, a crowd had collected at the north end of the bridge, enjoying the operation as though it were a football match. As Mac-Loughlin edged forward among them, he was recognized as a rebel by a woman who shouted, "There's another of them!" MacLoughlin turned and ran until he reached the safety of Commandant Daly's headquarters in Church Street. Daly, commanding the Four Courts region, had chosen to direct operations from the Father Mathew Hall.

The military, meantime, pressed home their attack. One party crept stealthily under cover along the wall fronting the Mendicity, then leaped up suddenly and tossed bomb after bomb through the windows. Inside there was pandemonium. But the young rebels, quickly recovering themselves, grabbed for the bombs as they dropped to the floor and hurled them back—a desperate effort which cost them four men. After a ferocious and sustained attack, lasting just under fifteen minutes, Heuston hung out a white flag, and within an hour after the whole operation commenced, twenty young rebels marched out to a rough reception from the infuriated Dublin Fusiliers.

All was ready now for General Lowe to draw his noose tight around the Four Courts.

Inside the noose, Daly struggled to maintain the brave spirit of the early hours of the insurrection. Approximately one hundred yards to the north of North King Street lay Linenhall Barracks, among the oldest military establishments in Dublin. By 1916, the barracks were no longer used to house fighting troops, but had been turned over to the Army Pay Corps, forty of whose members had been cooped up inside it since the Rebellion started. Toward noon, a rebel party under Captain Denis O'Callaghan marched up to the main gates and demanded the garrison's surrender. Courageously the half-trained soldiers refused to give in, forcing O'Callaghan to blow a hole in the barracks wall. Once the rebels began to pour in, the garrison raised the white flag and were marched to the Father Mathew Hall (where their services were requisitioned to help bake bread and fill sandbags).

Although Daly knew that this was hardly tit for tat, the op-

202

eration succeeded in its primary aim—which was to make his men feel that all was not yet lost.

Toward midday the weight of military fire directed against the east side of Lower Sackville Street had finally begun to tell. Volunteer Lieutenant "Blimey" O'Connor (he had a cockney accent), and Volunteers O'Kelly and Bourke, finding they could no longer operate the wireless transmitter, obtained permission from Connolly to transfer vital parts to the G.P.O., where they hoped to set it up again. During a lull, the party ran across Sackville Street, carrying pieces of apparatus in an upturned table, but when it became apparent that it would take at least half a dozen trips to transport all the material, the idea was called off.

By 12:30 firing had become desultory again and a crowd gathered beside the monument to the Emancipator, Daniel O'Connell, immediately north of the bridge. This seemed to irk the sniper in McBirney's, who opened fire. At once a machine gun started up in sympathy, and bullets danced off O'Connell's Monument, sending sparks in all directions. The crowd scattered across the bridge to the comparative shelter of D'Olier Street corner.

Connolly had been carefully observing the effect of the sustained fire on the Dublin Bread Company cupola. He was afraid that machine-gun bullets would pierce its fragile lead covering and wipe out the handful of men he had placed there. It was far more important that they make observations for him than it was to use the cupola as a sniper's post. He had to know from what direction and in what strength the military were closing in upon him, for he felt certain that the long-awaited direct assault on the Post Office would not be delayed much longer. Accordingly he dispatched a messenger ordering these men to stop firing and give the military the impression that the place had been evacuated. The message, delivered orally, was misinterpreted and the tower *was* actually evacuated. Shortly before one o'clock, reporter O'Leary watched its garrison run across Sackville Street in single file, bullets kicking all around them.

It was a poignant moment in O'Leary's day when a door

opened along Eden Quay less than twenty yards from Hopkins and Hopkins', and a blind man emerged. O'Leary saw him putter toward the corner, his white stick probing the way in front of him. After a moment of hesitation he stepped off the footpath and headed toward the Monument. Perhaps the McBirney sniper failed to realize that the man was blind; whatever the reason, he fired on him and the old man fell. From the south side of the bridge, Mr. Henry Olds, of the St. John's Ambulance Brigade, ran to his assistance. He knelt down, took off the blind man's coat and vest and folded a bandage with which he bound the wound. Then he helped the man to his feet and led him across the bridge. The McBirney sniper ruthlessly fired again, twice, both shots finding their mark. Down went the two men—and lay prone. A little later an ambulance drove onto the bridge, picked up the two bodies, and drove away. . . .

A hush fell over the battlefield. O'Leary thought it an ominous prelude.

(19)

On Tuesday night, from ten o'clock on, units of the 178th Brigade had been arriving at Kingstown. They consisted for the most part of a bewildered and seasick bunch of English Midlanders. Half of them still had the impression that they had landed in France, and even next morning a soldier greeted a girl, "Bonjour, ma'moiselle."

Food was short, because kitchens and transport had not yet arrived. Most of the men had only iron rations to munch on, supplemented by tuppeny sandwiches from stalls quickly set up by some local entrepreneurs. Men of the 2/5th and 2/6th were luckier—for them there was crisp bacon and eggs under the pine trees in school grounds about a mile outside of town.

For the officers, there was a civilized breakfast at the Yacht Club and animated conversation with the members, who had information about the fighting. At 8:30 A.M. the Brigadier, Colonel Maconchy, called a conference of officers and issued these verbal instructions:

"(1) The rebels are known to be preparing to oppose the movement of troops from Kingstown to Dublin.

"(2) Troops will therefore advance in two parallel columns; the left, consisting of the 2/5th and 2/6th Sherwood Foresters (Derbyshire troops) will advance by the inland Stillorgan-Donnybrook route; the right, comprising the 2/7th and 2/8th (Nottinghamshire troops) will follow the coast road through Ballsbridge. Destination in both cases—the Royal Hospital, Kilmainham. Starting point: Kingstown Harbour 10:30 A.M.

"(3) The right column will be led by the Robin Hoods (the

2/7th). Order of Companies: first 'C' Company (Captain F. Pragnell), second 'A' (Captain H. C. Wright), three 'B' (Major H. Hanson), four 'D' (Captain L. L. Cooper). O.C. Advance Guard will dispose his platoons as follows: one in advance, one to clear houses overlooking the road, one to deal with side roads, one in support. Every house and side road will be searched and cleared.

"(4) Fall in: 10:15 A.M."

At 10 A.M. the troops charged magazines. Lieutenant-Colonel W. Coape Oates, an old Munster Fusilier who commanded the 2/8th, conscious that most of his men had seen less than three months' service, ordered them down to the quayside to do it "so that," as he put it later, "apart from the limited amount of danger to fishing smacks, little risk was run." Even so, shots peppered the clear Irish sky and Colonel Oates rode down on horseback and angrily warned, "Any man in any platoon who lets off a shot will be considered to have disgraced the whole platoon and will be sent back to England." Aboard a transport approaching the harbor was Wilfred Tunley of Field Ambulance, who remembers that they were ordered, "Keep your heads down, the rebels are sniping."

In fresh, glorious sunshine, then—the Irish countryside so quiet and peaceful that Colonel Oates found it impossible to imagine that less than six miles away bloody murder was happening—the 2/5th and 2/6th Sherwoods moved off. Fifteen minutes later the right column followed, with the 2/7th in the van, and the C.O., Lieutenant-Colonel Cecil Fane, C.M.G., D.S.O.—an experienced cavalry officer and Mons veteran—leading the advance guard. Major F. Rayner headed the main body. The 2/8th followed at an interval of four hundred yards, touch being maintained between the two battalions by Lieutenant W. Hewitt, commanding a party of battalion scouts. Their minds filled with bloody details supplied in embellished form by a newspaper seller on Kingstown pier, the men were hardly prepared for the welcome they received. As they reached the outer, well-to-do suburbs, hot and laden down with full marching equipment, doors opened and maids came down the steps with steaming pots of tea, followed by their

206

mistresses bringing trays with cups. Chocolates, oranges, bananas, sandwiches, sweets were pressed on the men.

The officers welcomed the break. Expecting to be ambushed at any moment, they were grateful for the scraps of information eagerly offered. Some residents brought out maps and field glasses.

Fortified, the right column resumed its march toward Ballsbridge. The left, after experiencing similar hospitable treatment, pressed on warily. Lacking a leader who knew Ireland as well as Colonel Oates did, officers of the 2/5th and 2/6th suspected all hospitality and word was passed down the line that the troops were not to accept any gifts, especially of food and drink. Word filtered among the troops that the Sinn Feiners were trying to poison them, and by the time the column reached Donnybrook, men were swearing blindly that they had personally seen chaps keel over, foaming at the mouth and gripping their bellies.

For Captain F. C. Dietrichsen, a Nottingham barrister in private life, then Adjutant of the 2/7th, the march brought a pleasant surprise. Fellow officers saw him drop out of the column and fling his arms around two young children. Unknown to him, his wife, fearing the Zeppelin raids, had sent the children from England to stay with her parents outside Dublin. Neither the father nor the children had anticipated such a fortuitous meeting—nor could they guess that they would never see each other again.

By midday the right wing had reached the Ballsbridge Showgrounds, where they glimpsed a melee of prize bulls, heifers, fine hunters, and innumerable agricultural implements, before Brigadier-General L. B. Carleton of the 177th Brigade and Colonel Maconchy established temporary headquarters in the Town Hall. Staff quickly gathered intelligence—most of it inaccurate—and Colonels Fane and Oates were told to expect opposition at Mount Street Bridge *where the rebels were known to be holding some schools* on the right-hand side of the road. Fane was ordered to take this position and then push on into the city.

After a short halt, the column resumed its march, moving

warily. At approximately 12:15, it rested again near an imposing residence known as Carrisbrooke House. People were friendly and gathered around to talk. Then, abruptly, several shots rang out. Taken by surprise, and under fire for the first time in their lives, the young soldiers reacted admirably. On orders from Colonel Fane and Major Rayner, they dispersed rapidly. The shots seemed to be coming from Carrisbrooke House, so, from the cover of walls and shop doorways, the troops answered back fiercely, and smashed all the front windows. Rapid fire was kept up on both house and gardens (where some of the Blackrock Company of Volunteers were lurking) while a small party advanced to the attack. They found the house empty and, leaving a platoon to search the grounds, Fane continued his advance.

Flankers were sent forward in Indian file. Behind them the main body advanced at short intervals, dropping flat on the roadway between times while scouts reconnoitered. Fane led the van, along with a Nottingham accountant, Captain Frank Pragnell of "C" Company, Captain Dietrichsen, and a party of stretcher bearers under Captain E. P. Stachell, R.A.M.C. Anxious about his right flank, where the rebels were known to be holding the railway line, Fane detached a platoon under twenty-year-old Lieutenant William Foster of Southwell, Nottinghamshire, to make a reconnaissance. Then, while still about a quarter of a mile from Mount Street Bridge, Fane halted his men. They were now into Northumberland Road and expected action at any moment. Fane ordered the main body under Major Rayner to wait in St. Mary's Road, running off to the left, while he and Captain Pragnell's company reconnoitered.

Fane could not yet see the Schools—they were beyond a slight bend in the road. On each side were substantial middle-class homes, with trim front lawns and tiled passages leading up to the front steps. Northumberland Road was as quiet and well-ordered as Kensington itself. Bloodshed and violence seemed far away and quite unreal.

In the drawing room of Clanwilliam House, seven young rebels sat around an ornate table munching steak sandwiches. Beside them lay their rifles, sights set at three hundred yards.

208

All morning they had listened to the far-off boom of a field gun and the crackle of steady rifle fire. Time had dragged slowly. Young Tom Walshe, moving around the house, picked up a magazine or newspaper, glanced at it, put it down again; then went to the window to gaze out at a vista which had become irksomely familiar.

The Walshe brothers had spent the night at the back drawing-room windows, crouched on a red plush settee and two armchairs, watching the sinister shadows in Lower Mount Street and fighting off a desire to sleep. Beside them lay a box of Mauser ammunition, the seals unbroken, bearing the label "Hamburg." Tom had two hundred rounds for his Howth Mauser and a .45 revolver with sixty rounds, Jim a .32 with fifty.

At eleven that morning, as Tom Walshe was taking in a parcel of food brought by his young brother, a man cycled past and shouted up, "The British have landed in Kingstown and are marching on the city—yez'd better watch out!"

Reynolds at once gave orders to fix sights at three hundred yards, at the same time warning the men not to waste ammunition by firing aimlessly. All knelt and prayed, then rose and went to their posts.

There were three windows in the room. Patrick Doyle and Dick Murphy knelt at the one on the right, Reynolds took the one in the middle, and young Jimmy Doyle and Willie Ronan the one on the left.

Scared though he was, Tom Walshe opened his food parcel and, realizing that this could well be their last meal on earth, decided to share it.

"Here," he said, placing the parcel on the table, "help yourselves."

They were sitting there, quietly munching, glancing now and then out of the window up the Northumberland Road, when suddenly they heard a volley.

Toward noon Jimmy Grace saw his sister Bridget and a Miss May Cullen of the Cumann na mBan come along the Northumberland Road, carrying what appeared to be a package of food. They approached No. 25 and hammered on the door. Cautiously Grace leaned out and explained that he could not let them in—the door was barricaded.

"We've got a dispatch," said his sister.

"You'd better put it in the letter box," he said.

"What about the food?"

"Thanks all the same—but I'm afraid we'll have to do without it."

The dispatch was from Connolly, warning Malone that British troops had arrived at Kingstown during the night and were reported to be marching on Dublin. If they advanced along Northumberland Road, every effort was to be made to stop them.

"Well," said Malone, handing the slip of typed paper to Grace, "this is it!"

Grace read the message and murmured, "Yes, this is it."

Malone said, "I wonder . . . should we move into Carrisbrooke House?" The mansion, situated roughly half a mile farther out toward Kingstown should have been occupied by fourteen Volunteers from the Blackrock Company, but Malone had discovered, reconnoitering during the night, that they had left it, and taken up isolated positions in the grounds and in nearby fields. Carrisbrooke House was in many ways a more important position than No. 25. It stood at the fork of Pembroke and Northumberland roads—Pembroke continuing left toward Baggott Street Bridge, Northumberland right toward Mount Street Bridge. If the English troops took the Pembroke route, they would outflank the rebel positions at Mount Street, and there would be nothing to stop them until they reached St. Stephen's Green. Malone had made up his mind to move into Carrisbrooke House when he decided to have a quick look out the bathroom window, which gave a view up Northumberland Road toward Ballsbridge. Grace heard Malone call out and rushed to join him.

"Look, Seamus!" said Malone.

Through the field glasses Malone handed him, Grace could see, near St. Mary's Road, several military officers, backed by a large body of troops, poring over maps. When he focused the glasses along the quarter-mile of Northumberland Road which lay between him and the officers, into his sights jumped the tight, strained faces of young English soldiers, advancing toward them with fixed bayonets.

The first volley from No. 25 Northumberland Road, recalls Captain Frank Pragnell, claimed ten Sherwood Foresters—youngsters who, a few months previously, had been clerks or shop assistants or workers in the leather, lace, and tobacco industries; lads who had hardly learned how to fire a rifle.

A little surprised, because neither he nor Fane had expected to meet opposition until they were nearer the schools, Pragnell yelled, "Drop!" and hit the ground. In that first terrible second it was impossible to tell where the shots had come from. A second fusillade resolved some doubts. "There!" shouted Pragnell, pointing, "that house there. Prepare to fire!" And the youngsters, taking aim, fired a volley in reply. Suddenly a young soldier dropped his rifle, clutching at his shoulder and crying out, "Oh, God, I've been shot!" Pragnell wriggled over to help him. Then he bawled, "Good God, man! You're not hurt—it's only the recoil. Pick up that rifle!"

For several minutes the troops remained pinned. Beside Pragnell a young soldier screamed in agony as a bullet tore away a piece of his backside. Then, as Malone and Grace paused for breath, Fane and Pragnell rose to their feet, drew their swords, and shouted, "Charge!"

In Clanwilliam House, Patrick Doyle, the oldest man there, warned his comrades hoarsely, "For God's sake, keep steady!" Section-Commander Reynolds said coolly, "Remove safety catches." Then away up at Haddington Road James Doyle saw a mass of khaki uniforms charging toward No. 25. Some dropped on one knee in the roadway to fire up at the windows while the rest courageously charged up the stone steps to the door.

"Fire!" yelled Reynolds, and the crash of the Howths in the confined space sounded as terrible as artillery. Young Doyle saw seven soldiers fall and the rest scatter. Flashes of fire spurted from No. 25 and Reynolds shouted, "Good old Mick!" Doyle was pleased with himself after his first taste of action. He felt capable of stopping the whole British Army if they marched down Northumberland Road.

To Malone and Grace, firing bullets into the Robin Hoods at point-blank range, the young Tommies seemed utterly lost. To Captain Pragnell, crouched in the lee of railings with Colonel Fane, after retreating from No. 25, the problem was to find out exactly where the fire was coming from; it appeared to come from half a dozen directions at the same time. Fane decided to lay down heavy fire along both sides of the road, with special emphasis on No. 25, from which firing was certainly coming, and the Schools near the bridge, which, according to Intelligence, would provide the main opposition. He also decided to outflank and then encircle No. 25 by sending Major Hanson and "B" Company to secure Baggott Street Bridge and then filter back down along the Canal bank to Mount Street Bridge. For the tall, good-looking Fane it was to prove a costly decision.

Hanson led his men toward the corner of Haddington Road, supported by heavy fire from other companies who simply sprayed the area indiscriminately. "We listen to the sound of battle," wrote a lady living nearby. "There seem to be many men engaged: we think there are some in our garden or on the steps. The soldiers are attacking the two corner houses—No. 25 opposite and No. 26 and 28 on our side of Northumberland Road."

As Hanson led his men into Haddington Road, Malone, crouched at the bathroom window with his high-powered "Peter the Painter," cut down most of them.

Despite his losses, Hanson pressed on. Once through, he found everything peaceful, yet he advanced toward Baggott Street Bridge with extreme caution. He had already learned that appearances in this weird kind of fighting could be deceptive. Far cry, indeed, from the type of warfare for which he and the regiment had been trained—the trench warfare of France.

In Northumberland Road, Colonel Fane buckled as a Howth bullet did terrible havoc to his left arm. Stretcher bearers rushed forward, but he waved them away. Then, calling on Major Rayner to take command, he staggered to the lee of the houses on the same side of the road as No. 25 and had his wound treated.

When Lieutenant Foster returned from his reconnaissance toward Beggar's Bush Barracks, he found Major Rayner scorning cover, directing the battle from the center of the road. It was an inspiring act, equaled only by the Colonel's own example when he returned, with his arm in a sling, and clearly in pain, to resume command. The young recruits, undergoing their baptism of fire, bewildered by their inability to find or hit back at the lurking enemy, were steadied by the example of their two senior officers. Foster took cover in the garden of a house opposite No. 25, directing the fire of his men through the iron railings. Other companies occupied the windows of the houses beside him and kept up furious fire on the beleaguered rebels while their comrades attempted to advance toward Mount Street Bridge. But before they reached Haddington Road, concentrated fire from Malone and Grace claimed heavy casualties.

Inside No. 25, the two rebels found themselves in a strong position. Grace, firing from a top window, found enemy bullets either ploughing into the ceiling or striking the sill in front of him in a continuous patter. The enemy at this time appeared to be directing their main fire at the ground- and first-floor windows. Malone, from the bathroom window at the side of the house, found he could enfilade and cut to ribbons every attempt to advance past Haddington Road.

From Clanwilliam House, young Jimmy Doyle watched stretcher bearers carrying the British wounded back to Ballsbridge. Now and then firing would cease altogether to allow ambulance men to pick up the dead and wounded. So far the military had not actually fired on Clanwilliam House, apparently still unaware that it was unoccupied. Presently the first chatter of machine-gun fire was heard, and George Reynolds asked if anyone could locate it. "It seems to be in the Baggott Street direction," he suggested. "By the way, be careful if you see anybody on the roofs over there—it could be Mick or Jimmy Grace trying to get away."

Doyle nodded and turned his attention back to Haddington Road. He watched as the military again attempted to storm Malone's post. There were brief flashes of fire from the house and again Reynolds roared, "Good old Mick—that's the stuff!"

At Baggott Street Bridge, Major Hanson, satisfied that the area was free of rebels, posted a platoon to guard the bridge and started doubling back along the Canal bank into Percy Place. He saw the low, huddled clump of buildings which were the Schools, the windows bright with the reflection of sunlight. He advanced cautiously.

The battle had been raging for almost an hour now. As yet, neither Tom Walshe nor his brother had been in action. Suddenly Tom, his ears cocking to the crackle of rifle fire from beyond the bridge, saw a khaki figure dart out of Percy Lane and run up the steps of a house four doors from the bridge. As the man hammered on the door, Tom had an easy target. He fired—for the first time in his life—and he paid for his inexperience and his neglect of company lectures: he felt a stunning blow and knew no more. His brother, who had been sent upstairs a short while before, watched a second soldier join the first at the door of the house, and fired. He saw one man drop and the other dive from the door and start running. Jim feverishly reloaded. His next shot hit the second man and he, too, tumbled over.

To Hanson and his men, crouching under the Canal railings, it looked as though the two soldiers had been shot down from the house they had been attempting to enter. Immediately they opened fire on it. A lady in the house next door, who had been watching from her window through field glasses, screamed and tumbled back into the room as a stray bullet hit her. Within seconds no less than fifty bullets had embedded themselves in the bedroom ceiling of the house under attack. Yelling fiercely to give themselves courage, the men charged forward under a screen of fire and began battering on the front door. When they got inside, they found a terrified lady, Miss Scully, and her maid cowering behind a settee, and promptly arrested them.

Tom Walshe regained consciousness to find that a chunk of the window sill in front of him—which was made of granite—had been blown away, and that he had been knocked out by the recoil of his own rifle. It took him several minutes to recover and he still felt shaky when he picked up the Howth again and peered out cautiously to see where the enemy were

214

now. A number of them were trying to make their way down Percy Place, crouching and kneeling, then running in short dashes, before making for cover.

Under attack from the other men in the front drawing room, they were dropping all over the place. It seemed as good a moment as any to join in. He cuddled the butt of the Howth tight against his shoulder and, swiftly running over in his mind all he could remember of the lectures on how to fire a rifle correctly, he squeezed the trigger. This time he did it right. The bullet crossed the bright Canal and struck somewhere among the crouching, darting soldiers, but Tom was unable to tell whether he had hit anyone.

At two o'clock that afternoon the military began occupying buildings along Aston Quay, where reporter John O'Leary sat watching Sackville Street through his twin-mirrored periscope. Quickly they positioned themselves at windows or swarmed out onto the roofs, placing a machine gun behind the parapet of Purcell's, which stood on the apex of the triangular block dividing Westmoreland and D'Olier streets. From across the river the rebels in Kelly's observed this movement, and bullets began to pepper O'Leary's window. Two carried away the upper mirror of his periscope, showering glass over him and toppling him from his comfortable seat. He picked himself up, discovered he was unhurt and, quickly regaining courage, crouched down below the level of the window sill and peered out.

The two 9-pounders from Trinity College opened fire almost simultaneously. At their first report every pane of glass in the vicinity shattered; in Trinity itself the solid buildings quaked. In the G.P.O., the boom shook the walls, and the rebels looked at each other in consternation. No one quite knew what had happened and somebody shouted that the bombs downstairs must have blown up, but a second great boom resolved all doubts. It was artillery.

The shells cleaved the river and tore two fairly large holes in the façade of Kelly's. Simultaneously machine guns on the tower of the Fire Station, the roof of the Custom House, the Tivoli Theatre, and Purcell's corner added to the battle noise. When James Stephens arrived at O'Connell Bridge a few minutes later, he counted six machine guns in action. Rifles

216

were also potting at Kelly's from every conceivable angle and, at regular intervals of half a minute, the 9-pounders would lob a shell through its windows.

The guns had been manhandled into position under the very noses of the rebels, who put up no opposition. After fruitless hours had been spent trying to dig holes for the re-coil, Colonel Portal impatiently ordered that the guns were to be trundled into position, with or without holes, and brought into action at once. The Brunswick Street gate of Trinity was swung open shortly afterward and horses were driven out, trailing the guns on limbers. The horses drew them into side streets where they were unlimbered and then manhandled onto the Quay by a party of O.T.C. and civilians. Under bombard-ment, clouds of red dust and smoke soon rose over Kelly's.

"Not even a fly can be alive in that house," said an awe-struck man beside Stephens, who already sensed that Sackville Street was doomed.

"What chance have they in the Post Office?" someone asked.

A tough-looking laborer answered fiercely, "None! And they never had, or never thought they would have." He nodded toward Kelly's. "That'll root them out quick enough."

A dozen or so men were clustered in a nearby lane, and suddenly Stephens heard a terrible flow of language coming from their direction. He turned. A young girl, no more than nineteen, was hurling the obscenities at them.

"Cowards—that's what you are! Why don't you march out into the streets like men? And them dying there for you in Kelly's!" And then a stream of oaths.

Halfway up Sackville Street, Brennan Whitmore watched British bullets ricochet off the tramlines and hit the G.P.O. His own men, face down at the open windows, were doing their best to reply to the fire, especially from the military on the roof of Trinity College and on the D'Olier Street triangle. Suddenly he saw a small man in moleskin trousers, blue reefer coat, and peaked cap stagger out of Henry Street and sprawl flat on his face in the gutter. Behind him a woman screamed and then flung herself on top of him. Whitmore thought that she had also been shot, but a second later she got up and started calling out. Three men dashed from the G.P.O. and carried

217

the body into the shelter of Henry Street, the woman following, loudly lamenting.

Whitmore had been so engrossed that he had failed to notice a tall, lanky man in a bowler hat, carrying a light shower coat over his shoulder, careering down the middle of the tramlines amid a torrent of rifle and machine-gun bullets. Gloriously, ecstatically drunk, he was singing and waving his hands wildly as he zigzagged along in a series of fits and starts, which probably saved his life. One second he lurched forward, in a kind of jog trot; the next he wavered to a dead halt, blissfully unaware of danger.

From both sides of the street rebels bawled fierce warnings, but he stood there in the middle of the road, pivoting first on one heel and owlishly glaring about him at an extraordinarily noisy world that was entirely unfamiliar to him, then twisting back on the other. In the end he went careering away toward the O'Connell Bridge, still somehow miraculously preserved, until at last he disappeared from sight.

When Whitmore was able to turn his attention to more important matters, he found that his telephone link to the G.P.O. had been wrecked. He therefore wrote out a message for Connolly and called for someone to volunteer to take it across the street. The senior Cumann na mBan woman stepped forward. "I need bandages, lint, and anesthetics, anyway," she explained. "We're not likely to escape casualties."

"I'm sorry," said Whitmore shortly. "Obviously you can't go, but the man who goes across can bring those things back for you."

"But he wouldn't know where to look for them in the G.P.O.," she insisted with courageous obstinacy. In the end, despite misgivings about allowing a woman to carry out such a dangerous mission, Whitmore gave in.

The woman was not in uniform and her skirt was the fashionable hobble. It had to be slit down one side from just above the knee so that she could run. From the relative safety of his position in North Earl Street, Whitmore watched her race across Sackville Street, the slit skirt flapping wildly. Bullets flew at her, but she reached the far side safely.

Fifteen minutes later he saw her reappear in the doorway of

218

the G.P.O. She put her head down and, with her arms full of medical supplies, commenced her return dash. Even while she was in the roadway another shell hit Kelly's, sending up a choking cloud of dust, and the machine guns opened up again. Sparks flew off the street near her, but somehow or other nothing hit her and, panting fiercely, she reached North Earl Street where she collapsed in Whitmore's arms.

On the G.P.O. roof, Desmond Ryan was making the discovery that he possessed a stoic quality. Perhaps it was because he was weary and desperately needed sleep; perhaps it was because he was hungry, or possibly it was only because of the incessant noise. Whatever the cause, he began to lose the feeling that things were happening. Noise, shells, rifle shots, machine guns, even visual experiences such as the vast traceries of dust appearing along the façades of the buildings down near the river, all ceased to have meaning or reality.

Quartermaster Fitzgerald asked Lieutenant Mahoney to accompany him to the ground floor. "I want to show you our hospital," he said.

He led Mahoney through a maze of men, sweaty, begrimed and somewhat apprehensive-looking, to a corner of the great public office where a number of wounded men lay on mattresses. Mahoney ran an expert eye over the equipment arranged neatly on a counter. There were sterilizing needles, forceps, and surgical knives. At the other end of the counter, chucked down in a higgedly-piggedly fashion was a collection of stuff obviously commandeered from various chemists' shops by somebody who had no idea of medical needs. Among them was a veterinary thermometer for registering the temperature of cows.

A man lying on a mattress had been shot through the lung, so Mahoney gave him an injection of morphia. While he was engaged in this, a young man came up and introduced himself as MacLoughlin of Derry. He was a "chronic," he said; for ten years he had been trying to qualify as a doctor and still could not get his degree.

"And then I was simply walking down Sackville Street when some of the boys saw me and shouted out 'Come in and help us.' Anyway, in I came—like a mug, I suppose. Now I don't see any way of getting out." And he grinned.

Up on the roof, Richard MacAuliffe lay flat and watched the machine-gun bullets ripping clouds of mortar from the D.B.C.'s Restaurant and peppering the Imperial Hotel. When the stream swept against the G.P.O., the men around him replied with an indiscriminate volley from their Howths. Pearse, accompanied, as usual, by his brother Willie, came up on the roof to observe the fighting and encourage his men. He looked calm and still gave an impression of great confidence, although rumors had been heard all morning that a military assault was imminent. Throughout the great building, indeed, men crouched anxiously by bowls containing their shotgun ammunition, with stacks of reserve pikes and revolvers close at hand.

As each man steeled himself for the big attack, a venerable white-haired priest stumbled out onto the roof and, crouching down as far as he could, made his way toward the front where the defenders lay. Behind him crawled a young Dublin urchin, hardly twelve years old, who had managed to sneak into the building because the guards on the door thought he was with the priest. The priest gathered the men around him and explained that, as an attack was imminent, he intended to give them all conditional absolution. As the men lowered their heads reverentially a sudden flow of obscenities interrupted the solemn moment. The urchin was standing at the parapet, his face transfigured with a look of sheer exaltation.

"Janey, what don't I wish the fuggers!" he yelled at the top of his voice. "They're all s- - - and wind. Listen!" His face blazed excitedly as a shell thumped against Kelly's, followed by the low roar of Howth guns in reply. "D'ye hear that now! Ye'll wipe them all out before you're done with them!"

"Clear out of here!" shouted a rebel. "What the hell are you doing here anyhow? . . . Pardon me, father."

The priest smiled understandingly. Then he addressed the boy. "Listen, my son, this is no place for a lad like you. Go home now and leave the fighting to those whose business it is."

"But, father . . ." protested the boy. He left the sentence unfinished as another shell boomed out across the city. "Janey,"

220

he said excitedly, "there goes another one! By God, I'd see them all in hell!"

The priest shrugged in mild despair and returned to the business of absolution.

"You understand what I mean by conditional absolution, men, don't you?" he asked, taking up where he had left off. "I shall ask each one of you in turn if he is sorry, then pronounce absolution." The men remain kneeling, heads bowed, their hands clasping the long rifle barrels, as the priest pronounced the Latin words.

He had scarcely left the roof, taking the urchin with him, when the men on the roof had to listen to a fresh hurricane of oaths and obscenities. Jack White, son of a British Field-Marshal and now a Citizen Army officer, was a picturesque ex-sailor who had picked up an extraordinary vocabulary of scabrous words in seaports all over the world. The imminence of eternity had not diminished his gusto for life, and as he handed out canister bombs from a bundle that he was carrying, oaths poured from him in a wild and eloquent cascade. The contrast between the preceding quiet moment of reflection and exhortation and this terrible flow of language proved too much for most of the men. Surrounded by the habiliments of death and violence as they were, White brought a breath of familiar life to them. They roared with helpless laughter.

White left the roof in a final blaze of sulphurous language to which he was still giving vent when he reached the ground floor.

"Heaven help us all!" protested an extremely religious Volunteer. "Do you want the ground to open under us?"

"To hell with you and the ground both!" said White pleasantly, and strode on.

The outraged Volunteer was not prepared to leave it at that. He collected some friends, and they went after White to insist that he attend Confession.

"But I haven't been for fifteen years," spat the ex-sailor. "Why the hell should I go now?" and to emphasize his point, he let loose a string of blasphemies.

Father John Flanagan, unofficial chaplin to the garrison, intervened. Gently he explained to White that time was not

221

an obstacle to the making of a good confession. The blaze died out of White's eyes and his face grew almost pensive. To everybody's relief, he finally agreed to make his peace with God.

There was little the rebels could do now but sit and wait. Sometimes they said the Rosary. A few, more fervent than the rest, fingered Rosary beads or the holy scapulars around their necks. The waiting was worst for the men on the ground floor; as yet they had no targets—only empty streets to look at. For those on the upper floors or on the roof, there was at least the occasional flash of khaki as a soldier ran across a street opening. It had become obvious to everyone, of course, that they were hemmed in on at least three sides. Southward, the military held Dame Street, Trinity College, D'Olier Street corner and the quays on the college side of the river as far down as Butt Bridge. Eastward, they held the Custom House, Liberty Hall (or what was left of it), and Amiens Street railway station as well as numerous positions in Lower Abbey, Gardiner, and Talbot streets. Here they were reported to have adopted rebel tactics and to have built barricades. Westward, they had been spotted moving now and then across the head of Upper Sackville Street, and they had a machine gun on the roof of the Rotunda Hospital.

The insurgents—their senses and nerves increasingly under assault by the incessant chatter of Lewis and Vickers guns and the intermittent noise of the artillery still attacking Kelly's— sought to hit back at their largely unseen enemy. From the roof of the Hibernian bank, little John Reid, armed with a Howth Mauser almost as big as himself, attempted to pick off the khaki specks as they dashed briefly across Butt Bridge. Finally, however, the tremendous volume of machine-gun and small-arms fire, and the loss of Captain Tom Weafer, drove him and his comrades below.

From the Henry Street corner of the G.P.O., Volunteer Joseph Sweeney tried equally hard to knock over some of the khaki blurs dodging across Upper Sackville Street at the Parnell Monument. Once it seemed as if the big attack had really begun when an extraordinary contraption suddenly lurched into view. Sweeney blinked in astonishment; nothing

222

like it had ever been seen in Dublin. Two months before Sir Douglas Haig would surprise the Germans by throwing thirty-six newly invented tanks into the Battle of the Somme, General Lowe and Colonel Portal were trying out their own improvised armored vehicles. They were Portal's idea. First he secured two big iron boilers from Guinness's Brewery and the Inchicore Railway Works. He asked the railway people to mount these on two motor lorries and in the sides had holes and slits bored through which troops could fire. Dummy holes were painted beside the real ones to confuse the rebels. Each boiler accommodated eighteen soldiers in some discomfort, but certainly offered comparative safety.

Sweeney watched the first of these iron-clad nightmares lumber down Sackville Street until it got as far as the Gresham Hotel, where it halted momentarily. Beside him Volunteer Sammy Reilly and several other men were blazing away at it, despite a terrible feeling of helplessness. No one was sure whether it had advanced merely on reconnaissance or whether it was the spearhead of an attack. Sweeney's weapon was a modern Lee-Enfield and he was a good shot; taking careful aim, he fired at the narrow slit in the front, hoping to hit the driver. His first three or four shots bounced off the armor, but one must have gone home because, after a jerky attempt to restart, the iron-clad stopped dead. For the remainder of the afternoon it lay immobilized, a stuffed prehistoric monster which belonged in a museum.

From the roof of the Metropole Hotel in the next block, Volunteer Charles Saurin enjoyed a superb panorama of the battle. Dublin, had it not been for the noise which never let up, seemed an almost-deserted city. The military hardly ever showed themselves. Saurin could see his comrades on the far side of the street, a few floors below him, lying flat at the windows, firing away, but he saw no targets. The most incongruous sight was of men and women sitting in the windows of Wynn's Hotel in Lower Abbey Street, watching the battle as from a theater seat.

Pearse did little during this waiting phase except speak a quiet word or two now and then to some of his more intimate friends. Members of the Provisional Government had congregated on the ground floor, where they sat on some upturned barrels and talked. Pearse's favorite perch was a high stool near the main entrance. Beside the barrels were mattresses on which the leaders slept. Plunkett, now very ill, rarely rose from his. Connolly still moved among the men like a relentless machine, ticking them off for sloppy work, making them strengthen their defenses, constantly finding them new tasks. He had already begun preliminary work toward securing an escape route, ordering the erection of barricades in Henry Street and Moore Street on the north side of the Post Office. Clarke and MacDermott, neither of them military men, interfered as little as possible with Connolly's direction of the battle. Both still remained cheerful, Clarke especially so. Miss Mary Ryan, a member of Cumann na mBan, remembers him beaming every time another shell burst. "I have never seen him look happier—he was like a bride at a wedding," she recalls. And this despite the knowledge that time was running out; that their lives would soon be forfeit. Neither man had any illusions about the position. The population of Dublin had not risen to join them. Not a single trade, political, or municipal society anywhere in Ireland had declared for the Republic. There had never been any chance of a German landing or a massive Irish-American invasion. The British had them surrounded and were bombarding Sackville Street. Yet what did it matter? Every hour they held out, every shell that destroyed yet another brick of Dublin, was a victory.

Feeling restless, Pearse, accompanied, of course, by his brother Willie, climbed out onto the roof again just as a tremendous cross fire of bullets drenched Sackville Street. As Pearse and his brother, bending low, moved toward the front of the roof, Lieutenant Michael Boland, O.C., out of sheer habit, rapped out an order to keep under cover. Suddenly realizing that he was talking to Pearse, he hastily apologized.

Pearse smiled. "Thank you, Lieutenant Boland," he said gently. Then, looking around at the exhausted men, some of whom had been continuously on duty on the roof since Monday afternoon, he promised, "I'll try to see to it that you are relieved shortly."

The brothers stood for a while looking out over the roofs of

224

the city. "A curious business," remarked Willie at last, in his slow, lisping way. "I wonder how it will all end." Pearse, absorbed in the scene below, did not reply. . . .

"What do you think of it all?" one of the men asked Lieutenant Boland (a Boer war veteran) after Pearse had left the roof.

Boland shook his head. "It's a mad, bloody business," he said. "Here we are, shut in, with all our leaders and the flags flying over our heads to let the enemy know exactly where we are. Why didn't we take to the hills—and fight like Boers? But I suppose all we can do now is stick it out!"

Brennan Whitmore, having moved into the Imperial Hotel, now faced the problem of keeping in touch with Headquarters, since dispatches could no longer be carried across the street through the bullets. If he could rig up a line, he decided, messages could be passed back and forth. A search yielded several balls of twine and some quarter-pound weights. One man flung a ball of twine from the window, hoping it would land near the G.P.O. It barely cleared the pavement. A second reached the middle of the road. A third rolled into the gutter, and someone dashed out and pitched it up to the men in the first-floor windows of the Post Office. A message attached to the twine asked the men in the G.P.O. to run the line around a post and then fling it back. This would make a two-way cable. It was soon done, but the first attempt to send a message failed. When the canister holding the message was hauled in, there was a neat bullet hole in it. Half an inch higher and the string cable would have been snapped.

"For God's sake, simply tie the message on by itself," ordered Whitmore. "They'll never see a bit of paper."

This was tried and it worked. But even as Whitmore stood at the hotel window studying the progress of a message through field glasses, he heard a sudden whistling sound nearby and instinctively ducked. A tongue of smoke, flame and debris belched into the air beside the Post Office and a loud detonation followed. For a moment he thought G.H.Q. had been hit. Then, as the smoke and dust cleared, he saw that the shell had struck the offices of the *Freeman's Journal*, organ of

225

Redmond's Parliamentary Party. His men cheered loudly, and an answering shout floated back from the G.P.O.

Then suddenly, away to the right, a long way off, probably up near the Broadstone Station, a great cloud of black smoke ascended into the air. Whitmore learned later that this was the work of Commandant Daly's men. Pressure in the Four Courts area had also been increasing steadily, although not with the intensity of that building up against the Post Office. The men guarding Daly's northern outposts, holding the high buildings beside Moore's Coach Factory, and in Clarke's Dairy at the corner of North Brunswick Street were constantly dueling with military snipers in the Broadstone Station and houses in that area. The whole of Church Street was under long-range fire from across the Liffey—especially from a military sniper in the Bermingham Tower (who had chalked up fifty-three rebel casualties before he himself was killed on Saturday morning) and from the bell tower of Christ Church Cathedral. A machine gun on the roof of Jervis Street Hospital constantly sprayed the area, but accurate sniping, with the aid of powerful field glasses, by Volunteer Frank Shouldice, high up in Jameson's Malthouse off North King Street, drove them down.

With the steadily increasing military activity in the area, the beleaguered Lancers, holed up in the Medical Mission in Charles Street since Monday, grew bolder. Their snipers began to make it hot for the rebels inside the Four Courts. A carpenter called Murphy finally hit on the idea of burning the Lancers out by shooting a crude flaming arrow (made from a piece of ash tied with rags soaked in petrol) through one of the Mission windows. The arrow successfully crashed through the window, but when it fell on the floor inside, the Lancers quickly put it out.

Daly's men—on the whole, probably as tough and as able as any of the rebel commandos—still retained most of their early buoyancy and confidence. They launched a sudden raid on the Bridewell Police Station and made prisoners of twenty-four policemen they found hiding in the cells. The D.M.P. had been there since the beginning of the rebellion, subsisting on the skillet they normally served to their prisoners.

226

Captain Denis O'Callaghan and young Garry Holohan went back to the Linenhall Barracks, which they had captured earlier that morning. Daly, because of a shortage of men, had been unable to garrison it, yet somehow he had to deny it to the military who, if they recaptured it, would place themselves in the heart of his position. He therefore decided it should be set on fire. O'Callaghan and Holohan carted several drums of oil and paints from a nearby chemist's shop, sloshed them around the large room on the first floor, then set the place alight. O'Callaghan flung open the windows to feed the flames. These flared so rapidly and so fiercely that the two men found themselves almost trapped, and Holohan still recalls the terrible heat as they ran toward the door. Behind them smoke and flame ascended into the clear air. For a moment they lingered to look at the blaze, almost appalled at what they had done.

From the rebel positions in Lower Sackville Street, that smoky cloud looked ominous. All day long, nerves had been wracked by the military onslaught. None had slept properly or eaten well since the Rebellion began; early feelings of triumph had given way first to boredom, then sheer weariness, and now fear. Under the circumstances, Connolly's order to the men in the D.B.C. cupola to cease firing—misinterpreted as an order to leave the whole building—was easily translatable into further sanction for a general evacuation of all the Lower Sackville positions. By late afternoon every building up to the Imperial Hotel had been left empty. First, under a Red Cross flag, a party of women and nurses had scrambled across Sackville Street from the Hibernian Bank, where a large Red Cross flag had been flying all day, the military holding their fire to allow them to cross. Then the men of different garrisons crossed singly. Something like panic had gripped them. Small in numbers, robbed of the steadying influence of their captain, Tom Weafer, who had died an agonizing death after being shot through the lung, they were scared by their first military attack.

Brennan Whitmore, watching the military close in, suddenly realized that by allowing themselves to be trapped inside the city instead of fighting from open country, they had lost the

227

battle. A man beside him summed it up: "Another Irish rebellion ending in blood and tears."

To Whitmore it seemed hopeless to continue fighting. The Howth rifle, which had to be reloaded after every bullet, was no match for artillery and machine guns. Surrender was unthinkable. There was one alternative—to break out through the military cordon and escape into the countryside. There they might regroup and start the guerilla warfare which Professor MacNeill had envisaged if ever the Irish Volunteers were forced to fight. Whitmore gently hinted at the idea to a couple of his senior men, asking them what the chances were of breaking northward through the military cordon. One thought it could be managed; he knew several back streets and alleyways through which he thought they might filter without being detected. Whitmore suggested that they sit down and work out a plan.

In the G.P.O., James Connolly lost his temper for the first and last time that week. He had a shrewd idea that the hurried evacuation of the D.B.C. cupola had been due less to a genuine misinterpretation of an order than to simple panic. The pattern of modern warfare, he knew, was to soften up the enemy by artillery fire before launching an infantry attack; and it seemed obvious that, once the guns had ceased firing, the military would advance at the charge across O'Connell Bridge. He intended to make that move as costly for them as he could. He asked for thirteen volunteers to reoccupy the block of buildings along Lower Sackville Street. Gallantly thirteen men, including most of the original garrison, recrossed the fire-swept street, utilizing the cover of Nelson's Pillar. They gained North Earl Street without loss. From there they infiltrated along Marlborough Street and thence into Lower Abbey Street, where they had to run a gantlet of fierce fire, so fierce that only eight men managed to reoccupy the D.B.C. block.

At five o'clock to the minute, following three hours of intermittent bombardment, the military fire ceased. Damage caused was slight despite the uproar. Kelly's looked much as it always had. Far from reducing it to rubble, the shrapnel shells had caused only slight damage. Five shells, piercing the brickwork,

228

had left distinct holes not much bigger than a man's hand. Not one window remained whole, but single panes of glass were left here and there. The interior, however, had been wrecked, and if the few rebels who had initially occupied the place had stood their ground, they must certainly have all been killed. As it was, once they had found themselves under fire, they had hurried back through the holes they had bored in the walls.

One thing was clear. At this rate of progress, it would take several weeks of intensive bombardment to drive the rebels out of Sackville Street.

Meanwhile Captain Bowen-Colthurst continued his personal campaign of extermination. While searching suspected premises in Camden Street, not far from Portobello Barracks, his men flushed out Volunteer Lieutenant Richard O'Carroll, a Dublin city councilor. Bowen-Colthurst marched O'Carroll into the backyard at the point of a revolver, remarking, "So you're a Sinn Feiner?"

"From the backbone out!" said O'Carroll defiantly.

Bowen-Colthurst hardly hesitated. He fired a bullet through O'Carroll's lung, and the rebel collapsed. As he lay writhing in pain, a soldier said, "Sir, he's not dead yet."

Bowen-Colthurst, who was striding away, glanced back. "Never mind, he'll die later. Take him into the street." Two soldiers dragged O'Carroll outside, where he lay in the gutter until a passing bread van eventually picked him up. After living for ten days in agony, he died, exactly a fortnight before his wife gave birth to a baby.

Still on the rampage, Bowen-Colthurst claimed yet another victim. This time it was a youngster in his early teens, from whom the crazy captain demanded information. When the boy refused to speak, Bowen-Colthurst ordered him to kneel in the street and summarily shot him in the back of the head as he raised his hand to cross himself.

An hour later, Captain Edward Kelly of the Royal Irish Rifles walked into the mess at Portobello and found Bowen-Colthurst lying half across a table, his head resting on his arm. Kelly took a seat and watched him for a while. Occasionally Bowen-Colthurst would look up and stare across the room, then fall forward again. After a while Kelly went to Captain James MacTurk of the Royal Army Medical Corps. "For goodness sake, keep an eye on Colthurst," Kelly warned. "I think he's off his head."

MacTurk decided to see Colthurst. He found him apparently rational enough, though obsessed by his behavior that morning. "It's a terrible thing to shoot one's own countrymen, isn't it?" said Bowen-Colthurst.

By this time his maniacal activities—he had disposed of at least half a dozen persons in cold blood and with some degree of cruelty—had become known to both Dublin Castle and Irish Command H.Q. Neither evinced any interest in his behavior or did anything about the murders. Bowen-Colthurst, after all, had considerable "pull" at the Castle; he had been A.D.C. to the former Viceroy, Lord Aberdeen, Wimborne's immediate predecessor. Major Rossborough, who was temporarily in command of Portobello, was a kindly man, but even when he learned of the cold-blooded shootings, felt inclined to leave well alone.

Bowen-Colthurst might well have continued his insane career until the Rebellion ended had it not been for Major Sir Francis Vane. No longer a young man, Vane had spent the greater part of the war traveling up and down Ireland addressing recruiting meetings, doing what he could to arouse the conscience of young Irish farmers to their duty as citizens of the Empire. On the outbreak of insurrection, he had hurried back from Bray, where he had been lunching with friends, to help organize the defenses of Portobello under Major Rossborough. On his way back from posting snipers in Rathfarnham Town Hall early on Wednesday, he was disturbed to hear a crowd near the barracks shout at him, "Murderer, murderer!" Once inside he asked if anything had been happening, and was told about Bowen-Colthurst. Indignant—from what he already knew of Bowen-Colthurst he thought him a hysterical fanatic—he stormed in to see Rossborough, demanding Bowen-Colthurst's arrest. Rossborough pointed out that apparently neither the Castle nor Irish Command to whom the matter had been reported, wanted him to

230

take action with regard to the captain, and that he was not prepared to defy his superiors. There was the feeling in the regiment, too, to be considered; there was hardly an officer in the place who favored anything but the harshest penalties against the rebels.

"But think of the effect these murders will have on the reputation of the Army!" expostulated Vane. "Worse still, think of the effect they will have on America and on the Colonies where there are large numbers of Irish people."

In the end Vane persuaded Rossborough to confine Bowen-Colthurst to barracks, at least until the insurrection was over. Then he summoned a meeting of all officers under his command and read them a severe lecture on their duties and responsibilities under martial law. "If there are any other shootings like this," he warned them, "I will see to it that the perpetrators are held responsible for murder under common law, as soon as martial law has ceased."

Later that afternoon, General Lowe was able to issue a communiqué stating: "There is now a complete cordon of troops round the centre of the town on the north side of the river."

In Westminster, the Prime Minister, Mr. Asquith, reassuringly announced: "Steps have been taken to give full and accurate information to our friends abroad as to the real significance of this most recent German campaign."

Mr. Augustine Birrell, in turn, added: "We were anxious, indeed, during these last few days that news should not reach the neutral countries and particularly our friends in America, which would be calculated to give them an entirely false impression as to the importance of what has taken place. Therefore during the short period there has been a censorship— that, I hope, will be taken off almost at once."

21

Somewhere up Northumberland Road a piercing whistle sounded. Young Jimmy Doyle, kneeling at the left-hand window of the drawing room in Clanwilliam House, saw an almost solid mass of English troops charging straight toward him. It was such a foolhardy thing to do that at first he was almost too astonished to fire. He saw some of them charge up the steps of No. 25, but the main force came on, led by their officers, easily identifiable by their Sam Browne belts and revolvers. Then suddenly the whole drawing room erupted with explosive noise and he was firing as rapidly as his Italian Martini would allow.

It was sickening slaughter. Even as Doyle picked out two men and, one after the other, knocked them over, he could see that the soldiers who had charged No. 25 were being cut to ribbons. Fierce rifle fire had burst from the Parochial Hall, too, as the main body got abreast of it—apparently they did not know that this also was held by the rebels. Of the sixty young Englishmen who had commenced the brave charge, less than a dozen got farther than the Parochial Hall. Doyle saw with surprise that they were nearly all as young as he was. Somehow, it shocked him; he had never dreamed that the British Army could be simply young boys. But youngsters or not, as they funneled up to the bridge, George Reynolds yelled, "Pick up your revolvers and let them have it!" A sheet of bullets flailed into them, knocking them over like ninepins, and the survivors halted in their tracks, bewildered. They appeared to be confused as to their real objective and apparently had no idea from where exactly they were being hit. So they flattened on the roadway.

232

Their confusion was understandable. For most of the battle Colonel Fane and his officers were to maintain the fixed idea that their principal objective was the schools. The hail of fire which caught them obliquely as they tried to charge No. 25 was, they thought, coming not from Clanwilliam House but from the school buildings on the near side of the bridge. This fallacy and confusion persisted until late afternoon. It compounded the difficulties which were certainly not all of Fane's making.

The truth was that the 2/7th and 2/8th Sherwood Foresters had set off to march into Dublin (through territory known to be held by rebels) without a single bomb (hand grenade) or machine gun—all of which had been left behind on the docksides at Liverpool. There the disorganization had been so complete that a whole company ("D" company) of the 2/8th had been left behind when the rest of the battalion had sailed. A little later, an entire battery of heavy guns was dropped into the River Mersey during loading operations. In addition both Irish Command and Brigade had erred in giving Fane incomplete and therefore inaccurate information about the strength of the rebel forces at Mount Street Bridge. And finally they had erred in ordering Fane to advance into the city by Northumberland Road and Lower Mount Street when there was at least one safer route open. Although badly wounded and suffering agonizing pain, Fane's personal bravery and coolness under fire did much to steady his bewildered young soldiers.

In Clanwilliam House, George Reynolds told his men: "If they charge again, the two men in the right window fire to the left: the two in the left fire to the right footpath and road. I'll take the middle of the road."

Below, on the far side of the bridge, the wounded were trying to slip off their heavy equipment, maneuver water bottles to their parched lips. In Percy Place, the heavy fire coming unexpectedly from the side of Clanwilliam House picked off Major Hanson's "B" Company men in devastating fashion. Hanson himself took cover behind the coping stones along the Canal bank and motioned his men to do likewise. To Tom Walshe, huddled in the back drawing room of Clanwilliam House, a dry, cokey feeling filling his mouth, there was little

233

to fire at but the slight humps of khaki haversacks on the far side of the silent Canal. He blazed away at these, though he had no way of telling whether his bullets were hitting their mark or not. Then he noticed that there was a small gate roughly opposite the fourth house up Percy Place and that inevitably, the khaki humps would have to negotiate this. He held his fire and waited for them to show.

Suddenly there was a khaki blur there. The Howth roared in his ears as he fired, but he could not tell whether he had hit anything or not. Again a blur showed and again he fired. From the room above he could hear the roar of his brother's Mauser as he joined in. Yet their fierce fire appeared to be having little or no effect: on came the camel humps. Then something astounding happened. Suddenly several doors opened along Percy Place and the residents came to their doorways holding aloft white sheets. Before Tom Walshe grasped their intentions, they had dashed down the steps. He saw them—men and women both—lifting khaki figures into the sheets, then staggering with them back up the steps and into the houses. He made no attempt to fire on them, nor did his brother.

Hanson's company had suffered severely. Hanson himself, Second-Lieutenant Lamb, and Second-Lieutenant Hartshorn were early casualties. The officers gone, it had been left to Company Sergeant-Major Towlson to drive the men forward. But as he led them out onto the bridge, Section-Commander O'Donoghue and the three men with him in Roberts Yard for the first time opened fire. With only seven or eight men to back him up, Towlson could get no farther. Tom Walshe, in a frenzy, was pouring bullets onto the bridge. The big Howth bullets lay on a chair just beside his knee. He had to keep stooping, picking up a bullet and inserting it, firing, then ejecting the spent cartridge and firing again. The Mauser grew so hot in a short while that he had to stop firing altogether to allow it to cool. While waiting, he decided to go up and see how his brother was faring. He took a ramrod with him, for if Jim kept on firing as frantically as he had, his rifle would burst eventually. The din in the upstairs room was so intense that Jim did not hear him enter.

234

Tom moved carefully and tapped him on the shoulder. "For God's sake, mind yourself!" he warned, handing him the ramrod. "You'd better clean your rifle, the way you're firing it. Is it hot?"

Jim, his face blackened with powder, stroked the metal and grinned. "It isn't exactly cool."

When Tom got back to the room below, he found three holes neatly drilled through the wooden shutter, near where his head would have been had he not gone upstairs. What was particularly interesting was their angle of penetration. He glanced around the room. Near the wainscoting behind him were three scorched marks where the bullets had ploughed their way through the carpet. He crawled over, put his head down, and squinted back at the holes in the shutter. In the far distance rose the spire of St. Mary's Church, Haddington Road. They had evidently come from there. So he called Reynolds, and showed him the shutter holes and the burns in the carpet.

"H'm!" said Reynolds. For devout Catholics this posed a difficulty. Could they fire on the house of God?

Meantime, Colonel Fane was busy trying to turn the right flank of the Schools. He had ordered Captain H. C. Wright and "A" Company to work their way around by Beggar's Bush Barracks and the railway line, in the hope of coming in from the far side of the bridge. Wright circled around by Beggar's Bush Barracks (where the C.O., Colonel Frederick Shaw, unfortunately nabbed a platoon from him to help defend the place) and the first the rebels knew of this outflanking attempt was when Section-Commander O'Donoghue spied a single figure darting out of Grand Canal Street, furtively trying to pull aside one of the bread vans Simon Donnelly had put there as part of the barricade. O'Donoghue opened fire and the soldier "leaped into the air as though stung," and abruptly vanished.

Wright, of course, had almost blundered into De Valera's main position, and his men, circling cautiously around an enormous turf stack in Grand Canal Street, came under fire from Volunteer Joseph Guilfoyle, perched on a narrow platform high up in a railway tower between two giant water tanks. Guilfoyle's field of fire was almost blocked by one of the tanks, and he had to lean out to shoot around it. His attack on Wright's men, therefore, was hardly distinguished marksmanship, but at least it scattered them. Wright managed to regroup them and sent back for further instructions, the men, meantime washing and shaving in the streets while they waited out of the line of rebel fire.

At 2:45 P.M. Colonel Fane finally informed Brigade that, although he had taken Baggot Street Bridge, he was held up at Northumberland Road and urgently needed bombs and machine guns if he were to make progress. Irish Command suggested that, as the Sherwoods' own supplies were still in Liverpool, Fane could try Captain Jeffares of the Elm Park Bombing School of Instruction, near Ballsbridge. Jeffares was contacted and agreed to help. Yes, he could let them have plenty of bombs. Better still, he would come along himself and throw a few.

As the long, golden afternoon advanced, Colonel Fane's efforts became increasingly desperate. The failure of Hanson to distract rebel fire from the frontal attacks, and of Wright to outflank the bridge, left him with little alternative but to proceed more forcefully with his frontal attack. After an interval, he launched another determined charge. This met with exactly the same fate as the one which had preceded it. "D" Company, under Captain L. L. Cooper, which until then had been kept in reserve back in St. Mary's Road where the whole 2/8th Battalion waited for the Robin Hoods to clear a way for them, was hurriedly called up and told to occupy what windows and roofs they could around No. 25. Captain Pragnell was ordered to take "C" Company and reinforce Hanson, with the object of breaking through to Mount Street bridge.

As Pragnell led his men round Haddington corner under covering fire from Cooper's men, Malone again brought his "Peter the Painter" into action with devastating effect. In the space of twenty yards, Pragnell lost at least ten men, including Lieutenant Hawken, but he had won through the gantlet and was in the clear. Behind him Cooper's men opened what was perhaps the heaviest and most sustained assault yet on Malone's position. James Grace, inside No. 25, began, for the

236

first time, to know the desperate feeling of being trapped, of experiencing the shattering effect of bullets zipping and zinging into the room he occupied. All he could do was to keep his head down and "tremble from head to foot in a panic of fear." The trembling disappeared only in the brief intervals when he was able to fire back.

There had been no movement for some time in Percy Place. Tom Walshe, crouching on his little settee, could hear the continuous crackle of rifle fire from the front of the house, but he could see little or nothing himself. At the beginning of the fight George Reynolds had come in now and then to drop him a word of encouragement but for some time now, he had apparently been far too busy. Walshe decided to go upstairs again and see his brother.

Jim Walshe knelt quietly on an easy chair, waiting patiently for the military to show themselves again in Percy Place. For almost an hour there had not been a single movement along the far side of the Canal. The tree shadows had grown perceptibly longer on the still waters, broken now and then by a slight ripple as a gentle breeze stroked across it. With a jerk of his head Tom indicated that Jim should follow him. Together they padded down the stairs and crawled into the drawing room on their hands and knees. Reynolds motioned them to the middle window. Jimmy Doyle and Willie Ronan were on their left, Richard Murphy and Patrick Doyle on their right. (James and Patrick were not related).

In front of them stretched an unforgettable sight. There were khaki troops everywhere—crouched behind flights of front steps, behind the garden hedges, behind the trees lining Northumberland Road. And lying in the road; especially lying in the road. Four great khaki caterpillars pulsated toward them like an obscene monster. Two lines had stretched themselves in the gutters and two more crawled along on their bellies, jammed against the coping stones. It was not like killing men; it was more like trying to slaughter a great insect or animal. Tom Walshe at once opened fire and just kept on firing—at the men in the gutters. As one man was killed, another crawled up and over him. When he, too,

237

reached the head of the line, he was either killed or wounded. Sometimes, as the caterpillar tried to move forward—it could never advance beyond the group of dead and wounded at the entrance to the bridge—it appeared to be weaving from side to side as men elected to move around a dead or wounded body rather than risk crawling over it. Sometimes a few men at the head of the line would rise up and attempt to charge the bridge, generally led by an officer with drawn revolver. None ever got beyond the halfway mark.

Tom Walshe had forgotten all fear; he never, despite his intense religious emotions, dreamed of praying. No one talked. Every now and then, when a terrific spurt of fire flashed out from No. 25, George Reynolds would bellow, "Good old Mick!"—but that was all. Tom sometimes glanced quickly at Jim to make sure that he was all right, and they would exchange grins. Then suddenly Tom saw a clergyman dart forward from Lower Mount Street, coming from their rear, and run out onto the bridge, followed by two young girls. In sheer surprise he stopped firing and watched them kneel down among the bodies.

"Hold it, boys!" roared Reynolds, and then, leaning forward slightly, he shouted out the window, "Get back, you women!" and ducked in again. Neither the girls nor the clergyman paid any attention, however, and other people also began to run forward. In a moment all firing died away and the battle stood, quite incredibly, suspended.

Redmond-Howard had never envisaged a battlefield as strange as this; as different from the trench warfare of the Western Front as chalk from cheese. On the city side of the bridge, continually edging closer to Clanwilliam House, was a massed crowd of civilians; the whole neighborhood, it was clear, had turned out to watch the Thermopylae so improbably taking place on their own doorsteps. "The soldiers were crouched along the roads and hedges like a great khaki caterpillar," he wrote later. "They were in the most exposed order so that if a rebel shot missed the first, it was bound to hit the second. For the most part the soldiers were boys, ignorant of the town. There was not an enemy in sight, only a mass of civilians up to within fifty yards in front of them and blocking the street. I saw them lying writhing in the roadway, struck by the terrible leaden bullets of the Sinn Feiners. I wanted to rush over and help."

Somebody warned him, however, that the rebels would open fire on him. "They'd fire on anybody, the blackguards," said the man.

"I don't believe that," said Redmond-Howard.

"Nor do I," said the Reverend Mr. Hall, a local Methodist minister. Together they walked down a laneway in the rear of Clanwilliam House, which took them to Sir Patrick Dun's Hospital on Grand Canal Street, directly facing Boland's Bakery. Here a number of doctors, surgeons, and nurses stood in the doorway trying to decide what they could do to help. Among them were two well-known Dublin medical men—Dr. Myles Keogh and Dr. C. B. O'Brien. All of them felt desperately that the wounded Tommies could not be left to die out there on the bridge. At Redmond-Howard's suggestion, they finally decided to advance under cover of the Red Cross and put the matter to the test. Redmond-Howard rigged himself out in a white coat and the small party holding a Red Cross flag aloft, walked around to Mount Street Bridge.

The crowd opened a path for them and as they came into the clear space just before the bridge, Redmond-Howard saw bodies lying on the bridge itself in prodigal confusion, and on the far side, two great caterpillars still pulsing forward irresistibly. As they reached the side of Clanwilliam House, two young girls—sixteen-year-old Kathleen Pierce and seventeen-year-old Lou Nolan—came out from among the crowd carrying two big white jugs of water. Impatiently the girls ran ahead of Mr. Hall, and the clergyman, anxious for their safety, also broke into a run. A great shout went up from the crowd as the girls rushed into the firing zone and knelt to give water to the wounded and dying. The military fire died away and the battlefield grew silent save for the moanings of the wounded and the faint shouts of "Water, water!" Meanwhile Dr. Keogh and Dr. O'Brien marched to the front of Clanwilliam House, their hands raised above their heads, and shouted up that they wanted rebel permission to remove the wounded.

George Reynolds briefly raised his head and looked down at them. "Go ahead!" he shouted.

Onto the bridge ran fourteen nurses and several young doctors and civilians. There were not enough stretchers, so the wounded had to be hoisted onto the backs of the doctors, or carried away one at a time by two or three nurses.

The lull was brief. Young Jimmy Doyle saw the military begin edging up, taking advantage of the cease fire to work themselves into more favorable positions. Suddenly from the direction of Haddington Road there sounded a whistle blast, and down the road came the Robin Hoods, shouting, "Good old Notts!"

"Fire!" shouted Reynolds, "but for God's sake be careful of the nurses!"

Spurts of flame broke from the Parochial Hall, and from O'Donoghue and his men in Robert's Yard. Once again only a handful of the brave youngsters reached the bridge. Their bodies fell in heaps at its approach, and the aprons of the nurses, who darted to their succor in the brief interludes between firing, grew more and more bloodstained.

As progress continued slow and casualties mounted, the Brigadier, Colonel Maconchy ordered Colonel Oates, whose Battalion, the 2/8th, had so far taken no direct part in the battle, to detach a company on the right flank and try and turn the position at the bridge. Oates at once ordered Captain Quibell to take "A" Company and work his way round Beggar's Bush Barracks along the same route taken earlier by Wright. The men had scarcely moved off, however, when a countermanding order arrived from General Lowe. He wanted no diversionary tactics; the Sherwoods must press the matter frontally. The order was delivered in a peremptory, impatient manner; clearly Lowe had the impression that the Sherwoods were making surprisingly heavy weather of what was only a relatively simple job. Maconchy decided to move up to Northumberland Road and see for himself what was wrong. He rode on horseback through the township of Ballsbridge, where the Spring Show still carried on as though nothing untoward were happening less than a mile away. Nearing Mount Street Bridge, he saw crowds gathered in the roadway

240

and white-aproned maids out on the doorsteps or leaning out of upstairs windows. Some people cheered him and it was clear that most of the inhabitants, at least, were friendly toward his troops.

Fane made no attempt to belittle the serious nature of the position. "The second-seventh can't take it alone," he said firmly. "If it has to be taken—and I don't see why—then it will take the second-eighth as well to do it."

Maconchy nodded grimly and rode back toward Balls-bridge where he got through by telephone to General Lowe personally. Quickly he sketched in the difficulties of the situation emphasizing that the 2/7th Battalion had been badly cut up.

"The bridge *can* be taken," said Maconchy, "but I'll have to throw in the second-eighth as well, and there'll be heavy casualties. Is the situation sufficiently serious to demand the taking of this position at all costs?"

"I think it is," replied General Lowe, shortly.

At 4:40 Maconchy sent for Oates, who at once rode back on his horse to Ballsbridge.

"The second-seventh have suffered terribly, as you know," began Maconchy. "Fane is wounded and so are most of his officers. I've just heard that Captain Dietrichsen has died. I don't think it's fair to expect them to take the Schools; their casualties have been heavy and they've been under fire all afternoon. I want you to come through with the second-eighth and get on with the job. I want your battalion to storm the Mount Street Schools—at all costs, *at all costs*, mind you, and penetrate further if you can."

"Very good, sir," said Oates and saluted.

Captain Pragnell nearing the Schools, paused to admire the courage of the nurses, who were still working on the bridge despite the heavy rifle fire. Then he led the way out of Percy Lane, where he and his men had taken shelter as they filtered down Percy Place, and dashed across the road toward the Canal, only to be caught in a tremendous cross fire from the other side of the water.

In Clanwilliam House, George Reynolds had watched him

coming and had warned his men: "That lane must be kept open—it's the line of retreat for Mick and Grace." Every rifle in the drawing room was therefore focused on Pragnell's company.

In Robert's Yard, Section-Commander O'Donoghue placed his rifle in a fixed position so that it covered the gap in the railings noticed earlier by Tom Walshe; now he lay flat on the roof of a small shed and, protected by a low wall, fired blindly as one of his men, "spotting" for him, cried excitedly, "You're on target; one has just rolled down the grassy bank."

Pragnell reached the bridge with fewer than half a dozen men, bullets zipping about them like angry insects. He flung himself on the roadway at the entrance to the bridge and started to crawl, shouting at his men to follow. Abruptly he gave an agonized cry as an excruciating pain shot up his left arm. His revolver clattered to the ground and, as he twisted around trying to escape the pain, a terrible thump hit one shoulder, and blackness descended on him.

Still the Sherwoods continued to attack. At twenty-minute intervals the whistle would blow and yet another wave would make a frontal charge on the bridge. When this, too, had been mowed down, the doctors and nurses from Sir Patrick Dun's would rush out and rescue as many of the wounded as they could before the whistle blew again and the tactics were repeated. In Robert's Yard, O'Donoghue wondered why the English did not advance in more rapid waves—if they had, he believed, he and his comrade must inevitably have been quickly overwhelmed.

Once, indeed, the Sherwoods actually got across the bridge. Lacking officers or even N.C.O.'s, however, the young soldiers, by the time they had got this far, were in disarray. They leaped over the Canal wall, taking cover on the Clanwilliam side of the bridge, right under the rebel guns, and huddled there, unable even to raise their heads. From their shouts of distress, O'Donoghue realized that many of them were wounded and ordered his men to hold their fire, which gave some of them a chance to crawl to safety under the bridge.

Physically his own men had begun to suffer from the continuous action and the strong sun. The heat bouncing back

242

off the tar and sanded roof of the shed on which they were lying caused discomfort little short of real torture. They were behaving well, however, remaining calm and saving precious ammunition by firing only when they had chosen a precise target. Midway through the afternoon O'Donoghue sent a man back to Boland's to ask when they could expect relief.

He returned with the discouraging order, "There are no reliefs. Hang on."

Failure to reinforce or relieve the hard-pressed garrison at the bridge remains one of the most extraordinary aspects of the battle of Mount Street. Seventeen men had kept a whole English battalion at bay for almost five hours of bloody and continuous fighting, yet De Valera never made any attempt to help them. Some six hundred yards up Northumberland Road, the 2/8th Sherwoods had lain inactive for most of the afternoon in St. Mary's Road. Although his men held the nearby railway line and could have sallied forth along a number of avenues to sow chaos and panic in the enemy's rear, De Valera did nothing toward relieving the pressure being inexorably exerted against the Mount Street Bridge positions. All afternoon his Battalion H.Q. staff lay doggo, apparently waiting for their outposts to give way—as they inevitably must—and the military to attack Boland's.

At 5 P.M. a dramatic change came over the situation. Captain Jeffares arrived with bomb and machine-gun reinforcements and inside half an hour no less than three separate bombing attacks were launched against Malone's position. One bomb, landing on five hundred rounds of Howth ammunition, left lying on a bed, almost wrecked the room. But both Malone and Grace kept up a ferocious fire, darting from the front to the side of the house and back again, changing weapons when those they were using grew overheated. Somehow or other they repulsed the early charges. But at the end of the third charge, a squad of Captain Jeffares' men was ready to blow in the door. Corporal H. Hutchinson and Private J. E. Booth, of the 2/7th Battalion bombing section, crawled forward on their stomachs under heavy covering fire and attached slabs of guncotton to the door handle. Then they retreated and the door, or most of it, disappeared in an explosive cloud. The men of "B" Company charged inside as the defenders pumped lead into them at point-blank range, but for some time they made no attempt to penetrate the stairs which were booby-trapped.

At 5:50 P.M. Colonel Oates called a conference of his officers and senior N.C.O.'s in St. Mary's Road and explained that the 2/8th were about to enter the fight.

"Round the bend of the road, on the right, is the School and several houses strongly held. These must be taken tonight at all costs. 'B' Company will lead, 'A' will be in close support to press the attack home and 'C' Company will remain in reserve. Start in three minutes. Once under fire, move quickly." And the old Boer War veteran gave his venerable white mustache a businesslike twirl.

With Colonel Machonchy, the Brigadier, accompanying him, Oates led the way down Northumberland Road. By this time No. 25 had been silenced and the old Colonel, with the Brigadier watching, stood on the west side of the road just beyond the intersection of Haddington Road and pointed out the Schools. At 6 P.M. precisely, "B" Company, led by Lieutenant Daffen began moving along the west side of the road, losing men right from the start and being finally checked just opposite the Schools. Captain Quibell, leading "A" Company and realizing that the hottest fire was being directed to the west side of the road, moved over to the right.

Lieutenant Foster led his men after Quibell's. Directing withering fire both on the Schools and on Clanwilliam House up ahead, they succeeded in climbing the railings and breaking into the schoolyard. Foster himself rushed a window, broke it, and flung himself in, expecting to be blasted at point-blank range by the Sinn Feiners. Incredibly, he found the place empty and a hurried search disclosed only the dead bodies of the caretaker and his wife, lying in the grounds. With a platoon, Foster edged out of the Schools and darted toward the low parapet wall immediately facing Clanwilliam Terrace.

His men began firing over this wall and the Canal, raking Clanwilliam House and the house next to it. Foster was delighted to find himself so cool and unflustered under fire (it

244

was his first time in action) and he was almost enjoying himself. He ordered his men to distribute their fire carefully, each picking a window. To his annoyance their first efforts were amateurish; not a single man even managed to hit Clanwilliam House. In disgust he roared at Corporal Warren, "How is it that normally this platoon has plenty of excellent marksmen and first-class shots and yet now you can't hit a whole terrace at fifty yards' range?" As the fight continued on, however, their marksmanship improved.

Meantime Lieutenant Daffen led yet another charge across Mount Street Bridge. Backed up by Lieutenant Browne, he almost succeeded in reaching Clanwilliam House, but just beyond the northwest corner of the bridge, he was killed outright and Browne fatally wounded. The 2/8th, like the 2/7th, were finding it no easier to shift the rebels.

From the bell tower of St. Mary's Church, Haddington Road,
three sharpshooters plugged away steadily at No. 25 Northumberland Road, at intervals varying the target to back up the
troops charging Clanwilliam House. From five o'clock on they
were reinforced by a machine gun.

In No. 26 Northumberland Road, where Captain Dietrichsen had died, and the wounded lay stretched on the dining-
room floor, the lady resident and her mother narrowly escaped
death as a bullet crashed through a window, shattering the
mirror over the mantelpiece. Upstairs was no safer.

They had hardly taken shelter there when a window was
blown out. On the far side of the Canal a bullet entered No.
20, Delahunty's Buildings, passed through Mrs. Elizabeth
Kane, killing her and wounding her daughter Nan, standing
immediately behind her. Miss Henrietta Mitchell, a rheumatic
invalid, forgetting her illness for a moment, ran out of her
house into Mount Street to watch the Sherwoods attack and
found herself—as though by a miracle—permanently cured.
Miss Ethel Walsh, looking from her window, saw little Mr.
Hayter, a local grocer, foolishly dart into the road and get himself killed; then twelve bullets shattered the window where she
was standing, showering her with glass. Emily and Gertrude
Byrne, aged seventeen and nineteen respectively, sent to get
milk, crawled on their stomachs across the garden and, in
Warrington Place, saw a man just in front of them shot dead.
Little Mary Brady excitedly tugged at her mother's hand demanding "What are all the bangs about, Mammy?" "Hush,"
soothed her mother. "They're only firecrackers."

246

By this time both Malone and Grace had undergone almost every emotion it is possible to experience so near the edge of death; they had, in turn, felt both exhilarated and panic-stricken; yet at no time had they considered surrender or its alternative—escape. As their ordeal grew worse, as hopes of relief or even reinforcement vanished, they resigned themselves to the inevitable. But while they had a bullet left to fire, they were determined to fire it.

According to Grace's own account written afterwards, it was almost 8:30 in the evening (the military say it was shortly after 6 P.M.) when, after a particularly heavy bombing attack —probably when the door was blown in—Malone ordered him to the ground floor. He got downstairs safely and was standing in the hall, waiting for Malone to join him, when he heard movements in one of the rooms off it and saw a door handle turning. He opened fire through the door and heard a sudden rush of feet scuffling away in the opposing direction. Seconds later there was a crash of glass, the back door was burst open, and troops rushed in. Grace, emptying a fresh clip at them, dived for the stairs to the basement even as he heard Malone shout down, "All right, Seamus, I'm coming."

There was another rush of feet, several soldiers appeared at the head of the basement stairs, and he fired on them. There was a lot of scuffling above, shouts of "Get him! Get him!" and then a volley of shots in which Malone must have died as he came down the stairs.

Grace rushed to a small cellar window and saw an officer leading men up the steps of the front entrance. He opened fire, dropping the officer and scattering the men. Then his automatic jammed. Desperately he ran into the basement scullery and held the barrel under the water tap to cool it, quickly dried it, and loaded a fresh clip. As he prepared to fire again through the chinks in the kitchen window shutters, two bombs were flung into the basement—one exploding at the kitchen door to his right, the other beside the window of a small cellar opening off the kitchen—driving him to take shelter behind the gas cooker. It had grown dark now, so that when the military came down to search for him, they passed within a few feet without seeing him. And there he remained until the noise of the search died away and the sounds of battle grew less.

247

Sheer weight of numbers and weapons had begun to tell. With No. 25 Northumberland Road gone, the four insurgents holding the Parochial Hall attempted to escape by the back, but were caught in Percy Lane. By 7 P.M. only Clanwilliam House itself and the men in Robert's Yard barred the way to Trinity College.

Suddenly the machine gun positioned in the belfry of Haddington Road Church began chattering furiously and within seconds every window sash in Clanwilliam House had been cut to pieces. Through field glasses Reynolds tried to fix the gun's position accurately. He had again spotted soldiers filtering out of Percy Lane onto the side of the Canal, and repeated fiercely, "That lane must be kept open. It's the only line of retreat Mick and Grace have." Moments later he had muttered something about Patrick Doyle and himself going across into Warrington Place to take up a position at the Canal wall opposite the lane so as to give the two men cover if they should make a break for it. The machine gun opened up again as he spoke and he quickly abandoned the idea as impracticable.

On came the 2/8th again in a really determined advance. Jimmy Doyle's Martini jammed and Reynolds scrambled into a corner and asked the men to pass their rifles to him for quick cleaning. Doyle watched horrified as the military rushed the bridge and some half-dozen soldiers actually reached the railings right below him. He saw one soldier fling back his arm and throw something. This was followed by an immediate explosion downstairs. But Reynolds continued calmly to clean the rifles, even as there were further explosions below. Second by second it was becoming more and more difficult to return the heavy fire and to hold back the soldiers. Several gained the cover of an advertisement hoarding directly opposite and, although Doyle and his comrades plastered it until it looked like a sieve, they were unable to drive back the English.

The drawing room was thoroughly wrecked by now, but somehow or other the crystal chandelier had not been destroyed. The bullets, however, were beginning to carry away bits of it, adding a curious tinkling harmony to the odd orchestration caused by pieces of plaster crashing down onto the

248

grand piano and bullets pinging against the wires. Fire became so intense that Reynolds, hoping to draw some of it off, ordered Jimmy Doyle and Willie Ronan to go to the windows upstairs. They crawled out of the room on their hands and knees and then discovered that the stairs were almost unusable. Two steps had been practically obliterated and the remains were hanging together tenuously. Walls had been completely stripped of plaster and a water pipe sliced into, so that a great jet of water was springing out. By flattening themselves against a wall and sidling up an inch at a time they were able to get upstairs. Ronan took over the room directly facing Mount Street Bridge, Doyle the one at the side of the house overlooking Lower Mount Street, Warrington Place, the Canal itself, and on the other side of it, Percy Place.

Downstairs in the drawing room, the bullets continued to jangle into the piano wires as though a mad musician were playing. The great chandelier disgorged its last shower of crystal and parts of the room were already smoldering. Unpleasant-smelling smoke curled up from the upholstery, chairs, settees, carpets, and curtains.

Still Patrick Doyle was enjoying himself. Even as the military pressed forward with new energy and the rate of fire reached a new intensity, he kept roaring, "Boys, isn't this a great day for Ireland?"

"Isn't it that!" said Tom Walshe, between bullets.

"Did I ever think I'd live to see a day like this!" bellowed Doyle happily. "Shouldn't we all be grateful to the good God that He's allowed us to take part in a fight like this?" Then suddenly he was no longer saying anything.

"What's wrong with him?" Tom asked his brother. Jim spoke to Doyle, but got no reply, so he tugged at his coat. Doyle fell over into his arms—shot through the head. Jim laid him gently down and, together with Dick Murphy, the brothers said a short prayer.

To make up for Doyle's loss, Tom Walshe decided to rig up a dressmaker's dummy he had discovered downstairs the previous night and had brought up to play a joke on the lads. He had placed it on the landing with a hat on its head, and in the dark it had been easy to mistake it for a human figure.

249

There had been a few moments of panic when it was first seen. Now he dragged the dummy in, placed Doyle's hat and his own jacket on it, and set it near the window. Within seconds it had been riddled. Then the small red settee he and his brother were kneeling on caught fire. Jim picked up the siphon bottle with which they had been cooling their rifles, squirted a jet of water on the fire, and put it out. He turned the nozzle toward his own parched mouth and prepared to drink. Just then the bottle shattered in his hand.

A few moments later Dick Murphy went quiet. Jim touched him gently and found he was dead. By now the room was in a frightful condition. Bullets still shattered into the walls and ceilings, cut the chopped-up window frames into slivers; pictures and bric-a-brac littered the floor while plaster dropped from the ceiling in a continual rain. The piano still jangled out its crazy tunes, and choking smoke filled the room as more pieces of carpet and upholstery burst into flame. Outside whistles were sounding all along the Canal bank. Someone bawled "Surrender!"—and Reynolds replied by emptying his revolver. Then he left the room to see how the men upstairs were faring.

By themselves now, the Walshes found it no longer possible to keep firing from their positions. They decided that they were next for it, so they crawled out onto the landing and began negotiating the wrecked stairs. In the upper back bedroom, Jimmy Doyle climbed onto a table he had pushed over to the window and had begun firing on troops moving from Percy Lane toward the bridge when there was an explosion near him. . . . He regained consciousness to find himself lying on the floor with George Reynolds bending over him, wiping blood from his face.

"You're all right, Jimmy," said Reynolds, "but I'm afraid the rifle is finished." Doyle saw his Martini lying on the floor, its stock split. Reynolds said, "Here, take mine—there's a spare one downstairs." As he spoke, there was a series of explosions below and, satisfied that Doyle was all right again, Reynolds left the room. He had hardly done so when there was a terrific explosion on the roof. A shower of plaster clonked down on Doyle's head and Ronan called out from the front room, "The place is on fire!"

Doyle crawled on hands and knees into the front room where he found the carpet smoldering. He was helping Ronan to stop it from spreading when Reynolds called him from the landing. Still on hands and knees, he crept out to join his officer. Smoke was coming from under the door of the room where the Wilsons had stored their valuables. "Here, give me a hand," said Reynolds, and together they rammed the door with their shoulders, forcing it open. Most of the ceiling had fallen and a mattress on the bed was burning furiously. They dragged the suitcases onto the landing, put out the fire, and shut the door again. Doyle pointed out that he was getting short of ammunition.

"Don't worry," said Reynolds. "We'll have more men and plenty of ammunition soon. So get back to your position. In the meantime take this." He handed Doyle ten rounds, then left him and went down the stairs.

Doyle returned to his position and saw that some military had managed to cross the bridge and were now crouched behind the Canal wall in Warrington Place. Tom Walshe, who had crawled back into the room just below Doyle when he found the wrecked stairs being plastered with bullets, watched them come down along the near side of the Canal while the main body massed ominously just beyond the bridge, under cover of both the parapet and the bridge wall. There were more shouts of "Surrender!", followed by a sudden rush from Warrington Place. One soldier had his hand raised to toss a bomb when Walshe shot him; the bomb fell from his hand and exploded in a burst of light. Walshe knew then that the end could not be far off. The military were so close now that the house seemed to be rocking from bomb explosions. Somewhere behind him he heard George Reynolds shout, "Come on, lads, we can't do any more. . . ."

Up until this time the fire from Clanwilliam House had been extremely fierce and accurate. To the desperate military, trying to carry the narrow pass, it seemed as though a whole army of men had ensconced themselves in the house—trained riflemen, whose every bullet seemed to claim a victim. Some were convinced that the rebels were using a machine gun, the casualties were so appalling. Lieutenant Hewitt's platoon, for example, had been reduced to two men. Lieutenant C. P. Elliott's had been cut to ribbons and Elliott himself severely wounded. All officers including the Sergeant-Major and N.C.O.s of "B" Company had been either killed or wounded. Colonel Oates decided to call up his reserve company—"C" Company—under Captain Frank Cursham, a Notts solicitor. Captain A. B. Leslie-Melville, Battalion Adjutant, anxious to experience action, joined Cursham's men but had advanced only a few paces toward the bridge when he was severely wounded. Cursham was forced to retreat.

Captain Quibell now led a strong assault force, consisting of Captain L. L. Cooper and Lieutenant William Foster and his platoon, out through the back of the Schools and onto the Canal path almost opposite Robert's Yard. Here they were reinforced by Cursham and Captain Branston, Second-Lieutenant Curtis, and the survivors of "C" Company (whose losses during the day had been trifling). The low Canal wall gave ample protection, but the field of fire was impeded by the advertisement hoarding. Rebel fire penetrated and inflicted casualties). After a brief halt here, Quibell decided to try and rush the bridge. To support him, Colonel Oates led six men along Northumberland Road toward the bridge and concealed them carefully behind stone steps.

Quibell shouted to Lieutenant Hewitt, crouched behind the stonework on the Percy Place side of the bridge with the only two survivors of his platoon, and then rose to his feet and charged. Both Hewitt and Foster backed him up and were followed by "C" Company under Cursham and Branston.

In Robert's Yard, O'Donoghue and his men knew that they had reached their last gasp. It had been a tough, desperate day, if a glorious one. In the considerable heat they had not had a single drop of water to drink, and it was now almost eight o'clock in the evening. Exhaustion was setting in and in the brief lulls while the military regrouped it was easy to dwell on the full extent of their plight. O'Donoghue had watched Quibell's men coming across the yard walls of the house opposite, exposing themselves to his fire as they leaped to the ground to take up positions for the final assault. At such close range it was difficult to miss, and he almost felt revulsion at the slaughter. Still, he had to keep banging away at the hoarding behind which most of the attackers were sheltering.

Quibell's charge from behind the hoarding was carried through with bravery and determination. Even so he was stopped dead halfway over Mount Street Bridge. "It was a bad moment," Foster recalls. "All we could do was to sham dead and lie still. There were piles of dead and wounded all around me. So I picked up a dead man's rifle [officers carried revolvers only] and opened fire."

For a moment the fire from Clanwilliam House died away and Quibell leaped to his feet. "Up and at them, lads!" he shouted, and the party—cheering wildly, jumping over the dead and wounded, tripping and falling over the widely strewn equipment—darted and weaved toward Clanwilliam House. They found the door heavily barricaded.

In the final rush Quibell had been slightly nicked by a bullet, so Foster took charge and began battering at a window. He found this also heavily barricaded, but finally managed to force a way into the darkened room. The house was rocking from the explosion of bombs hurled by the other officers. At the front door Captain Cursham tried to lob a bomb through the drawing-room window on the first floor, but missed, and the bomb, bouncing back off the sill, exploded on top of him, wounding him fatally. Inside, Lieutenant Foster tiptoed across the room toward the hall door.

In the upper back bedroom of Clanwilliam House, Jimmy Doyle was knocked almost senseless by a tremendous explosion—which brought part of the ceiling down. He recovered to find himself choking in the thick smoke filling the room. From outside the military were still shouting, "Surrender! Surrender!" Then he heard Ronan call out and staggered through the smoke into the front room. "I think the roof's on fire," said Ronan, pointing. But he was interrupted by a wild shout from downstairs. It seemed to come from Tom Walshe. "Come on!" Doyle said to Ronan, and they raced for the stairs.

253

Tom Walshe had been firing more and more desperately as the soldiers closed in on the house, and George Reynolds, standing on the landing behind him, emptied his revolver through the drawing-room window. He had risen to his feet to do it, a gesture hard to understand, for bullets had riddled the landing all day. Walshe heard a crash behind him and, glancing around, saw that Reynolds had fallen. He crawled over, calling out to the others, and found that Reynolds had been shot in the thigh and was bleeding badly.

When Doyle and Ronan got down the stairs, they saw Reynolds lying in a pool of his own blood just inside the drawing-room door, and Tom Walshe trying to stanch the bleeding. Doyle noticed two dead men over near the window —Patrick Doyle crumpled on his side and Dick Murphy propped up as though still living, clutching his rifle. He helped Walshe drag Reynolds, who was apparently dying, out onto the landing. Reynolds asked for water and Doyle crawled into the back room to get some while the Walshes tried to make the wounded man comfortable—Tom saying an Act of Contrition into his ear. The military were now cheering wildly outside. Doyle filled a cup from a dirty basin—the water was scummy with fallen plaster and dust—and then crept back and put it to Reynolds's lips. The dying man drank greedily. When the cup was withdrawn, he murmured, "God," followed by "Mick, Mick!" and then his head slumped to one side.

Even today, Doyle cannot recall exactly what happened to him after that, not, that is, until he found himself ouside Clanwilliam House, lying flat on the grass close to a garden wall, the area behind him lit by flames. Tom Walshe, however, remembers that when Reynolds died (and he is certain that he was dead when they left him), they all went down into the kitchen, in the basement. Here they were trapped, because they had barricaded the back door. There was a quick way out, however; through a small window not much bigger than a foot square. They wriggled through this into the back garden, then climbed the garden wall and finally separated when they got to the far side.

Lieutenant William Foster's account of the last moments inside the doomed house differs in one important detail from the rebel version. Foster says that when he began to ascend the staircase from the hall downstairs, he saw a rebel standing on the half-landing at the turn of the stairs. "I am absolutely confident that a man stood on the half-landing. He was in civilian clothes and, I think, armed, but it was dark and I can't be sure he had a revolver. I certainly shot this man when he was standing and looking at me, and as far as I can remember he fired also." Foster shot from the hip, then bayoneted the rebel (who could only have been the wounded Reynolds) and finally, satisfied that he had killed him, plunged forward as far as the door of the drawing room. In a hasty glance in, he saw two men crouched by the windows. He had the impression that they were still firing, so he rolled a Mills bomb across the floor and slammed the door shut. There was an explosion and when he opened the door again the two Sinn Feiners lay sprawled out on the floor and a great spout of flame was jetting from the center of the room and striking into the ceiling where the bomb had burst a gas pipe. Behind him his men passed up the stairs, and he heard more bombs going off in the upper rooms. He himself went downstairs and out into the street and found, with the fighting over, that he was shaking like a leaf. Clanwilliam House was burning furiously and Major Rayner said, "Perhaps we ought to send for the Fire Brigade."

"How *do* you send for the Fire Brigade?" somebody asked, and Foster, struck by the sheer incongruity of Rayner's remark, broke into laughter.

Three of the surviving rebels—William Ronan and the two Walshes—were meantime making their way over one garden wall after another at the back of the houses in Lower Mount Street. They reached Love Lane finally and, in desperation, knocked on the door of a cottage. A young girl answered.

"Can you give us something to cover our uniforms?" asked Ronan. From upstairs the girl's mother shouted, "Put them out, put them out, or we'll all be shot!" So they carried on, climbing over several more garden walls until eventually they found a basement flat whose tenants were out. Here they found clothes—of a kind. Jim Walshe draped a lady's coat around his shoulders: Ronan dressed himself in a tramwayman's uniform, and Tom Walshe pulled on an overcoat. Thus

255

crudely disguised, they took the risk of walking out into Lower Mount Street. Away up at Mount Street Bridge they could still hear bombs and shots going off. People crowded every door and window and Tom Walshe, sighting a friend, shouted that they were going to hide in nearby stables, and would he ask their mother to bring them food and clothes.

They reached the stables and a little later their mother took them food and civilian clothes. They changed, then left the stables and hid for a while in the grounds of a nearby convent, where they lay in the grass and listened to the girls singing "Hail Glorious St. Patrick." In the early hours of the morning they quit the convent grounds and found refuge with a friend, as had been arranged in the meantime by their mother.

James Doyle got safely away also, although he was fired at by the military as he ran through a garden. Near Merrion Square he was set on by a hostile crowd as he staggered blindly along the street. He managed to get away from them, only to collapse eventually near Stephen's Place. Here some people carried him into a house, removed his uniform, and dressed his wounds. James Grace hid in the kitchen of No. 25 until Clanwilliam House had fallen and then left it and hid in a woodshed; later that night he attempted to escape by swimming the Canal with his boots tied around his neck, but was challenged by military sentries and forced back into the woodshed, where he remained until found by a search party three days later.

Meanwhile Clanwilliam House blazed fiercely, lighting up streets for miles around. The house next door caught fire and the occupants, Mr. and Mrs. Mathis, who had crouched in terror in their cellar throughout the battle, sat on deck chairs in their back garden and watched their home burn down. In the angry crimson glow, Brigadier Maconchy rode stiffly along Mount Street through picquet lines of troops with fixed bayonets stretching as far as Fitzwilliam and Merrion Squares, the crowds cheering madly and calling out for "The Gineral." In Powers Court, just off Lower Mount Street, officers and men were served gargantuan meals of Irish ham and scalding cups of tea by the celebrating residents.

In the meantime, scarcely three hundred yards away, panic

256

gripped the rebels in Boland's Bakery and their comrades strung out along the railway line.

By seven o'clock in the evening the strange, unnatural quiet which had fallen over most of Dublin had begun to rest like an eiderdown upon Sackville Street itself. Sometimes when a figure staggered out into the open—a drunk, perhaps, who had forgotten about the curfew—a burst of firing would break the heavy silence. In the G.P.O., Pearse tried to cheer his men by reading out communiqués he had received from his subordinate Commandants in the city. These were universally optimistic in tone, but now few men were capable of responding to such artificial hopes. Realization that defeat was not only inevitable but imminent, had sunk into most of them and they felt it was only a question of time before the khaki hordes flung themselves upon the G.P.O.

In St. Stephen's Green, Mallin's men, cut off from General Headquarters and lacking information as to what was happening in the rest of the city, remained in good spirits, although shortage of food and a certain disorganization resulted in young rebels who were mere boys being left at their posts without food or relief for days on end. Fred O'Rourke, aged sixteen, for instance, was discovered in a faint by Citizen Army woman Maeve Ward and, on being revived, explained that he had had nothing to eat except a handful of biscuits since he left home on Monday morning. Mary Donnelly, after hauling herself through the holes in the walls a dozen times during the night to deliver food, discovered another youngster who had been existing on nothing but plum jam since Tuesday morning. The Countess, however, refused to let small details like this spoil her considerable satisfaction. As alert, lively, and bloodthirsty as ever, she declared ringingly, "Think of it! We've done more already than Wolfe Tone." As darkness crept over Dublin, the men and girls gathered in the big lecture room of the College of Surgeons and, led by Joseph Connolly, sang rebel songs with contented cheerfulness.

Margaret Skinnider, a young Glasgow schoolteacher, was impatient with this kind of thing. She wanted to get at the enemy, and suggested that she and Joseph Connolly should

257

ride past the Shelbourne on their bicycles and toss a few bombs through the windows.

"Too dangerous," smiled Mallin.

A little later, however, she talked him into allowing her to accompany a patrol to the Russell Hotel; orders were to get rid of a troublesome sniper on the roof. The patrol ran into trouble. The patrol leader, Councillor William Partridge had just broken the glass front of a shop premises beside the hotel, which was on the corner of the Green and Harcourt streets, with the aim of getting onto the roof when a volley cracked out from the other side of the street. Margaret Skinnider was turning to speak to seventeen-year-old Fred Ryan, when he fell dead and she herself was hit and severely wounded. Partridge, with another member of the patrol, carried her to the corner of Cuffe Street, where they got help to carry her back to the Surgeons.

Mallin had no qualified medical men on his staff and gave orders that she was to be taken to the nearest hospital. She refused, however, and Miss Margaret Ffrench-Mullen had to bandage her up as best she could. In her subsequent delirium, Miss Skinnider heard someone declare, "That's the death rattle," and decided she was done for. A little later, when she heard big guns booming nearby, she thought: Oh, everything's all right now—it's the Germans attacking the British.

Meanwhile, northward on the other side of the city, flames from the blazing Linenhall Barracks had lit up North King Street like broad daylight. It was easily the biggest fire Dublin had ever seen. The heat was such that neighboring tenements and shops seemed inevitably doomed, especially when the Dublin Fire Brigade refused to turn out. Commandant Edward Daly, afraid that the conflagration would destroy the entire city, ordered his men to find fire hoses and tackle the blaze themselves. A search of the nearby North Dublin Union uncovered a few, and throughout the night the rebels fought the fire, despite constant and heavy military sniping.

Shortly before midnight Daly called a conference of officers to decide whether it would be wise to attack eastward in an attempt to break through the military lines in Capel Street and link up with the General Headquarters garrison in the G.P.O.

258

There was little to discuss; an attack under such conditions clearly had no hope of success, and that there was nothing for it but to hold on and defend themselves with their last ounce of determination.

In the G.P.O., Pearse, Connolly, MacDermott, and Clarke took turns resting on mattresses placed behind the central counter on the ground floor. Here each, with the aid of a sleeping draught prepared by the medical section, slept for brief spells. Once, in the early hours of the morning, The O'Rahilly shook Connolly awake to tell him that the British were "stealing over the roofs in Henry Street." Connolly raised his head slightly and then commented laconically, "They are *not*," and went back to sleep like a man with no care in the world.

About nine o'clock on Wednesday evening, Lord Kitchener's secretary called on Lord French with a message saying that the Government desired to send a senior general of some reputation to Ireland and that the Army Council had therefore chosen Sir John Grenfell Maxwell. As C in C, Egypt, Maxwell had done much to organize assistance for the troops in Gallipoli and had checked the one serious Turkish thrust in the Delta. French broke open the sealed letter and read:

I am commanded by the Army Council to inform you that Lieut. General Sir John Maxwell has been appointed G.O.C., forces in Ireland from 27th inclusive. His Majesty's Government desire that in this capacity Sir John Maxwell will take all such measures as may in his opinion be necessary for the prompt suppression of insurrection in Ireland and may be accorded a free hand in regard to the movement of all troops now in Ireland or which may be placed under his command hereafter and also in regard to such measures as may seem to him advisable under the Proclamation dated 26th April under the Defence of the Realm Act.

French immediately sent word to Maxwell who, idle since his replacement by Sir Archibald Murray, the former C.I.G.S. (Chief of the Imperial General Staff), was known to have a slight chip on his shoulder, and arranged for him to call at 10:30 the next morning. Then, thoroughly on his mettle, the irascible little Army chief telephoned the Prime Minister to inform him that he was holding the 60th Division in readiness to go to Queenstown and had also alerted the cavalry at Aldershot.

That night Mr. Birrell left Holyhead for Dublin on the Mail Boat, accompanied by a large retinue of newspaper reporters.

The flames of Clanwilliam House licking into the sky, and the recollection of the day-long booming of artillery had sown its due measure of demoralization among the men under De Valera's command: without waiting for orders, for instance, Lieutenant Joseph Fitzgerald abandoned a row of small cottages in Grand Canal Street as "a waste of time" after hearing —and accepting—a rumor that Battalion H.Q. had abandoned the Bakery and taken to the mountains. De Valera, his puttees discarded and his red socks showing up brightly, moved up and down the line, from one shallow trench to another, exhorting his men to remain in their positions and get ready to withstand repeated bayonet charges. He felt certain that the military would now switch their attention to the Bakery and the railway line and would attack continuously throughout the night after a short rest for regrouping. His desperately fatigued men quickly flung up low banks of earth in front of the inadequate trenches, but instead of occupying these holes, they stretched themselves flat a few yards back from them, with the idea of catching the military napping as they clambered over the earth banks and lunged with their bayonets into the empty trenches.

Captain Simon Donnelly, however, more accurately aware of just how exhausted most of the men were and—from his study of British military textbooks—just how unlikely it was that the British would launch a night attack, tried hard to get De Valera to cancel these dispositions. He had nothing like De Valera's faith in the capability and will of the men to withstand a charge of cold steel. To Donnelly, these lads, gripping their strange assortment of rifles with a nervous energy, almost as though they thought the weapons were about to bite them, jittery as young virgins when anybody approached in the dark, were not at that moment the stuff of great heroes but young fellows whose romantic notions of dying for Ireland could be easily smashed by a determined charge and the terrifying glint of naked bayonets. "I never had any faith in the men acquitting themselves well in a bayonet charge," he insists today, "especially in the dark."

Toward dawn, when long hours had passed with no sign of a British attack and he knew his theory was right, he countermanded De Valera's orders and brought the men down off the railway line so that they could rest and eat before meeting the stern challenge he was certain daylight would bring. As a measure of the rebels' situation, officers and N.C.O.'s passing down the line with these orders had, in most cases, to kick awake the men who should have been on the alert.

At 2 A.M., the 2/6th South Staffordshire Regiment, part of the 176th Brigade which had landed at Kingstown on the heels of the Sherwood Foresters, moved forward from Ballsbridge under the command of Brigadier-General L. B. Carleton, and relieved the weary remnants of the Notts and Derby lads who had battled so desperately and so bloodily all the previous day. These now retired upon Ballsbridge Showgrounds where, in the Agricultural Hall, Colonel Oates was pleased to find his "lost" Company ("D" Company) which had been left behind at Liverpool. With them was his second in command, Captain "Mickey" Martyn and, what was possibly of more immediate interest to him, his son, Captain J. S. Oates, O.C. "D" Company.

In the G.P.O., Commandant-General James Connolly, active and vigorous again after a short nap, sought to raise his men's spirits by getting them to sing the songs they usually sang on route marches. This annoyed Captain Michael Collins who, awakened from sleep by the noise, barked at Miss Carney, "If this is supposed to be a concert, they'll want that piano in the next room."

261

(23)

The weather—down the years it would be remembered through a mist of gold as "rebellion weather"—was superb. At 6 A.M. on Thursday, Volunteer Richard MacAuliffe, for example, woke to a spring morning as beautiful as any he could ever remember. All over Dublin trees and flowering shrubs were bursting into life and he could scent a wonderful effervescence in the air.

But unknown to Volunteer MacAuliffe, into this most pleasant city of venerable buildings and Georgian squares stole hunger. Compounded by chaos. The great Rebellion, far from being any longer a matter of mere curiosity, excitement, or even exhilarating danger, had become a nuisance to most of Dublin's citizens. There was no traffic in the streets. Within the military cordon there were no bread or milk deliveries. There was no theater, no cinema. There was no time, indeed; for every public clock in the city had stopped—in need of rewinding. There were no newspapers. There was no work, no wages, no banks open, no separation allowances being paid, no postal services. All factories were closed; no ships had sailed in or out of the Port of Dublin since Easter Monday, save for troop transports or supply vessels. The streets had not been swept. Waiters and cooks in hotels stood idle. In all the city perhaps only doctors and nurses carried on as usual—if at an accelerated pace. And over all lay the strange, unnerving stillness, as though the city had become a giant cemetery.

Hunger, of course, was the worst menace. In Commandant Daly's area, the people were still being fed, though inadequately. Bread was handed out sparingly every day under rebel

262

supervision, to the people living around Monk's Bakery. But in De Valera's area, the military—under the impression that the shawlies, appearing at Boland's for the daily handout, were bringing in supplies to the rebels—opened fire to deter them. In the nature of things, they shot and wounded several, thus forcing De Valera to end the arrangement.

In the back streets, the poor grew desperate. One man, trapped in his home with five children to feed, took an ax and broke his way through the roofs of five neighboring houses until he found something to eat. Shopkeepers riveted heavy planks to their shop fronts and stuck up notices saying: "This shop sold out." In the Ringsend district a crowd of yelling women broke into a grocer's shop, beat up the proprietor, and dispossessed him of his entire stock. Unable to carry away heavy sacks of rice, they angrily broke them open and started flinging great handfuls at one another like guests at a wedding. In other areas shopkeepers tried to stave off attacks by selling foodstuffs well under normal prices. (Some shopkeepers exhibited great kindness; one grocer-publican housed a dozen of his neighbors for the whole week of the Rebellion, feeding them regularly and accepting no payment.)

The situation grew so bad that not even money could always buy food. People sidling up to hotel doors, prepared to pay anything for a meal, were asked, "Have you brought the food with you?" Inside conditions were sometimes chaotic and extremely uncomfortable. Several English and Scottish visitors, over for the Spring Show, spent most of the week cooped up in their hotels, eking out a bored existence with increasingly meager meals. Doors and windows in the Gresham Hotel had been kept shut since Tuesday afternoon and the air grew stale and odious, worsened by the stench of the Lancers' dead horses outside, corrupting rapidly under the blazing sun.

From the suburbs, well-dressed men and women journeyed for miles into the surrounding countryside to bring back bread, sides of bacon, and vegetables. One clergyman arranged for a fleet of private cars to bring in supplies from Belfast for his parishioners. Some prices skyrocketed,—butter rose to 6 shillings a pound, oranges sixpence each, bananas two shillings sixpence a dozen. The military commandeered what meat there was available and tentative arrangements were made to distribute it to the population, once the rebels were crushed. Many troops had to subsist on short rations. In Trinity College, there was neither bread nor sugar by Thursday, and soldiers crowded into the kitchens where they were given hard ship's biscuits to munch on. In the College of Surgeons, the rebels were so short of food that a major tunneling operation was begun to reach a nearby pastry shop.

Dublin had become a lunatic world. Ceremonial funerals, an important ingredient of the city's social life, were forbidden; only the driver and one mourner were allowed to accompany the hearse to Glasnevin. People on the outskirts of the city continued to play golf and tennis as though nothing out of the ordinary were happening. At Clontarf, a couple got married while a machine gun swept the street outside. In Trinity College, soldiers played football on the tennis courts, grazed their horses on the immaculate lawns, slept in the quadrangles. In Charles Street, the dead lay unburied for three days. In the Castle, they buried seventy dead in a single night, all wrapped in sheets and thrown into a common grave.

Death often came to those who least expected it. A shopkeeper was shot dead as he walked up the stairs carrying a glass of water to his sick wife. A nun was killed as she was shutting a convent window. A woman died simply of fright. A priest was shot fatally as he went to the aid of a wounded man. A girl was killed as she stood in her own doorway. A woman was shot through the hand as she sat at her own fireside. A woman patient propped up in a hospital bed was hit by three bullets which zipped through a window at the far end of the ward. A County Court crier, raising his hand in the street to salute a friend, was shot dead because a military sniper thought he was about to throw a bomb.

All over the central fighting areas, rebels, soldiers, and dead civilians alike were buried in back gardens.

The *Times* thundered at Birrell, blaming him for the troubles because he had spent too much time in Chelsea's literary salons and had shown an aptitude for shelving his responsibilities. In the same issue the newspaper reported John Redmond's speech, declaring that "as for the overwhelming majority of the people of Ireland, the proceedings filled them with detestation and horror," and Sir Edward Carson's offer of the services of fifty thousand Ulster Volunteers "for the maintenance of the King's authority." The Russian newspaper *Novoc Vremya* headlined the news "The New German Farce." The Germans on the whole played the story down. Under the small headline "Serious Disturbances in Dublin" the *Frankfurter Zeitung* commented: "These serious riots cannot be regarded as important for the course of the war, but they are certainly not child's play."

The morning waxed hot and still. On the roof of the G.P.O., men rolled over, breathed deeply, and cautiously raised their heads. The paving stones below, worn shiny, flung back a sharp light which hurt the eyes. Somewhere, away toward Jacobs, a heavy burst of firing broke the stillness and a sudden tension gripped the defenders. All night long they had waited for the military to begin the assault; now they believed it must come at any moment and accordingly braced themselves. Behind them, to the northwest, the blazing Linenhall Barracks still sent fierce, billowing clouds into the clear sky.

At precisely ten o'clock, timed to the second by an officer's watch, a field gun barked and a shell landed in Lower Abbey Street. Connolly, believing—almost hoping—that this was the prelude to attack and that the main thrust would be across O'Connell Bridge from Trinity College, dispatched twenty men to reinforce his garrison in the Metropole Hotel. The solitary shell, however, indicated nothing of the sort. Instead, it inflicted a kind of damage none of the rebel leaders had ever thought of. Within moments of its landing, a thin spiral of smoke rose into the air from what appeared to be Wynn's Hotel, next door to the Royal Hibernian Academy. The shell had, in fact, crashed into the *Irish Times* printing office, setting fire to giant newsprint rolls stored there. Gradually huge flames leaped and flickered. From a vantage point on the roof of the G.P.O., Willie Pearse eyed the blaze and remarked, "That fire won't be easily stopped." He did not guess it then, but it was the end of Sackville Street. When it rose from its ashes, it

265

would have become O'Connell Street—and much of its symmetry and grace would have gone forever.

Father John Flanagan had said Mass that morning to the smallest congregation he could remember. The Pro-Cathedral was closed to the public and there were only three other priests present. They had all been up most of the night preparing for the removal of the sacred books and vessels to a safer place, lest the Pro-Cathedral catch fire. A strong wind fanning the glowing embers of nearby Lawrence's Toy Shop had sent showers of sparks floating over the church roof. Father Flanagan had telephoned the Fire Brigade, to be told surprisingly: "Our orders are that we're not to go out—even though further fires can be expected before the end of the week." Luckily, the wind had died away toward morning and the great church had been saved.

At 10:30 A.M. there was a knock on the presbytery door and Father Flanagan answered. It was a young lady. Highly agitated, she blurted out her request: "Would you come to the G.P.O., Father. There's a Volunteer dying?"

The priest's first reaction was to consider the request unreasonable. Two priests had already been stationed in Jervis Street Hospital, which lay just behind the G.P.O., specially to attend to the spiritual needs of the men in rebel G.H.Q. Still . . . He went back into the church to pick up the Viaticum and, accompanied by a friend, set off for the Post Office by a circuitous route. The military allowed him to pass through their lines in Great Britain Street and near Moore Street without difficulty. But while negotiating the latter street, a sniper, whether military or rebel he was unable to tell, opened fire on them and his friend was shot dead. Father Flanagan, despite the bullets which continued to fly around him, knelt and anointed the dead man. Then, shaken, but still determined to fulfil his priestly duty if God so willed, he pressed on toward Henry Street where rebels spotted him and signaled him to enter through buildings at the rear of the Post Office. He was escorted through the crude holes which had been broken in the walls and into the great public office of the G.P.O. where, he wrote later, he found "as gay and debonair an army as I have ever seen." He was led to the wounded Volunteer and, after attending him, saw Pearse, who urged him to stay, pointing

266

out that the men felt the need of a chaplain. Aware that it was essential not to compromise the Catholic Church by appearing to aid or comfort rebels, Father Flanagan at first refused, but in the end decided that his priestly duty overrode every other consideration, and stayed.

Even the most naïve no longer believed in victory. Yet the men garrisoning General Headquarters were still far from being dispirited. Their main anxiety, indeed, was that in some way or other they might be cheated of the chance to get a real crack at an English uniform. Far from experiencing the emotions of the defeated, a man turned to his comrades when another shell hit Lower Sackville Street, and remarked, "Isn't this great gas, boys?"

The fire in Lower Abbey Street had by this time begun to spread rapidly. Sparks caught the great barricade of furniture and newsprint rolls which Captain Tom Weafer's men had thrown up across the top of the street, and from here the flames jumped to Wynn's Hotel on the south side. Premises along both sides of the street were soon blazing furiously, the fire spreading both north and south. Taking advantage of this gap which suddenly opened a ready way into Sackville Street, the military began infiltrating until they were stopped by fire from the rebels under Lieutenant Oscar Traynor who, during the night, had tunneled from the Metropole Hotel to Messrs. Manfields' premises on the corner of Middle Abbey Street. Traynor's men brought on themselves a double wrath—first, of the military in Lower Abbey Street and second, of the Canadians and Anzacs on the buildings at the corner of D'Olier and Westmoreland streets, but they returned the fierce fire so effectively that the military advance was halted.

Meanwhile in the cellars below the D.B.C. Restaurant, seventeen-year-old James O'Byrne took cover with the rest of his company when artillery fire opened up again. Acrid smoke soon filled the cellar and above the noise of the big guns and the heavy rifle fire outside, he could hear the crackle of burning wood. Rocked and shattered by the bombardment, O'Byrne and his comrades no longer knew what to do and could only turn in their extremity to the familiar refuge of prayer.

267

If the 2/6th South Staffords had attacked De Valera's head-quarters at dawn, they almost certainly would have scattered the rebels like children. Rebel nerves, after a taut, jittery night, had reached breaking point, and actual physical weariness was such that when Volunteer George Lyons attempted to report to Captain John MacMahon, his Company C.O. in the Bakery, he found him stretched out across an orange box like a carcass of dead meat. Several other officers and men lay on the cement floor, utterly exhausted. It would have taken little to demoral-ize them completely. A night spent watching the flames of Clanwilliam House and the scarlet glow that stained the rest of the Dublin sky, plus fresh information that more troops from England were arriving every moment, had flung the men into something like despair. There was the continuing lack of sleep and the never-ending strain of waiting for the English attack. Additionally, with dawn, came the knowledge that they were now cut off completely from General Headquarters and could not hope for help.

Officers were beginning to find De Valera, for all his in-tellectual pretensions, a perhaps too unorthodox and mercurial leader. Tall, lanky, feverish-eyed, De Valera contrasted un-favorably with the curt, sharp-tongued Simon Donnelly, whose ordinary, relatively unimaginative common sense and ability to master detail inspired a confidence which "the Spaniard," in his tensed, exhausted state was quite unable to arouse.

De Valera's physical condition, indeed, had become alarm-ing. He had not slept (so far as anyone knew) since the open-ing of the Rebellion, and for the two days preceding it. None had been more conscious than he of the reckless and irrespon-sible nature of what Pearse and the I.R.B. proposed doing, and of its only too-inevitable end, an undertaking which appeared even more reckless, irresponsible, and inevitable because of the *Aud's* sinking and MacNeill's countermand. Rumors that De Valera had given way under the strain and would not appear in the field again swept his command that morning. Officers, including Donnelly, begged him to rest for a while, but he trusted no one, afraid that if he napped for even half an hour men would desert their posts or fall asleep. The sight of his restless, continually prowling figure did nothing to relieve the jitters which had been so bad during the night that a few men were shot by their own comrades simply for failing to give the correct countersign. De Valera himself narrowly missed death when he gave the wrong password.

These, then, were the young men who found themselves under artillery fire shortly before noon on Thursday. The attack began without warning. Suddenly there was a boom, followed by a whistling noise overhead, and a 1-pound shell landed heavily in the mud less than twenty yards from Boland's Bakery. It caused demoralizing consternation among the rebels, but it was at this juncture that Donnelly showed his real worth. He ordered a squad of men to erect a rough, shellproof shelter, using the flour bags stored in the Bakery, and withdrew all units from their exposed positions along the railway line. A second shell landed while his orders were being carried out, bursting the wall of the Bakery and blowing a bread van to pieces.

With commendable ingenuity, Irish command—still short of the 59th Division's artillery, which did not arrive at Kingstown until the following day—had rigged up their own fieldpiece, a quite admirable improvization, if hardly on a par with Portal's armored cars. They stripped a naval 1-pounder gun from the gunboat *Helga* and mounted it upon a lorry. Towed through the streets by bluejackets the previous evening, the gun had been cheered by crowds eager to see a quick end to the nonsense and, toward the end of the battle of Mount Street Bridge, had been hauled into position in Percy Place. By the time it was ready for firing, however, Clanwilliam House had fallen. The gun remained in Percy Place all night, under guard, General Carleton's intention being to advance, with it in support, toward Trinity College first thing on Thursday morning.

24

The day had begun in lively fashion for the yet untried South Staffords, tough, unyielding men drawn from some of the most highly industrialized slums in the world; men whose horizons until now had stretched no farther than the great kilns and smelters, the pitheads and the slag-heaps of the Black Country; men, in short, who were prepared to put up with "no bloody nonsense" from the Sinn Feiners. English troops did not, of course, as yet feel hate for the rebels. This was to grow as the fighting got tougher and rebel tactics became less commendable to men trained for a different kind of warfare. It would seem mean and cowardly to hide behind a chimney stack or suddenly blast a man from an open window. It seemed even worse, perhaps, to not wear a uniform; to shoot down unsuspecting troops, then throw away your rifle and stroll out through the back garden with your hands in your pockets. Very soon every street, every house, almost every individual in Dublin—whether man, woman, or child—would begin to look like evil spawn to the South Staffords. Nobody, it seemed, could be trusted.

There were tales of troops breaking into houses from which there had been firing only to find them occupied, perhaps, by a grandmother or other innocent with a "Peter the Painter" rifle-pistol stashed under the bed. Catholic priests became highly suspect, supposably having disgraced their cloth by signaling or acting as spies for the rebels. Almost any fairytale became credible. Even today Captain G. J. Edmunds of the 2/6th Sherwood Foresters believes that a party of priests who attempted to pass his column in the Stillorgan Road were

270

"Sinn Fein priests," anxious to cycle ahead and warn the rebels. Other priests were believed to have solemnly pronounced curses on the troops. Indeed, any sort of invented rubbish was thought authentic by men who discovered Dublin to be as strange as Timbuctoo (the sight of Catholics crossing themselves in the streets was regarded as a bizarre manifestation almost on a par with jungle voodoo), and who thought street-fighting a treacherous kind of warfare. The fact that a soldier, posted on the roof of a house in Lower Mount Street, eventually went off his head and began to slaughter passers-by indiscriminately is an indication of the tension under which the troops had to fight.

However, at noon on Thursday, April 27, 1916, the 2/6th South Staffords were still a calm and steady lot. But as the brilliant sun warmed the day, and chased away the rebels' night terrors, their courage returned, and soon the Staffords were being heavily sniped. The shooting came from long-range positions in Boland's Mills—an immense gray structure towering over the Canal basin—and the complex of railway yards and buildings around it. In quick succession Lieutenant Halliwell was shot dead, Lance-Corporal Barratt was hit in the head, and Captain P. S. Bayliss was severely wounded. The men were forced to take cover behind the Canal wall and in the grounds of the Schools until something was worked out. Then houses along Lower Mount Street were rapidly taken over and, in an adoption of the rebel's own tactics, sharpshooters were hidden behind chimney pots and on the roofs. Civilians were ordered to stay indoors. Those who ignored the instructions paid the penalty. Charles Hyland, for instance, who had spent all the previous day helping to carry the wounded into Sir Patrick Dun's Hospital, was shot dead on his own doorstep.

It was some time before the *Helga*'s gun could be brought to bear on what was generally understood to be the rebels' main position, because here, as with the 9-pounders opposite Kelly's the previous day, there was difficulty with the recoil. Working rapidly, however, in the shade of spreading trees and enjoying a certain liberty because the nearest rebel post was four hundred yards away and rebel fire consequently inaccurate, the men eventually jacked out the paving stones and the gun was made ready. Its opening blast shattered what remained of the windows in Percy Place, and landed, apparently without much effect, among the rebel positions. After a suitable interval it was followed by a second.

It was the most critical moment of the week for De Valera; upon his behavior now was to rest his later reputation as a soldier and a leader. Certainly with a man who had less confidence in himself, who was less intellectually vainglorious and less determined to make what heroes he could out of his unpromising raw material, the Boland's garrison might easily have scattered and broken. De Valera realized that it would not take much to batter down Boland's Bakery (an adequate-enough structure against rifle or machine-gun fire, but flimsy in relation to heavy gunfire) and that even a small-caliber shell would quickly demoralize his men. He called for a green flag and, when it was brought to him, ordered Captain Michael Cullen and three men to occupy a tall disused distillery tower, some three or four hundred yards from the Bakery and perhaps the dominating landmark in the area. Even today there are those who insist that De Valera, when he ordered Cullen to occupy the tower, had no other thought in mind than to prevent the military from seizing it first, but the majority "are inclined to allow him the benefit of the doubt" and give him the credit for a brilliant strategem. Before a third shell could be fired, Cullen and his men had hung the rebel flag from the top of the tower and had then hastily retreated down a spiral staircase to the ground floors.

The military at once took new bearings and another shell arced triumphantly into the cloudless sky. It missed the tower by several yards, however, and plunged into the Liffey near Sir John Rogerson's Quay, while De Valera danced up and down in high glee, shouting, "Hurray! What a rotten shot!" The burst landed in the water within feet of the *Helga*, at that moment lying alongside the Quay. It immediately led to one of those mad contretemps which inevitably appear to attend the English when they find themselves breathing in the pure, crystal air of Ireland. The *Helga*, believing herself under bombardment, replied with a salvo which also missed the tower by yards and fell just short of Percy Place. Nothing daunted, the 1-pounder had another go at the tower and once again missed —the shell following almost precisely the same trajectory as its predecessor and plunging into the Liffey so close to the *Helga* that it drenched the crew. As the gunner prepared for yet another go, Sergeant George Norton of the South Staffs heard him remark, "If I miss again, it means tuppence off my pay!" Luck was with him this time, however, and the shell cracked heavily against the top of the tower, knocking the green flag askew and bursting a water tank, which showered its contents upon the defenders and almost drowned them.

De Valera was so delighted that the English had been fooled into firing on the wrong target that he ran up and down the railway line cheering like a schoolboy. The rank and file hardly shared his enthusiasm. For them the whole business was grim, and they wondered what would happen when the tower was finally demolished. This would obviously happen fairly soon, for after his initial lapses, the gunner in Percy Place had got his aim straight, and every time the gun boomed, great chunks of masonry plunged toward earth. The *Helga* caught on to what was happening and was finding the mark. But inexplicably, after less than a dozen shells had cracked stunningly into the tower, the bombardment ceased.

A few minutes later Volunteer Jackson was seen to stagger from the tower. To Captain Donnelly, who ran to meet him, he cried, "You must relieve us. Send someone else in there— we can't stick it!" Behind him emerged the rest of the party, all badly shaken. Donnelly told them to withdraw, but did not try to send another party in. The tower, in drawing off the heavy gunfire, had served its purpose, and the green flag, however askew, still flaunted defiantly. It was, morally, a victory.

During the lull which followed, Donnelly decided an infantry attack must be imminent and ordered his men into position to repel it. The South Staffords, however, were concerned only with continuing their advance into the city. This, according to their own reports, they found "arduous and perilous," in no way like fighting an open battle in France or among the ruins of Ypres or Albert. It was not until evening, in fact, that they felt confident enough to push forward in strength.

The bombardment of the tower had ended prematurely because the 1-pounder gun had been borrowed by the 2/7th and 2/8th Sherwoods. At daybreak, the two battalions had received orders from General Lowe to march to the Royal Hospital at Kilmainham along the same route which their left wing had taken without incident the previous day. With that stanch old warrior, Colonel Oates, in command of the advance guard and the main body—including Brigade H.Q., Royal Engineers, and A.S.C., with the rest of the 2/8th and the remnants of the 2/7th following—the column set off from Ballsbridge Show grounds intending to cross Leeson Street Bridge and proceed by the South Circular Road. They hoped to negotiate all this without fighting. No one expected a repetition of Wednesday's battle during the crossing of the bridge, but the 1-pounder was borrowed as a precaution, since there was a report that the Sinn Feiners were holding a few houses in the vicinity. The gun, as it turned out, was not needed. All, indeed, went as well as had been anticipated until the column reached the vicinity of the South Dublin Union where, at Rialto Street, a flurry of shots stampeded the horses of the Royal Engineers. Colonel Oates and the advance guard had already passed the spot and were approaching Rialto Bridge when the shots were fired.

The Colonel at once called his second in command, Captain "Mickey" Martyn, and ordered him to clear Rialto Street and all buildings in the vicinity. Martyn was a short, dashing bundle of energy, imbued with the French spirit of *elan,* who had served with the first-line battalion at "Plug Street" and Neuve Chapelle. While the Colonel was giving these orders, his son, Captain John Oates, who had gone scouting ahead with a small advance party, reported that he was being fired on from the front and also from a rhubarb field southwest of the bridge.

Colonel Oates halted the entire column, deciding that both flanks would have to be cleared before it was safe to allow the Brigade transport—a long column of vehicles—to risk the crossing. He ordered Captain Dimmock with "A" Company to clear the rhubarb field, brought "D" Company up to secure the line of advance along the South Circular Road, and sta-

274

tioned a platoon at the approach to the bridge where he established his Advanced H.Q. The 2/7th and 2/8th appear to have been gluttons for punishment: a short detour could have been made easily and action avoided.

As it was, Captain Martyn entered the Union grounds and began by investigating the Auxiliary Workhouse from which the firing appeared to be coming. He found the place deserted but from it, spotted a Sinn Fein flag flying above a fairly strong-looking building five or six hundred yards away. A sudden black puff of powder from one of its windows showed where the shooting really was coming from. Characteristically Martyn decided to have an immediate go at it. Even if he failed to take it, he reasoned, he would at least keep the Shinners occupied long enough to let the Brigade transport get through. He left a small party under Captain Oates near the Rialto Gate to give him covering fire, and led forty men across the open ground. The crossing was no picnic.

"I found a bullet in Dublin every bit as dangerous as a bullet in No-Man's-Land," recalls Martyn. "In some ways the fighting in Dublin was worse. In France you generally had a fair idea where the enemy was and where the bullets were going to come from. In Dublin you never knew when or from where you were going to be hit."

The fire from the Nurses' Home—for this was the building which Martyn had spotted from the Auxiliary Workhouse—was heavy and accurate and Martyn knew he was suffering casualties (one was Lance-Corporal Chapman, gamekeeper to the Duke of Newcastle), but he had no time to look round. In short rushes—advancing, dropping to return the fire, then jumping up to make another short dash before flopping down again—the party advanced toward the great straggle of Union buildings lying between them and the Nurses' Home. In the meantime Brigadier Maconchy decided to risk sending a transport across the bridge to see what would happen. Reins gripped in one hand, rifle in the other, the Army Service Corps driver galloped his horses toward the bridge. The animals strained eagerly and sparks flew as the iron-rimmed wheels skidded and bounced along the road, the transport swaying crazily. A volley of bullets sang over the driver's head and all

275

around him, some piercing the wooden slats, but the horses never slackened. The lesson was clear though: the rest of the transport was not likely to get through without being severely damaged.

Captain Oates watched Martyn and his men vanish toward the first Union building and waited for some sign that they had come in contact with the rebels. Heavy fire from the main position in the Nurses' Home continued, however, and Oates, with only his orderly, decided to reconnoiter and see what had happened to Martyn. Screened by the trees near the Canal wall, he managed to reach the building near which he had last seen Martyn and his men. He turned a corner and bumped into the platoon Martyn had borrowed from him. Martyn was not with them. They were in a long quadrangle, enclosed by tall stone buildings on either side and the Nurses' Home, with its Sinn Fein flag hanging limply, still lay four or five hundred yards away.

Sergeant Walker reported that Captain Martyn had gone off alone to see if it were possible to get into the Nurses' Home. Even as he spoke, a window shot up and a rebel opened fire. Oates thought the men took the surprise well—at least they did not run away. Foolishly, however, they leaped from one side of the quadrangle to the other with the muzzle moving after them as though they were attached to it by a piece of string.

"Come on, let's get inside!" shouted Oates, and raced toward a doorway at the corner of the quadrangle. The men followed him, and as they burst into the building, they bumped straight into Martyn. He rapidly explained that he had worked his way along the left flank of the Union through a series of workhouse wards until he was stopped by a brick wall and realized that there was no direct way from there into the Nurses' Home. He thought they should advance through the Maternity Hospital they were now in, for they would probably find windows overlooking the rebel position.

"That sounds fine," agreed Oates.

"Right then," said Martyn. "Come on."

They advanced without difficulty through several maternity wards, their appearance creating a hubbub among the pa-

276

tients, and gained the windows overlooking the Nurses' Home. Here Martyn posted riflemen. A brisk exchange of shots, however, made him decide that they were not likely to make progress by firing at heavily barricaded windows and hoping with luck to hit a Sinn Feiner. To the left of the Nurses' Home, directly facing them, lay a line of low buildings which appeared to be connected to it. "If we get in there, there must be a way into that building where the flag is," said Martyn. "I'm going across to recce."

Oates and the main body gave him covering fire, and Martyn, with a platoon in support, raced across the intervening ground under scattered fire. He returned shortly to explain that he had worked his way up through the low buildings—which were in fact an old people's ward—until he had come up against a blank wall.

"The only way through is to knock a hole in that wall," said Martyn. "Where can we find battering tools?"

Oates ordered Sergeant Walker to search for hammers and picks. Then, under covering fire, he and Martyn raced across the quadrangle, followed by the main body, two or three men at a time. Luckily the rebels proved to be "fairly poor shots" and there were no casualties. At the same time, an eight-man party made for the Bakehouse, just beyond the Nurses' Home, with the idea of enveloping the building on the right flank while Martyn enveloped it on the left. They were met by fierce, if again inaccurate rebel fire, but managed to reach their goal, although one man was shot dead as he entered the doorway and another was severely wounded. Two soldiers remained in the Bakehouse to give covering fire, while the other four crept around the side into a courtyard flanking the Nurses' Home. Here they dropped a bomb through a barred window of a building just behind the Bakehouse, killing one and wounding eight unfortunate members of the Union who had taken shelter in the dormitory there. On the left flank, meanwhile, Martyn and Oates had hurried through the Old People's Ward and reached the blank wall barring the way into the Nurses' Home. They waited until Sergeant Walker came up with a coalpick (hammer at one end, pick at the other) and got to work on the wall. It presented little difficulty (it was only two bricks thick) and it was quickly weakened to a point where only a push was necessary to break through. At this point Martyn casually turned to Oates and said, "Would you nip back, John, and get some bombs?" Never dreaming what Martyn might be up to, Oates went back into the Old People's Ward for a box of bombs. He returned to find Martyn gone and only a big whole gaping in the wall.

"The blighter!" swore Oates softly, and ducked through the hole.

It was quite dark and noisome inside; the windows had been well barricaded and the place was still full of choking dust. At the far side of the room—it seemed to be an office—was an open door. As Oates started toward it, there came a shattering burst of fire from just beyond it and instinctively he flung himself to the floor. There was a sudden thumping noise at the door and a member of his platoon came charging through, a shocked, incredulous look on his face.

Good God—he's running away! thought Oates, and shouted. But the man stumbled blindly past him and fell headlong through the hole. Oates went after him. The soldier was lying stretched out on his face, quite still. Oates bent over him and found he was dead. He had been shot through the heart and —just as a chicken flops around after his neck has been wrung —must have been dead even as he had charged through the door.

Oates rose quickly and tiptoed across to the door, where he halted. "I shall never forget that scene," he recalls. "I was looking into a lobby. To my right was the main door of the Nurses' Home, which had been blocked up with all sorts of rubbish. To my left was a wide doorway or archway—a kind or ornamental affair dividing the lobby. This had been barricaded with the most extraordinary conglomeration of everything you could possibly think of—sandbags, stones, rocks, bricks, furniture, mattresses. Opposite me was a door. It was open and I could see that it led into some kind of offices with a big barred window at the far end. "Mickey" Martyn and Sergeant Walker were stretched flat on the floor just under the barricade with the Sinn Fein rifles sticking out of the barricade just over their heads. The rebels, apparently, were unable to

278

depress them to the right angle. I saw Walker take the pin out of a bomb and try to throw it over from where he lay. Unfortunately there were only a few inches of space between the top of the barricade and the ornamental arch and it was not an easy thing to do. Instead of going over, the bomb hit the top of the barricade and fell back into the room. I thought 'My God—that's the end of them!' and I'm ashamed to say, I ducked back. Then I heard a tremendous explosion."

Miraculously Martyn and Walker still lived. When the bomb fell beside him, Martyn picked it up and threw it again. This time it sailed cleanly over the barricade and exploded on the far side. There was a great deal of shouting and yelling by the rebels then sounds of running feet, followed by an almost absolute silence. Martyn glanced round the little lobby and took stock. Two of his men lay dead near the door. Then he saw Oates in the doorway.

"You damn fool!" he shouted. "Come on! If you stay there you'll get shot!"

Oates emptied everything he had at the barricade—an automatic Colt and a Ross rifle—and dived full length under it to join Martyn and Walker. Rebel rifles still poked through the barricade, but they were no longer firing. The three men waited for some sound or movement. After a few moments they heard a rustle and scraping, as though someone were dragging himself along the floor.

"We'll never get through this," whispered Martyn, indicating the barricade. "We'd better try the annex," and he pointed to the door on the left. Oates nodded and they crawled through it on their stomachs. Once in the safety of the doorway they got to their feet and rushed toward the windows. If they got through them, they might, by creeping round the side of the Nurses' Home and entering it from the rear, successfully outflank the barricade. Martyn broke the window with his revolver and seized the bars. He shook them like a lunatic, but they held firm.

"Blast!" he swore. "It's no use—we'll have to go back and try some other way." Then, as they started toward the door, a simply tremendous firing broke out in the lobby. "It was completely indiscriminate firing," recalls Oates. "They were just blazing away across the room at nothing in particular as though they had lost their heads." The three men lay flat and crawled forward cautiously. There seemed nothing for it now but to cross the lobby somehow, go back to the hole, and try to work their way around the outside of the Nurses' Home. Waves of suffocating cordite beat into their faces and they began to cough. Immediately another tremendous blast of fire swept the lobby.

At the beginning of this extraordinary battle, the Nurses' Home was occupied by exactly twenty-seven insurgent officers and men (sixteen more rebels occupied the buildings fronting James Street, but they were not immediately involved in the fighting). From the beginning they had been under heavy strain. Nine sentry posts had to be manned nightly, and there were only twenty men available to do duty—Kent, Brugha, Cosgrave, the cook Doyle, a Red Cross man, and a man who had suffered a nervous breakdown being excused. By Thursday no one had had a proper sleep for days. Casualties, too, had been relatively heavy—eight men killed, a dozen wounded and more than a dozen captured. Morning, that Thursday, however, had been marked by a strange quietness. The city appeared to have relapsed into normality. Not a single shot had disturbed the serenity and people could be seen walking in the streets, or idly talking with their neighbors. It was so quiet, indeed, that the garrison had seized the opportunity to shave and freshen themselves up. A dispatch from Pearse shortly before noon had raised their spirits, too, so it was with a faint feeling of surprise that the first sounds of shots were heard shortly before 3 P.M. These, in fact, had been fired by rebels cooped up in Jameson's Distillery in Marrowbone Lane. Here 120 men and their women auxiliaries were so confident of victory that they had even arranged a ceilidhe— an Irish dance—for the following Saturday night. It was these shots—from their sentries posted on the roof—which stampeded the Royal Engineers' horses.

When Captain Martyn began advancing across the Union grounds, the covering fire given him was so fierce and sustained that the men in the Nurses' Home found themselves

280

pinned down and, for all practical purposes, unable to return it. Bullets streamed through the windows from all angles, stripping what remained of the plaster from the walls and ceilings, blasting window frames and cutting off each man from his fellows. Movement up or down the stairs became impossible. Martyn was thus able to gain his first objectives with little loss. It was only when he and his men began their rush across the courtyard in front of the Nurses' Home, one party heading for the Bakehouse, the other—under Martyn himself —making for the Old People's Ward, that the rebels were able to get in reasonable shots. Despite this, both parties gained their objectives with minimum losses.

The rebels had been holding out well, but now the military missed an excellent opportunity to bring the battle to a swift conclusion. Had the Bakehouse party, when they dropped their bomb into the dormitory, continued along the wall of the building, they would have come upon a hole giving them access to the rebel positions along the James Street frontage. Had they even, as an alternative, swung left, they would have taken the Nurses' Home in the rear, and could have captured the entire garrison with a minimum of trouble. As it was, they retreated to the Bakehouse.

The truth was that, at this moment, each side had gathered rather exaggerated ideas of the other's strength. The rebels, picking out the long column of transports and the two Sherwood battalions through field glasses, calculated that they were up against two thousand men, although in fact Colonel Oates had actually dispatched less than fifty men to deal with them. Martyn himself, from the outset eager for action and perhaps a trifle contemptuous of the opposition, had little or no idea of the rebel strength until a Union official, (perhaps deliberately) told him that there were more than two hundred rebels holding out in the Home. This sobered him a trifle but failed to deter him, and although heavily outnumbered at the actual point of battle, he almost managed to pull it off. In fact he would have, indeed, but for the sheerest ill luck.

When he and his small party smashed their way into the lobby, Commandant Kent decided that all was lost. He had seen the military gain the Bakehouse and knew that his line of retreat was in danger. When the military got into the lobby, also, Kent decided it was time to get out. Volunteer David Sears, who later wrote an account of what happened in the South Dublin Union, insists that there was no panic among the garrison. He says that he and the men with him received a definite order to evacuate the Nurses' Home and that their retreat was carried out in an orderly, if hurried, fashion. Lieutenant William Cosgrave, the Battalion Adjutant (later to become President of the Irish Free State) who was on the rebel side of the barricade when Martyn broke in, also says that a definite order to retire was given to him. "It was given to me by Captain Douglas Ffrench-Mullen and I understood it was a definite order from Vice-Commandant Brugha who was upstairs and in a position to see where the British were." On the other hand, Section-Commander John Joyce, who was on the top floor, did not receive any order. He recalls that after he had been firing on the Bakehouse party for some time his ammunition ran low and, when he turned to ask for more, he discovered he was alone.

Kent left by the rear of the Nurses' Home just as Captain Martyn broke into the lobby and was met by the first fierce volley which killed three of his men. Sears says that Kent, realizing the full peril of the position, hurried off to call up the sixteen men in James Street as reinforcements, and that this action, coinciding with panicky shouts of "The British are in!" was misunderstood by the rest, who thought the enemy had broken through the barricade. This, in turn, led to Brugha ordering a retreat. Whatever was the cause of the confusion, the rebels were already fleeing before Martyn tossed his bomb over the barricade and called on them to surrender.

It was a stroke of ill luck for the military that Walker decided to throw the bomb. It killed no one. It did not cause the rebel retreat. But it wounded Cathal Brugha (Charles Burgess), the fierce, courageous little Vice-Commandant, who was the last man down the stairs (except for Joyce who was still busy firing away at the Bakehouse). As Brugha crossed the lower landing (which was roughly the same height from the ground as the top of the barricade), the bomb exploded. Small fragments hit him and as he collapsed in agony, Captain

282

Oates, standing in the lobby doorway and raking the barricade first with his Colt automatic and then with his rifle, hit him again. Somehow, not a single shot proved fatal and although it was said of him years afterward that "every time he walks, he jingles," Brugha was able to drag himself to the bottom of the stairs and crawl into a small kitchen opening off the passageway. He managed to turn over onto his stomach, and with his "Peter the Painter" rifle pointing at the barricade, prepared to hold off the military singlehanded.

This is how Joyce found him when he came down the stairs. Firing had ceased temporarily as Martyn, Oates, and Walker crawled toward the annex.

Joyce bent over Brugha. "Good God! What's happened?" he asked.

"Oh, they've left," said Brugha laconically.

"But what about you?" asked Joyce.

"I'm staying here," said Brugha. He fumbled in his pocket and extracted a watch. "If you ever get out of here alive, will you give this to my wife?" he asked weakly. "Now, will you get me a drink of water?"

Joyce, pocketing the watch, rose and got water from the kitchen. While Brugha drank, there was a shout of "Surrender!" from the far side of the barricade. Brugha immediately fired a terrific burst in defiance. Then turning to Joyce he said, "You'd better go after the others. Tell Kent I'll hang on here as long as I'm able."

Crouching low, Joyce darted past the foot of the stairs and doubled round to the rear of the Home and into the open courtyard. At the far side a hole had been broken in a wall; he went through it and found himself in the dormitory next to the Bakehouse where more holes in the wall led to the offices on James Street. The rest of the battalion were in the dormitory. When Joyce arrived, Cosgrave was arguing with Kent that the military had not, in fact, broken into the Nurses' Home and that they should return and continue fighting. Joyce told Kent that he had left Brugha lying desperately wounded and alone at the barricade, but that he would hold on for as long as possible. To Joyce's astonishment, Kent just shook his head and wearily shrugged his shoulders.

283

"I got the impression that it was all up then," recalls Joyce. "I remember sitting down on a chair or a sofa and thinking, 'This fellow Kent thinks it's the end.'"

Sears, who was present, admits that at this point the rebels felt so dispirited that they could only sit there and wait for the military to arrive. Kent said that they had all put up a good fight, that there was still no question of surrender, and that they would go on fighting to the last man. Then he led them in a decade of the Rosary, following which anybody who had cigarettes had a last smoke. "If the military had come in then," wrote Sears afterward, "they could have raked us with fire and we were in no position to reply." As the military would have had to cross an open courtyard, this is a measure of the rebels' demoralization.

Then, while they sat gloomily around, their thoughts fixed on defeat, they heard someone singing "God Save Ireland," in short, intermittent snatches. One man ventured out to see who it was and returned shortly to report that it was Brugha, who had apparently dragged himself into a small yard at the rear of the kitchen. He had, in fact, propped himself up with his back to a wall and through the open back door had been able to enfilade the barricade at an angle of forty-five degrees. From time to time he fired at the barricade. When the military refused to charge over it, he began singing in defiance, repeatedly challenging them to come over and fight.

"That singing seemed to stir Kent from his lethargy," recalls Joyce. "It stirred every one of us, in fact. I remember Kent suddenly saying, 'Come on, boys,' and then the whole crowd of us rushed back. Some of us manned the barricade while others lay flat on the landing behind the partly erected barricade there, and from there we blazed away. Brugha had in fact saved us, for the military never got through."

Captains Martyn and Oates and Sergeant Walker scuttled back across the lobby to the safety of the small room they had entered through the hole long before the main body of rebels had plucked up enough courage to return. From the annex doorway Oates had plastered the barricade with bullets, while Martyn and Sergeant Walker scrambled across to the

284

far side. Then Martyn from the other side, gave cover to Oates. Safely across, the three men sat down in the small room to decide their next move. At brief intervals a burst of bullets in the lobby showed that the rebels [*this was Cathal Brugha*] were still there, and still quite aggressive.

"We decided that none of us felt brave enough to storm the barricade," remembers Oates. "Martyn said he would go back and report, and see if anything else could be done. He left me in the room with orders to see that the rebels didn't break out. I remained with about half a dozen men. It was growing dark and the lights had been turned on in the Old People's Home next door, where the rest of my platoon waited. I ordered these to be turned out so that we would not be caught in silhouette if the rebels broke out. And here we stayed. I had two boxes of Mills bombs. I placed my men round the walls and told them to keep their eyes fixed on the doorway and if they saw the slightest movement, to toss a bomb. For a long time everything remained quiet. Then suddenly there was a terrific burst of fire in the lobby [*this was when the rest of the rebels returned*] and I thought: Oh, well, here they come! It really sounded quite tremendous in that confined space and immediately my recruits bolted. I hadn't the sense to do the same . . . I just sat there with the two boxes of bombs between my feet. The easiest way to save my life, I decided, was to chuck a bomb into that lobby every two or three minutes. I had about 48 bombs in all and I calculated that that would keep me going long enough, anyway, for Martyn to come back. That is what I did. I felt sorry for the old people behind me in the Ward—the noise must have been horrible—but I never heard a sound from them. Every now and then these chaps kept firing into the lobby and then I'd give them another one. I'd got through one box and was halfway through the other, beginning to wonder what I was going to do next, when Martyn returned. He said, 'It's all right now—Brigade and the transports have got through—we've managed to keep these chaps so busy that they haven't had time to give trouble. Orders now are to withdraw.' So we decided to give the Sinn Feiners the rest of the box. We stood in the doorway and tossed the bombs at the barricade—possibly some went over, probably most didn't. Then we went back into the Old People's Ward where I found Sergeant Walker and another stalwart called Negus, looking thoroughly ashamed of themselves; when they realized that I'd stayed on, they'd come back. We rejoined the other men in the yard and made our way through the Union grounds back to Rialto Bridge and from there to the Royal Hospital. When we finally got there, everyone, of course, had gone to sleep long ago. So we dossed down in front of the altar in the Chapel and fell asleep."

It was then 10:15 P.M. Outside—away down toward Sackville Street and the center of Dublin—the whole sky had turned blood red.

[25]

By early afternoon, the flames were relentlessly consuming Lower Abbey Street, but despite their spectacular nature, they were still moving slowly; the buildings, at least a hundred years old, were solid. By 2:52, however, with the cannonading continuing, the flames had reached Sackville Place, which meant that at least half the block between Lower Abbey Street and Nelson's Pillar was on fire.

Captain Purcell, Chief of the Dublin Fire Brigade, looking through his field glasses from the high tower of the Fire Station near the Custom House, watched it spread slowly along both sides of Abbey Street. Now and then, he would put down his glasses and clench and unclench his fists in anger. He was so furious at times that none of his men dared to approach him. He had been warned by the military that it would be dangerous for him to tackle the fires and he now watched the city he loved, which his courage and skill had saved more than once, perish in front of him.

To reporter John O'Leary, in his eyrie on Aston Quay, burning Dublin was a scene of a "grandeur almost indescribable"; a tremendous holocaust of flame and smoke billowing into the air in such vast clouds that the street itself appeared to be dwarfed. Flames advanced from Lower Abbey Street toward the river, and he saw people emerge from the houses along Eden Quay like "terrified animals running before a forest fire." As they ran toward the Custom House, their tiny bundles joggling crazily up and down, gunfire ceased. He heard, floating across the river, the sound of the crackling and hissing flames, loud and roaring in the new silence. He

287

saw a soldier knocking at doors along Eden Quay, and more people emerging. Another soldier appeared with a megaphone and O'Leary caught the echo of his flat voice, "Come out, come out!" One by one reluctant people—young and old, sick and infirm, strong and weak—came out and were escorted toward Beresford Place. And then the gunfire restarted. A violent boom shivered over the water and a puff of smoke rose into the air beside the G.P.O.

Two shells hit the *Freeman's Journal* building in Princes Street, shortfalling the G.P.O. by scarcely twenty yards. Another shell screamed across the roof of the Metropole Hotel and crashed into the slates just above Volunteer Charles Saurin, on guard at a top-floor window. Dust and dirt billowed down the chimney into the room and yellow fumes swirled through the window. Spluttering and coughing, Saurin staggered into the corridor outside, as yet another shell hit the roof and a huge crack appeared in the wall beside Lieutenant Oscar Traynor. Saurin was again almost hit when a jet of machine-gun bullets, whipping in over the G.P.O. roof from Upper Sackville Street, scorched down the corridor. When the murk had finally cleared, Traynor ordered his men to evacuate the two top floors and left a man called Neale alone to keep watch in case the place caught fire. Neale, a Londoner, who spoke with a Cockney accent, and, as a good Socialist, addressed everyone as "camarade," perched nonchalantly on the top parapet, his legs dangling over Sackville Street, and studied the scene through his field glasses as though it were a play.

With characteristic recklessness James Connolly risked the dangerous streets to set up fresh outposts in preparation for a last stand by the Army of the Irish Republic. Undismayed by the sight of flames all along Lower Sackville Street, he stomped energetically up Henry Street, placing some men in a warehouse there, others in O'Neill's pub in Liffey Street (to command the Mary Street and Denmark Street approaches), and then retraced his steps to supervise the building of a large barricade in Princes Street, the short cul-de-sac at the south side of the G.P.O. Here he was hit. Without allowing his men

288

to realize that he had been wounded, he strolled casually back into the G.P.O. and walked around to the hospital section.

"Have you a screen here?" he carelessly asked McLoughlin, the medical student.

"There's one in that corner," said McLoughlin.

"Well, I want you for a moment," said Connolly, nodding to McLoughlin to follow him.

Behind the screen he took off his jacket. A bullet had pierced the upper flesh of his right arm. Lieutenant Mahoney was called quietly and he dressed the wound and bandaged it. This done, Connolly slipped on his jacket again, warning McLoughlin, "Now, don't say a word about this." Then he walked back into Princes Street as little concerned, apparently, as if he had nicked himself shaving.

Elsewhere in the G.P.O., a man went off his head and had to be locked up. Richard MacAuliffe, writing later, recalled the long-drawn-out tension of interminable hours of waiting. Desmond Ryan remembers voices calling out, "Go upstairs to meals," or "Two men are dying, be quiet." There were constant alarms that the military had begun their attack. Once almost the entire garrison rushed to the northern side of the building, with a few craning dangerously out of the windows to see, after someone had reported an armored car coming down Henry Street. From the roof of the warehouse in Henry Street, Volunteer John Reid and his comrades opened fire on the monster. Bullets bounced harmlessly off its plating, until somebody tossed a bomb and stopped it.

At three o'clock, Connolly posted sentries and lined the rest of his men up on the marble floor of the main office, numbering them off as smartly as though they were still on parade. Pearse left his high stool and took his place beside him. Then Connolly stepped back a pace and Pearse began speaking. The armored car, he announced, had been overturned by a bomb. All their principal positions were still intact; Commandant Daly had taken the Linenhall Barracks and captured twenty-three prisoners; the country was rising in support and a large body of Volunteers was marching on Dublin from Dundalk. Between thirty and forty police had been captured in an engagement at Lusk, and panic had been unleashed among the authorities, especially in the counties of Dublin and Meath. Wexford had risen and a column was marching on Dublin. Stocks of food had been found and the Dublin men would have no difficulty in holding on until the country forces arrived to relieve them. He ended by declaring that as the Irish Republic had held out for three full days, they were, by international law, entitled to the status of belligerents and the right to send a delegate to the Peace Conference which would follow the war.

It sounded almost like victory. Cheers rang out through the building and the men began singing the "Soldiers' Song." All fears of a military attack vanished and the men went back happily to their positions. Then, suddenly, from somewhere just off Upper Sackville Street, a field gun boomed briefly and shrapnel spattered over the roof, wounding several men. Connolly ordered everyone down at once and in their haste the men tumbled through the safety manholes (rough holes torn in the roof through which ropes had been lowered), and MacAuliffe saw some men ignore the ropes altogether and drop the whole distance of eighteen feet.

As this was happening, Mary Ryan saw The O'Rahilly, wearing a Tyrolean hat, parade a small party of men in the rear courtyard. She watched him strut up and down, before warning them: "Let every man remember this—as custodians of the prisoners every man must keep in mind the honor of his country. Whatever happens to the rest of us—they must be our first concern."

The omens worsened. Pearse and Connolly, although both believing in the right of women to make a full contribution, decided that the moment had come when they must leave. They had been gay, helpful, brave, and unflinching. Louise Gavan Duffy, chief assistant to Quartermaster Desmond Fitzgerald, had not slept since Tuesday; had served tea, sandwiches, and hot meals even while the shelling was at its height. Peggy Downey had gone on cooking; Mae Murray had tended the wounded. Long before other armies of the world would allow women to take places in the front lines, the Army of the Irish Republic accepted the principle that women were

290

entitled to stand there if they so wished. Pearse, however, knew it was time they went and issued orders accordingly.

Peggy Downey, a fiery little Liverpool girl, refused to accept the order. "I'm going to see Mr. Pearse," she told Miss Gavan Duffy. "I insist on staying."

"So do I," said Miss Gavan Duffy.

"In that case, so do I," said Mae Murray.

All three saw Pearse, and demanded to be allowed to stay. The rebel Commander in Chief could not refuse them. "If that is what you want, then you have my permission to stay," he said, looking very pleased. Three other determined women were also permitted to stay: Winifred Carney—Connolly's secretary—and two young nurses, the Misses Elizabeth O'Farrell and Julia Grenan.

Disaster, when it came, arrived unexpectedly.

Connolly ordered a "Stand to" in the main office and then marched along the ranks and picked out thirty men, among them fifteen-year-old John McLoughlin. He dismissed the rest and led the picked men into the courtyard, where he told young McLoughlin that he was putting him in charge and had an important job he wanted carried out. The military, he thought, would attack from both ends of Abbey Street— moving up Lower Abbey Street from the direction of the Custom House and down Middle Abbey Street from Capel Street or one of the bridges near the Castle. He wanted McLoughlin to occupy the *Irish Independent* newspaper offices in Middle Abbey Street and prevent the military moving down it. Then he led the party into Princes Street and through a back alleyway to Middle Abbey Street.

It was because Connolly was short of officers that he was forced to place a boy of fifteen in charge of a vital outpost at this critical moment. McLoughlin, as it turned out, proved an inspired choice—so far as anybody could have been in the circumstances. Tall and strong for his age, McLoughlin had come to the notice of Pearse and Connolly when he was carrying dispatches to them from John Heuston and Commandant Daly in the early part of the week. He had talked good sense, had shown he possessed sound ideas, and seemed to have that energy and persistence which usually lifts a man to prominence. Among men of limited talents and abilities, the tall self-assured youth no longer seemed merely a fair enough choice. Connolly, anyway, seized on him thankfully. Telling ten men to occupy Lucas's Lamp depot, Connolly stepped from the shelter of the alleyway into Middle Abbey Street and beckoned McLoughlin and the remainder of the party to make a dash for the *Independent* offices. Then, contemptuous of danger, he edged out to the curb to watch. He saw them safely inside and had just turned toward the alley again when a bullet ricocheted wildly from the pavement and struck him in the ankle.

He fell and lay for a moment twisting with pain. Then realizing that he was alone and no one was likely to answer his cries, he began dragging himself along the alleyway, inch after agonizing inch. He covered exactly one hundred and ten yards before flopping into the gutter in Princes, where he was seen at last by his men, and carried into the Post Office.

To Lieutenant John Mahoney, I.A.M.S., it did not seem wrong or in any way disloyal to assist in the rebel hospital. As a prisoner of war he had the right to refuse, but his natural inclinations as a doctor led him to do what he could. Each night, after a spell in the hospital below, he was returned to the room on the second floor which he shared with Chalmers and King. When Connolly was brought in, bleeding heavily, Mahoney immediately applied a tourniquet, while a rebel, like a magician producing a rabbit, wheeled up a bed. The bullet had smashed into the bone just above Connolly's ankle, and Mahoney suggested to "The Chronic" that he improvise a splint from a piece of board. While McLoughlin and Volunteer James Ryan, a medical student whom MacDermott had put in charge of the "hospital," applied the splint, Mahoney watched silently. Ryan was punctilious about Mahoney's position and took care to have as little truck as possible with him in contrast to "The Chronic," who regarded himself as a neutral. It was to "The Chronic" that Mahoney turned when he saw Connolly wince with pain. There was nothing to keep the torn ankle fixed and so the ends of the bones were protruding through the flesh.

"I couldn't stand that," recalls Mahoney today. "I was, after

292

all, first and foremost a doctor—so I asked McLoughlin ("The Chronic") if he had any way of giving an anesthetic?" He produced some chloroform—or at least a compound of spirits and chloroform of a strength of one in two thousand.

"It would have taken a whole lake of that to put Connolly under," says Mahoney, "and I began to understand why McLoughlin hadn't qualified after ten years of trying. 'Oh, that'll be all right,' he insisted, when I pointed out its inadequacies. Eventually Ryan sent a small lad for some chloroform and anesthetic ether. Ryan administered this while I released the tourniquet, fished out the small fragments of broken bone and ligatured the small vessels. Then I fashioned a back splint with a footpiece, applied it, and gave Connolly an injection of morphia. When I'd finished, Desmond Fitzgerald came to me and said, 'You're not to go back to your friends tonight—you're to stay here in the hospital.' So they produced a mattress for me and I lay down on it. Sometime later Connolly called me over, and eying me critically, said, 'You know, you're the best thing we've captured this week!' "

Although Connolly's spirit and courage remained as strong as ever, physically he grew very weak. Despite the injection he twisted and turned restlessly throughout the night, and Harry Walpole, his bodyguard, heard him cry out once, "Oh, God, did ever a man suffer more for his country!"

At 4:30 that morning, the 2/5th and 2/6th Sherwood Foresters had left the Royal Hospital, Kilmainham, for Dublin Castle. During the night, the men had been quartered in the armory of the hospital; the officers, in the little chapel among the exquisite carvings by Grinling Gibbons. Nearby, Kingsbridge Station had been taken over as Battalion H.Q. (the colonels establishing themselves in the Directors' Boardroom) where a complex system of outposts was established by Captain Stebbing to protect the lines and railway sheds while snipers of the Royal Irish Regiment potted away at the South Dublin Union. Following an early meal of bully beef and tea, the two battalions marched toward the Castle along a route protected by men of the Irish regiments, posted on roofs or the floors of houses. Camp was set up in Castle Yard where the troops remained until late afternoon, amusing themselves by watching snipers in Bermingham Tower operate against the Four Courts and Jacob's Biscuit Factory. Great drapes of canvas had been wrapped around the Tower to give cover and one sharpshooter had already been credited with over twenty victims.

Shortly after five o'clock the first units moved from the Castle down Parliament Street toward Gratton Bridge, where they were abruptly scattered by a volley from the Four Courts. Rebel command of the bridge threatened to disrupt the tying up of the two inner cordons—round the G.P.O. and the Four Courts. One of the armored cars, therefore, was loaded with sharpshooters and, under heavy fire, drove along the Quay and set down its sixteen occupants in a churchyard opposite the Four Courts. Private Bob Bury of Ashbourne, Derbyshire, was one of the men who jumped from the "boiler." He flung himself flat on a moss-covered grave and opened fire from between two headstones. This maneuver helped to keep down the Sinn Feiners' fire to some extent, but the bridge was still swept by bullets and crossing it was difficult. Eventually the armored car towed a field gun into position at the corner of Essex and Exchange streets and began bombarding the Four Courts, registering four clean hits on the east wing.

Military tactics, of course, were distinguishable from rebel ones by a marked superiority of method. Each Sherwood Company was assigned a specific sector to work in. Captain Tompkins and "D" Company were allocated the area from Coles Lane to Sackville Street, Captain Edmunds with "A" Company a sector from Capel Street to Coles Lane, while "C" Company under Captain Jackson was made responsible for Upper Abbey and Liffey streets. Captain Orr and "B" Company were to contain the Four Courts itself. Once the first troops crossed Gratton Bridge, they began erecting barricades to prevent the rebels infiltrating. Captain Edmunds discovered an apparently inexhaustible supply of sacks in a factory in his sector and ordered them filled with earth (most hovels in the area were so poor that they had only earthen floors, which the troops hacked up). The improvised sandbags were then loaded into the armored cars, which dropped them off at strategic points.

The "boilers" allowed the Sherwoods to work with almost utter impunity in the narrow, crisscrossed area of hovels and tenements. Each was capable of transporting a minimum of fifteen men at a time and their use counterbalanced, to some extent, the unorthodoxy of the rebels' own tactics. Shinners, the infantry had realized by now, might be hidden behind any of a couple of hundred chimneys and were exceedingly difficult to locate, telltale puffs of smoke from the rifles being rare; or they could be behind any curtained window. In the circumstances, the troops at times became jittery and trigger-happy. Private Thomas Fidler of Renishaw, Derbyshire, remembers one hectic ten-minute action in the gathering dusk that Thursday evening, when units of "A" and "B" companies mistook each other for Shinners and began blazing away at each other.

The armored cars, generally used only to transport men charged with holding key posts, would back up to houses on the corner of right-angled streets and disgorge troops armed with crowbars and hatchets for breaking in. They would then reload and drop more men at houses opposite, commanding the street along which they had just driven. In this way the cordon was slowly contracted. A first fruit was the release of the Lancers who had been holed up in the Medical Mission since Monday. At nightfall, however, operations ceased except where it was absolutely safe, as for example when the Royal Irish Regiment handed over their sector to "C" Company, Sherwoods. That night troops slept on the pavements, with sentries posted at each corner.

Toward midnight, flames from the burning Linenhall barracks finally spread to the premises of Messrs. Moore and Alexander, wholesale druggists in Bolton Street, and the area became so brightly lit that it was possible to pick out a pin lying on the pavement. The highly inflammable materials exploded in a roar, creating a searing furnace which challenged the spectacular flames along Sackville Street. At intervals barrels of oil shot into the air like fiery rockets and burst into pieces with a sound like artillery.

Captain Purcell still retained a faint hope that somehow or other the tall D.B.C. building in Lower Sackville Street might

295

withstand the flames. He watched Reis's, next door to it, go up, and still the D.B.C. held fast. Then suddenly, a long time afterward, an ominous light appeared in its upper lantern window and smoke and flames finally burst through the ventilators and windows. Within half an hour the roof had caught fire and the great lantern on top was encased in flames. "The whole made a weird sight", wrote Purcell afterward. Reporter O'Leary saw the flames kiss the ball on the top of the pagodalike dome, and for a while watched it stand high above the smoke and flame, thrown into relief by the scarlet clouds. "A scene of greater grandeur I have never witnessed, even in the cinema," he wrote. "It was only topped by the avalanche of flame and smoke that cascaded to the ground when the top itself collapsed," Richard MacAuliffe watching from the G.P.O., saw the crash as "a gigantic waterfall of fire."

And still the fires raged on and spread. At 7:30 P.M. the façade of the Waverly Hotel fell with a terrible roar and a vast cloud of smoke, glistening with blazing embers, oozed into the street like volcanic lava, and billowed off into the sky, leaving behind a rubble of smoking brick. At 9 P.M. the whole dolorous magnificence was brought to a climax by the collapse of Hopkins and Hopkins, whose blazing fall crushed and melted down thousands of pounds' worth of gold and silver.

At 10 P.M. Hoyte's oil works opposite the G.P.O. burst into flames and a sheet of death-white fire spurted several hundred feet into the air with an explosion which shook the walls of the G.P.O. This was followed by what sounded like a heavy bombardment, as thousands of oil drums exploded over Sackville Street. The light became so harsh and terrible that the men inside the G.P.O. had to shut their eyes. The heat struck them "like a solid thing," and across Sackville Street a million sparks floated in a starry cascade.

Long hoses snaked their way over the marble floors of the G.P.O. as windows and barricades were drenched time and again to keep them from catching fire. Men, dazed with the heat and the fearsome possibility that they would be burned to death, moved like sleepwalkers. With Connolly weak and suffering great pain, more and more of the actual direction of the battle devolved upon Tom Clarke and John MacDermott, who could not even boast military rank. Plunkett, courageously cloaking his own extreme pain and weakness, rose from the mattress where he had lain for most of the Rebellion and did what he could to relieve their burden. Once, staring out at the terrible fires, he remarked, "It's the first time it's happened since Moscow—the first time a capital has been burned since then!" which drew a weak, uncomprehending smile from some of the men, while others turned from him as though doubting his sanity. To Lieutenant Mahoney he seemed a weird apparition, striding about in a creased uniform, wearing a glittering bangle, big rings and, for some reason, a single spur jangling on one boot. As Mahoney stood watching him, Quartermaster Fitzgerald approached and said, "Lieutenant, I want you to know that we'll probably have to evacuate this position tomorrow. We're putting Chalmers and King down in the cellar for safety; if you manage to get away, you can tell your friends where they are."

Still the cordon contracted. Machine-gun and rifle fire went on continuously throughout the night. Once an armored car made a fleeting appearance in Westmoreland Street, as though it intended to cross O'Connell Bridge, but it soon retreated. Despite the harassment, Pearse strove desperately to keep a system of reliefs and duties going; even at the height of the bombardment, those off duty were glad to wrap themselves in a coat or blanket and, with their rifles beside them, stretch out on a shelf or a table or even on the floor.

And all the while the fire, creeping along the far side of the street and getting closer every second to the Imperial Hotel and Clery's, caused the temperature inside the G.P.O. to rise. It grew so hot, in fact, that when hoses were turned onto the coalbags and books which formed the window barricades—to prevent them catching fire—the water at once turned to steam. On the far side of the street a shining river of molten glass flowed along the pavement.

Suddenly a shout from across the street reached the G.P.O. and a figure was picked out, framed in a window of the Imperial Hotel. The cable line had long since been shot to pieces, so the man made a trumpet with his hands and shouted that the hotel had caught fire at the rear. "What are the orders?" he roared.

"Come over here, if you can," he was told.

In a moment four men were seen standing in the doorway of Clery's, which occupied the ground floor. Pearse ordered the front door of the G.P.O. thrown open, and the four men dashed for it one by one. The last man across, who had wrapped himself in a mattress as protection, fell on his face in the middle of Sackville Street, and a great "Oh!" went up from the watchers in the G.P.O. The man lay still for a moment as bullets chipped pieces out of the roadway, then amid cheers, picked himself up and resumed his run. Ten minutes later the flames burst through the hotel windows.

The O'Rahilly stood beside young James O'Byrne watching the hotel burn down. "Do you know what they're doing that for?" he remarked quietly.

"Yes," said O'Byrne. "With that out of the way they can get a good bang at us."

"No," said The O'Rahilly sadly, "that's not the reason. It's to show you and me exactly what they think of poor old Ireland."

The great fear shadowing the mind of every rebel was that if he were captured by the military, he would be instantly put up against a wall and shot. This was what troubled Brennan Whitmore certainly, as he and his comrades slipped down a ladder from the Pillar Café into North Earl Street and, with Hoyte's oil barrels exploding spectacularly over their heads, doubled across the street to an alleyway on the far side. General Headquarters having neither confirmed nor countermanded his plan, he had decided to make a break for it on his own responsibility. They ran through the alleyway into Cathedral Street and then into Marlborough Street and Brennan Whitmore began to feel optimistic. "This is what Headquarters should be doing," he remarked to one of the aides, Volunteer Gerald Crofts.

He was handicapped, however, by the presence of the four Cumann na mBan ladies. Crofts suggested that they should be left in the Pro-Cathedral Presbytery. Whitmore agreed, so they stopped on their way past and rang the bell. The priest who came to the door said, "I presume you want sanctuary?"

"Well, it's not for ourselves, Father, but for these four girls,"

298

said Whitmore. The girls, however, were not willing to be left behind. Their protests were followed by a struggle, but eventually they were hustled inside and the priest slammed the door shut as Whitmore and Crofts ran off.

For the first five hundred yards or so all went well, but as Whitmore led his men across a street opening, a bullet caught him in the leg. A young man called Lemass, who was running beside him, also collapsed, wounded. In the resulting panic, the men scattered. When Whitmore managed to drag himself to the shelter of a corner, he found he had only nine men left and only the vaguest idea of where he was. Nearby was a tenement and, helped by one of his men, he led the way into it. The place simply swarmed with women and children and, while they were trying to find a corner in which to hide, a man appeared and ordered them to get out. Whitmore told him to go to hell and led his men into the first unoccupied room he found. He told them to place the wounded Lemass on a bed and disposed the rest of them around the room with their backs to the wall. Warning them to keep a constant watch and waken him before daylight, he rolled under the bed. Within seconds he could feel the fleas biting, but he was so tired that, despite them, he was soon fast asleep.

Rebel nerves had reached breaking point. In the South Dublin Union, a man pointed a gun at Kent, threatening to shoot him. In Church Street, a young man flung himself to the floor of the Father Mathew Hall and screamed aloud for God to save him from all devils around him. It took six men to hold him down and two administrations of chloroform to quiet him. In Boland's, a man ran amok and shot a sentry, a popular city councillor called Peter Macken, and was, in turn, shot by a comrade.

From the roof of the College of Surgeons, the Countess Markievicz watched Dublin burning. "Think of it," she said to Chris Caffrey. "That's not Rome burning—but Dublin!"

A short distance away Professor O'Briain sat awestruck, and then commented, "Lord, we are destroying the city."

From Killiney Hill, nine miles away, people could pick out Nelson atop his pillar.

In a cellar near the docks where he and several other "suspects" had been incarcerated by the military, Sean O'Casey laid down his volume of Keats and gazed at the scarlet stain spreading across the sky. One of the men playing cards followed his gaze for a moment and then said, "Christ help them now!"

Sparks showered down upon the roof of the G.P.O. as though from a cornucopia. With the building threatened by fire, Pearse ordered all bombs and grenades taken into the cellars. Again men drenched the walls and barricades with water. Yet for a while their efforts seemed useless. Dramatically, then, a breeze whipped in from the mountains and the flames were swept to the southeast away from the G.P.O.

Desmond Ryan sat down wearily on a barrel and gazed at the flames licking the sky. After a while Pearse sat down beside him, his face red and scorched under his upturned hat. They chatted idly for a while, then Pearse said, "We might all come through—perhaps."

"I've only one reason for wishing to survive," said Ryan, "Someday I'd like to write a book about this."

Pearse smiled, but remained silent for a moment. Then almost abruptly he asked, "It was the right thing to do, wasn't it?"

"Yes," said Ryan slowly, "yes, it was."

"Failure, of course, means the end of everything," said Pearse sadly, "the Volunteers, Ireland, all!" A shadow crossed his face as outside yet another building crashed. "Well, when we're all wiped out, people will blame us for everything, I suppose, and condemn us," he continued. "Yet if it hadn't been for this protest, the war would have ended and nothing would have been done. After a few years people will see the meaning of what we tried to do."

He fell silent again. Then, as another flurry of gunfire boomed down Sackville Street he suddenly seemed to come alive once more. "What a great man The O'Rahilly is," he said enthusiastically. "Coming in here with us although he's been against a Rising. You know, Emmett's [two hour] insurrection is as nothing to this. They will talk of Dublin in the future as

300

one of the splendid cities—as they speak today of Paris. Dublin's name will be glorious forever!"

Across the street, the whole front of Clery's and the Imperial Hotel crashed to the ground in a rending, tearing roar, and great tongues of fire leaped hundreds of feet high. Above the sound of the rushing flames the rebels all around them began to sing:

> "Soldiers are we,
> Whose lives are pledged to
> Ireland!"

From the window of the Chief Secretary's Lodge in Phoenix Park, Augustine Birrell looked out and wept.

26

When General Sir John Grenfell Maxwell, K.C.B., K.C.M.G., and his staff (it included Prince Alexander of Battenberg) sailed up the River Liffey at two o'clock on Friday morning, April 28, 1916, the entire city of Dublin appeared to be given over to the holocaust.

"When we got to the North Wall," Sir John wrote later to his ailing wife, "it was not quite so bad, yet a great deal of that part north of the Liffey was burning. Bullets were flying about, the crackle of musketry and machine-gun fire breaking out every other minute. We were met by three motors and drove to the Royal Hospital. The tower is picquetted with soldiers and most of the rebels are in a ring fence and we are gradually closing in on them. I think that after tomorrow it will be clearer, but a lot of men will be knocked over. These infernal rebels have got a lot of rifles and apparently a fair supply of ammunition. Everything is hung up. No food or supplies of any sort can be got; it is not safe to walk into the town. Grafton Street and all the shop part has to be cleared of these infernal fellows."

Sir John, still vigorous and full of ambition at fifty-six, had arrived back in Ireland still smarting from what he considered the raw deal which had been handed him by the politicians. As C in C Egypt he had checked the Turk in his one serious advance into the Delta, and it was certainly not his fault that everything had gone wrong at Gallipoli. Why they had not left him to fight out the war on the terrain he knew best he would never know. In addition, they had left him languishing in idleness for almost a month since his return from Egypt. In a letter to his friend, Sir George Arthur, only a few days previ-

302

ously, he had allowed himself to give expression to the bitterness he felt: "I have been in a nursing home for the past ten days for a complete overhaul as it was thought I had a stone. But happily I am passed fit. I am idle and fear likely to be as the political people have got their knives into me." At one stage he had toyed with the idea of turning down the Dublin job—he could offer Lady Maxwell's ill health as an excellent excuse—but mature reflection had convinced him that his career still might be advanced if he could deal with this affair quickly and efficiently. Within hours of his arrival, therefore, he issued a Proclamation:

The most vigorous measures will be taken by me to stop the loss of life and damage to property which certain misguided persons are causing by their armed resistance to the law. If necessary I shall not hesitate to destroy all buildings within any area occupied by the rebels and I warn all persons within the area specified below, and now surrounded by H. M. troops, forthwith to leave such area under the following conditions: women and children may leave the area by any of the examining posts set up for the purpose and will be allowed to go away free. Men may leave by the same examining posts and will be allowed to go away free provided the examining officer is satisfied they have taken no part whatever in the present disturbances. All other men who present themselves at the examining posts must surrender themselves unconditionally together with any arms and ammunition in their possession.

Then, getting down to the sure military aspects of the problem, he confirmed Lowe's orders in relation to the operations in and around Sackville Street; ordered the 2/4th Lincolns (part of the 176th Brigade which had arrived during the night, bringing the 59th Division to is full complement) to fling an outer cordon around the entire southern suburbs of the city, and in the afternoon ordered the 2/5th and 2/6th South Staffs to concentrate on reducing the Four Courts area, while the Sherwoods and the Irish Regiments dealt with rebel General Headquarters. He then interviewed the Lord Lieutenant and Mr. Birrell.

"They do not altogether appreciate being under my orders,"

he wrote Lady Maxwell, "but I told them I did not mean to interfere unless it was necessary and I hoped they would do all I asked them to. The Sinn Feiners are all over Ireland; when we have done with them in Dublin we will have to clear the outstations. But from all I can gather the nerve centre of the movement is in Dublin and in that part we have surrounded. I got your telegram. I am glad you are going on all right; mind, no set backs and try to do what the doctor orders. It's strange being back in Dublin, living in the Royal Hospital [he had been Chief Staff Officer to the Duke of Connaught when the latter was C-in-C Ireland in 1902]. Since I began this letter a good deal has happened: I think the signs are that the rebels have had enough of it. I will know this for certain tonight."

To Maxwell all was as it should be. He had arrived on the scene promptly and all that it had been necessary for him to do was to give a few quick blasts on his trumpet and the walls had begun to fall down.

Dawn, in fact, had lighted a scene of destruction and desolation paralleled up to that time only by the ruined towns and cities of Northern France. To those familiar with newspaper photographs, Dublin overnight had become a second Ypres. Here rose up the same sliced, skeleton buildings, here spread the same acres of flattened and obscene rubble. Directly opposite the G.P.O. stood bare, blackened walls, smoke still wreathing around them. It was no longer possible to see as far as O'Connell Bridge. Now and then yet another wall would fall with a stupendous crash, shooting up a fresh shower of burning fragments and clouds of billowing smoke. Debris was scattered halfway across the street; steel girders hung twisted and blackened. The heat still remained and a heavy smell of burning cloth hung in the air.

To reporter O'Leary, bleary-eyed after a sleepless night, the most poignant sight of all was that of the stiff body of an old man lying across the tram tracks on O'Connell Bridge— shot down sometime during the night—for this was the only figure of a human being amid the entire wasteland. The Post Office seemed even more majestic, more stately than ever in contrast to the ruin and devastation all about it. Above it still flaunted the green flag and the Sinn Fein tricolor of green, white, and orange. Then he began to notice the military, singly and in twos and threes, creeping furtively across the bridge, probing for cover among the debris. Now comes the final assault, he decided, and braced himself for a thrilling bayonet charge.

Inside the G.P.O., a lull had set in. Breakfasts were served according to routine, and the women—who had been warned the previous evening that they would eventually have to go—prepared now to leave. Pearse, conscious that the end could not be far off, had spent the early hours of the day working on a manifesto, writing it with conscious irony, on Post Office notepaper bearing the Royal Arms of England in the top left-hand corner. In his own grandiose language he declared:

> Headquarters, Army of the Irish Republic,
> General Post Office, Dublin.
> 28th April, 1916. 9:30 A.M.

The Forces of the Irish Republic which was proclaimed in Dublin, on Easter Monday, 24th April, have been in possession of the central part of the Capital since 12 noon on that day. Up to yesterday afternoon, Headquarters was in touch with all the main outlying positions, and, despite furious, and almost continuous assaults by the British Forces all those positions were then still being held, and the Commandants in charge were confident of their ability to hold them for a long time.

During the course of yesterday afternoon and evening the enemy succeeded in cutting our communications with our other positions in the city and Headquarters is to-day isolated.

The enemy has burnt down whole blocks of houses, apparently with the object of giving themselves a clear field for the play of artillery and field guns against us. We have been bombarded during the evening and night by shrapnel and machine gun fire, but without material damage to our position, which is of great strength.

We are busy completing arrangements for the final defence of Headquarters, and are determined to hold it while the buildings last.

I desire now, lest I may not have an opportunity later, to pay homage to the gallantry of the soldiers of Irish Freedom who have during the past four days been writing with fire and steel the most glorious chapter in the later history of Ireland. Justice can never

305

be done to their heroism, to their discipline, to their gay and un-conquerable spirit in the midst of peril and death.

Let me, who have led them into this, speak, in my own, and in my fellow-commanders' names, and in the name of Ireland present and to come, their praise, and ask those who come after them to remember them.

For four days they have fought and toiled, almost without cessation, almost without sleep, and in the intervals of fighting they have sung songs of the freedom of Ireland. No man has complained, no man has asked "Why?" Each individual has spent himself, happy to pour out his strength for Ireland and for freedom. If they do not win this fight, they will at least have deserved to win it. But win it they will, although they may win it in death. Already they have won a great thing. They have redeemed Dublin from many shames, and made her name splendid among the names of cities.

If I were to mention names of individuals, my list would be a long one. I will name only that of Commandant-General James Connolly, Commanding the Dublin Division. He lies wounded, but is still the guiding brain of our resistance.

If we accomplish no more than we have accomplished, I am satisfied. I am satisfied that we have saved Ireland's honour. I am satisfied that we should have accomplished more, that we should have accomplished the task of enthroning, as well as proclaiming, the Irish Republic as a Sovereign State, had our arrangements for a simultaneous rising of the whole country, with a combined plan as sound as the Dublin plan has been proved to be, been allowed to go through on Easter Sunday. Of the fatal countermanding order which prevented those plans from being carried out, I shall not speak further. Both Eoin MacNeill and we have acted in the best interests of Ireland.

For my part, as to anything I have done in this, I am not afraid to face either the judgment of God, or the judgment of posterity.

(Signed)   P. H. PEARSE
Commandant-General
Commanding-in-Chief, the Army of the
Irish Republic and President of the
Provisional Government.

Connolly, indeed, was still the guiding brain. He had slept fitfully during most of the night. With morning, and a realization that the end could not be put off much longer, his iron will asserted itself. "Put me on some kind of stretcher and take me into the front hall where I can resume command," he demanded.

James Ryan, the medical student who was officially in charge of the "hospital" demurred. So did Mahoney and McLoughlin. Ryan stressed the gravity of his wound, but he brushed the objection aside. "It is more important that I give confidence to the garrison," he insisted.

He was lifted onto a small iron bed, therefore, and half-wheeled, half-carried into the front hall, where his reappearance, despite the obvious pain he was suffering, cheered the men immensely. Harry Walpole, his bodyguard, reporting for duty, found him reading a detective story. Connolly put down the book while Walpole lit a cigarette for him, then, exhaling luxuriously, he said, "A book like this, plenty of rest, and an insurrection—all at the same time. This certainly is revolution de luxe."

Yet the man refused to stay idle for long. He sent for Miss Carney and began dictating a dispatch to her which would prove his last. It contained little that bore resemblance to the facts, yet from Connolly's point of view, it performed its main function, which was to keep up the morale of his men. Her Webley beside her, Miss Carney typed the following order:

> Army of the Irish Republic
> (Dublin Command)
> Headquarters, April 28th, 1916.

To Soldiers,

This is the fifth day of the establishment of the Irish Republic, and the flag of our country still floats from the most important buildings in Dublin, and is gallantly protected by the officers and Irish soldiers in arms throughout the country. Not a day passes without seeing fresh postings of Irish soldiers eager to do battle for the old cause. Despite the utmost vigilance of the enemy we have been able to get information telling us how the manhood of Ireland, inspired by our splendid action, are gathering to offer up

307

their lives, if necessary, in this same holy cause. We are here hemmed in because the enemy feels that in this building is to be found the heart and inspiration of our great movement.

Let us remind you of what you have done. For the first time in 700 years the flag of free Ireland floats triumphantly in Dublin City.

The British army, whose exploits we are for ever having dinned into our ears, which boasts of having stormed the Dardanelles and the German lines on the Marne, behind their artillery and machine-guns are afraid to advance to the attack or storm any positions held by our forces. The slaughter they have suffered in the last few days has totally unnerved them, and they dare not attempt again an infantry attack on our positions.

Our Commandants around us are holding their own.

Commandant Daly's splendid exploit in capturing Linenhall barracks we all know. You must know also that the whole population, both clergy and laity, of this district are united in his praises. Commandant MacDonagh is established in an impregnable position reaching from the walls of Dublin Castle to Redmond's Hill and from Bishop Street to Stephen's Green.

(In Stephen's Green, Commandant Mallin holds the College of Surgeons, one side of the square, a portion of the other side and dominates the whole Green and all its entrances and exits.)

Commandant de Valera stretches in a position from the Gas works to Westland Row, holding Boland's Bakery, Boland's Mills, Dublin South-eastern Railway Works and dominating Merrion Square.

Commandant Kent holds the South Dublin Union and Guinness's Buildings in Marrowbone Lane and controls James Street and district.

On two occasions the enemy effected a lodgement and were driven out with great loss.

The men of North County Dublin are in the field, have occupied all the Police barracks in the district, destroyed all the telegram system on the Great Northern Railway up to Dundalk, and are operating against the trains of the Midland and Great Western.

Dundalk has sent 200 men to march upon Dublin, and in the other parts of the North our forces are active and growing.

In Galway Captain Mellowes, fresh after his escape from an English prison, is in the field with his men. Wexford and Wicklow are strong and Cork and Kerry are equally acquitting themselves creditably. (We have every confidence that our Allies in Germany and kinsmen in America are straining every nerve to hasten matters on our behalf.)

As you know, I was wounded twice yesterday, and am unable to move about, but have got my bed moved into the firing line, and with the assistance of your officers, will be just as useful to you as ever.

Courage, boys, we are winning, and in the hour of our victory, let us not forget the splendid women who have everywhere stood by us and cheered us on. Never had man or woman a grander cause, never was a cause more grandly served.

(Signed)   JAMES CONNOLLY
Commandant-General,
Dublin Division.

It all sounded magnificent; and really that was all that mattered. Victory, in the military sense anyhow, had never been possible, but every extra hour they held out, every additional English soldier who set foot in Ireland, every shell which wrecked another building was another step toward ultimate victory. Never more would the Citizen Army "and their popguns" be a subject for public merriment; no longer would those who dreamed of a separate Ireland be contemptuously regarded as cranks and visionaries—for the dreamers had finally proved themselves to be men of action. They had at long last made their noise in the world; and the louder it was, the more certain their eventual victory.

The coils flung round them by the military still contracted however, if more slowly and less spectacularly than on the previous day. The 5th Leinsters, the Dublin Fusiliers, and the Ulster Composite Battalion along with dismounted troops of the Mobile Column held a tight arc stretching from the Castle along Dame Street and the Quays to Trinity College and the Custom House, and thence to Amiens Street Station and Gardiner Street. In Great Britain Street, the Royal Irish Regiment held the line, gradually moving eastward as the 2/5th and 2/6th Sherwood Foresters filtered into the labyrinth of streets behind the G.P.O. Captain Jackson's "C" Company

309

pushed in from Capel Street toward Abbey Street while "A" Company cleared Jervis Street and Denmark Street, and "B" Company set up a field gun in Great Britain Street at the junction of Coles Lane, which would prevent any rebel escape along Henry Street. Rapidly the ring fence round the G.P.O. began to bristle with barricades, machine guns, artillery, and mortars: a machine gun on the roof of the Rotunda Hospital at the head of Sackville Street, a mortar in Findlater Place just off the east side of Sackville Street, snipers as far down as the Gresham Hotel, a machine gun on top of Purcell's on the D'Olier Street corner, a field gun in Westmoreland Street, and finally a machine gun on the roof of Jervis Street Hospital.

The Sherwoods found their task distasteful. Casualties were persistent and the men were inclined to lose their tempers when they saw the terrible wounds caused by the Sinn Fein bullets. Operations were hampered, too, by the women of the neighborhood, who in their eagerness to loot the shops in Henry Street continually cut across the line of fire. Every house in the area had to be thoroughly searched, and as many were filthy, the job became more and more of a nightmare.

Just before noon an 18-pounder had been dragged into position in Great Britain Street and aimed down Coles Lane straight at Arnott's, a big drapery shop at the rear of the G.P.O. in Henry Street. Private Thomas Fidler recalls that the Colonel shouted, "Open all windows in the area!"; that another officer misinterpreted the order and bawled, "Close all windows!"; and that someone else then shouted, "Open those windows!" "While confusion reigned," says Private Fidler, "I remember the gun was fired off anyhow, and every bally window in the area was shattered." The military concern to avoid shattering windows in Great Britain Street was a trifle inexplicable in view of their bombardment of Arnott's, which was not even occupied by the rebels. The building caught fire immediately but was saved by its water-sprinkler system. Within a few minutes a small lake appeared in Henry Street.

In the Post Office the women and girls who were about to leave lined up in the main office where they listened, for the last time, to an address by Pearse. They deserved a foremost place in the nation's history, he told them; their bravery, their

310

devotion and their heroism in the face of danger surpassed even that of the women of Limerick in the days of Patrick Sarsfield; without them, he insisted, the men could not have held out so long. And then, with that diffident awkwardness which characterized his relations with women, he shook each of them by the hand and said good-bye. Clutching their Red Cross flag, the women stepped out into Henry Street and with pale, anxious faces, set off to meet the military.

Upstairs in their prison room overlooking Princes Street, Lieutenants Chalmers and King crouched under the table while bullets ricocheted around the room, and wondered how they would get out alive; it seemed ironical that, having escaped thus far without having their throats slit, they might end by being shot by their own side. Three rooms away Constable Dunphy of the D.M.P. and the other military prisoners lay flat on the floor to avoid the machine-gun fire. Then the O'Rahilly, anxious for their safety, ordered them transferred to the cellars where they at least would have protection. The move did nothing to remove Chalmers' deep misgivings, although The O'Rahilly promised: "I give you my word that you'll escape with your lives." They were locked in a cellar where, in semidarkness, they were able to feel the foundations tremble every time the artillery fired.

The bombardment, by now, had intensified. In Westmoreland Street the gunners were firing across O'Connell Bridge over open sights. They were finding it difficult, however, to get the exact range of the Post Office and kept smacking their shells into the Metropole Hotel beside it instead. To Volunteer Saurin, inside the hotel, the detonation sounded terrific, but in actual fact little damage was being done, the shrapnel splintering harmlessly over the roof. For a while, indeed, the main fury of the military assault seemed to be directed against the Metropole block (which extended from Manfield's shop on the corner of Middle Abbey Street to Princes Street). Even so Lieutenant Traynor's twenty-man garrison still held out in Manfield's desperately stemming the advance of the military up Lower Abbey Street and also preventing any direct attack across O'Connell Bridge. Two machine guns sprayed their positions incessantly, but the rebel fire remained dangerous.

311

Once Lieutenant Traynor returned to the Metropole from Manfield's through the holes in the wall and declared, "Thank God, I can die now—I've just shot one."

In contrast to the rebels in other positions—especially in the College of Surgeons where they were experiencing real hunger—the men in the Metropole were at least able to enjoy good food. Saurin—ordered into the basement to help a G.P.O. forage party fill sacks with tea, flour, fruit, and bottles of preserves—found that the management had cannily locked the silver room and the wine cellar before leaving. Comrades sent to prepare a meal for the garrison high-spiritedly donned the uniforms of the chefs and enjoyed themselves clowning around. Yet despite the circumstances and the fact that they had a wide choice of meats available, they refused to prepare any meat dishes, remembering that it was a Friday and therefore, for Catholics, a meatless day. One man asked Saurin to go down to the storerooms and send up some flour so that he could bake some bread. Saurin discovered in the semidarkness a sack of what seemed to be flour and sent a sample up to the "chef." A few seconds later there was a whistle on the speaking tube from the kitchen and he answered it. It was Volunteer Joe Tallon, the "chef."

TALLON: Do you know what your sample is?

SAURIN: No.

TALLON: The same stuff as your head's made of—sawdust!

Back in G.H.Q. it had dawned on Pearse and Connolly that the incredible was actually happening—that the military were not going to attack. Even so, Connolly ordered an enormous barricade of coalbags erected just inside the main entrance door. With its appearance, the rank and file realized how close they had come to the moment of truth and began to cast around for personal cover. Some, for the first time that week, thought of their families. A man beside Brian O'Higgins remarked that his wife was sick and he had six children, the eldest of whom, aged fourteen, was looking after them all. He wondered what was going to happen to them. On the roof the men recited the Rosary every half hour, between intervals of shrapnel fire.

At a few minutes past four o'clock Volunteer Joseph

312

Sweeney instinctively ducked as he heard a shell whistling toward him, and something crashed onto the roof only a few yards from where he crouched. When he looked around, spurts of flame were shooting out in all directions. The roof, half-penetrated by an incendiary shell, had caught fire.

Captain Brennan Whitmore awoke to the intolerable bites of fleas and a roomful of military, standing poised with grenades in their hands. Befuddled with sleep, he instinctively opened fire on the young officer in charge—luckily missing him. The soldiers, surprisingly failed to react, but the officer, angrily pointing to the burn on his sleeve, demanded, "Who fired that shot?" Nobody spoke. Glaring at the prisoners he again roared; "I'll have you all shot! Now, who fired that bullet?" Still nobody answered. Enraged, he ordered them all out to the street, and told his sergeant to search them. "The young basket's off his head!" murmured the sergeant as he searched Brennan Whitmore. Behind them, from the steps of the tenement they had left, the crowd urged the soldiers: "Shoot them, the bloody Shinners!" The sergeant turned, saluted smartly, and reported, "No weapons, sir."

"Right, sarg'nt. Line them up on the other side there. And then shoot them."

At this a wild cheer broke from the tenement crowd.

The sergeant grimaced, but ordered "March!" and the dejected-looking rebels stepped forward. Whitmore had just begun to say a last prayer when a British captain came around the corner, and the sergeant shouted "Halt!"

"Where are you taking those men, Lieutenant?" asked the captain casually when he came up.

Angrily the lieutenant displayed the hole in his sleeve. "I was going to shoot them, sir."

The captain turned to the sergeant. "March these prisoners to the Customs House, sarg'nt."

"You lucky lot of baskets!" the sergeant murmured to Brennan Whitmore.

In the Custom House, they were imprisoned at the foot of an airshaft and guarded by two sentries. Sometime later they were brought in small batches before a colonel of the Queens

Regiment, where their names, addresses, and occupations were noted. Brennan Whitmore tried to bluff his way out by saying that he was a Wexford journalist who had come up to Dublin for the races on Easter Monday and had found himself caught in the Rising. The colonel, however, showed no inclination to accept this yarn.

The rebels could not complain of bad treatment. The military apologized for not being able to offer them better food, and said that they were living on iron rations themselves. Their officers wanted souvenirs of the Rebellion and Captain Frank Thornton had to part with his uniform buttons. Shortly afterward the rebels were put through a second interrogation. Thornton's Volunteer contribution card was found and an officer wanted to know what it meant.

THORNTON: We contributed what we could to buy arms.

OFFICER: Do you seriously mean to tell me that you men have been saving out of your wages to buy rifles?

THORNTON: Yes.

OFFICER: Didn't your leaders get all the money they wanted from Germany?

THORNTON: Certainly not. Any German rifles we've got we paid for with our own money.

OFFICER: Well, I never could understand this damned country anyway!

Later an Australian sergeant came to the doorway and shouted obscenities at them. Then he asked, " 'Ere, what about the German sniper?"

"We had no German snipers," insisted Brennan Whitmore indignantly. "By the way, you British had some pretty good snipers yourselves. We had a cable across Sackville Street and one of your fellows hit the canister from Trinity."

The Aussie gave a whoop. "Do you mean I got it?"

"You mean it was you?" asked Whitmore astonished. "Well, you didn't cut the cable, but you were within half an inch of doing so."

"Listen," said the Aussie, suddenly friendly. "I'll try to find you something to eat." Smiling happily he went away.

"You know, that fellow's crazy," said Thornton.

314

In a short time the Aussie returned carrying a big biscuit tin and a jug of cold tea.

I'm sorry, but this is all I could scrounge," he apologized. "But anyway, here, take it," and added, "for Auld Lang Syne!"

Brennan Whitmore looked at the tin of biscuits—every one broken—at the jug of cold tea, and at the eager, friendly face of the Australian. Then he reached out for them. "For Auld Lang Syne," he said.

In Jacob's, the rebels simply sat and waited, itching for some kind of action. Behind the tall, solid walls they could feel themselves impregnably positioned, although Major Mac-Bride, the handsome, soldierly, divorced husband of the great beauty, Maud Gonne, thought the whole thing was "daft." "Why don't we fight them as the Boers did," he said, "instead of locking ourselves up in a whole lot of buildings?"

In the South Dublin Union, they watched a "funeral" taking place from the courtyard in front of the Nurses' Home. Kent had given the Union authorities permission to remove any military killed in the Bakehouse in Thursday's fighting. The rebels watched an old cart lumber away, carrying two plain coffins, never dreaming that inside one was a very live "corpse"—one of Martyn's men who had been cut off and was now being helped to escape.

In Boland's, a new form of terror had seized upon the garrison. As Volunteer George Lyons wrote later: "You had a feeling that your comrades might go mad—or, what was even worse, that you might go mad yourself." No one was immune from suspicion. Captain Michael Cullen, who had been in charge of the party which had erected the flag on the distillery tower began to talk a little wildly and was knocked on the head by Captain Donnelly. Worse, De Valera himself seemed to have lost a little of his wits. Lieutenant Joseph Fitzgerald tried to persuade him to rest for a while. "I can't," De Valera protested, "I can't trust the men—they'll leave their posts or fall asleep if I don't watch them."

"Look," said Fitzgerald, "I promise to sit beside you and if anything happens, waken you immediately."

On this understanding, De Valera lay down on the bed in

315

the Grand Canal Dispensary and fell asleep almost immediately. Then he began to toss restlessly, disturbed by some nightmare. Suddenly, his face beaded with sweat, his eyes wild, he sat bolt upright and in an awful voice bawled, "Set fire to the railway! Set fire to the railway!"

Fitzgerald, certain that De Valera had gone off his head, called other officers immediately. They managed to calm the overwrought commandant a little, but he still insisted that Westland Row Station must be set on fire. Lieutenant John Quinn, in charge of the party occupying the station, thought the order was mad, but felt he had to obey it.

Bundles of papers soaked in whiskey were tossed into booking offices, waiting rooms, and empty trains—and a good blaze had been started when Captain John MacMahon eventually persuaded De Valera to listen to reason and the fires were put out.

In retrospect, these minutes appear the most critical of De Valera's career. Bold schemes followed by arbitrary cancelations had already weakened many of his subordinates' confidence in him and the purposeless order to set fire to Westland Row seemed to prove that the strain of leadership had been too much for him. De Valera, however, quickly recovered his composure and canceled the wild order.

In the College of Surgeons the actual fighting was no longer the main problem. So long as you kept your head down and away from the windows, machine guns could chip as many bricks as they liked out of the façade. The battle was now almost wholly one of wits. First, the military dressed a sniper in maid's uniform and placed him in a window of the Shelbourne where he enjoyed considerable success until Volunteer Captain Harry Nicholls, operating from the Turkish Baths, discovered the ruse and shot him through the head. Then, the military rang up a shop held by the rebels, their snipers standing ready to shoot any man who lifted the receiver, which was beside a window. Captain MacCormack rose to the bait the first time the trick was tried, and only a crash tackle by Frank Robbins saved him.

Countess Markievicz remained brave and belligerent as ever, determined to hold out until the last man lay dead. Professor O'Briain recalls that her main worry was that she "had no stabbing weapon for close quarters work—I'll have to get a bayonet or sword or something," and Mallin's wry comment: "My, my, but you're very bloodthirsty!"

The main problem was food. Men fainted at their posts through lack of nourishment. Late in the afternoon O'Briain, who was posted in a house farther down the block, returned to the Surgeons and saw Miss Nellie Gifford, in charge of the commissariat. "There are fourteen men over there starving, and I can't go back without something," he said desperately. Yet all she could spare him was a little rice. "And that," he recalls without relish, "was my first bite to eat since Tuesday."

27

Next time I'll make sure I'll get him, thought little John Reid. Crouched behind a sack of coal on the second floor at the Henry Street corner of the G.P.O., he had been carefully watching a head bob up and down at the parapet of the Gresham Hotel. He was so weary that he found it difficult to hold the barrel steady, to keep his finger tensed. He wanted to squeeze the trigger and just hope for the best. Yet he was determined to get that Tommy.

Beside him someone said quietly, "There's a fire." Reid glanced up at the glass dome. Flames were bursting forth, but before he could say anything an officer hissed fiercely, "Shut up!" Reid readjusted his sight, but his concentration was gone now and the bead wobbled wildly. He knew then that he would never get the Tommy.

Suddenly there was a tremendous uproar behind him, and when he looked around, men were charging across the floor, dragging great hoses which wriggled about like gigantic boa constrictors.

A babel of shouts and commands filled the Post Office and the encircling military, had they but known, could almost have thrown away their weapons and advanced with bare hands. Men wrestled to fix two lines of hose onto the hydrants and direct twin jets of water onto the fire. Sweating, cursing, and struggling, they formed several bucket lines and passed water along in a fearful race to douse the flames. Within ten minutes only a cloud of steam remained to show that there had been a fire, and everyone relaxed a little. Seconds later another incendiary shell struck the roof, shooting off a splash of

318

flame. Amid renewed uproar, a hose was turned on and a strong jet of water smacked against the blaze. From his perch on the far side of the river, reporter O'Leary watched smoke rising like an Indian signal above the Post Office. Suddenly his eye caught a limping dog which ran across Sackville Street, shrieking madly—the only thing alive, it seemed to him, in all that desolation.

Pearse, with Joseph Plunkett at his heels, stomped through the smoke and water toward the new outbreak. Then he stopped short and in quick, jerky sentences, spoke to Plunkett. For once his air of quiet, calm confidence seemed to have deserted him—and he no longer moved among the rebels as a man loftily above the battle. His face was red and excited, and the words tumbled from him in a stream lacking all traces of the usual stutter. Plunkett, too, was excited and they both stood shouting at each other, oblivious of everything except the paramount need to restore order before panic set in among their men. It was the supreme moment for cool, highly disciplined thinking, for the firm word of command, which would freeze men in their tracks. Connolly could have done it. It was not, however, the role, for which nature had cast Pearse. The uproar continued. The Irish temperament, sometimes wild and uncontrollable, was now, under pressure, showing its weakness. MacAuliffe recalls: "Everybody appeared to consider it his duty to give orders at the top of his voice while the fire gained ground very fast."

Yet Pearse, despite the difficulties and the handicap of his own nature, slowly managed to bring some order out of all this confusion. A large party was put to work dealing with the fire while the rest were peremptorily ordered back to the windows to hold off the enemy. The O'Rahilly, calm and not easily ruffled, helped Pearse a great deal, and for a while, as things gradually sorted themselves out, he became the effective director of operations. Through smoke and flooding water, parties made their way up ladders and, with picks and axes, hammered at the ceiling, breaking holes through which the hoses could be brought closer to the flames. One or two men toppled back, caught by a stream of bullets zipping through the windows as the military launched yet another barrage of machine-gun and rifle fire. Twice bullets cracked into the plaster near Pearse's head as he watched his men struggle up a ladder gripping a wriggling, slippery hose.

At 4:45, O'Leary noticed that the cloud of smoke rising from the G.P.O. had assumed "dangerously large proportions." He could see rebels out on the roof trying to deal with it, but they were finding it difficult to raise their heads because of the heavy machine-gun fire. Five minutes later he saw a great tongue of flame leap through the roof.

From the Telegraph Room on the top floor, glimpses of sky could be seen through the blazing gaps in the roof—there were now quite a number of them. On the roof itself a party led by Captain Michael O'Reilly daringly crawled along thin steel frames holding together the panes of the glass dome, guiding a hose toward the flames. "You didn't think about it," recalls O'Reilly (now chairman of Ireland's largest insurance company) "in fact you didn't realize until afterward what a risk you'd been taking. The only thing that mattered was that the fire had to be put out."

As fast as they extinguished a blaze in one part of the roof, however, another shell landed a few yards away. One or two, or even three, fires might have been brought under control, but not a dozen. The rebels realized that the Post Office was doomed.

The fire ate fiercely through the roof in several different places, and slates, plaster, and mortar showered down into the flood water, turning it into a great, slimy, coal-blackened lake. Bullets tore into the hosepipes and jets of water spouted like fountains; MacAuliffe saw one man holding on grimly to the hose as a spout drenched him from head to foot. Lines of men continued to pass buckets up the ladders to the men on the roof. It was all useless. Clouds of smoke filled the room, dirty, black choking stuff that had the men soon coughing badly. A whole side of the roof had caught fire now, and there was a rending, tearing noise as a huge lump of it crashed into the room below, scattering the fire fighters, who slipped and fell among the tangle of hoses and buckets, drenching themselves in filthy water. The very floor shook and a yell went up, "The floor's giving way!" Burning wood and charred

320

plaster sizzled in the water and clouds of steam rose to mingle with the smoke. From a corner of the room Volunteer Sweeney kept firing at the military who, taking advantage of rebel difficulties, were attempting an advance from the Parnell Monument.

"They must have thought we were done for," recalls Sweeney. "Our rifle fire was returned by machine guns, with interest, but we were well sandbagged and loopholed and now and then we were able to get our heads up. They were firing from all round Upper Sackville Street and we could hear the chatter of a gun from somewhere near Amiens Street Station. Fortunately the Pillar blocked their fire to some extent or they might have driven us out sooner."

And yet the military still showed no signs of making an assault. Now and then, when a khaki blur showed itself for an instant along Upper Sackville Street or on some rooftop, reporter O'Leary saw puffs of rifle smoke issue from the burning Post Office, proving that the rebels were still defiant. At every barricade the military gripped their rifles harder and waited with tight nerves. At any moment, they believed, a mob of trapped and desperate men, driven by reckless fanaticism, would pour out of that blazing building and charge down upon them, determined to slaughter or be slaughtered. Meantime, they must wait and fight the gnawing tension; wait for the fire to drive out the rats.

At 5:30 P.M., Father John Flanagan, summoned with everyone else into the general sorting office as more and more fragments fell into the main public office, asked The O'Rahilly what was to happen to the wounded, now numbering sixteen. The O'Rahilly replied that he wanted them taken to Jervis Street Hospital. Lieutenant Mahoney, told to accompany the party, tried to persuade James Connolly to go with them.

"No, my place is with my men," answered Connolly brusquely.

At 6 P.M., led by Captain Michael O'Reilly, the party, consisting of Father Flanagan, Lieutenant Mahoney, the sixteen wounded men and twelve of the fifteen women who had stuck it out until then, started crawling through the tunneled walls toward the Coliseum Theatre in Henry Street. A few men

321

went with them to help carry the wounded, who were lifted on mattresses or blankets. Three women remained behind: two Red Cross nurses—blonde, pretty Elizabeth O'Farrell and dark, petite Julia Grenan—and Connolly's indomitable secretary, Miss Winifred Carney, who when urged by Pearse to leave with the others, replied in curt, unladylike terms. Before ducking through the hole in the wall, Father Flanagan was approached by The O'Rahilly, who asked for a Last Absolution and blessing, saying, "Father, I'm afraid we'll never meet again in this world." Father Flanagan did as he was asked, and then, with a last look at a gallant and resolute face, stepped through the crude hole in the wall.

Through two intervening shops, across a roof (where they were exposed to military fire), then up a ladder, the party made their way in a slow, painful effort which lasted more than half an hour. They finally reached the Coliseum where, in the saloon bar, the wounded were made comfortable on a thick pile carpet, and Captain O'Reilly and Quartermaster Fitzgerald talked over what they should do next. Although the bar had been held by the rebels since Monday afternoon not a single bottle of beer or spirits had been touched, a point Father Flanagan noted with pleasure. Lieutenant Mahoney was impressed by Quartermaster Fitzgerald's determination to prevent any of the party from sampling the contents now, although in the circumstances he thought it would have been reasonable. Fitzgerald, however, sensitive to rebel honor, declared he would allow only nonalchoholic drinks to be taken.

Meanwhile, back in the Post Office, Pearse and Connolly had decided that their position was no longer tenable. The problem now was whether the onrushing flames would force them to leave while it was still daylight, or whether they might be able to hold on until darkness. More important was *where* and *how* they would go. The two Poole brothers offered to explore the sewers to see if an exit could be found that way, but were driven back by the filth. Pearse, after consulting his fellow members of the Provisional Government, finally announced that an attempt would be made to establish new Headquarters in Messrs. Williams and Wood, soap and sweet manufacturers in Great Britain Street, which was the nearest large building. A dash would be made from the side door in Henry Street and then up Moore Street to the factory. The O'Rahilly had volunteered to lead an assault party of forty men in an attempt to reach Williams and Wood, seize the building and establish a route for the remainder of the Post Office garrison.

Toward seven o'clock, however, and before The O'Rahilly's charge could be mounted, the threat to the G.P.O. was suddenly intensified. The fire, which—due to the gallantry of the fire fighters—had been more or less confined to the front part of the Post Office, began to surge rapidly along both sides of the building, threatening to engulf everything. Flames roaring near the head of the ventilator shaft sent sparks floating into the basement where the gelignite and bombs had been lodged for safety when the fire first started. Captain Dermot Lynch led a party into the basement to remove the stuff to a safer place. Volunteers John MacLoughlin, John Reid, and Brian O'Higgins staggered along a passageway under Sackville Street to a courtyard in the rear of the building on the Princes Street side, carrying their dangerous burden. Other rebels, holding lighted candles, were stationed at short intervals to show them the way and guard against a collision or a fall, which might cause catastrophe. MacLoughlin found the job "hair-raising." The homemade bombs had been stored at the foot of the ventilator shaft and as The O'Rahilly flushed a steady stream of water up the spark-filled area, the three volunteers scooped up armfuls. Once, as MacLoughlin stooped, The O'Rahilly momentarily lost control of the hose-pipe and a staggering stream of water hit MacLoughlin full in the chest, crashing him to the ground with the bombs in his arms. In that dangerous instant he thought the end had come, but the drenching water must have affected the bombs; anyway none exploded. Then abruptly the water gave out and, as blinding fumes eddied from the ventilator shaft, The O'Rahilly ordered everyone to leave.

Upstairs he remembered Lieutenants Chalmers and King and the thirteen other prisoners locked in the cellars. He told Lynch, who immediately saw Connolly. The Commandant-General, directing operations from his bed beside the Henry

Street exit, ordered that the prisoners should be placed in what was now the safest part of the building, a ferro-concrete rear annex which had been added during the recent remodeling. Lynch left at once to attend to the transfer.

For Lieutenant Chalmers at least, his appearance was not a moment too soon. For almost three hours he and his fellow prisoners had yelled themselves hoarse as smoke filtered along the passageway, and they realized that they were trapped in a burning building. Chalmers could scarcely control himself as Lynch remarked soothingly, "It's all right now, boys," and led the highly strung party into the Princes Street courtyard and then into a room where they were left temporarily in charge of, as Chalmers put it later, "a woman in male attire who flourished a big, loaded revolver and threatened us." Who that could have been it is difficult to imagine, as none of the three women left in the building were so dressed. A little later the prisoners were escorted to the Henry Street exit where The O'Rahilly awaited them. Private Peter Richardson of the Connaught Rangers told reporters afterward: "We were placed near the door where we could rush for our liberty. Then, shaking hands with each one of us in turn, The O'Rahilly said, 'Good-bye . . . I may never see you again. Good-bye, and good luck to you.' Then the door was pulled open."

Chalmers led the party, with a Dublin Fusilier following close behind. He ran into the street, crossed into Henry Place opposite, and then turned a corner. He was running west toward Moore Street when a machine gun opened up and caught him in the thigh. Beside him the Dublin Fusilier fell dead with a bullet in his head. Chalmers dodged about for a moment, utterly bewildered, until he was fired on again by a second machine gun. He jumped over a low wall, followed by the rest of the party, and ran into an alleyway, where he collapsed and was carried into a cellar by a sergeant of the Royal Irish Regiment.

Behind them The O'Rahilly, gripping his Mauser pistol, walked from the Post Office, leading thirty smoke-begrimed, haggard-eyed men into Henry Street. Here they lined up and listened to Pearse, who explained once again that their job was to establish new headquarters in Williams and Wood. When

324

Pearse finished, The O'Rahilly looked his men over and then told them briefly, "It will be either a glorious victory or a glorious death, boys," and, turning, led the way toward Moore Street.

All went well as they filtered slowly west toward the corner, taking cover in doorways, then darting forward for a few yards before again taking cover. Making as little noise as possible, they opened a way through their own barricade in Henry Street and scrambled through. At Moore Street corner they halted to sort themselves into two parties—The O'Rahilly explaining that he would lead the charge northward up Moore Street along the left-hand pavement, leaving the second party to advance at the double along the right.

The O'Rahilly and his party fanned out across the end of Moore Street and the Sherwood Foresters, massed behind a barricade at the top of the street where it ran into Great Britain Street, at once opened up on them. Men were hit, and Volunteer Charles Steinmayer, running along the right-hand side of the street, recollects that it was "a case of taking cover wherever it could be found—and this consisted of doorways about six inches deep." The charge did not get very far, being stopped within twenty-five yards. From the cover of a doorway, Steinmayer saw The O'Rahilly fall at the corner of Sampson's Lane, an opening on the left. He himself dived into a laneway on the right and took refuge in a tenement as another volley swept the street—it now seemed "humanly impossible for anything to get up that street."

Meanwhile The O'Rahilly, although badly wounded, managed to drag himself into Sampson's Lane where he was joined by a few men, while the others huddled in doorways in Moore Street or took refuge in Henry Place on the far side of the street. The military still blazed away mercilessly, raking Moore Street from one end to the other, but eventually there came a lull. At once the indomitable O'Rahilly rose to his feet and, firing blindly toward the barricade, led another advance up Moore Street. He cut across Moore Street as he ran, perhaps hoping to get into Sackville Lane, and regroup his men there; or possibly he wanted to draw the enemy fire on himself while his men charged on to the barricade. Whatever his reasons, his men responded bravely to his gallant leadership, but of his original party only a handful remained, and the military, reinforced by picked marksmen, cut them down easily with a withering fire. Again The O'Rahilly was hit. This time, wounded mortally, he collapsed at the entrance to Sackville Lane. Realizing that he had not long to live, he propped himself against a wall and scratched a last note to his wife, explaining briefly why he had joined in the Rebellion and how he had come to lead the charge.

Within a few moments silence fell over the empty street. When it became clear that the rebels would no longer attack, Captain G. J. Edmunds sent a sergeant down to search The O'Rahilly's body. The man brought back the note The O'Rahilly had written to his wife, and Connolly's last order, copies of which were immediately sent to General Maxwell.

Out of the thirty men who went out with The O'Rahilly on his last charge, twenty-one ended up as casualties.

In those last hours inside the burning Post Office, the thoughts of Joseph Plunkett had turned often to Grace Gifford, the artist daughter of a Dublin solicitor whom he might have married on Easter Sunday. In his breast pocket—as he and Pearse made a last tour of the blazing building, calling together the few men still at their posts—lay a short note and his will, bequeathing her everything "of which I am possessed and may become possessed." In the main hall he stopped and asked Winifred Carney, "Will you do something for me?"

Miss Carney had not particularly admired him—his bizarre getup and his strange, almost histrionic manner had caused her to make uncomplimentary remarks about him to Connolly earlier in the week, to which the rebel leader had replied that Plunkett "is such a brilliant military man that I don't care how he dresses." But his behavior throughout the Rebellion, his courage and his cheerfulness despite his weakness and pain, had gradually won her sympathy and she allowed him to slip the filigree bangle from his wrist and put it on hers. Then he took from his finger one of the great antique rings—which had particularly roused her ire—and pressed it, along with the note, into her hand, asking her if she would deliver them to

Grace Gifford. Miss Carney promised she would and he went on toward the Henry Street exit, where Connolly waited on his couch, Clarke and MacDermott by his side.

There was still spirit left in the rebel army. Most of them looked brave as they listened to Pearse's last words to them, his exhortation to "go out and face the machine guns as though you were on parade." Lieutenant Mahoney, recalled from the Coliseum because a man had fallen over Connolly's foot and smashed the "cradle" (Mahoney fixed it), saw them gather around their Commander in Chief and stand calmly as if they were still on maneuvers. "I found it impressive," recalls Mahoney. "I could see no panic, no obvious signs of fear—and in the circumstances that would have been excusable, for parts of the building were already an inferno and the roof and ceilings had already given way in places. To me, in that hasty moment, it seemed that Pearse, in the way he held them all together, was a gifted leader and a man supremely fitted to command. Then I went back to the Coliseum."

The men in the Metropole Hotel had joined the Headquarters garrison by now and Charles Saurin remembers how they sang defiantly as they edged toward the exit. The words of "The Soldier's Song" which had gripped their imagination (it has since become the National Anthem of the Republic of Ireland) were roared out with all the fervor of men who intended to go on resisting stubbornly, however often they were beaten. This was the human spirit at its most obstinate, expressing a particular inheritance, centuries of resistance to England and the determination to be free. The song rose above the noise of the flames, and, from the front of the building, the constant explosion of small-arms ammunition and the homemade bombs which, perhaps fortunately for themselves, they had never had a chance to use. There was a good-natured patience about the men. They were crowding toward the door when a shotgun went off accidentally and hit Volunteer Andrew Furlong's ammunition pouch. It exploded, sending bullets in every direction—nine pierced Furlong's leg. Beside him, the strange cockney Socialist called Neale, swayed and fell against Saurin. "Can't you stand away and let a fellow lie down?" asked Neale gently. He was laid on a pile of mail-bags and Lieutenant Traynor asked, "Are you badly hurt?" to which Neale replied wryly, "I'm dying, comrade."

When young John MacLoughlin reached the door, Pearse and MacDermott were explaining the route to the Williams and Wood factory. This was the first MacLoughlin had heard of the plan and he protested that the factory, and indeed the whole of Great Britain Street, had been in the hands of the military since Thursday. He knew of this personally, for he had sneaked through the area on his way to the G.P.O. from Commandant Daly's headquarters following the fall of the Mendicity Institution.

"Why don't we go up Henry Street, through the markets and on into the Four Courts?" he suggested.

Pearse considered this, while someone shouted, "Stop The O'Rahilly—he's gone into Moore Street with some men."

Unhesitatingly MacLoughlin darted through the door and ran across into Henry Place opposite. He reached Moore Street just as The O'Rahilly and his men were being cut to pieces. He turned, to discover that most of the garrison, led by Captain Michael Collins with a drawn revolver, had fol-lowed him. It was dusk now and in the quickening darkness the burning Post Office, the flames licking so high that they threatened to cremate Nelson himself, looked an awesome sight to young MacLoughlin.

With the rebels in the streets the military now opened up in real earnest. Among the fleeing men order and discipline were fast disappearing in the confusion. Some followed MacLough-lin and Collins up Henry Street; others, obeying the direct instructions of their Commander in Chief, dashed toward Moore Street and, turning the corner, ran straight into the blazing guns of the military, most of them being hit. The rest ran wildly across into Henry Place and then around the cor-ner toward Moore Street, but were stopped at the bottom of Moore Lane (a parallel to Moore Street) because it was under machine-gun fire from the roof of the Rotunda Hospital.

While Collins sought refuge for his men in the houses along Moore Street, MacLoughlin grabbed an officer's sword and took over command at the bottom of Moore Lane. When he ordered the men to search for materials to make a barricade, they found a motor van in a nearby yard and pushed it into position barring the mouth of the Lane. It wasn't much use as protection, but it partially screened the men as they ran across the opening. Some of them, scared to run the gantlet, broke into O'Brien's mineral water premises nearby, others into stables. Still others, seeing their comrades hit by the machine-gun bullets, cowered in the laneway, too terrified to move. Plunkett, coming up behind them, drew his sword and rallied them on. "Don't be afraid, don't be cowards, any of you. On, on, on!" Clarke and MacDermott took up positions in the lane as fresh arrivals, frightened by the intense machine-gun fire, scattered madly, and shouted at them to behave like men. Amid all the confusion, young MacLoughlin stood out like a rock, and seeing that the men were ready to obey him, MacDermott shouted, "You're the only one who seems to know where we are—you'd better give the orders around here."

Few of the men had any idea where they were going. Some-one shouted at Volunteer John Nunan to "go into the ware-house," and he climbed into O'Brien's Mineral Water store, where he stayed until the firing died down. James Ryan found himself clambering aimlessly over the roofs, but got down finally into a courtyard at the rear of Moore Street, from where he was able to rejoin the main party.

Volunteer Kevin O'Carroll was hit in the leg and carried into the nearest house, filled with hysterical women. This was the home of the McKane family—mother and father and fourteen children. For two days the family had huddled to-gether in a tiny cottage, the last house in a row of workmen's cottages in Henry Place, crouched under the beds, saying their Rosaries and growing more and more hungry. They had not dared to go out after seeing a looter shot and his body thrown up on a barricade by the military. Elizabeth, then ten, still recalls today how the "boys came up in twos and threes while we were all kneeling saying our prayers."

"My father jumped up when he heard the commotion in the yard," she remembers. "A rifleman, without waiting for him to open the door, broke the glass panel. It was terrible. The rifle went off and pierced my father's shoulder—he was carrying the baby in his arms at the time—and went straight through him and hit my eldest sister Bridget in the forehead, killing her instantly. I remember my mother getting to her feet, looking completely stunned—everything had happened so suddenly."

Pearse and Connolly were still in the Post Office. Connolly, despite his pain, insisted on staying with Pearse until the rest of the garrison had got safely away. Finally he allowed them to carry him out in a stretcher, the faithful Miss Carney hovering by and a young boy, proud to be of service to his general, walking beside the stretcher, shielding Connolly's body from bullets. Smoke had by now clouded Henry Street; so black and thick, Joseph Sweeney recalls "that it was almost impossible to see your finger in front of your face." He was with the last party to hurry across. Behind him came the two Red Cross nurses, Elizabeth O'Farrell and Julia Grenan, who were escorted to the safety of Henry Place corner by Pearse himself. He returned to check that there was no one left in the burning building. By then, floors were collapsing spectacularly, heaving giant tongues of fire into the glowing night, beams were falling and interior walls crashing down. Pearse, standing alone for a moment amid all the terror and the beauty, stared at the ruin, symbolic in a way of all his hopes. As he turned to leave, a small party stumbled from a hole in the wall, led by Captain Michael O'Reilly and Willie Pearse, who had been helping to carry the wounded to the Coliseum Theatre. Willie went out first, followed by the Commander in Chief himself, Volunteer Patrick Colwell, and Captain O'Reilly.

At the bottom of Moore Lane, where the screening barricade had been made larger, Miss O'Farrell slipped and fell as she ran across. She was helped up and led into Cogan's, a grocer's on the corner of Henry Place and Moore Street, where she found Connolly, Plunkett, Clarke, and MacDermott. Connolly lay on his stretcher in the middle of the floor, his face white and shadowed with pain. She knelt beside him and asked how he felt.

330

Connolly: "Bad—the soldier who wounded me did a good day's work for the British Government."

When Pearse reached the bottom of Moore Lane, he, too, slipped and fell—and in exactly the same spot as Miss O'Farrell, but he jumped up immediately and safely reached Cogan's. Mrs. Cogan had told the rebels they could have a ham she was boiling, and then vanished with her family into the cellar. When the ham had been cooked, Miss Carney portioned it out among the famished men, kneeling to feed Connolly. MacDermott took an egg from a box, bored a hole in it and sucked it. Two rebels stood on guard at the windows, which had been barricaded, and another stood guard at the door. Then Miss Carney collected small personal possessions from each of the men for their wives or their mothers. When she bent over one young boy, he asked her nervously, "Do you think we'll win? . . . You see, I've never been in a rebellion before."

"Neither have I," said Miss Carney, and smiled.

Outside MacLoughlin and Plunkett worked frantically to build a barricade at the junction of Henry Place and Moore Street. In the glare of the Post Office flames the rebels were an easy target and there were casualties. Strangely, the military still made no attempt to come to close grips.

From the far side of the Liffey, Reporter O'Leary watched, absorbed, as G.P.O. continued to burn spectacularly. "The fire," he wrote, "grows and grows, seems to bubble over as heaps of glowing debris crash over the granite walls and through the flame-eaten windows. High above the doomed building, the Republican flag flutters in the stifling atmosphere of smoke. Leaping flames lick and kiss the pole on which it hangs. With my field glasses, I can see the letters IRISH REPUBLIC scorch to a deep brown. Now and then the flag is buried as thousands of fragments of burning paper belch up as it were from a volcano. Now it begins to hang its head as if in shame. At 9 P.M. the G.P.O. is in ruins, its granite walls look like the bones of a skeleton skull. Its core is nothing but smouldering debris. The fluttering of the flag grows feebler. In the dimness of the night I see it give an occasional flutter, as if revived by a gust of air. At length at 9:51 P.M. the staff supporting it begins to waver and in a second falls out towards the street. The Sinn Fein fortress is no more."

In Cogan's, Pearse ordered a party of men to start breaking through the walls toward Great Britain Street, then held a brief council of war. A decision was taken to give the boy, MacLoughlin, high military command.

"He should hold my rank," insisted Connolly, impressed as were MacDermott and Plunkett with the boy's vigor and energy and his evident qualities of leadership. In their predicament, ovewhelmed but reluctant to admit defeat, they considered the youth capable of lifting some of the burden from their exhausted shoulders. Pearse, too, perhaps remembered Cuchulain, the boy hero of ancient Ireland. There was no alternative, anyway. Connolly was *hors de combat,* as was Plunkett, despite his display of courage. Clarke and MacDermott were not military men, while Pearse himself was almost spent. MacLoughlin received news of his appointment soberly and immediately suggested that everyone should get as much sleep as possible, so that they would be ready for what the morning might bring. As accommodation downstairs was crowded, Pearse and his brother went upstairs, where they spread two blankets on a table and lay down on them. MacLoughlin went outside and posted sentries at the barricade, checked the positions of all the men and then retired himself, bedding down under the table on which the Pearse brothers slept.

At the barricade, John Nunan hunched wearily beside Volunteer Frank Kelly and Captain George Plunkett and listened to a wounded man moaning on the far side of Moore Street. They listened to his faint cry: "Water, water!"

"That must be one of our lads," whispered someone.

"Give me you water bottle, Frank," said Plunkett.

Kelly slipped it from his shoulder. "Keep me covered," said Plunkett, "but don't fire unless you have to." He edged his way through the flimsy barricade and bending low, ran toward Sampson's Lane. A volley crashed out immediately and sparks flew where the bullets hit the street. Plunkett dived into the laneway where Nunan, by the glare of the fires, saw him bend over a prone figure. He watched Plunkett lift the man onto his shoulders and start back. A few ragged shots blew dust from the bricks; then the firing ceased as the military realized Plunkett was rescuing a wounded man. When Plunkett reached the barricade, Nunan saw with surprise that the wounded man was not a rebel but a British soldier. Plunkett dumped him rather unceremoniously over the barricade and gasped out: "Here, take him—I want to get his rifle." Nunan and Kelly pulled the wounded man in while Plunket jinked his way across the street again. This time the military fired on him with all they had, but he reached the far side, grabbed the rifle and managed to dash back safely.

In the Coliseum, meanwhile, Father Flanagan and Quartermaster Fitzgerald, watching the flames advance, decided that the time had come to try to reach Jervis Street Hospital. Neither was familiar with the theater and they had difficulty finding any way out other than the main exit into Henry Street. Eventually they found a door leading to Princes Street. Father Flanagan placed himself at the head of a little procession which, Red Cross flags held high, wended its way along an alleyway, climbed over a burning barricade, and emerged cautiously into Middle Abbey Street. Here it was fired upon, but when the Red Cross flag had been waved several times, Captain Orr of the Sherwood Foresters stepped forward with drawn revolver and shouted, "Bearer of flag and one other advance and parley." Father Flanagan gestured to Lieutenant Mahoney, who flung back his coat to show his khaki jacket; then they both stepped forward.

In Moore Lane, Mrs. Thomas McKane, hysterical following the death of her daughter Bridget and the wounding of her husband, Thomas, ran toward the British barricade, waving a white sheet over her head.

"Get back for God's sake, or we'll fire!" shouted a Tommy.

"My husband! My husband!" yelled Mrs. McKane. "I must get a priest!" She continued running toward the barricade and a rifle cracked, the bullet tugging at her sleeve. "Get back," yelled the Tommy. "Get back, you silly bitch!"

333

"My husband!" screamed the half-crazed woman. "I must get a priest." And she kept on running.

"For Christ's sake, sir, what shall we do?" shouted the Tommy desperately.

"Use your head, man," barked the officer. "Stop firing at once!"

[28]

Certainly Brigadier-General Lowe, the tall, austere officer who continued to conduct field operations despite the arrival of Maxwell, ought to have realized that North King Street was the worst place that could have been chosen through which to draw the northern boundary of the inner cordon around the Four Courts. As early as Easter Tuesday, small probing operations had shown that the rebels, in considerable strength, were well bedded down in the area. A Red Cross ambulance, trying to get through to the Richmond Hospital on Thursday had been fired on from a barricade, and an armored car, cautiously pushing forward early that (Friday) morning, had been liberally sprayed with Mauser bullets. It was clearly a place to be wary of; perhaps first encircled and then worked over thoroughly before troops were sent in.

Maxwell ordered otherwise. Left with two North Staffs battalions on his hands at Kingstown, he decided to bring up the South Staffs from Mount Street and give them the task of finally making the cordon link-up through North King Street. Orders given to Lieutenant-Colonel Henry Taylor of Wolverhampton, C.O. of the 2/6th South Staffs, were to press westward from Capel Street and join with the 2/5th South Staffs advancing eastward from Queen Street. Taylor left Trinity College about five o'clock in the evening, marching his battalion over Butt Bridge, skirting the Post Office area by way of Gardiner and Great Britain streets and eventually halted at the junction of Bolton and Capel streets. From the Sherwood Foresters he learned that North King Street was too strongly held by the rebels to allow for an unsupported infantry assault.

335

He would need to call up the armored cars. At 5:45 P.M. he took over the Bolton Street Technical Schools as a base of operations and ordered a rifle party on the roof to open fire on the rebel barricades. The arrival of one armored car allowed him to commence serious operations. The car opened the attack by rolling slowly forward and depositing assault parties in several houses along the street. Behind it advanced the infantry, pouring fierce and indiscriminate fire into all the houses before entering and occupying them. Civilians who had not followed General Maxwell's instructions to leave the area were shepherded back to the Technical Schools for safety.

Two hundred yards up North King Street, Volunteers Thomas Sherrin, William Murphy, William Hogan, John Williamson, and John Dwan watched the "tank" slew across the street and fire a broadside at them. They returned the fire, but saw their bullets rattle harmlessly against the armor plating. It was the beginning of the most vicious and most sustained fighting of the whole week, although casualties were to be well below those at Mount Street Bridge, due largely to the less open nature of the ground and because most of the battle was fought in darkness. The employment of the armored car also helped to keep casualties down, as did Colonel Taylor's decision to adopt rebel tactics and tunnel through houses. For both sides the fighting rapidly became an edgy, nerve-testing battle, fought out in an unusually narrow street, with men firing from behind bedroom windows or chimney pots.

The focal point turned out to be "Reilly's Fort"—an empty public house at the corner of North King and Church streets, where a green flag still hung defiantly from the lance of the dead British trooper. These premises commanded a stretch of North King Street some two hundred yards long. Opposite Reilly's, across North King Street, was a barricade. Two hundred yards down on the right-hand side, and at a slight bend in the road, lay Beresford Street. Towering over it was Jameson's Malt House and Granary, from whose top floor Volunteer Frank Shouldice and two other insurgents had command of the whole area. Out of sight around the bend, and on the left-hand side, lay Coleraine Street and it was at a barricade here that Sherrin and his comrades met the first onslaught of the South Staffs. As night fell, their battle became a lonely, desperate fight against spitting flashes of fire from each side of the street (which was all they could see of the enemy) and the constant roar of the armored car, whose engine revved loudly as it advanced and then reversed to back up against a door.

Inside the armored car rebel bullets created a terrible racket. Sergeant Sam Cooper of "B" Company, 2/6th South Staffs, remembers how "Every bullet clanged and jarred through your head. It wasn't possible to fire back, either—you couldn't discharge a rifle in that confined space." Nor did the car guarantee complete invulnerability. "I remember we backed up to a pub as bullets rattled madly against 'the tank'—and one fellow broke a window and we all poured out. It wasn't until daylight we discovered one fellow had been hit apparently just as he got out. He was lying dead under a window."

For the military, on the whole, the fight was sheer nightmare. The Shinners were foxy, shadowy foes, ready to fight dirty; they would use anybody, old women, young girls, old men, boys. Sergeant Cooper remembers that the worst thing was the strain of staring out into North King Street from a pub window, scanning the rooftops constantly, peering into the night until his eyeballs felt like footballs. He recalls: "One young fellow was certain we were being fired on from behind a chimney. I kept watch, but could see nothing. I had hardly left the window for a second when he yelled out, 'They're firing from behind that chimney'—so we let them have it. We riddled the chimney stack, knocking every pot to hell and eventually bringing the whole lot tumbling down. A complete waste of ammunition—there wasn't a Shinner in sight."

Progress was slow. From the high Malt House, Frank Shouldice, lying out on an iron platform at the top of the outside stairway, poured down an accurate fire on the houses along the north side of the street, picking out his targets by the answering flashes of their rifles. Sherrin and his comrades blazed away in a terrible fury. "Once when the armored car ventured too near, they tossed a handful of grenades at it, and caused it to retire. They themselves faced a constant hail of bullets. Somehow none of them was hit, although annihila-

337

tion clearly could be only a matter of time. Small parties of military had begun to work their way along the rooftops in an attempt to lob hand grenades down on the barricade. Caught in the heavy, relentless rebel fire, this proved suicidal and the grenades fell in front of the barricades, exploding brilliantly, but harmlessly.

By midnight Colonel Taylor's gains were precisely nil. The rebel barricade still held. Thousands of rounds of ammunition had been poured out wildly and recklessly into the flickering night by his young recruits. Faced with failure, Colonel Taylor decided that the only way to beat the rebels was to adopt their own tactics. He sent a strong party to tunnel through some houses with the idea of outflanking the barricade. Then, about 2 A.M., the armored car struggled up to within thirty yards of the barricade and a party armed with picks and crowbars broke into No. 172 North King Street, a house owned by Mrs. Sally Hughes, where twenty neighboring families had taken refuge.

If the struggle so far had been a hard, frightening battle for the men forced to fight it, it now became a matter of pure terror for the impoverished inhabitants. General Maxwell had warned that anybody who remained within the battle zone did so at his own risk, but since Easter Monday only the rebel writ had run in North King Street and few people were aware of their risk. Some who learned of it elected to remain anyway in what they took to be the safest place they could stay—their own homes. Early in the week the rebels had tried to persuade most inhabitants to move to the nearby North Dublin Union, but except with people living in houses which were entered and fortified, this attempt was not successful. Now, into the midst of these frightened people crashed the South Staffords, infuriated by their own slow progress, and, with a lust for blood in their hearts.

"We heard the soldiers banging at the street door," testified Mrs. Ellen Walsh later. "Mr. Hughes called out to his wife, 'Don't open the door, Sally, we shall all be killed.' But as the soldiers kept thundering at the hall door, Mrs. Hughes at length opened it. 'You are just in the nick of time, we were going to blow you up,' shouted the first soldier through the door. We then heard a voice cry, 'Are there any men in this house?' Immediately about 30 soldiers . . . ran at us like infuriated wild beasts or like things possessed. They looked ghastly and seemed in a panic. There was terrible firing going on outside in the street . . . and an armored car was near the door. One of the soldiers with stripes on his arm seemed in command. He shouted, 'Hands up!' and they presented their rifles at us. We all stood round the room in groups, and my husband and Mr. Hughes seemed petrified at the wild looks and cries of the soldiers and stood motionless with their hands clasped in front of them. . . . The man in command shouted, 'Search them,' and they searched the two men and the two boys. At the same time the others rushed about the house, furiously searching everywhere. They thrust their bayonets through a feather tick . . . and ripped it to bits, and stabbed the furniture in a hunt for ammunition. One of our men said, 'There was no one firing from this house.' The corporal with the stripes said, 'Not firing, eh?' and pointing to a rip in his hat said 'Look what a bullet did for me. I nearly lost my life.' The women and children were then all ordered down into the back kitchen and my poor husband and Mr. Hughes were brought upstairs. We were locked in the kitchen. I shall never forget the horror of it. Sometime after I heard a voice upstairs crying, 'Mercy! Mercy! Don't put that on me!' and someone resisting as if being tied up, or having his eyes bandaged. The old man [a lodger] in the upper room close by heard my husband crying, and as they killed them he heard his last words: 'O, Nellie, Nellie, jewel!' "

And so the episodes known in Dublin as "The Massacres of North King Street" began.

At the barricade, young John Dwan fell with a bullet through his head. William Hogan lifted the inert body onto his shoulders, crawled back to the entrance of Coleraine Street where he laid his friend down and stood guard until stretcher bearers could be found to take him to hospital. By now the hammering of picks as the Staffs tunneled through the houses could be heard above the rifle fire and Sherrin and his comrades, realizing the military's intentions, decided to retreat. They crawled one by one toward Coleraine Street where, once

339

under cover, they doubled round by a back lane to Church Street, and rejoined Lieutenant Jack Shouldice and his men in Reilly's. Behind them the South Staffs continued to fire upon the deserted barricade until at length, realizing it was no longer manned, they rushed forward and occupied it. In Reilly's Fort, they heard a constant breaking of glass and smashing of woodwork and the excited shouting of orders as the military battered their way into more and more houses. Now and then a star shell would rocket into the night, bathing the scene in a weird, blue light.

At Commandant Daly's Heaquarters in the Father Mathew Hall, eighty yards from Reilly's Fort, priests from a nearby church listened to the confessions of the rebels, and afterward administered Holy Communion. Addressing the men, a priest explained: "The situation at present is very grave and we all know that if the military break in, there will be no mercy shown to anyone. I want you all, therefore, to offer your lives to God as a willing sacrifice for Ireland, if it is so needed. I will stay with you to the end." He had scarcely finished speaking when an unexpected sound came floating in from the street outside. It was the sound of the men at the barricades singing.

Firing ceased abruptly as the astonished South Staffords listened to a rebel song drift over the barricades, sung with all the fervor of patriotic hearts. The voices rose defiantly into the sudden quietness of the night. As the song ended, the South Staffords poured volley after volley into the darkness in a fury of frustration. The rebels replied with two songs: "The Boys of the West" and "The Green Flag." Each time the South Staffords ceased firing until the song had finished, then unleashed a further furious storm of lead. The rebel reply was an outburst of ironical cheers and yet another song.

"Frank McCabe sang a most inappropriate song," recalls Volunteer Thomas Sherrin. "It was called 'The Bucket of Mountain Dew.' It runs:

> On yonder little hill,
> There's a darling little still
> Its smoke curling up to the sky.

340

And it's easy to tell
By the whiff and the smell
That there's poteen, me boys,
Close by.

For it fills the air
With perfume rare,
And betwixt both me and you,
As home we roll,
We'll drink a bowl,
Or a bucket
Of the Mountain Dew.

Oh, we certainly sang good-ho that night!"

Colonel Taylor, short and slightly pompous, did not appreciate the concert. As dawn began to light the gray streets, he sent his angry troops charging over the captured barricade in an impatient effort to finish the job. It was twelve hours since he had seized the Bolton Street Technical Schools and ordered his men down North King Street and in that time they had managed to advance barely two hundred yards—casualties, fortunately, had been light. Now four platoons of "C" Company, led by Major J. Sheppard, went into the charge with bayonets thrust determinedly forward.

They were met by the concentrated fire of seven riflemen in Reilly's pub. In the narrow street, bedded down behind their loopholed windows, big sacks of maize and meal protecting their heads, the rebels had ample time and opportunity to pick out their men. A sheet of heavy, killing bullets stopped Sheppard's men dead. Sheppard himself fell wounded. His men, scattering for cover, dashed into Beresford Street where, high above their heads, Volunteer Frank Shouldice waited for them.

"Our fellows at Reilly's were firing into them, and some more from six cottages then being built on waste ground on our left. About fifteen Tommies turned into Beresford Street right under me. I was on the iron platform and all I had to do was fire down upon them. One by one we knocked them all over.

It was a terrible slaughter, and to this day I can't understand why they decided to rush things." Thus Frank Shouldice.

"If they'd kept boring through the walls, creeping up on us gradually, we'd have stood no chance," says Sherrin. "Some officer, however, clearly lost his head and sent those lads out to their death."

Captain Fionan Lynch and Lieutenant Jack Shouldice, who had been touring posts all night, had just come down from the Malt House when the South Staffs launched their charge. "When the last of those fellows was knocked over, we leaped over the barricade in Beresford Street and ran out into the road and picked up their rifles and ammunition. One young fellow, still alive, was moaning pitifully for his mother, but what could I do to help him?" says Jack Shouldice.

Still the battle raged on. Lieutenant Shouldice worked his way back into Reilly's to reinforce the other riflemen. The military pushed their way from one house to another, aided by a heavy covering fire from the houses through which they had tunneled. On the other side of the street they reached the corner of Beresford Street. Shouldice and his men blanketed the street with fire, taking turns when their rifles got too hot to hold. The interior of Reilly's was a shambles. Worse, the sacks of meal and flour used to loophole the windows were pierced by bullets and the contents poured out, leaving them with no protection. "We weren't frightened," recalls Sherrin. "We were simply past being frightened by then." Their ammunition, however, was running low.

"On two occasions I sent messengers down to the Father Mathew Hall to bring back supplies," recalls Lieutenant Shouldice, "but neither could get back. By this time we were under heavy fire not only from the frontal attack by the 2/6th South Staffs, but also from the 2/5th South Staffs, advancing at our rear from Queen Street through Smithfield. They had a machine gun with them and constantly swept the roadway outside. Shortly after 7 A.M. I sent young Patrick O'Flanagan out in a last desperate attempt to get fresh ammunition. We were almost exhausted physically, and we hadn't had a decent meal or anything to drink for some time, but we were still determined to keep fighting as long as the stuff held out."

342

Young O'Flanagan reached the Father Mathew Hall and was on his way back when Shouldice saw him halt briefly, then dash suddenly into the road. He was more than halfway to Reilly's door when Shouldice saw him trip. "Then I saw him falling forward, carried on by his own impetus." When Shouldice got down into the hallway to help him, the boy lay dying in the doorway. The ammunition pouches he had collected lay in the roadway, just out of reach.

By 9 A.M. it was all over in Reilly's. Shouldice took a vote among his men, then lined them up in the hallway, and during a momentary lull they made a run for it.

They were halfway across the street before the military began shooting, but they flung themselves to the pavement and scrambled furiously on their hands and knees to safety.

With a shout of triumph the Staffords swept forward victoriously. Captain Percy Bayliss, of Wolverhampton, rushing ahead impetuously with his platoon, became isolated from the main body. From both ends of Church Street the rebels swept the crossing with bullets. Colonel Taylor, his brow black as thunder, strode up North King Street followed by his orderly. For sixteen damned hours, now, he had struggled fiercely to take this wretched slum and still the battalion was hung up. Warily he approached the crossing. And there, straight in front of him, ruffling slightly in the breeze, a green flag hung mockingly.

At dawn the main army of rebels cut off in Moore Street, commenced burrowing again through the houses toward Great Britain Street. In Cogan's, the three rebel women prepared a scrappy meal for the members of the Provisional Government, after which the whole party moved forward through the holes in the wall as far as Hanlon's fish shop at No. 16. The holes had been broken through at different levels and the job of getting Connolly's stretcher up and down flights of stairs and through the holes was laborious. For Connolly, whose foot had turned gangrenous, every step of the way meant torture. It was decided he could go no farther and a halt was made at No. 16. Here, in the back parlor of a fishmonger's shop, the final Headquarters of the broken army of the Irish Republic were established. The five leaders, Pearse, Connolly, Plunkett, Clarke, and MacDermott, along with Pearse's young brother, flopped down wearily wherever there was room. Near Connolly were placed four wounded men, including the British prisoner rescued by George Plunkett.

A field gun thundered somewhere in Sackville Street as the leaders and their principal officers held a last council of war. Asked to outline the position as it appeared to him, MacLoughlin, the boy commandant, said he thought the important thing was to escape from Moore Street before the military realized exactly where they were and how weak they had become. Once they found out, the troops were certain to set fire to Moore Street and as the rebels ran from the flames, they would be mowed down without mercy. He thought there was no hope of breaking through the barricade at the top of Moore Street; the way to go, he suggested, was down Henry Street,

344

through the old Ormonde Markets and then on to the Four Courts. If twenty men, well-armed and with bombs, were first to hurl themselves in a diversionary charge against the British barricade, they would distract the military's attention long enough to allow the rest to break out from the houses and dash across the street into the laneways opposite. From there, they could filter into Capel Street and on to the Four Courts. Scouts might be sent ahead to contact Commandant Daly and a strong escort party provided to secure a link-up. The leaders listened in silence while the boy put forward his ideas. When he had finished, Pearse asked, "How many lives would we lose?"

MacLoughlin: "Twenty to thirty in Moore Street. If the British are in strength in Denmark Street, most of us probably will not get through. But in any event, we're simply doomed if we stay here."

There was silence. Then the leaders leaned forward, their heads almost touching, and in low, careful tones, began talking over the merits of the plan. Pearse raised his head finally and, clearing his throat, said that they were all agreed; the plan seemed worth trying. MacLoughlin went among the weary men, asking for twenty volunteers and when he had found them, they set to work to bore a way through the intervening houses to Sackville Lane. From here, only twenty yards short of the British barricade, they would mount their diversionary charge. Some hours later, when they had finally broken into the last house, MacLoughlin carefully stepped into the lane to reconnoiter. The dead body of The O'Rahilly lay on its back, face up to the sky, two of his men crumpled up nearby. MacLoughlin tiptoed to the corner and peered cautiously around. He was followed closely by John Mac-Dermott, weeping a little at the sight of The O'Rahilly. Then a rebel shouted that they were both wanted urgently back in No. 16.

When they returned to the house, they were told that the plan had been called off. An incident had occurred which had decided Pearse that surrender was necessary. Robert Dillon, licensee of The Flag, a public house in Moore Street, his premises set on fire by a burning fragment from the G.P.O., had ventured out into the street with his wife and his daughter, carrying a white flag. The military had chopped them down mercilessly under the very eyes of Pearse, who turned away sickened.

When MacDermott and MacLoughlin entered the room, Pearse asked the boy, "Will the retreat not involve the loss of civilian life? Won't it be bound to lead through populous districts, whatever route we take?"

"I'm afraid it will," said MacLoughlin.

"In that case, will you issue cease-fire orders to last for the next hour," ordered Pearse abruptly.

Stunned, MacLoughlin, without speaking further, quit the room to pass on the order. When he returned, some fifteen minutes later, old Tom Clarke, his face sad and haggard, beckoned him over to sit beside him. Miss Carney, still cheerful, made them both a cup of tea. Then Clarke gently broke the news that the decision had been made to ask for terms and that a messenger had been sent out to treat with the military. MacLoughlin stared astonished and Clarke added thoughtfully, "Perhaps we ought to go on with your plan and fight it out, for terms or no terms, probably we'll all be killed anyway."

"Deep gloom settled over the place," wrote MacLoughlin later. "No one spoke; the only sound was the groaning of the wounded soldier. On the wall above the fireplace was a lithograph of Robert Emmett, standing defiantly in the dock. Underneath it was a caption which said: 'Until my country takes its place among the nations . . . let no man write my epitaph.' "

Although by now they had the ruined Post Office invested on all sides, still the military seemed to have no inkling at all as to the real plight of the rebels. General Maxwell remained in Dublin Castle, while Lowe refused to put a foot outside Trinity College. So uninformed, indeed, were the military of the real state of affairs that Colonel Hodgkin, C.O. of the 2/6th Sherwood Foresters, summoned Captain G. J. Edmunds to Battalion H.Q. in Great Britain Street and ordered him to take one hundred men and report to Colonel Owen of the Royal Irish Regiment.

"The position is, Edmunds," explained the Colonel briskly,

346

"that the Royal Irish are getting ready to assault the Post Office to try and take it, and they need some extra men to help out. So take a hundred chaps and report to Colonel Owen in Summerhill at once, will you, there's a good fellow?"

In Sackville Street a shell crashed through the upper stories of the Metropole Hotel, and sent a loud, reverberating echo sighing away down the ruined, desolate street. Not even a bird moved any longer. Thin smoke still wisped into the air from the smoldering Post Office, whose flagpole hung crazily askew, the scorched green flag hanging down in sorrowful defeat. Machine-gun bullets ate viciously into the façade of the empty hotel. Again and again artillery rumbled, the shells picking great holes in the deserted buildings. Soon reporter O'Leary noticed the first traces of fire eating their way along the Metropole roof. Fanned by a breeze, the flames gained strength and once again smoke clouds drifted across Sackville Street, obscuring for long intervals the figure of Nelson.

In No. 16 Moore Street, Pearse and Connolly talked together long and earnestly in very low tones. At last Pearse arose from the wounded man's couch and spoke to MacDermott, who turned and asked Miss O'Farrell to obtain a white flag. She left the room to search for a Red Cross insignia, and MacDermott went into the house next door where he discovered Captain Michael O'Reilly shaving.

"Can you get us a white flag of some sort?" asked MacDermott.

O'Reilly took a large white linen handkerchief from his breast pocket. "Will this do?" MacDermott nodded, his face gray. Quietly he tied the handkerchief to a stick, then handed it back to O'Reilly, who went to the front door and stuck the "flag" out. A volley of bullets caused him to duck back. In the silence which followed O'Reilly again stuck the handkerchief out. This time he waved it gently, and the military did not fire. MacDermott beckoned Miss O'Farrell forward, and the young woman, holding her Red Cross flag, walked out into the street. It was 12:45 P.M.

The nurse stood for a moment gazing up the street toward the barricade and waving her flag. A shout came from the military, telling her to come forward. Defiantly, the young

347

woman started walking. At the barricade hands stretched out to assist her. Slightly out of breath, she jumped down on the far side, and demanded to see the general.

She was brought before Colonel Hodgkin, to whom she explained that she had been sent by Mr. Pearse, who wished to treat with them.

"How many girls are there down there?" asked Hodgkin brusquely.

"Three," replied Miss O'Farrell.

"Well, take my advice and go down again and bring the other two girls out of it," said the Colonel shortly.

He was about to help her back over the barricade when he changed his mind and said, "No. Don't go; you'd better wait —I suppose this will have to be reported." He called another officer and told him to escort Miss O'Farrell along Great Britain Street. The nurse walked along the street passing Tom Clarke's shop, and then stopped outside either No. 70 or 71, while the escorting officer called for the C.O.

In a short time Colonel Portal came out, and there was the following dialogue:

O'Farrell: "The Commandant of the Irish Republican Army wishes to treat with the Commandant of the British forces in Ireland."

Portal: "The Irish Republican Army?—the Sinn Feiners, you mean."

O'Farrell: "No, the Irish Republican Army they call themselves and I think that is a very good name, too."

Portal: "Will Pearse be able to be moved on a stretcher?"

O'Farrell: "Commandant Pearse doesn't need a stretcher."

Portal (turning to another officer): "Take that Red Cross off her and bring her over there and search her—she's a spy."

The officer obeyed. The Red Cross insignia was taken off her arm, then off her apron. Then the officer took her into the hallway of a nearby bank and searched her. Satisfied that she had no concealed arms, he took her into Tom Clarke's shop where she was held prisoner.

In No. 15 Moore Street, Julia Grenan knelt in the hallway

348

and said a prayer for the safety of her friend. When she had finished, she rose to her feet and went over to John MacDermott. Hesitantly she asked him, "Will they shoot her?"

"Ah, not at all," said MacDermott comfortingly, patting her on the arm. He turned away and went into the next house, No. 16. A few minutes later she heard Connolly call out to her, and went through the hole in the wall to the wounded leader's bedside.

"Now, don't be crying for your friend," said James Connolly soothingly; "they won't shoot her. She may be away for some time, but don't worry, they won't shoot her."

In Trinity College, General Lowe's telephone rang. It was Dublin Castle on the line to say that a Red Cross nurse had come to the Moore Street barricade with a verbal message from Pearse, saying he wished to treat as to terms of surrender—the girl had been detained pending further orders. Lowe at once left for Great Britain Street, accompanied by Captain H. de Courcy Wheeler.

"General Lowe treated me very gentlemanly," wrote Miss O'Farrell afterward. "I gave him the message and he said he would take me in a motorcar to the top of Moore Street. I was to go back to Mr. Pearse and tell him that 'General Lowe would not treat at all until he would surrender unconditionally,' adding that I had to be back in half an hour as hostilities must go on."

Colonel Portal then wrote a note to this effect, which General Lowe signed, and they both took her in a motorcar as far as Moore Street. Here she was permitted to go back over the barricade again to rebel headquarters at No. 16. She delivered the messages, explaining that she had to be back within half an hour.

"The situation was discussed and then I was sent back with a written message," she goes on. "I went back to the top of Moore Street where General Lowe was waiting in the car. He was vexed because I was a minute over the half hour coming, but I pointed out that I wasn't by my watch. Then one of the officers set his watch by mine. I did not know what was in Mr. Pearse's note [he had requested terms for his men, although not for himself], but General Lowe's reply was 'Go back and

349

tell Mr. Pearse that I will not treat at all unless he surrenders unconditionally and that Mr. Connolly follows on a stretcher.'" Lowe then warned her that unless she and Mr. Pearse were back within half an hour he would resume hostilities. Once more she returned to Moore Street carrying this message, and the members of the Provisional Government held a short council. "Then Mr. Pearse decided to go back with me," adds Miss O'Farrell.

No one spoke in the little parlor as the Commander in Chief, his face more somber than any of those present could remember it, shook everyone there by the hand for what they sensed might be the last time. MacLoughlin had the impression that Pearse did not altogether believe that this was a final good-bye, but felt that he would be permitted to return and make whatever arrangements were thought necessary. The women wept bitterly and Miss Grenan pressed Rosary beads on Miss O'Farrell. Then the two stepped out into the street—Pearse tall and still commanding in presence, Miss O'Farrell blonde and diminutive, trotting briskly beside him.

At exactly 2:30 P.M. officially (Miss O'Farrell's watch said 3:30, but it would seem that her watch was an hour fast) General Lowe received the rebel commander on the British side of the barricade at the top of Moore Street. Lieutenant King, who had been held prisoner in the Post Office, was called forward to identify Pearse, but said he could not as he had not seen him there.

"Were you in the G.P.O.?" asked King.

"Yes," answered Pearse briefly.

"Well, I didn't see you there."

Pearse, a trifle irritated by this nonsense, did not answer but simply took off his sword and handed it to Lowe. The general took it and then said, "My only concession is that I will allow the other Commandants to surrender. I understand you have the Countess de Markievicz down there?"

"No, she isn't with me," said Pearse shortly.

"Oh, I know she's down there," said Lowe sharply.

"Don't accuse me of speaking an untruth," replied Pearse, somewhat heatedly.

350

"Oh, I beg your pardon, Mr. Pearse, but I do know she's in the area."

"Well, she's not with me, sir."

At a loss for a moment Lowe then suggested that Miss O'Farrell should be detained by the military for the night in order that she could take Pearse's surrender order round to the other rebel commandants.

"Will you agree to this?" asked Pearse, turning to the nurse.

"Yes, if you wish it," replied Miss O'Farrell.

"I do wish it," said Pearse slowly and sadly, and shook her hand. She watched him as he was led away, escorted by General Lowe's son and another officer.

Lowe, accompanied by Captain Wheeler, drove off down towards Sackville Street, the car carrying Pearse, with an armed bodyguard standing on the running board, following immediately behind. Then the two cars disappeared from sight round the Parnell Monument. As Miss O'Farrell stood there, her head bowed in misery, she heard a military officer remark casually, "It would be interesting to know how many [German] marks that chap has in his pocket."

In Moore Street, the small party left behind sat together in strained and anxious silence. After a while MacLoughlin crossed to Connolly's bedside. "What do you think will happen?" he asked the wounded leader. "Oh, I think those of us, including myself, who have signed the Proclamation, will be shot. Some good, however, might come from what we have done," said Connolly. He advised MacLoughlin not to reveal his rank. "You're a young man; you'll be able to pick up the thread; men such as you will be needed." As the Commandant-General spoke, MacDermott gently laid a hand on young MacLoughlin's shoulder and led him away. As they left the room, the young man saw Miss Carney kneel at Connolly's bedside, weeping bitterly, asking, "Is there no other way?"

CONNOLLY: "No—I couldn't bear to see my brave boys burned to death—there is no other way." He called for the medical student, James Ryan, and asked to be prepared for the journey. A stretcher was brought in and Connolly gently lifted onto it and then carried into the house next door.

Meanwhile Pearse had been driven to the Headquarters of Irish Command at Parkgate where, on arrival, he was ushered before General Maxwell. The interview, according to Maxwell's biographer, Sir George Arthur, "was both short and stern. Pearse seemed stunned by the thought of what he had brought on his followers and unhesitatingly yielded to the demand to write and sign notices ordering the various 'commandoes' to surrender unconditionally." The instrument of surrender read:

In order to prevent the further slaughter of Dublin citizens, and in the hope of saving the lives of our followers now surrounded and hopelessly outnumbered, the members of the Provisional Government present at Headquarters have agreed to an unconditional surrender, and the Commandants of the various districts in the City and Country will order their commands to lay down arms.

(Signed)   **P. H. PEARSE**
29th April, 1916,
3:45 P.M.

This done, Captain Wheeler was instructed to go to the Red Cross Hospital in Dublin Castle where by this time Connolly had been taken and to obtain his countersignature. When Wheeler arrived, Connolly had already been put to bed and was under medical care. Wheeler read out Pearse's statement and explained that General Lowe thought he—Connolly—should endorse the order as far as his own commands were concerned. Connolly scribbled: "I agree to these conditions for the men only under my own command in the Moore Street District and for the men in the Stephen's Green Command." (Signed) James Connolly, April 29/16."

Copies of both orders (written on the same piece of paper) were then taken to Miss O'Farrell to deliver to Moore Street along with a written note telling the men how they should surrender: "Carrying a white flag, proceed down Moore Street, turn into Moore Lane and Henry Place, out into Henry Street

352

and around the Pillar to the right hand side of Sackville Street; march up to within a hundred yards of the military drawn up at the Parnell Statue, halt, advance five paces and lay down arms."

When the nurse reached Moore Street with these orders, there were still some hotheads who wanted to fight on. They were quieted, however, by Tom Clarke, who pointed out that he had given his life to the struggle and was satisfied as things were; he thought Ireland "would be all right in the future." Thereupon MacDermott and MacLoughlin rounded up most of the men in the backyard of No. 16, and MacDermott, looking as though he might break down at any moment, read Pearse's letter aloud, stumbling over the words, then haltingly adding some of his own: "I am proud of you. You have made a great fight. It is not our fault that you haven't won. You were outclassed, that is all."

It was evening before all the wounded were placed on stretchers on the pavements. The Moore Street shops were closed and shuttered; the bodies of the dead still lay where they had fallen. Together MacDermott, MacLoughlin and Captain Michael O'Reilly marshaled the fit men into ranks in the middle of the street. O'Reilly was ordered to lead the way, carrying the white flag.

He set off at the head of fifty men, the main body following. When the latter, led by MacLoughlin, flanked by Willie Pearse and John MacDermott, reached Sackville Street, they saw no sign of O'Reilly's party. O'Reilly, with that instinct for farce which somehow obtruded on even the most dramatic moments of the insurrection, had taken the wrong turning and gone marching past the burned-out G.P.O. and the still blazing Metropole Hotel toward O'Connell Bridge, where he proceeded to lay down arms to an astonished military party advancing to meet him from Westmoreland Street. After a short parley O'Reilly's men picked up their arms again, and O'Reilly led them back up Sackville Street to rejoin the rest of the rebel army. Drawn up on each side of the street in front of the Gresham Hotel were 250 or 300 rebels. The command rang out: "Step five paces forward and deposit your arms!"

As the order echoed down the great, devastated thorough-

353

fare, where every principal building had been either destroyed or was still burning, where the dead horses of the Lancers, killed six long days ago still lay in stinking obscenity, the haggard, weary, hungry, and bedraggled army threw down its arms angrily and stepped back five paces to stand weaponless at the mercy of their conquerors.

The attitude of the military toward their beaten adversaries hardly smacked of generosity. Officers and men, on the whole, believed that the rebels were in the pay of the Germans, doing their dirty work for them, and considered that they deserved little better treatment than to be placed against a wall and shot. Rebellion, even if not fomented by Germany, was a heinous crime, too, and certainly no authority anywhere had ever been known to treat those who attempted to suborn it with anything but the most excessive harshness. In England, in highland Scotland, and, of course, in Ireland itself, rebels throughout the centuries had always been mercilessly punished by the Crown. A rebel's life was forfeit, as were his goods and possessions. Only the most naïve might have imagined that they would be accorded the honored treatment prescribed by international law for recognized prisoners of war.

Physically, the military behaved most correctly. Rebel complaints of ill-treatment can be whittled down to a series of insults delivered almost entirely by a single officer. Typical of this man's attitude was a sneer directed at John MacDermott. "So you've cripples in your army!" To counter balance this kind of childishness there were generous gestures. One officer walked behind the line of prisoners murmuring, "If you men have any incriminating papers, tear them up quietly and drop them in the gutter behind you." Again, as the rebels were marched to the grounds of the Rotunda Hospital (a small plot of greensward opposite the Parnell Monument), Joseph Plunkett, hardly able to walk, swayed and almost fell. A soldier gave him a rough shove forward and threatened to bayonet him, only to have a sergeant pull him fiercely by the arm and bark angrily, "Do your duty and do no more; *that's* not your duty."

By 10 P.M. some four hundred rebels (including Daly's men from the Four Courts who had by this time surrendered) had been squashed into this small plot of ground. (A small

354

detachment of Daly's men, under Volunteer Patrick Holohan, were cut off in North Brunswick Street and had refused to surrender although, at the urgings of the Capuchin monks of the district, they had agreed to a truce while confirmation of Pearse's order was brought to them). Here, as the night came down and a bitterly cold wind swept Sackville Street, the main body of the rebel army squatted, crushed close together, with ample time to look back on its errors. Fires still smoldered, or burst intermittently into life along the great street. Armored cars rattled past every now and then and there was a constant stream of Red Cross ambulances "gliding by silent as ghosts." At intervals Tommies would gather up rebel arms and trot away with them. An officer, examining a Howth gun, remarked as he fingered a Mauser bullet, "You know, this damn thing would kill a bally elephant!" From the roof of the Rotunda, a machine gun stood trained throughout the night, while a ring of bayonets encircled the plot. The Misses Grenan and Carney, sat on the grass beside John MacDermott and sucked compressed food lozenges he gave them, which "tasted awful."

In the early hours the quiet, well-behaved officer in charge was relieved by Captain Lea Wilson, a dark-browed, florid-faced, thick-lipped Irishman, a little the worse for drink. Wilson began to hurl insults at them. "He strides around looking for looters and threatening to have us all shot and telling us not to smoke, not to stand up, and not to lie down and, if we want lavatories, use the beds provided and lie down in both," Desmond Ryan wrote later. "He roars madly at his own men and issues contradictory orders. Rushes at this man and that shouting he'll have them shot. Strikes matches and holds them in the faces of the men and shouts 'Anyone want to see the animals?' He bends over Plunkett and snatches a document from his inner pocket: 'Ah, his will! He certainly knew what he was coming out to get!' He snatches a whistle from Willie Pearse, has another man's Red Cross armlet ripped away with bayonets. "You're a nice specimen of an English gentleman!' snarls an exasperated victim. He yells at Clarke: 'That old bastard is the Commander in Chief. He keeps a tobacco shop across the street. Nice general for your ——army.' One Volunteer mutters: 'A dark night, a dark lane, a stout stick—and that fellow!' " (Three years later Michael Collins had Wilson shot during the height of the Black-and-Tan campaign).

At nine o'clock on Sunday morning, thoroughly miserable, stiff and half-frozen after their night in the open, the rebels were lined up in Sackville Street and told to start marching. Wilson, in a fit of rage, had confiscated MacDermott's walking stick during the night. MacDermott pleaded that, without it, he would be unable to keep up with the others and so was permitted to march by himself under separate escort. As for the rest, an eyewitness in the Gresham Hotel who saw them march down Sackville Street that morning had left this description of the scene:

"It's a sight I shall never forget. That thin line, some in the green uniform of the Volunteers, others in the plainer equipment of the Citizen Army, some looking like ordinary civilians, the others looking mere lads of fifteen, not a few wounded and bandaged, and the whole melancholy procession wending its way through long lines of khaki soldiers. But down-hearted—no! As they passed, I heard the subdued strains of the scaffold songs of many an Irishman before them—'God Save Ireland.' Dockers, labourers, shop assistants, all conditions of men; all have the same look of defiance which will haunt me to my dying day. Whatever else they were, they were not cowards. If they had been at the front and accomplished what they had accomplished in the face of such odds, the whole Empire would have been proud of them, and the whole world ringing with their praises."

This was a lone voice, a lone view. As the prisoners marched toward Richmond Barracks, crowds stood at the curbsides to hoot and jeer them. "Shoot the traitors!" they cried, "Bayonet the bastards!" In one of the poorer quarters, the shawlies pelted them with rotten vegetables, the more enthusiastic disgorging the contents of their chamber pots over the beaten, yet somehow still undefeated men.

The G.P.O. and the Four Courts had fallen. Patrick Pearse had surrendered and lay captive in Arbour Hill barracks. Connolly was in the hospital in Dublin Castle. The people of

Dublin flocked into the city to see the still smoldering ruins and hunt for souvenirs, while the City Fathers totted up the cost of it all, and General Maxwell prepared his courts-martial. Yet the Rebellion was still not over. Commandants Kent, MacDonagh, De Valera, and Mallin had not yet surrendered. Escorted by Captain Wheeler, Nurse O'Farrell, a brave and lonely little figure set off through areas where bullets still flew, carrying the instrument of surrender. She went first to Boland's Bakery, where De Valera, who did not know her personally, refused at first to believe its authenticity. She left, not knowing whether he intended to surrender or not. Here, as with other commands, there were men who wanted to go on fighting and the authority of De Valera and his senior officers was openly flouted by a few diehards who supported Lieutenant John Guilfoyle and his plan to escape to the mountains and carry on fighting. In the end, on the plea that only by surrendering immediately were they likely to save De Valera's life, they gave in. De Valera, escorted by Cadet Mackay, a military prisoner, left the Bakery, stopped the first respectable person he saw—Dr. Myles Keogh of Sir Patrick Dun's Hospital—and informed him that he wished to surrender. Keogh immediately passed the message on to Trinity College.

De Valera made two memorable remarks that morning. To the military officer who took his surrender he said, "Shoot me if you will, but arrange for my men." And then to the people who gathered in Lower Mount Street to watch his men lay down their arms: "If only you'd come out with knives and forks!"

Commander MacDonagh surrendered only after a good deal of discussion, insisting that, as Pearse was being held prisoner, the Commander in Chief was acting under duress in issuing his order. An interview was arranged with General Lowe by the Carmelite friar, Father Augustine, after which MacDonagh drove to the South Dublin Union to see Kent and talk over the position. In the end both surrendered at the same time.

Father Augustine also played a vital part in securing young Holohan's surrender, thus saving the South Staffords the distasteful task of winkling him out. After interviewing Pearse in Arbour Hill and securing a copy of the surrender order written in the Commander in Chief's own hand, the monk was permitted to pass through the embattled lines to see Holohan. In the face of such a document, the desperate young rebel reluctantly laid down his arms.

Constance Markievicz remained gay and utterly fearless right to the last. She and Michael Mallin marched out the side door of the College of Surgeons together and together surrendered to Captain Wheeler. Then she took off her great Mauser rifle-pistol and bright bandolier, raised them to her lips, kissed them, and then handed them over.

"I can place a motorcar at your disposal, madam," said Wheeler, with great courtesy.

"No," she answered, still defiant, and with all the pride and dignity of a lady of the Big House, added, "I shall march at the head of my men as I am second-in-command, and shall share their fate."

Epilogue

One thousand three hundred and fifty one people had been killed or severely wounded—officially. One hundred and seventy-nine buildings in central Dublin, enclosing sixty-one thousand square yards, had been irrevocably ruined and the cost, in terms of the monetary values then existing, was two and a half million pounds sterling. One hundred thousand people—approximately one-third of the total population—had to be given public relief.

It was a time for wisdom. Had General Sir John Maxwell, in the last analysis, been something more than an unimaginative soldier, he might have understood that from the Imperial point of view, the way to treat the insurrectionary leaders was to make them look ridiculous. Had he, in effect, spanked them and sent them home with a stern warning to be good boys in the future, Britain might well have avoided the disasters of the years which followed—which ate into the fabric of the Imperial idea as surely as any German army. The consequences were immense; not least among them the continual fostering by Irish-Americans of the traditional dislike felt by the United States for colonialism.

Yet, all in all, perhaps it was asking a little too much to expect Maxwell to foresee any of this. Possibly almost any man, placed suddenly in his position, faced with the precedents he had to face, would have done very much as he did. The sentences he confirmed were hardly barbaric and he allowed the leaders to die a soldier's death when he might so easily have hanged them as common felons. Against the charges that the courts-martial were set up and carried through with

359

an almost indecent haste, is to be set the fact that, while the menace of a German invasion remained, time was of the essence. Rebels and rebellion must be crushed, and the quicker it is done, the better. Perhaps the real irony lay in the fact that by executing Pearse and his comrades in the way that he did, Maxwell was only doing what they really wanted him to do. Only in death, most of them knew, could they achieve victory.

Pearse, MacDonagh, and Clarke were shot at dawn on the morning of Wednesday, May 3, 1916, in the yard of Kilmainham prison. In his court-martial speech Pearse went to some lengths to refute the suggestion that the insurrection had been financed with German gold as was genuinely believed by most people at the time:

"I desire in the first place to repeat what I have already said in letters to General Sir John Maxwell and Brigadier-General Lowe. My object in agreeing to unconditional surrender was to prevent the further slaughter of the civilian population of Dublin and to save the lives of our gallant fellows, who, having made for six days a stand unparalleled in military history, were now surrounded and (in the case of those under the immediate command of headquarters) without food. I fully understand now, as then, that my own life is forfeit to British law, and I shall die very cheerfully if I can think that the British Government, as it has already shown itself strong, will now show itself magnanimous enough to accept my single life in forfeiture and to give a general amnesty to the brave men and boys who have fought at my bidding. In the second place I wish it to be understood that any admissions I make here are to be taken as involving myself alone. They do not involve and must not be used against anyone who acted with me, not even those who may have set their names to documents with me. [The Court assented to this.]

"I admit I was Commander-General Commander-in-Chief of the forces of the Irish Republic which have been acting against you for the past week and that I was President of the Provisional Government. I stand over all my acts and words done or spoken in these capacities. When I was a child of ten I went down on my knees by my bedside one night and promised God that I should devote my life to an effort to free my country. I have kept that promise. First among all earthly things, as a boy and as a man, I have worked for Irish freedom. I have helped to organise, to arm, to train, and to discipline my fellow countrymen to the sole end that, when the time came, they might fight for Irish freedom. The time, as it seemed to me, did come and we went into the fight. I am glad that we did, we seem to have lost, we have not lost. To refuse to fight would have been to lose, to fight is to win, we have kept faith with the past, and handed a tradition to the future.

"I repudiate the assertion of the prosecutor that I sought to aid and abet England's enemy. Germany is no more to me than England is. I asked and accepted German aid in the shape of arms and an expeditionary force, we neither asked for nor accepted German gold, nor had any traffic with Germany but what I state; my aim was to win Irish freedom; we struck the first blow ourselves but I should have been glad of an ally's aid.

"I assume I am speaking to Englishmen who value their own freedom, and who profess to be fighting for the freedom of Belgium and Serbia. Believe that we too love freedom and desire it. To us it is more desirable than anything else in the world. If you strike us down now we shall rise again and renew the fight. You cannot conquer Ireland; you cannot extinguish the Irish passion for freedom; if our deed has not been sufficient to win freedom then our children will win it by a better deed."

On the morning of his execution Pearse wrote to his mother:

My dearest mother,

I have been hoping up to now it would be possible to see you again, but it does not seem possible. Goodbye, dear mother. Through you I say goodbye to "WowWow" [a sister], Mary, Brigid, Willie, Miss B., Michael, cousin Maggine and everyone at St. Enda's. I hope and believe Willie and the St. Enda's boys will be all safe.

I have written two papers about financial affairs and one about my books which I want you to get. With them are a few poems which I want added to the poems in MS in my bookcase. You asked me to write a little poem which would seem to be said by you about me. I have written it, and a copy is in Arbour Hill barracks with other papers.

I just received Holy Communion. I am happy, except for the great grief of parting from you. This is the death I should have asked for if God had given me the choice of all deaths—to die a soldier's death for Ireland and for freedom. We have done right. People will say hard things of us now, but later on will praise us. Do not grieve for all this but think of it as a sacrifice which God asked of me and of you.

Goodbye, dear mother, may God bless you for your great love to me and for your great faith and may He remember all you have so bravely suffered. I hope soon to see papa, and in a little while we shall all be together again. I have not words to tell you of my love for you and how my heart yearns to you all. I will call to you in my heart at the last moment.

Your son,
Pat

The poem to which he refers was called *The Mother:*

> I do not grudge them; Lord, I do not grudge
> My two strong sons that I have seen go out
> To break their strength and die, they and a few,
> In bloody protest for a glorious thing
> They shall be spoken of among their people,
> The generations shall remember them,
> And call them blessed!

Little of what Tom Clarke had to say—if he said anything much—has survived to us. To his court-martial judges he announced that he would do the same again if spared. To his wife, on the last night of his life, he said, "I am to be shot at dawn. I'm glad it's a soldier's death I'm getting. I've had enough of imprisonment."

MacDonagh wrote his own epitaph:

> His songs were a little phrase
> Of eternal song
> Drowned in the harping of lays
> More loud and long

His deed was a single word
Called out alone
In a night where no echo stirred
To laughter or moan

But his song's new soul shall shrill
The loud harps dumb
And his deed the echoes fill
When the dawn is come

At midnight the news was broken to MacDonagh that he would be shot at dawn. His wife was not able to get to him but his sister, a nun, found him in "a dank, vile cell" lighted by the butt of a candle. He had already confessed by the time she arrived, had had Holy Communion, and had written to his wife. When his sister entered the cell and saw that there was no water, she asked the sentry, "Will you give him some water to wash in?" The sentry, acting under orders, refused. MacDonagh's sister then handed him a rosary which had belonged to their mother and he put it around his neck. "I hope they will give me this when it is all over," she said. "Ah, no," he said quietly, "they will shoot it to bits." (They did not— only four beads were shot away and the rosary was eventually returned to his sister).

In his court-martial speech MacDonagh said:

"Gentlemen of the Court-martial. I choose to think that you have but done your duty, according to your lights, in sentencing me to death. I thank you for your courtesy. It would not be seemly for me to go to my doom without trying to express, however inadequately, my sense of the high honour I enjoy in being of those predestined in this generation to die for the cause of Irish freedom. You will, perhaps, understand this sentiment, for it is one to which an Imperial poet of a bygone age bore immortal testimony: 'Tis sweet and glorious to die for one's country.' You would all be proud to die for Britain, your Imperial patron, and I am proud and happy to die for Ireland, my glorious Fatherland."

(A member of the Court) "You speak of Britain as our Imperial patron."

(MacDonagh): "Yes, some of you are Irishmen."

"And what of your Imperial patron; what of Germany?"

"Not if Germany had violated and despoiled my country and persisted in withholding her birthright of freedom."

(President) "Better not interrupt the prisoner." (The prisoner bowed.)

"There is not much left to say. The Proclamation of the Irish Republic has been adduced in evidence against me as one of the signatories; you think it already a dead and buried letter, but it lives, it lives. From minds alight with Ireland's vivid intellect, it sprang; in hearts aflame with Ireland's mighty love it was conceived. Such documents do not die. The British occupation of Ireland has never for more than one hundred years been compelled to confront in the field of fight a rising so formidable as that which overwhelming forces have for the moment succeeded in quelling. This rising did not result from accidental circumstances. . . ." [The rest of the manuscript, whose authenticity has been questioned, but which is accepted as wholly true by MacDonagh's family, is missing.]

Late the same night, Mr. Stoker (the Grafton Street jeweler who had been standing outside the General Post Office when Joseph Plunkett had headed the rebel charge into it) was just about to close his shop when "a taxi stopped at the front door and a beautiful young woman stepped out and asked me to show her some wedding rings. The best, as she put it, that money could buy. She had a thick veil, but I could see that her eyes were red with weeping and noticing continual convulsive sobs as she spoke, I ventured to ask the reason. It was then that she revealed the terrible tragedy she was about to suffer. 'I am Joe Plunkett's fiancée' she said, 'We are to be married in prison tomorrow morning, an hour before his execution. Oh, I can't tell you how I love him and he loves me. We belong to each other. And even if we are to be together for only a single hour I mean to marry him in spite of everything in order to bear his name through life.' "

The "beautiful young woman" was Grace Gifford. At 1:30 A.M. on May 4, 1916, she was led into the small chapel of Kilmainham Jail and stood waiting until the ailing Joseph

364

Plunkett was brought in, in handcuffs, and led up beside her before the altar. Owing to a lighting failure, the marriage was performed by the Reverend Eugene MacCarthy by the light of a single candle, held by a British soldier, while twenty others, with bayonets fixed, lined the walls of the chapel. Immediately after the ceremony the couple were separated, but just before Plunkett's execution at dawn, the bride was allowed to see him for a further ten minutes. During those last few minutes fifteen soldiers stood guard in the cell, and the time was regulated to the second by a soldier who stood by with a watch.

At dawn Plunkett, Commandant Edward Daly, Michael O'Hanrahan (MacDonagh's second in command at Jacobs), and Willie Pearse were all shot together.

The gallant Major John MacBride died alone on May 6.

On that same day, to her intense chagrin, the death sentence on the Countess Markievicz was commuted to life imprisonment.

On the following Monday morning, May 8, four more men were executed—Edmund Kent, Michael Mallin, J. J. Heuston, and Cornelius Colbert; nineteen other death sentences were commuted to varying terms of imprisonment.

On Thursday, May 11, the death sentence passed on De Valera was commuted to one of life imprisonment.

Finally, on Friday, May 12, John MacDermott and James Connolly were shot—the last men to pay the supreme penalty.

These last two executions shocked public opinion as none of the others had. The earlier ones had taken place while most Irish people were still stunned and still full of resentment against the Sinn Feiners. But as penalty followed penalty a feeling of revulsion set in; the belief took hold that the Government was indulging in an orgy of revengeful bloodletting. Strong voices were raised in protest; the United States Senate requested the President to transmit to the British Government an expression of "their hope that Great Britain would exercise clemency in the treatment of Irish political prisoners generally." Redmond and the Orange leader, Carson, appealed for clemency in the House of Commons. "No true Irishman calls for vengeance," said Carson magnanimously. "It will be a matter requiring the greatest wisdom and the greatest calmness in dealing with these men. Whatever is done, let it be done not in a moment of temporary excitement but in a moment of deliberation."

When eventually Irish Command announced that De Valera had been spared the death sentence (Maxwell had taken into account De Valera's American birth), there was general relief and a feeling that wisdom and statesmanship were likely to heal the breach rapidly. Sinn Fein, after all, had been crushed; its principal leaders were dead. True, Connolly lived, but the man had been severely wounded, and one thing was certain —he would never again lead another military rising. And who, anyway, could shoot a wounded man?

The people of Ireland were stunned to learn that General Maxwell could—and from that moment on he and the nation he represented earned their hearty opprobrium; even today his name is still execrated as "Bloody" Maxwell. The shock was the more severe because, on the day before Connolly's execution, an official announcement had stated: "The trials by court-martial of those who took an actual part in the rising in Dublin are practically finished. . . ."

The last persons, outside his jailors and executioners, to see MacDermott alive were the two Ryan sisters, Mary and Phyllis, who later married men well known in modern Ireland. Today Phyllis is Mrs. Sean T. O'Kelly; Mary, the wife of General Richard Mulcahy. In her contemporary account of the last meeting, Mary Ryan wrote: "The last time I saw him [MacDermott] was in his prison cell at Kilmainham Jail at 3 o'clock on the morning of May 12th. He was shot at 3:45 on the same morning. . . . The cell was small with walls whitewashed. There was a raised board in the corner—a plank bed. There was a small, rough table near a light on which was placed a tall, brass candlestick. . . . On the plank bed were a couple of soiled blankets. MacDermott had a smile on his face. He was cheerful. There were two soldiers there all the time. He sat on the plank bed discussing the revolution. He told of the insults hurled at them by the British after they'd laid down their arms—the inhuman treatment in Richmond barracks. He did not complain—almost as if he did not expect better treatment.

366

He preferred to talk of casual matters, asking about different people we knew, enjoying little jokes almost as though we were in Bewleys [a well-known Dublin coffeehouse]. The most pathetic scene was where he tried to produce keepsakes for different girl friends of his we mentioned. He sat down at the table and tried to scratch his name and the date on the few coins he had left and on the buttons which he cut from his clothes with a penknife reluctantly provided by a young officer who stood by. His beautiful head bent assiduously over the work. At 3 o'clock on the arrival of the prison chaplain, we bade farewell. He had a beautiful head, black hair with deep blue eyes, dark eyebrows and long lashes. Illness had left him lame and somewhat delicate—he often looked tired and frail. He had wonderful charm. He had worked and planned for Irish independence since boyhood. . . . His last words, aside from prayers, were 'God save Ireland.' At 4 o'clock, when the shooting was done, a gentle rain began to fall—the tears of Dark Rosaleen."

James Connolly's daughter, Nora, has left an account of the last days of her father as he lay wounded in Dublin Castle, uncertain as to his fate.

"On Tuesday [May 9] I went with mother. There were soldiers on guard at the top of the stairs and in the small alcove leading to Papa's room. They were fully armed and as they stood guard they had their bayonets fixed. In the room there was an R.A.M.C. officer with him all the time. His wounded leg was resting in a cage. He was weak and pale and his voice was very low. Mother asked was he suffering much pain. 'No, but I've been court-martialled today. They propped me up in bed. The strain was very great.' She knew then that if they had court-martialled him while unable to sit up in bed, they would not hesitate to shoot him while he was wounded. Asked how he had got the wound he said: 'It was while I had gone out to place some men at a certain point. On my way back I was shot above the ankle by a sniper. Both bones in my leg are shattered. I was too far away for the men I had just placed to see me and was too far from the Post Office to be seen. So I had to crawl till I was seen. The loss of blood was great. They couldn't get it staunched.' He was very cheerful, talking about plans for the future, giving no sign that sentence had been pronounced an hour before we were admitted. He was very proud of his men. 'It was a good clean fight. The cause cannot die now. The fight will put an end to recruiting. Irishmen will now realise the absurdity of fighting for the freedom of another country while their own is enslaved.' He praised the women and girls who fought. I told him about Rory [Connolly's son; the boy had been arrested with other rebels but had given a false name and was released along with all other boys under sixteen]. 'He fought for his country and has been imprisoned for his country and he's not sixteen. He's had a great start in life, hasn't he, Nora?' Then he turned to mother and said: 'There was one young boy, Lillie, who was carrying the top of my stretcher as we were leaving the burning Post Office. The street was being swept continually with bullets from machine-guns. That young lad was at the head of the stretcher and if a bullet came near me he would move his body in such a way that he might receive it instead of me. He was so young looking, although big, that I asked his age. "I'm just fourteen, sir," he answered. We can't fail now.'

"I saw father next on Thursday, May 11, at midnight. A motor ambulance came to the door. The officer said father was very weak and wished to see his wife and eldest daughter. Mama believed the story because she had seen him on Wednesday and he was in great pain and very weak, and he said he couldn't sleep without morphine. Nevertheless she asked the officer if they were going to shoot him. The officer said he could tell her nothing. Through dark, deserted, sentry-ridden streets we rode. I was surprised to see about a dozen soldiers encamped outside Papa's door. There was an officer on guard inside the room. Papa turned his head at our coming.

" 'Well, Lillie, I suppose you know what this means?'

" 'Oh, James, it's not that—it's not that.'

" 'Yes, Lillie. I fell asleep for the first time tonight and they wakened me at eleven and told me that I was to die at dawn.' Mamma broke down and laid her head on the bed and sobbed heartbreakingly. Father patted her head and said: 'Don't cry, Lillie, you'll unman me.'

368

" 'But your beautiful life, James. Your beautiful life!' she sobbed.

" 'Well, Lillie, hasn't it been a full life and isn't this a good end?' I was also crying. 'Don't cry, Nora, there's nothing to cry about.'

" 'I won't cry, Papa,' I said.

"He patted my hand and said: 'That's my brave girl. . . .'

"He tried to cheer Mama by telling her of the man who had come into the Post Office during the rising to try and buy a penny stamp. 'I don't know what Dublin's coming to when you can't buy a stamp at the Post Office. . . .'

"The officer said: 'Only five minutes more.' Mama was nearly overcome—she had to be given water. Papa tried to clasp her in his arms but he could only lift his head and shoulders from the bed. The officer said: 'Time is up.' Papa turned and said goodbye to her and she could not see him. I tried to bring Mama away but I could not move her. The nurse came forward and helped her away. I ran back and kissed Papa again. 'Nora, I'm proud of you.' Then the door was shut and I saw him no more. . . .

(Later) "We saw Father Aloysius who had attended him in Kilmainham. 'How did they shoot him . . . how could they shoot him?' asked Mama. 'He couldn't sit up in his bed.'

" 'It was a terrible shock to me' said Father Aloysius. 'I'd been with him that evening and I promised to come to him this afternoon. I felt sure there would be no more executions. Your father was much easier than he had been. I was sure that he would get his first real night's rest. The ambulance that brought you home came for me. I was astonished. I had felt so sure that I would not be needed that, for the first time since the rising, I had locked the doors. And some time after two I was knocked up. The ambulance brought me to your father. I'll always thank God as long as I live that He permitted me to be with your father until he was dead. Such a wonderful man—such a concentration of mind. They carried him from his bed in an ambulance stretcher down to a waiting ambulance and drove him to Kilmainham Jail. They carried him from the ambulance to the jail yard and put him in a chair. . . . He was very brave and cool. . . . I said to him 'Will you pray for the men who are about to shoot you?' and he said: 'I will say a prayer for all brave men who do their duty.' His prayer was 'Forgive them for they know not what they do . . .' and then they shot him."

Adding fuel to the flames of anger and resentment sweeping the country were "the atrocities"—first the rampaging personal acts of Captain Bowen-Colthurst and second, the behavior of the 2/6th South Staffordshire Regiment in the course of the savage fighting in North King Street. Allegations of at least six cases of cold-blooded murder were to be leveled against Bowen-Colthurst; fifteen against the South Staffs.

Army authorities might very effectively have dampened down the Bowen-Colthurst affair had it not been for the intervention of Major Sir Francis Vane who, as he put it, was "alive to the good name and reputation of the British Army" and was convinced that Bowen-Colthurst's behavior well warranted official investigation and censure. He first made it his business to protest to General Friend, Colonel Kennard, and Major Price at Dublin Castle, insisting that Bowen-Colthurst be relieved from command pending an investigation. The three men responded by deprecating "the fuss" he was trying to make, Price adding, "Some of us think it was a good thing Sheehy-Skeffington was put out of the way, anyway." So, early in May, Vane crossed to London and visited the War Office and on May 3 interviewed Lord Kitchener, who assured him that he would send a telegram ordering Bowen-Colthurst's arrest.

Maxwell, alleged Vane later, simply ignored Kitchener's telegram; not only that—instead of dealing with Bowen-Colthurst, he took action against Vane, depriving him of his rank and dismissing him the service. Skeffington's widow carried on the campaign for redress until eventually she was received by the Prime Minister, Mr. Asquith, who expressed himself as horrified at the allegations against Bowen-Colthurst but even more horrified at the suggestion that General Maxwell was assisting the resident military authorities in Dublin to hush up the case. "I confess I do not and cannot believe it. Does anyone suppose that Sir John Maxwell has any object in shielding officers and soldiers, if there be such, who have been guilty of such ungentlemanly, such inhuman conduct? It is the last thing the British Army would dream of."

When Mr. Asquith crossed to Ireland himself, a few days later, however, he found that the British Army, as it was constituted in Ireland anyway, was unfortunately quite capable "of inhuman conduct" and General Maxwell or his subordinates only too anxious to hush up anything unpleasant. As a result, Captain Bowen-Colthurst was formally court-martialed on June 6 and after a number of witnesses had testified as to his character and behavior before and after the Skeffington affair, he was found guilty, but insane, and incarcerated in Broadmoor Criminal Asylum.

No unprejudiced person could possibly attach blame to an army because it was unfortunate enough to have at least one lunatic—or near-lunatic—in its ranks. Resentment primarily arose—and still lingers in Ireland—because the Army authorities, by refusing to act promptly against Bowen-Colthurst, appeared to condone his behavior. Asquith and Maxwell, however, soon found themselves deep in the mire of something a great deal more unpleasant. This time a whole Battalion of English troops, it was alleged, were involved. Sent across to Dublin to act as the guardians of authority and upholders of the law, the 2/6th South Staffs had behaved like barbaric savages in North King Street. No less than fifteen innocent civilians, it was alleged, had been bayoneted to death during military operations in the area—fifteen men who, despite protests and expostulations, despite the pleas of their family, were dragged away and either shot or bayoneted simply "because they [the military] were determined to wreak vengeance on the helpless inmates whom they found in the houses."

Although stories of the horrors alleged to have occurred were rife in the city from May 1, it was not until the bodies of two victims whom members of the South Staffs had buried in a cellar were dug up that the authorities were forced to take note. The inquest was adjourned to give Colonel Taylor an opportunity to be represented, but he consented merely to forward a statement saying:

371

"I cannot discover any military witnesses as to the manner in which the two men, Patrick Bealen and James Healy, met with their deaths, but I cannot believe that the allegations made at the inquest can be correct. To the best of my knowledge and belief, during the military operations in Capel Street and King Street, which lasted from 6 a.m. on Friday, 28th April until the truce was declared on the afternoon of Saturday 29th (and which were, in fact, continued for some hours after that by the rebels in that area) only those houses were entered by the military which the exigencies of the case rendered actually necessary, and no persons were attacked by the troops other than those who were assisting the rebels and found with arms in their possession.

The premises, No. 177 North King Street, were indicated to me as one of the houses from which the troops had been repeatedly fired upon, and the troops were also continually fired upon both during the night of the 28th April and the whole of the following day from the distillery, at which the deceased man, James Healy, was stated to have been employed. The operations in the portion of King Street, between Linenhall Street and Church Street, were conducted under circumstances of the greatest difficulty and danger for the troops engaged, who were subjected to severe fire, not only from behind several rebel barricades, which had been constructed across King Street and other barricades in Church Street and the side streets, but practically every house in that portion of King Street and other buildings overlooking it.

Strong evidence of these difficulties and dangers is afforded by the fact that it took the troops from 10 a.m. on the 28th April until 2 p.m. on the 29th to force their way along King Street from Linenhall Street to Church Street, a distance of some 150 yards only; and that the casualties sustained by the regiment (the great majority of which occurred at this spot) numbered five officers (including two Captains) wounded, 11 N.C.O.s and men killed and 28 wounded.

I am satisfied that during these operations the troops under my command showed great moderation and restraint under exceptionally difficult and trying circumstances.

The Coroner's court saw things in a different light. They returned a verdict as follows: "We find the said Patrick Bealen

372

died from shock and haemorrhage, resulting from bullet wounds inflicted by a soldier, or soldiers, in whose custody he was, an unarmed and unoffensive prisoner. We consider that the explanation given by the military authorities is very unsatisfactory, and we believe that if the military authorities had any inclination they could produce the officer in charge."

It was clearly impossible now to simply bulldoze a way through the affair. In a statement to the *Daily Mail,* General Maxwell tacitly admitted that brutalities had been committed: "Possibly some unfortunate incidents, which we should regret now, may have occurred . . . it is even possible that under the horrors of this attack some of them 'saw red'; that is the inevitable consequence of a rebellion of this kind."

Inevitably there was an inquiry. An elaborate identification parade was laid on at Straffan camp, outside Dublin, where the whole Battalion was paraded, and the wives or mothers of the dead men were invited to pick out the soldiers who had committed the alleged crimes. They were unable to identify anyone—and certainly in the case of Bealen and Healy this would have been difficult as the two culprits who had shot the men and then buried them in the cellar were safely back in England, having been got out of the way quickly on the orders of their company officer. One of the culprits was a Corporal Bullock, who is now dead, the other a sergeant who is now living in quiet retirement in Wolverhampton.

The latter was the man referred to in a letter sent by Maxwell to Lord Kitchener: "In one case a sergeant acted like a madman, the redeeming feature being that he reported what he had done. It must be borne in mind that there was a lot of house to house fighting going on, wild rumours in circulation and owing to the darkness, conflagrationists, apparently a good deal of 'jumpiness.' With young soldiers and under the circumstances, I wonder there were not more."

Despite this, announcing the result of the inquiry to the House of Commons, the Prime Minister said: "The conclusion arrived at after a full hearing in all the cases was that the deaths occurred in the course of continued and desperate street and house to house fighting which lasted for nearly two days and in which soldiers were constantly exposed to sniping from windows and the roofs of houses. There can be little doubt that some men who were not taking an actual part in the fighting were in the course of the struggle killed by both rebels and soldiers. But after careful inquiry it is impossible to bring home responsibility to any particular person or persons."

So there it was; between them, the Army and Government had managed to get all the skeletons safely, as they thought, locked away in the cupboard. It mattered not that ordinary Irish people—who desperately wanted to believe that English "atrocities" had ended with the disappearance of the redcoats and the solution of the agrarian difficulties of the nineteenth century—now began to feel that the English leopard could never change his spots and that the only compatible solution for Ireland, if she was ever to enjoy any kind of peace, was to go along with the Sinn Feiners and cut all connecting links.

Of the other actors in the drama of the rebellion, Lord Wimborne, Mr. Birrell, and Sir Matthew Nathan handed in their resignations almost immediately after the cessation of hostilities and on the eighteenth of May a formal Royal Commission of Inquiry began its sittings in Westminster. In its findings, the Commission exonerated Wimborne from all blame, and partially exonerated Sir Matthew, but added: "We consider that he did not sufficiently impress upon the Chief Secretary during the latter's prolonged absences from Dublin the necessity for more active measures to remedy the situation in Ireland." They found Mr. Birrell "primarily responsible for the situation that was allowed to arise and the outbreak that occurred."

This left Maxwell undisputed Lord of Ireland, a position which he no longer really relished. He constantly agitated against the Government's policy of oscillation between conciliation and coercion, demanding that they at least make up their minds which policy they wished to employ. He himself favored the appointment of an executive who would "meet a warm-hearted people half-way in redressing grievances." He expressed himself as disgusted with the poverty and squalor he found in Dublin, which "could be easily prevented" and emphasized the evil of allowing absentee landlordism to continue in other parts of the country. Finally he blamed all the trouble on the Government's pusillanimity in allowing Carson to form

374

the Ulster Volunteers, naming this as the primary cause of the Rebellion and the growing unrest which succeeded it.

It would seem, certainly, that he grew more and more anxious to undo as much as he possibly could the damage he himself had caused by executing fifteen rebels. But such was the virulence of the campaign against him both in Ireland and in England that by October he was no longer in a position to exercise any further influence on Irish affairs. The Government terminated his appointment in Ireland and as a clear mark of their disapproval of the way he had handled affairs there, relegated him to the relatively unimportant post of G.O.C., Northern England. For the man who, both in the Middle East and Ireland, had enjoyed almost the status of a pro-consul, it was a bitter disappointment. He had washed the Government's dirty linen for it, and this was his thanks. . . . Thus, in bitterness and disappointment, ended his career.

Not that either Pearse or Connolly would really have wanted that. In sentencing them to death, he had only done what they wanted him to do—he had made them glorious martyrs.

And that, in the end, would free Ireland.